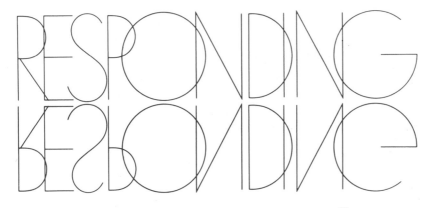

# RESPONDING

## BASIC SEQUENCE | THREE

ROBERT WEINBERGER

and

NATHAN S. BLOUNT

*Editorial Direction*
ALAN C. PURVES

*Advisers*
ROBERT F. HOGAN
RICHARD OHMANN
WILLIAM E. STAFFORD

*Ginn Interrelated Sequences in Literature*

GINN AND COMPANY
A XEROX EDUCATION COMPANY

# CONTENTS

iii

v

# FOREWORD

*"Do you believe in man?"*

It isn't always easy to believe in man. He is not as efficient as some of the machines he has created, and he's a lot less dependable. He can be much more cruel than the so-called "lower" animals—partly because he knows how to hurt others with just a word or a gesture. But in spite of these short-comings—and lots more—don't we have to keep the faith? Don't we have to believe in ourselves? in our ability to rise above ourselves? Isn't that what the history of the human race is all about?

But how can anybody believe in man when all around us is the evidence of his ability to destroy? Perhaps part of the answer is that man's capacity to love at least equals—sometimes even exceeds—his capacity to kill.

The stories and articles, the poems and plays you find in this book raise a lot of questions about man—about *you*. Most of them aren't easy questions to answer. In fact, no one really has any final answers. Maybe no one ever will. Some of the selections in the book show love growing out of suffering and despair. Others show suffering that produces only more suffering. Are both kinds of selections right? Are both kinds of selections to be believed?

Of course man is contradictory! Of course he's confusing! He's not a machine. He's a human being. And being human—finding out what it takes to be really human—that's what this book is all about.

So

    READ

        TALK

           QUESTION

              READ AGAIN

                TALK SOME MORE

                  ACT

                    AND

                      ENJOY!

                        —R. W.

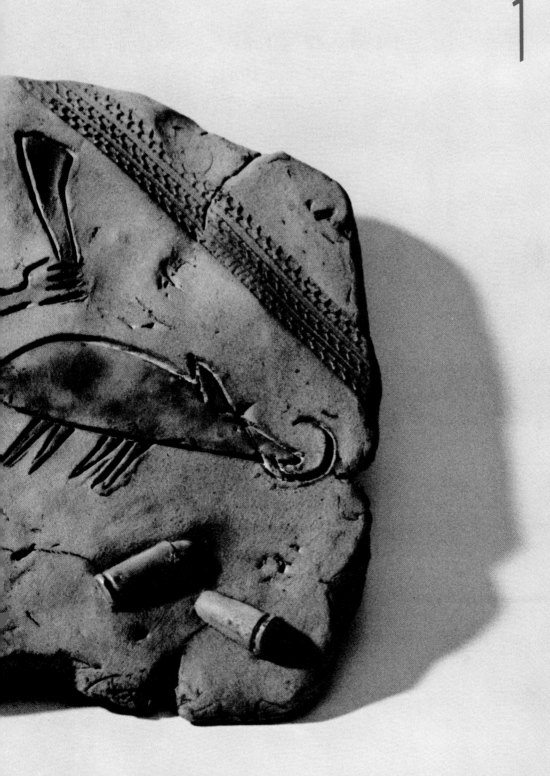

# The Day of the Last Rock Fight

*Joseph Whitehill*

FALLBROOK ACADEMY

May 16, 195–

DEAR DAD,

I expect this will be a very long letter, so I am sending it to your office marked *Personal*. I know you don't like to do family business at the office, but I wanted you to have a chance to read this all by yourself, and I didn't want Mother or Sue reading it before you did.

Thank you for sending my allowance, and also for the subscription to the home paper. Thank you also for the nice new wallet for my birthday. I really needed it, as my old one was afflicted with rot and falling apart.

I apologize for not having written sooner. As you said in your last letter, "*Something* must have happened in the last two months worth writing down." I have been very busy with things here at school, but mainly I haven't written because I didn't know how to say what I wanted to say. I hope this letter will make up for the long delay.

You keep asking me what I think of Fallbrook Academy and if I'm happy here, and so on. Well, I don't like it here, and I want to come home. That's what this letter is for—to tell you that now it's all right for me to come back home. I guess I know why you sent me here, and I admit that I wanted very much to come when I did. It's not that the people here aren't nice or anything. They are. They're so nice it's phony. In all the catalogues of the school they call it a *Special School,* but the boys here call it *Goodbar.* (Mr. Goodbar is a chocolate bar full of nuts.) They all kid about it, and pretend they don't care about being put in a school for misfits and boys with emotional problems. I guess most of them like it here. Most of them say they hate their parents, one or both, and are really glad to get away from them. All the faculty are so sweet and kind and sympathetic that a lot of the boys get away with murder. (That last word was sort of a poor choice, I suppose, but I'll leave it there anyway.) But I don't feel like I belong here any more.

It is going to be very complicated to explain everything in just one letter, because there are lots of different ways of looking at that mess that happened there at home, and I suppose I am the only one who knows the whole story. I guess you sent me here because you thought I was terribly upset by Gene Hanlon getting killed out there at Manning Day School at home, and seeing his body lying in the creek, and so on. Well, that was part of it, but only a little part. The rest of it I couldn't tell anybody until Detective Sergeant Gorman put the story in the paper last week. I got that paper in the mail yesterday and I have been reading the story over and over, and feeling relieved and awful at the same time.

I'm sure you read the same story, so you already know that Gene Hanlon was murdered, instead of getting killed accidentally as they said at first. But neither you nor anybody else knows that I saw the murder done, and knew all the time who did it. I guess if I acted upset afterwards it was from knowing all this and not being able to tell anyone about it. I'm going to work on this letter all night, if it takes that long, because I have to get all this out of my system. (When you stay up after curfew around here they don't actually *make* you go to bed, but the doctor who is on duty looks in on you every half hour or so to see what you're doing, and to try to make you *want* to go to bed.)

I suppose the beginning is the best place to start, so I will tell you first about Gene Hanlon, the boy who got killed. He came to Manning Day School last fall as a senior. They said he was fired from his last school, but I don't know about that. I didn't like him just from looking at him. I know you hate judgments that way on first impressions, but I couldn't help it. I wouldn't ever bring him over to our house, but if I had, you might have seen what I was talking about. He was big and beefy, and he played on the first string last fall. He was also blond, and the girls thought he was cute and from what I heard they fought over him for dates. But he was a bully, and he cheated in the classroom and he borrowed your stuff without asking you and then left it some place where you had to go hunt it up yourself.

In a school like Manning Day there are always a number of tight little groups—cliques, I guess you call them—that move around independently and generally stay out of the way of the others. I mean there is a football group, and a group of boys who drink beer, and a group who studies hard, and a group who loafs and tries to avoid everything that looks like work, and a group that meets in the locker room to talk about sex and tell dirty jokes. It was probably the same way when you yourself went to school, but you may have forgotten. When you go to a school like that, you pretty soon find the group that suits you best, and you stay there and don't try to mix with any of the others, because if you do you won't be let in.

What I am getting at in this long explanation is that Gene Hanlon was the Big Man in all the groups I wouldn't be seen dead in. He was tops among the football players and their fans. He could tell filthier stories and, he said, hold more liquor than anybody else. And he told stories about the things he had done to girls that you wouldn't believe if anybody else had told them, but with him telling them, you knew they were all possible. I guess he was feared more than he was liked, but one thing sure, he never went anywhere alone. There was always a loud bunch along with him horse-laughing and beating him on the shoulders.

I stayed out of his way. There is something about me that brings out the worst in bullies. That's what Peter Irish used to say. I guess it's because I'm slightly built, and because of those glasses I have to wear. Once, I was going upstairs to lab, and Gene Hanlon was coming down and we met halfway, and for no reason I could see, he belted me as hard as he could on my shoulder. My glasses flew off and bounced halfway down the stairs along with a whole armload of books and papers. I had to grab the bannister to keep from following them down myself. Two other guys with him saw him do it and didn't say anything at first, but then they looked at Gene and knew they'd better laugh, so they did. So I sat there on the stairs all confused inside, holding my shoulder to make it stop hurting. Gene Hanlon and the others went on down the stairs laughing to beat all at how I looked there with everything scattered around me. On the way down, Gene kicked my physics book ahead of him, bouncing it all the way to the bottom. When I could stand up all right I went down and got it. When I picked it up it fell apart in my hands with its binding broken and I guess I started to cry. I hate to see books treated that way.

When I had about got everything picked up, Peter Irish came up to where I was and wanted to know what had happened. Peter being my best friend, I told him all about it. Probably there were still tears in my eyes about the physics book because Peter said, "Do you want me to get him for you?"

I thought for a minute how swell that would be, but then I said no. It was almost yes because Peter was the only one in school who could have whipped Gene under any rules, and it was a very satisfying thing to think about. But then I thought about afterwards, when Gene would have gotten over his beating and would begin to wonder why Peter had done it, and he would remember that Peter was my best friend. Then he would put one and one together and start out after me seriously. So I said no.

Peter Irish was a good friend to have. I suppose he was the strongest kid in school, but he didn't ever use his strength to bully people, but just for things that were fun, like squashing a beer can in one hand. You knew him pretty well because of all the times he came over to the house to study with me. I remember the time he beat you at Indian hand wrestling on the dining-room table, and you were a real good sport about it because Mother was watching and laughing at your expression. But anyway, you know how strong Peter was, and you can feature what he would have done to Gene if I'd told him to. Peter always stayed out of fights unless they were for fun, and if they ever got serious he'd quit because he didn't want to hurt anybody. But he would have torn Gene Hanlon apart if I had asked him to.

That was something I don't think you understood—Peter and me, I mean, and why we hung around together. The simplest way to say it is that we swapped talents. I used to write a lot of his themes for him, and help him in labs so he'd finish when the rest of us did, and he'd show me judo holds and how to skin a squirrel, and such things. You would call it a good working agreement.

Now, there are just two more things you have to know about to see the whole picture. The first one is Peter Irish and Angela Pine. Peter and Angela went together all last year and the year before, and neither of them wanted anybody else. Both their folks made them date other kids because they didn't like to see them going steady, but everybody knew that Angela belonged to Peter, and Peter belonged to Angela, and that's all there was to it. He used to talk to me a lot about her, and how they were going to get married and run a riding stable together. And he told me that he would never touch her that way until they were married. They used to kiss good night and that was all, because Peter said that when the great thing happened, he wanted it to happen just right, and it could never be really right while they were both kids in high school. A lot of the fellows thought that more went on between them than I know did, but that's because they didn't understand Peter really. He had a simple set of rules he operated under, and they suited him very well. He was good to Angela and good to animals, and all he asked was to be let alone to do things his own way.

The other thing you have to know about is the noontime rock fights. From the papers and the inquest and all, you know something about them, but not everything. I guess most of the parents were pretty shocked to learn that their little Johnny was in a mob rock fight every day at school, but that's the way it was. The fights started over a year ago, as near as I can recollect, and went on all that time without the faculty ever finding out. The papers made a big scandal out of them and conducted what they called an "exposé of vicious practices at select Manning Day School." It was comical, actually, the way everybody got all steamed up over the things we knew went on all the time, not only at Manning but in all the other schools in town. Of course, we all knew the rock fights were wrong, but they were more fun than they seemed wrong, so we kept them up. (That time I came home with the mouse under my eye, I didn't get it by falling in the locker room. I just forgot to duck.)

We had a strict set of rules in the fights so that nobody would really get hurt or anything, and so the little guys could get into them too without fear of being killed. All sixty of us, the whole school, were divided into two teams, the Union Army and the Confederates, and after lunch in the cafeteria we'd all get our blue or gray caps and head out into the woods behind the school. The faculty thought we played Kick the Can and never followed us out to check up on us.

Each team had a fort we'd built out of sapling logs—really just pens about waist high. The forts were about two hundred yards apart, invisible to each other through the trees and scrub. You weren't allowed to use rocks any bigger than a hazelnut, and before you pegged one at a guy in the opposite army, you had to go *chk, chk* with your mouth so the guy would have a chance to find where it was coming from and duck in time. We had scouting parties and assault teams and patrols, and all the rest of the military things we could think up. The object was to storm the enemy's fort and take it before recess was up and we had to quit.

These rock fights weren't like the papers said at all. I remember the *Morning Star* called them "pitched battles of unrelenting fury, where injuries were frequent." That was silly. If the injuries had been frequent, it wouldn't have been fun any more, and nobody would have wanted to keep doing it. You *could* get hurt, of course, but you could get hurt a lot worse in a football game with the grandstand full of newspaper reporters and faculty and parents all cheering you on.

Now I guess you know everything that was important before the day Gene Hanlon got killed, and I can tell you how it happened so that you'll know why.

After our last morning class, Peter Irish and I went down to the washroom in the basement to clean up for lunch. All morning Peter had acted funny—silent and sort of tied up inside—and it was worrying me some. At first I thought I had done something he didn't like, but if I had, he'd have told me. He'd hardly said two words all morning, and he had missed two recitations in English that I had coached him on myself. But you couldn't pry trouble out of Peter, so I just kept quiet and waited for him to let me in on it.

While he was washing his hands I had to go into one of the stalls. I went in and shut the door and was hanging up my jacket when I heard somebody else come into the washroom. I don't know why, but I sat down—being real careful not to make any noise.

Somebody said. "Hi, Pete, boy." It was Gene Hanlon, and he was alone for once.

"Hi, Gene." That was Peter. (I am trying to put this down as near as I can just the way they said it.)

"Oh, man!" Gene said. "Today I am exhaust pipe!"

"Tired?"

"You said the word, man. Real beat under."

"Why so?"

"Big date last night. Friend of yours, Angela Pine." Just as if that stall door hadn't been there, I could see Gene grinning at Peter and waiting for a rise out of him. Peter didn't say anything, so Gene tried again. "You're pretty sly, Pete."

"What do you mean?"

"I mean about Angela. You've done a real fine job of keeping her in drydock all this time."

"She dates other guys," Peter said, sounding like he ought to clear his throat.

"Aaaah. She goes out with those meatballs and then comes home and shakes hands at the door. What kind of a date is that?"

"Well, that's *her* business."

Gene said, giggling, "I don't know what her business is, but I got a few suggestions for her if she ever asks me."

"What are you getting at?"

"Real coy, boy. She's crazy for it. Just crazy. Real crazy hungry chick, yeah."

"Are you through?"

"What? . . . Oh, sure. *Hey!* You sore or something?"

Peter said, "It's time for you to go to eat lunch."

"All right already. Jesus! You don't have to get *that* way about it. A guy gives you a compliment and you go and get sore. You *are* an odd ball. You and your screwy horses too. See you around." And Gene went out scuffing his feet along the floor.

When I came out of the stall Peter was hunched stiff-armed over the washbasin. He didn't even know I was around. I wished right then that I could have gone back and unlived the last five minutes. I wished they had never happened, and that everything was back just the way it was before. I was hurt and mad, and my mind was whirling around full of all the stuff Gene Hanlon had said. Just to be doing something, I got busy combing my hair, wetting and shaking the comb and all, trying to find a way to say what I was feeling. Peter was very busy turning both faucets on and off again in a kind of splashy rhythm.

Finally I said, "If you believe all that crap, you're pretty silly. That guy's a bragging liar and you know it."

Peter looked up at me as though he had just noticed I was there. "I've got to believe it," he said.

I jumped on him for that. "Oh, come on," I said. "Give Angela a little credit. She wouldn't give that pile of you-know-what the right time."

Peter was looking down the basin drain. "I called her this morning to say hello. She wouldn't talk to me, Ronnie. She wouldn't even come to the phone."

Now I knew what had been eating him all morning. There wasn't any more a friend could say to Peter, so I made him let go of the faucets and come with me to eat lunch in the cafeteria. All through lunch he just pushed dishes around on his tray and didn't say anything. As we scraped our plates I asked him if he was going out to the fight in the woods, and he surprised me by saying yes, so we got our caps and hiked out to the Confederate fort.

Almost everybody, Gene Hanlon too, was there before us, and they'd already chosen today's generals. Smitty Rice was General of the Armies of the Confederacy, and Gene Hanlon was the Union commander. Gene took all his boys off to the Union fort to wait for the starting whistle, and Smitty outlined his strategy to us.

There was to be a feint at the south side of the Union fort, and then a noisy second feint from the north to pull the defenders out of position. Then Smitty and Peter Irish were to lead the real massed assault from the south, under the lip of the hill where the first feint had come from. When five minutes had gone by on my watch, we all got up and Smitty blew the starting whistle and we piled out of the fort, leaving only five inside as a garrison, and a couple of alarm guards a little way out on each side of the fort.

I got the job I usually got—advance observation post. I was to note enemy movements and remember concentrations and directions and elapsed times between sightings. Even though you couldn't see more than a hundred feet through the woods, you could always get a fair idea of the enemy strategy by the way they moved their troops around. So all I had to do was stay in one place and watch and listen and remember, and every so often Smitty would send a runner over from field headquarters to check up on what had happened lately. I had three or four good posts picked out where I could hide and not be seen, and I never used the same one twice running.

Today's was my favorite—Baker Post, we called it. It was a dense thicket of young blackjack oak on a low hill on the inside of a bend in the creek, and because nothing grew on the gravel bars of the creek, you could see a long way to each side. The creek ran generally south, cutting the fighting area between the forts right in two, and it made a good defense line because there were only a few places you could cross it in one jump and not get your shoes wet. The east bank of the creek, directly across from Baker Post, is a vertical bluff about ten feet high so that the ground up there is right on eye level with Baker, and the creek and the gravel bars are spread out between you and the bluff bank. I always knew that Baker Post was good, because every time I took it up I had to flush out a covey of quail or a cottontail.

It was always quiet in the woods during the first few minutes of those fights. Even the birds shut up, it seemed like, waiting for the first troop contacts. Out of the corner of my eye I saw somebody jump the creek at the North Ford, and I rolled over to watch. Because of the brush up there I couldn't see who it was, but I knew he was there because once in a while a bush would stir, or his foot would slide a little on the gravel. Pretty soon he came out to the edge of the underbrush and crouched there looking around and listening. It was Gene Hanlon. His eyes crossed right over me, without finding me, and after a minute he came out and ran low along the creek. When he got even with Baker Post, he went down to his knees and began filling his cap with rocks. I had to laugh to myself at how stupid that was. He should have collected his ammunition earlier, when he and his army were on their way over to their fort. He was wasting maneuvering time and exposing himself for no good reason. It makes you feel good when a guy you hate does something dumb like that.

I got ready to go *chk, chk* with my mouth just to scare him and see him run. But then I looked up at the bluff above him and my heart flopped over inside me. Peter Irish was there, down on one knee, looking over at Gene Hanlon. Gene never looked up. Peter moves like that—floating in and out of the brush as quietly as if he didn't weigh anything. Peter was a good woods fighter.

So instead of going *chk, chk* I hunkered down lower in my thicket and thought to myself that now it wasn't a game any more. Peter looked a long time over at where I was hiding, then he looked up and down the creek bed, and then he moved back a little from the edge of the bluff. He put all his weight pulling on a half-buried boulder beside him until it turned over in its socket and he could get a good grip on it. Even from where I was I could see the cords come out in his neck when he raised it up in his arms and stood up. I hadn't heard a sound except the creek gurgling a little, and Gene Hanlon scratching around in the gravel. And also the blood roaring in my own ears. Watching this was like being in a movie and seeing the story happen on the screen. Nothing you can do or say will change what is going to happen because it's all there in the unwinding reel.

Peter held the heavy stone like a medicine ball and walked to the edge of the bluff and looked down at Gene Hanlon. Gene had moved a few feet south along the creek, so Peter above him moved south too, until he was even with Gene. Peter made a little grunt when he pushed the rock out and away and it fell. Gene heard the grunt and lifted his head to look up, and the rock hit him full in the face and bent his head away back and made his arms fly out. He sat right down in the water with his red and dirty face turned up to the sky and his hands holding him up behind. Then he got himself up with his head still twisted back like that, so he was looking straight up, and he wandered a little way downstream with the water up to his knees, and then he fell out on a gravel bar on his stomach. His legs and arms spread out like he was asleep, but his head was up rigid and his mouth was open. I couldn't look any more.

Peter hadn't made a sound leaving, but when I looked up, the bluff above was empty. As soon as I could move without getting sick I faded out of there and went up north a ways to Able Post and lay down in the foxhole there and held myself around the knees and just shook. I couldn't have felt more upset if I had dropped that rock myself. Just like the movie reel had the ends tied together, the whole scene kept rolling over and over in front of my eyes, and I couldn't stop the film or even turn off the light in the projector.

I lay there with my head down waiting for someone to find the body and start hollering. It was little Marvin Herold, Smitty's courier, who started screaming in his high voice, "Safety! . . . Oh, God! . . . Safetysafetysafety! . . . Help! . . . Help!" "Safety" was the call we used to stop the fights if anyone saw a master coming or somebody got hurt. I lay there for several minutes listening to guys running past me through the brush heading for Baker Post, then I got up and followed them. I couldn't move very fast because my knees kept trying to bend the wrong way.

When I came out of the brush onto the gravel bank, I was surprised that everything looked so different. When I had left just five minutes before, the whole clearing and the creek were empty and lying bright in the sun, and Gene Hanlon was there all alone on the gravel bar. Now, with all the guys standing around and talking at once with their backs to the body, the whole place was different, and it wasn't so bad being there. I saw little Marvin Herold go over and try to take the pulse of Gene Hanlon's body. Marvin is a Boy Scout with lots of merit badges, and I expected him to try artificial respiration or a tourniquet, but he didn't find any pulse so he stood up and shook his head and wobbled over to where we were. He looked terribly blank, as though the *Scout Manual* had let him down.

The assumption going around was that Gene had run off the bluff and landed on his head and broken his neck. I couldn't see Peter anywhere, so I finally had to ask Smitty where he was. Smitty said he had sent Peter in to the school to tell somebody what had happened, and to get the ambulance. Smitty was still being the General, I guess, because there was nothing else for him to do. I tried to think to myself what Peter must be feeling like now, sent off to do an errand like that, but I couldn't get anywhere. My head was too full of what *I* was feeling like, standing with the fellows on the gravel bar looking at Gene Hanlon spread out half in the water like a dropped doll, knowing just how he had gotten there, and not being able to say anything.

Then Smitty got an idea, and he said, "Ronnie, weren't you here at Baker Post all the time?"

I made myself look at him, and then I said, "No, damn it. I got to thinking their army might try a crossing up by Able Post, so I went up there instead."

He said, "Oh," and forgot it.

Not long after, we heard a siren. We all knew what it was, and everybody stopped talking to listen to it as it got nearer. It was the first time I ever heard a siren and knew while hearing it why it had been called, and where it was going. It was sort of creepy, like it was saying to us over the trees, "Wait right there, boys. Don't anybody leave. I'll be there in a minute, and then we'll see just what's going on." I wanted to run and keep on running, until I got away from all the things swarming around inside me. You always wish afterward you had never joggled the wasp ball.

Pretty soon we heard somebody moving in the woods on the bluff and then two big men in white pants, carrying a folded-up stretcher, and another man in a suit, carrying a black bag, came out to the lip of the bluff. They stood there looking at us a minute without saying anything until one of the stretcher-bearers saw Gene Hanlon lying there all alone on the gravel bar. The man said something to the other two, and they all three looked where he pointed. Then the doctor looked at us all bunched up where we were and said, "Well, how do we get down?" He sounded sore. None of us moved or said anything, and in a minute the doctor got tired of waiting and blasted us. "Wake up over there! How do we go to get down?" Smitty came unstuck and gave them directions, and they went back into the brush heading north.

From then on things got pretty crowded in the woods. Two uniformed policemen and a photographer and a plain-clothes man showed up, and then Peter Irish came back leading almost the whole school faculty, and later a reporter and another photographer arrived. Nobody paid any attention to us for a while, so we just sat there in a clump, not moving or saying much. I managed to get right in the middle, and I kept down, hiding behind the guys around me and looking between them to see what was going on. After the police photographer was through taking pictures of Gene Hanlon from all sides, the two ambulance men raised him onto the stretcher and covered him with a piece of canvas or something and carried him away. The photographer took pictures all around by the creek and then went up onto the bluff and took pictures of the ground up there too. The plain-clothes man poking around on the gravel bar found Gene Hanlon's blue cap half full of rocks and gave it, with the rocks still in it, to one of the policemen to save.

I finally got up nerve enough to look for Peter Irish. He was standing with Smitty and Mr. Kelly, the math teacher, and they were talking. Peter didn't look any different. I didn't see how he could do it. I mean, stand right out there in plain sight of everyone, looking natural, with all that in his head. He looked around slowly as though he felt me watching him, and he found me there in the middle of the bunch. I couldn't have looked away if I had tried. He gave me a little smile, and I nodded my head to show him I'd seen it, then he went back to his talking with the other two.

Then the plain-clothes man went over to the three of them, and I got all wild inside and wanted to jump up and say that Peter couldn't possibly have done it, so please go away and let him alone. I could see the plain-clothes man doing most of the talking, and Peter and Smitty saying something once in a while, as though they were answering questions. After a little the plain-clothes man stopped talking and nodded, and the other three nodded back, and then he led them over to where the rest of us were.

Smitty and Peter sat down with us and Mr. Kelly collected all the other faculty men and brought them over.

The plain-clothes man tipped his hat back and put his hands in his pockets and said, "My name is Gorman. Sergeant Gorman. We know all about the rock fight now, so don't get nervous that you'll let on something that'll get you into trouble. You're already *in* trouble, but that's not my business. You can settle that with your instructors and your parents. Uh . . . you might think some about this, though. It's my feeling that every one of you here has a share in the responsibility for this boy's death. You all know rock fighting is dangerous, but you went ahead and did it anyway. But that's not what I'm after right now. I want to know if any of you boys actually saw this (what's his name?), this Hanlon boy run over the bluff."

I was looking straight at Sergeant Gorman, but in the side of my eye I saw Peter Irish turn his head around and look at me. I didn't peep.

Then Sergeant Gorman said, "Which one of you is Ronnie Quiller?"

I almost fainted.

Somebody poked me and I said, "Me." It didn't sound like my voice at all.

Sergeant Gorman said, "Which?"

I said, "Me," again.

This time he found me and said, "Weren't you supposed to be lying here in this thicket all the time?"

"Yes," I said. All the kids were looking at me. "But there wasn't anything doing here so I moved up there a ways."

"I see," he said. "Do you always disobey orders?"

"No," I said, "but after all, it was only a game."

"Some game," said Sergeant Gorman. "Good clean fun."

Then he let me alone. There was only one person there who knew I would never have deserted the post assigned to me. That was Peter Irish. I guess, Dad, that's when I began to get really scared. The worst of it was not knowing how much Peter knew, and not daring to ask. He might have been waiting out of sight in the brush after he dropped that rock, and seen me take off for Able Post. I had always been his friend, but what was I now to him? I wanted to tell him everything was okay and I wouldn't for the world squeal on him, but that would have told him I knew he did it. Maybe he knew without my telling him. I didn't know what to do.

Sergeant Gorman finished up, "Let's all go back to the school now. I want to talk to each of you alone." We all got up and started back through the woods in a bunch. I figured Peter would think it was funny if I avoided him, so I walked with him.

I said, "Lousy damn day."

He said, "Real lousy."

I said, "It seems like a hundred years since lunch."

We didn't say any more all the way back.

12

It took all afternoon to get the individual interviews over. They took us from Assembly Hall in alphabetical order, and we had to go in and sit across from Sergeant Gorman while he asked the questions. He must have asked us all the same questions because by the time he got to me he was saying the words like they were tired. A girl stenographer sat by him and took down the answers.

"Name?"

"Ronnie Quiller." I had to spell it.

"Were you at the rock fight this afternoon?"

"Yes, I was."

"What side were you on?"

"The Confederates."

"What were you supposed to do?"

"Watch the guys on the other side."

"After this whistle, did you see anyone?"

"No."

"You sure?"

"No, I didn't. That's why I moved from Baker Post up to Able Post. There wasn't anything doing where I was hiding."

"In rock fights before, have you ever changed position without telling somebody?"

"Sure, I guess. You can't run clear back to the field headquarters to tell anyone anything. It's up to them to find *you*."

Sergeant Gorman squinted at me with his eyebrows pulled down. "You know that if you had stayed where you were supposed to be you would have seen him fall over that bluff there?"

"Yes," I said.

"I wish you had."

Afterwards I ran into Smitty out in the hall and I asked him why all this fuss with the police and all. I asked him who called them.

"It was Peter, I think. He told Mr. Kelly to, and Mr. Kelly did."

"What do you suppose they're after?" I asked Smitty.

"Oh, I guess they're trying to get a straight story to tell Gene's parents and the newspapers. From what I get from Mr. Kelly, the school is all for it. They want everybody to know they weren't responsible."

"Do *you* think Gene fell over that bluff?" I couldn't help asking that one.

"I don't know. I suppose so." He cocked his head to one side and grinned a little at me. "Like they say in the papers, 'fell or was pushed,' huh?"

I said, "I guess nobody'd have nerve enough to do that to Gene—push him, I mean." All of a sudden I was thinking about something I had seen. Going back in my mind I remembered seeing Sergeant Gorman pick up Gene's cap half full of rocks. Gravel rocks taken from the low bank of the

13

creek. Now, I figured that Sergeant Gorman wouldn't have been a sergeant if he was stupid, and unless he was stupid he wouldn't go on for long thinking that Gene had fallen from above—*when the cap half full of rocks said he'd been down below all the time!*

I got my bike and rode home the long way to give me time to think about Peter and what he had done, and what I should do. You were real swell that night, and I guess I should have told you the whole story right then, but I just couldn't. I put myself in Peter's place, and I knew he would never have told on me. That's the way he was. He hated squealers. I couldn't think about his ever learning I had squealed on him. That would put me right alongside Angela Pine in his book. To him, I would have been the second person he trusted who let him down.

I felt like a rat in a cage with no place to go and no way out. When you kept me home nights after that, I didn't mind, because I wouldn't have gone out after dark if I'd been paid to. I don't blame you and Mother for thinking I had gone loony over the whole thing. Every noon recess for two whole weeks they pulled us into Assembly Hall and one of the masters would give a speech about group responsibility or public conscience or something awful like that, and then, worst of all, they made us bow our heads for five minutes in memory of Gene Hanlon. And there I'd be, sitting next to Peter Irish on the Assembly Hall bench, thinking back to the day of the last rock fight, and how Peter had looked up there on the bluff with the cords of his neck pulled tight, holding that big rock like it was a medicine ball. I had the crawliest feeling that if anybody in the hall had raised up his head and looked over at us together there on the bench, he would have seen two great fiery arrows pointing down at us. I was always afraid even to look up myself for fear I would have seen my own arrow and passed out on the spot.

It was my nightmares that got you worried, I guess. They always started out with Peter and me on a hike on a dusty country road. It was so hot you could hardly breathe. We would walk along without saying anything, with me lagging a little behind Peter so I could always keep an eye on him. And then the road would come out on the football field there at school, and he would go over to the woodpile and pick up a thin log and hold it in one hand, beckoning to me with the other and smiling. "Let's go over to the drugstore," he'd say, and then I'd start running.

I would follow the quarter-mile track around the football field and I'd know that everything would be all right if I could only get around it four times for a full mile. Every time I turned around to look, there he'd be right behind me, carrying that log and running easily, just like he used to pace me when I was out for the 880. I would make the first quarter mile all right, but then my wind would give out and my throat would dry up and my legs would get heavy, and I'd know that Peter was about to catch me, and I'd never make that full mile.

Then I would jar awake and be sweating and hanging on tight to the mattress, and in a minute you'd come in to see why I'd screamed. Your face was always kind of sad over me, and there in my bed in the dark, with you standing beside me, I would *almost* let go and tell you why things were so bad with me. But then as I'd come awake, and the hammering in my heart would slow up, and the sweat would begin to dry, all the things I owed Peter Irish would stand out again and look at me, and I would know that I could never tell you about it until my telling could no longer get Peter Irish into trouble.

I'm tired now, Dad—tired in so many ways and in so many places that I don't know where to begin resting. This letter took all night, as I thought it would. It's beginning to get light outside and the birds are starting up. I just reread the story in the paper where it says that Sergeant Gorman knew all along that Gene Hanlon had been murdered. I told you he wasn't stupid. He knew what that cap half full of rocks meant, and he knew what it meant to find a big damp socket in the earth on top of the bluff, and the rock which had been *in* the socket down below in the creek. And after he had talked to each of us alphabetically there in the school office, he knew the name of the only boy in school strong enough to lift up a seventy-pound rock and throw it like a medicine ball. He knew all of these things before the sun went down on the day of the last rock fight, but he was two months putting the rest of the story together so he could use it in his business.

As I read it in the paper, Sergeant Gorman went over to Peter's house last Monday night and talked to him about the things he had learned, and Peter listened respectfully, and then, when Sergeant Gorman was through and was ready to take Peter along with him, Peter excused himself to go upstairs and get his toilet articles. He got his four-ten shotgun instead and shot himself. I suppose it was the same four-ten he and I hunted squirrels with.

There's only one good thing about this whole stinking lousy mess, Dad. Because Sergeant Gorman talked to Peter and Peter listened, there in the living room, when Peter Irish climbed up those stairs he did it knowing that I, Ronnie Quiller, had not squealed on him. That may have made it easier. I don't know.

Now please, Dad—please may I come home again?

Ronnie

If you were Ronnie, would you have done what he did?

Could something like what happened in this story take place at your school?

15

# The Boar Hunt

*José Vasconcelos*

*Translated by Paul Waldorf*

W E were four companions, and we went by the names of our respective nationalities: the Colombian, the Peruvian, the Mexican; the fourth, a native of Ecuador, was called Quito for short. Unforeseen chance had joined us together a few years ago on a large sugar plantation on the Peruvian coast. We worked at different occupations during the day and met during the evening in our off time. Not being Englishmen, we did not play cards. Instead, our constant discussions led to disputes. These didn't stop us from wanting to see each other the next night, however, to continue the interrupted debates and support them with new arguments. Nor did the rough sentences of the preceding wrangles indicate a lessening of our affection, of which we assured ourselves reciprocally with the clasping of hands and a look. On Sundays we used to go on hunting parties. We roamed the fertile glens, stalking, generally with poor results, the game of the warm region around the coast, or we entertained ourselves killing birds that flew in the sunlight during the siesta hour.

We came to be tireless wanderers and excellent marksmen. Whenever we climbed a hill and gazed at the imposing range of mountains in the interior, its attractiveness stirred us and we wanted to climb it. What attracted us more was the trans-Andean region: fertile plateaus extending on the other side of the range in the direction of the Atlantic toward the immense land of Brazil.

It was as if primitive nature called us to her breast. The vigor of the fertile, untouched jungles promised to rejuvenate our minds, the same vigor which rejuvenates the strength and the thickness of the trees each year. At times we devised crazy plans. As with all things that are given a lot of thought, these schemes generally materialized. Ultimately, nature and events are largely what our imaginations make them out to be. And so we went ahead planning and acting. At the end of the year, with arranged vacations, accumulated money, good rifles, abundant munitions, stone- and mudproof boots, four hammocks, and a half dozen faithful Indians, our caravan descended the Andean slopes, leading to the endless green ocean.

At last we came upon a village at the edge of the Marañón River. Here we changed our safari. The region we were going to penetrate had no roads. It was unexplored underbrush into which we could enter only by going down the river in a canoe. In time we came to the area where we proposed to carry out the purpose of our journey, the hunting of wild boars.

We had been informed that boars travel in herds of several thousands, occupying a region, eating grass and staying together, exploiting the grazing areas, organized just like an army. They are very easy to kill if one attacks them when they are scattered out satisfying their appetites—an army given over to the delights of victory. When they march about hungry, on the other hand, they are usually vicious. In our search we glided down river between imposing jungles with our provisions and the company of three faithful Indian oarsmen.

One morning we stopped at some huts near the river. Thanks to the information gathered there, we decided to disembark a little farther on in order to spend the night on land and continue the hunt for the boars in the thicket the following day.

Sheltered in a backwater, we came ashore, and after a short exploration found a clearing in which to make camp. We unloaded the provisions and the rifles, tied the boat securely, then with the help of the Indians set up our camp one half kilometer from the river bank. In marking the path to the landing, we were careful not to lose ourselves in the thicket. The Indians withdrew toward their huts, promising to return two days later. At dawn we would set out in search of the prey.

Though night had scarcely come and the heat was great, we gathered at the fire to see each other's faces, to look instinctively for protection. We talked a little, smoked, confessed to being tired, and decided to go to bed. Each hammock had been tied by one end to a single tree, firm though not very thick in the trunk. Stretching out from this axis in different directions, the hammocks were supported by the other end on other trunks. Each of us carried his rifle, cartridges, and some provisions which couldn't remain exposed on the ground. The sight of the weapons made us consider the place where we were, surrounded by the unknown. A slight feeling of terror made us laugh, cough, and talk. But fatigue overcame us, that heavy fatigue which compels the soldier to scorn danger, to put down his rifle, and to fall asleep though the most persistent

enemy pursues him. We scarcely noticed the supreme grandeur of that remote tropical night.

I don't know whether it was the light of the magnificent dawn or the strange noises which awakened me and made me sit up in my hammock and look carefully at my surroundings. I saw nothing but the awakening of that life which at night falls into the lethargy of the jungle. I called my sleeping companions and, alert and seated in our hanging beds, we dressed ourselves. We were preparing to jump to the ground when we clearly heard a somewhat distant, sudden sound of rustling branches. Since it did not continue, however, we descended confidently, washed our faces with water from our canteens, and slowly prepared and enjoyed breakfast. By about 11:00 in the morning we were armed and bold and preparing to make our way through the jungle.

But then the sound again. Its persistence and proximity in the thicket made us change our minds. An instinct made us take refuge in our hammocks. We cautiously moved our cartridges and rifles into them again, and without consulting each other we agreed on the idea of putting our provisions safely away. We passed them up into the hammocks, and we ourselves finally climbed in. Stretched out face down, comfortably suspended with rifles in hand, we did not have to wait long. Black, agile boars quickly appeared from all directions. We welcomed them with shouts of joy and well-aimed shots. Some fell immediately, giving comical snorts, but many more came out of the jungle. We shot again, spending all the cartridges in the magazine. Then we stopped to reload. Finding ourselves safe in the height of our hammocks, we continued after a pause.

We counted dozens of them. At a glance we made rapid calculations of the magnitude of the destruction, while the boars continued to come out of the jungle in uncountable numbers. Instead of going on their way or fleeing, they seemed confused. All of them emerged from the jungle where it was easy for us to shoot them. Occasionally we had to stop firing because the frequent shooting heated the barrels of our rifles. While they were cooling we smoked and were able to joke, celebrating our good fortune. The impotent anger of the boars amazed us. They raised their tusks in our direction, uselessly threatening us. We laughed at their snorts, quietly aimed at those who were near, and Bang! a dead boar. We carefully studied the angle of the shoulder blade so that the bullet would cross the heart. The slaughter lasted for hours.

At 4:00 P.M. we noticed an alarming shortage of our ammunition. We had been well supplied and had shot at will. Though the slaughter was gratifying, the boars must have numbered, as we had been informed previously, several thousands, because their hordes didn't diminish. On the contrary, they gathered directly beneath our hammocks in increasing groups. They slashed furiously at the trunk of the tree which held the four points of the hammocks. The marks of the tusks remained on the hard bark. Not

without a certain fear we watched them gather compactly, tenaciously, in tight masses against the resisting trunk. We wondered what would happen to a man who fell within their reach. Our shots were now sporadic, well aimed, carefully husbanded. They did not drive away the aggressive beasts, but only redoubled their fury. One of us ironically noted that from being the attackers we had gone on the defensive. We did not laugh very long at the joke. Now we hardly shot at all. We needed to save our cartridges.

The afternoon waned and evening came upon us. After consulting each other, we decided to eat in our hammocks. We applauded ourselves for taking the food up—meat, bread, and bottles of water. Stretching ourselves on our hammocks, we passed things to each other, sharing what we needed. The boars deafened us with their angry snorts.

After eating, we began to feel calm. We lit cigars. Surely the boars would go. Their numbers were great, but they would finally leave peacefully. As we said so, however, we looked with greedy eyes at the few unused cartridges that remained. Our enemies, like enormous angry ants, stirred beneath us, encouraged by the ceasing of our fire. From time to time we carefully aimed and killed one or two of them, driving off the huge group of uselessly enraged boars at the base of the trunk which served as a prop for our hammocks.

Night enveloped us almost without our noticing the change from twilight. Anxiety also overtook us. When would the cursed boars leave? Already there were enough dead to

19

serve as trophies to several dozen hunters. Our feat would be talked about; we had to show ourselves worthy of such fame. Since there was nothing else to do, it was necessary to sleep. Even if we had had enough bullets it would have been impossible to continue the fight in the darkness. It occurred to us to start a fire to drive the herd off with flames, but apart from the fact that we couldn't leave the place in which we were suspended, there were no dry branches in the lush forest. Finally, we slept.

We woke up a little after midnight. The darkness was profound, but the well-known noise made us aware that our enemies were still there. We imagined they must be the last ones which were leaving, however. If a good army needs several hours to break camp and march off, what can be expected of a vile army of boars but disorder and delay? The following morning we would fire upon the stragglers, but this painful thought bothered us: they were in large and apparently active numbers. What were they up to? Why didn't they leave? We thus spent long hours of worry. Dawn finally came, splendid in the sky but noisy in the jungle still enveloped inwardly in shadows. We eagerly waited for the sun to penetrate the foliage in order to survey the appearance of the field of battle of the day before.

What we finally saw made us gasp. It terrified us. The boars were painstakingly continuing the work which they had engaged in throughout the entire night. Guided by some extraordinary instinct, with their tusks they were digging out the ground underneath the tree from which our hammocks hung; they gnawed the roots and continued to undermine them like large, industrious rats. Presently the tree was bound to fall and we with it, among the beasts. From that moment we neither thought nor talked. In desperation we used up our last shots, killing more ferocious beasts. Still the rest renewed their activity. They seemed to be endowed with intelligence. However much we concentrated our fire against them, they did not stop their attack against the tree.

Soon our shots stopped. We emptied our pistols, and then silently listened to the tusks gnawing beneath the soft, wet, pleasant-smelling earth. From time to time the boars pressed against the tree, pushing it and making it creak, eager to smash it quickly. We looked on hypnotized by their devilish activity. It was impossible to flee because the black monsters covered every inch in sight. It seemed to us that, by a sudden inspiration, they were preparing to take revenge on us for the ruthless nature of man, the unpunished destroyer of animals since the beginning of time. Our imagination, distorted by fear, showed us our fate as an atonement for the unpardonable crimes implicit in the struggle of biological selection. Before my eyes passed the vision of sacred India, where the believer refuses to eat meat in order to prevent the methodical killing of beasts and in order to atone for man's evil, bloody, treacherous slaughter, such as ours, for mere vicious pleasure. I felt that foundland coast are the most visible. Here, they spawn on the beaches rather than in deep water offshore, and I have come to see their rush for eternity.

They gather a thousand feet offshore, coalescing into groups of a hundred thousand to break the water's surface with bright chuckling sounds. They gather, and grow. Soon they are in the millions, with other millions swimming up from the offshore deeps. They gather, now in the billions, so densely packed together in places that the sea shimmers silver for miles and flows, serpentine, with the swelling body of a single, composite creature.

The fish do, in fact, possess a common sense of purpose. Nothing can redirect their imperative to breed. I once swam among them and saw them parting reluctantly ahead of me, felt their bodies flicking against my hands. Looking back, I saw them closing in, filling up the space created by my passage. The passive fish tolerated me, in their anticipation of what they were about to do.

At this time of the year they are so engrossed that they barely react when a host of creatures advances to kill them. Beneath and beyond them, codfish pour up out of the deep. They overtake the capelin, eat them, plunge their sleek, dark bodies recklessly into shallow water. Some have swum so rapidly from such depths that their swim bladders are distended by the sudden drop in water pressure. The cod are gigantic by comparison with the capelin. Many weigh one hundred pounds or more, and will not be sated until they have eaten scores of capelin each. The water writhes with movement and foam where cod, headlong in pursuit, drive themselves clear out of the sea and fall back with staccato slaps.

The attack of the codfish is a brutal opening to a ritual, and a contradiction in their character. Normally, they are sedentary feeders on the sea floor. Now, however, they are possessed. Their jaws rip and tear; the water darkens with capelin blood: the shredded pieces of flesh hang suspended or rise to the surface.

Now a group of seabirds, the parrotlike puffins, clumsy in flight, turn over the capelin, their grotesque, axlike beaks probing from side to side as they watch the upper layers of the massacre. They are joined by new formations of birds until several thousand puffins are circling. They are silent, and there is no way of knowing how they were summoned from their nesting burrows on an island that is out of sight. They glide down to the water—stub-winged cargo planes—land awkwardly, taxi with fluttering wings and stamping paddle feet, then dive.

At the same time, the sea view moves with new invasions of seabirds. Each bird pumps forward with an urgency that suggests it has received the same stimulus as the cod. The gulls that breed on cliffs along a southern bay come first, gracefully light of wing, with raucous

voice as they cry out their anticipation. Beneath them, flying flat, direct, silent, come murres, black-bodied, short-tailed, close relatives of the puffins. The murres land and dive without ceremony. Well offshore, as though waiting confirmation of the feast, shearwaters from Tristan da Cunha turn long, pointed wings across the troughs of waves and cackle like poultry.

The birds converge, and lose their identity in the mass thickening on the water. Small gulls—the kittiwakes, delicate in flight—screech and drop and rise and screech and drop like snowflakes on the sea. They fall among even smaller birds, lighter than they, which dangle their feet and hover at the water's surface, almost walking on water as they seek tiny pieces of shredded flesh. These are the ocean-flying petrels, the Mother Carey's chickens of mariners' legends, which rarely come within sight of land. All order is lost in the shrieking tumult of the hundreds of thousands of birds.

Underwater, the hunters meet among their prey. The puffins and murres dive below the capelin and attack, driving for the surface. The cod attack at mid-depth. The gulls smother the surface and press the capelin back among the submarine hunters. The murres and puffins fly underwater, their beating wings turning them rapidly back and forth. They meet the cod, flail wings in desperate haste, are caught, crushed, and swallowed. Now seabirds as well as capelin become the hunted. Puffin and murre tangle wings. Silver walls of capelin flicker, part, re-form. Some seabirds surface abruptly, broken wings dangling. Others, with a leg or legs torn off, fly frantically, crash, skitter in shock across the water.

I see the capelin hunters spread across the sea, but also remember them in time. Each year the hunters are different because many of them depend on a fortuitous meeting with their prey. A group of small whales collides with the capelin, and in a flurry of movement they eat several tons of them. Salmon throw themselves among the capelin with the same abandon as the codfish, and in the melee become easy victims for a score of seals that kill dozens of them, then turn to the capelin and gorge themselves nearly stuporous. They rise, well beyond the tumult of the seabirds, their black heads jutting like rocks from the swell, to lie with distended bellies and doze away their feast. Capelin boil up around them for a moment but now the animals ignore them.

The capelin are hosts in a ceremony so ancient that a multitude of species have adapted to seeking a separate share of the host's bounty. The riotous collision of cod, seal, whale, and seabird obscures the smaller guests at the feast. Near the shore wait small brown fish—the cunner— one of the most voracious species. Soon they will be fighting among themselves for pieces of flesh as the capelin begin their run for the beach, or when the survivors of the spawning reel back into deep water, with the dead and dying falling to the bottom. If the water is calm and the sun bright, the cunner can be seen in two fathoms, ripping capelin corpses to pieces and scattering translucent scales like silver leaves in a wind of the sea.

Closer inshore, at the wave line, the flounder wait. They know the capelin are coming and their role is also predetermined. They cruise rapidly under the purling water in uncharacteristic excitement. They are not interested in capelin flesh. They want capelin eggs, and they will gorge as soon as spawning starts.

Now, the most voracious of all the hunters appear. Fishing vessels come up over the horizon. They brought the Portuguese of the fifteenth century, who anchored offshore, dropped their boats, and rowed ashore to take the capelin with handnets, on beaches never before walked by white men. They brought Spaniards and Dutchmen, Englishmen and Irish, from the sixteenth to the twentieth centuries. Americans, Nova Scotians, Gloucestermen, schoonermen, bankermen, long-liner captains have participated in the ritual. All of them knew that fresh capelin is the finest bait when it is skillfully used, and can attract a fortune in codfish flesh, hooked on the submarine banks to the south.

But presently, these hunters are Newfoundlanders. They bring their schooners flying inshore like great brown-and-white birds, a hundred, two hundred, three hundred sail. They heel through the screaming seabirds, luff,° anchor, and drop their dories with the same precision of movement of the other figures in the ritual. In an hour, three thousand men are at work from the boats. They work as the codfish work, with a frenzy that knots forearms and sends nets spilling over the sterns to encircle the capelin. They lift a thousand tons of capelin out of the sea, yet they do not measurably diminish the number of fish.

Meanwhile, landbound hunters wait for the fish to come within range of their lead-weighted handnets. Women, children, and old people crowd the beach with the able-bodied men. The old people have ancestral memories of capelin bounty. In the seventeenth and eighteenth centuries, when food was often short, only the big capelin harvest stood between them and starvation during the winter.

Many of the shore people are farmers who use the capelin for fertilizer as well as for food. Capelin corpses, spread to rot over thin northern soils, draw obedient crops of potatoes and cabbages out of the ground, and these, mixed with salted capelin flesh, become winter meals.

The children, who remember dried capelin as their candy, share the excitement of waiting. They chase one another up and down the beach and play with their own nets and fishing rods. Some are already asleep because they awoke before dawn to rouse the village, as they

° LUFF: to turn the nose of a ship into the wind

do every capelin morning, with the cry: "They've a-come, they've a-come!"

At the top of the beach, old women lie asleep or sit watching the seabirds squabbling and the dorymen rowing. They are Aunt Sadie and Little Nell and Bessie Blue and Mother Taunton, old ladies from several centuries. They know the capelin can save children in hard winters when the inshore cod fishery fails. They get up at two o'clock in the morning when the capelin are running, to walk miles to the nearest capelin beach. They net a barrel of fish, then roll the barrel, which weighs perhaps a hundred pounds, back home. They have finished spreading the fish on their gardens, or salting them, before the first of their grandchildren awakes.

They have clear memories of catching capelin in winter, when the sea freezes close inshore and the tide cracks the ice in places. Then millions of capelin, resting out the winter, rise in the cracks. An old woman with a good net can take tons of passive fish out of the water for as long as her strength lasts and for as far as her net reaches.

A cry rises from the beach: "Here they come!"

The ritual must be played out, according to habit. The dorymen and the seabirds, the rampaging cod and cunner cannot touch or turn the purpose of the capelin. At a moment, its genesis unknown, they start for the shore. From the top of some nearby cliffs I watch and marvel at the precision of their behavior. The capelin cease to be a great, formless mass offshore. They split into groups that the Newfoundlanders call *wads*—rippling gray lines, five to fifty feet wide—and run for the shore like advancing infantry lines. One by one, they peel away from their surviving comrades and advance, thirty to forty wads at a time.

Each wad has its discipline. The fish prepare to mate. Each male capelin seeks a female, darting from one fish to another. When he finds one, he presses against her side. Another male, perhaps two males, press against her other side. The males urge the female on toward the beach. Some are struck down by diving seabirds but others take their places. Cod dash among them and smash their sexual formations; they re-form immediately. Cunner rise and rip at them; flounder dart beneath them toward the beach.

The first wad runs into beach wavelets, and a hundred nets hit the water together; a silver avalanche of fish spills out on the beach. In each breaking wavelet the capelin maintain their formations, two or three males pressed tightly against their female until they are all flung up on the beach. There, to the whispering sound of tiny fins and tails vibrating, the female convulsively digs into the sand, which is still moving in the wake of the retreating wave. As she goes down, she extrudes up to fifty thousand eggs, and the males expel their milt.

The children shout; their bare feet fly over the spawning fish; the nets soar; sea boots grind down; the fish spill out; gulls run in the shallows under the children's feet; the flounder gorge. A codfish, two feet long, leaps out of the shallows and hits the beach. An old man scoops it up. The wads keep coming. The air is filled with birds. The dorymen shout and laugh.

The flood of eggs becomes visible. The sand glistens, then is greasy with eggs. They pile in driftlines that writhe back and forth in each wave. The female capelin wriggle into masses of eggs. The shallows are permeated with eggs. The capelin breathe eggs. Their mouths fill with eggs. Their stomachs are choked with eggs. The wads keep pouring onward, feeding the disaster on the beach.

Down come the boots and the nets, and the capelin die, mouths open and oozing eggs. The spawning is a fiasco. The tide has turned. Instead of spawning on the shore with the assurance of rising water behind them, each wad strikes ashore in retreating water. Millions are stranded but the wads keep coming.

In the background, diminished by the quantity of fish, other players gasp and pant at their nets. Barrels stack high on the beach. Horses whinny, driven hard up the bank at the back of the beach. Carts laden with barrels weave away. Carts bringing empty barrels bounce and roar down. The wads are still coming. Men use shovels to lift dead and dying fish from driftlines that are now two and three feet high. The easterly wind is freshening. The wavelets become waves. The capelin are flung up on the beach without a chance to spawn. They bounce and twist and the water flees beneath them.

It is twilight, then dark; torches now spot the beach, the offshore dories, and the schooners. The waves grow solidly and pile the capelin higher. The men shovel the heaps into pyramids, then reluctantly leave the beach. Heavy rain blots out beach and sea.

I remain to watch the blow piling up the sea. At the lowest point of the tide, it is driving waves high up on the beach, roiling the sand, digging up the partially buried eggs, and carrying them out to sea. By dawn most of the eggs are gone. The capelin have disappeared. The seabirds, the schooners, the cod, flounder, cunner, seals, whales have gone. Nothing remains except the marks of human feet, the cart tracks on the high part of the beach, the odd pyramid of dead fish. The feast is done.

The empty arena of the beach suggests a riddle. If the capelin were so perfectly adapted to spawn on a rising tide, to master the task of burying eggs in running sand between waves, to *know* when the tide was rising, why did they continue spawning after the tide turned? Was that, by the ancient rules of the ritual, intentional? If it was, then it indicated a lethal error of adaptation that did not jibe with the great numbers of capelin.

I wonder, then, if the weak died and the strong survived, but dismiss the notion after recalling the indiscriminate nature of all capelin deaths.

29

There was no Darwinian selection° for death of the stupid or the inexperienced. Men slaughtered billions, this year and last year and for three hundred years before, but the capelin never felt this pin-pricking on their colossal corporate bodies. Their spawning was a disaster for reasons well beyond the influence of men.

A nineteenth-century observer, after seeing a capelin-spawning, recorded his amazement at "the astonishing *prosperity* of these creatures, cast so wilfully away. . . ." It was in the end, and indeed throughout the entire ritual, the sheer numbers of capelin that scored the memory. The *prosperity* of the capelin preceded the disaster but then, it seemed, created it. Prosperity was not beneficial or an assurance of survival. The meaning of the ritual was slowly growing into sense. Prosperity unhinges the capelin. Prosperity, abundance, success, drive them on. They become transformed and throw themselves forward blindly. . . .

I turn from the beach, warm and secure, and take a blind step forward.

°DARWINIAN SELECTION: the idea that the continuance of any form of life depends on "survival of the fittest"; a part of the theory of evolution as advanced by Charles Darwin, English naturalist, in 1859.

30          In your opinion, is the running of the capelin and all that goes with it an example of nature's "madness"? Or is it an example of the natural order of the universe?

# On a Squirrel
# Crossing the Road in Autumn,
# in New England

*Richard Eberhart*

*It is what he does not know,*
*Crossing the road under the elm trees,*
*About the mechanism of my car,*
*About the Commonwealth of Massachusetts,*
*About Mozart, India, Arcturus,*

*That wins my praise. I engage*
*At once in whirling squirrel-praise.*

31

*He obeys the orders of nature*
*Without knowing them.*
*It is what he does not know*
*That makes him beautiful.*
*Such a knot of little purposeful nature!*

*I who can see him as he cannot see himself*
*Repose in the ignorance that is his blessing.*

*It is what man does not know of God*
*Composes the visible poem of the world.*

*. . . Just missed him!*

# 2

# Traveling Through the Dark

Traveling through the dark I found a deer
dead on the edge of the Wilson River road.
It is usually best to roll them into the canyon:
that road is narrow; to swerve might make more dead.

By glow of the tail-light I stumbled back of the car
and stood by the heap, a doe, a recent killing;
she had stiffened already, almost cold.
I dragged her off; she was large in the belly.

My fingers touching her side brought me the reason—
her side was warm; her fawn lay there waiting,
alive, still, never to be born.
Beside that mountain road I hesitated.

The car aimed ahead its lowered parking lights;
under the hood purred the steady engine.
I stood in the glare of the warm exhaust turning red;
around our group I could hear the wilderness listen.

I thought hard for us all—my only swerving—,
then pushed her over the edge into the river.

—William Stafford

33

Just who is it that's traveling through the dark?
And what is "the dark," anyway?

# Fifteen

South of the bridge on Seventeenth
I found back of the willows one summer
day a motorcycle with engine running
as it lay on its side, ticking over
slowly in the high grass. I was fifteen.

I admired all that pulsing gleam, the
shiny flanks, the demure headlights
fringed where it lay; I led it gently
to the road and stood with that
companion, ready and friendly. I was fifteen.          10

We could find the end of a road, meet
the sky on out Seventeenth. I thought about
hills, and patting the handle got back a
confident opinion. On the bridge we indulged
a forward feeling, a tremble. I was fifteen.

Thinking, back farther in the grass I found
the owner, just coming to, where he had flipped
over the rail. He had blood on his hand, was pale—
I helped him walk to his machine. He ran his hand
over it, called me good man, roared away.          20

I stood there, fifteen.

—William Stafford

35

36

# The Osage Orange Tree

William Stafford

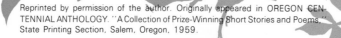

Reprinted by permission of the author. Originally appeared in OREGON CEN-
TENNIAL ANTHOLOGY. "A Collection of Prize-Winning Short Stories and Poems."
State Printing Section, Salem, Oregon, 1959.

On that first day of high school in the prairie town where the tree was, I stood in the sun by the flagpole and watched, but pretended not to watch, the others. They stood in groups and talked and knew each other, all except one—a girl though—in a faded blue dress, carrying a sack lunch and standing near the corner looking everywhere but at the crowd.

I might talk to her, I thought. But of course it was out of the question.

That first day was easier when the classes started. Some of the teachers were kind; some were frightening. Some of the students didn't care, but I listened and waited; and at the end of the day I was relieved, less conspicuous from then on.

But that day was not really over. As I hurried to carry my new paper route, I was thinking about how in a strange town, if you are quiet, no one notices, and some may like you, later. I was thinking about this when I reached the north edge of town where the scattering houses dwindle. Beyond them to the north lay just openness, the plains, a big swoop of nothing. There, at the last house, just as I cut across a lot and threw to the last customer, I saw the girl in the blue dress coming along the street, heading on out of town, carrying books. And she saw me.

"Hello."

"Hello."

And because we stopped we were friends. I didn't know how I could stop, but I didn't hurry on. I stood. There was nothing to do but to act as if I were walking on out too. I had three papers left in the bag, and I frantically began to fold them—box them, as we called it—for throwing. We had begun to walk and talk. The girl was timid; I became more bold. Not much, but a little.

"Have you gone to school here before?" I asked.

"Yes, I went here last year."

A long pause. A meadowlark sitting on a fencepost hunched his wings and flew. I kicked through the dust of the road.

I began to look ahead. Where could we possibly be walking to? I couldn't be walking just because I wanted to be with her.

Fortunately, there was one more house, a gray house by a sagging barn, set two hundred yards from the road.

"I thought I'd see if I could get a customer here," I said, waving toward the house.

"That's where I live."

"Oh."

We were at the dusty car tracks that turned off the road to the house. The girl stopped. There was a tree at that corner, a straight but little tree with slim branches and shiny dark leaves.

"I could take a paper tonight to see if my father wants to buy it."

A great relief, this. What could I have said to her parents? I held out a paper, dropped it, picked it up, brushing off the dust. "No, here's a new one"—a great action, putting the dusty paper in the bag over my shoulder and pulling out a fresh one. When she took the paper we stood there a minute. The wind was coming in over the grass. She looked out with a tranquil expression.

She walked away past the tree, and I hurried quickly back toward town. Could anyone in the houses have been watching? I looked back once. The girl was standing on the small bridge halfway in to her house. I hurried on.

The next day at school I didn't ask her whether her father wanted to take the paper. When the others were there I wouldn't say anything. I stood with the boys. In American history the students could choose their seats, and I saw that she was too quiet and plainly dressed for many to notice her. But I crowded in with the boys, pushing one aside, scrambling for a seat by the window.

That night I came to the edge of town. Two papers were left, and I walked on out. The meadowlark was there. By some reeds in a ditch by the road a dragonfly—snake feeders, we called them—glinted. The sun was going down, and the plains were stretched out and lifted, some way, to the horizon. Could I go on up to the house? I didn't think so, but I walked on. Then, by the tree where her road turned off, she was standing. She was holding her books. More confused than ever, I stopped.

"My father will take the paper," she said.

She told me always to leave the paper at the foot of the tree. She insisted on that, saying their house was too far; and it is true that I was far off my route, a long way, a half-mile out of my territory. But I didn't think of that.

And so we were acquainted. What I remember best in that town is those evening walks to the tree. Every night—or almost every night—the girl was there. Evangeline was her name. We didn't say much. On Friday night of the first week she gave me a dime, the cost of the paper. It was a poor newspaper, by the way, cheap, sensational, unreliable. I never went up to her house. We never talked together at school. But all the time we knew each other; we just happened to meet. Every evening.

There was a low place in the meadow by that corner. The fall rains made a pond there, and in the evenings sometimes ducks would be coming in—a long line with set wings down the wind, and then a turn, and a skimming glide to the water. The wind would be blowing and the grass bent down. The evenings got colder and colder. The wind was cold. As winter came on the time at the tree was dimmer, but not dark. In the winter there was snow. The pond was frozen over; all the plains were white. I had to walk down the ruts of the road and leave the paper in the crotch of the tree, sometimes, when it was cold. The wind made a sound through the black branches. But usually, even on cold evenings, Evangeline was there.

At school we played ball at noon—the boys did. And I got acquainted. I learned that Evangeline's brother was janitor at the school. A big dark boy he was—a man, middle-aged I thought at the time. He didn't ever let on that he knew me. I would see him sweeping the halls, bent down, slow.

38

I would see him and Evangeline take their sack lunches over to the south side of the building. Once I slipped away from the ball game and went over there, but he looked at me so steadily, without moving, that I pretended to be looking for a book, and quickly went back, and got in the game and struck out.

You don't know about those winters, and especially that winter. Those were the dust years. Wheat was away down in price. Everyone was poor—poor in a way that you can't understand. I made two dollars a week, or something like that, on my paper route. I could tell about working for ten cents an hour—and then not getting paid; about families that ate wheat, boiled, for their main food, and burned wheat for fuel. You don't know how it would be. All through that hard winter I carried a paper to the tree by the pond, in the evening, and gave it to Evangeline.

In the cold weather Evangeline wore a heavier dress, a dark, straight, heavy dress, under a thick black coat. Outdoors she wore a knitted cap that fastened under her chin. She was dressed this way when we met and she took the paper. The reeds were broken now. The meadowlark was gone.

And then came the spring. I have forgotten to tell just how Evangeline looked. She was of medium height, and slim. Her face was pale, her forehead high, her eyes blue. Her tranquil face I remember well. I remember her watching the wind come in over the grass. Her dress was long, her feet small. I can remember her by the tree, with her books, or walking on up the road toward her house and stopping on the bridge halfway up there, but she didn't wave, and I couldn't tell whether she was watching me or not. I always looked back as I went over the rise toward town.

And I can remember her in the room at school. She came into American history one spring day, the first really warm day. She had changed from the dark heavy dress to the dull blue one of the last fall; and she had on a new belt, a gray belt, with blue stitching along the edges. As she passed in front of Jane Wright, a girl who sat on the front row, I heard Jane say to the girl beside her, "Why look at Evangeline—that old dress of hers has a new belt!"

"Stop a minute, Evangeline," Jane said, "let me see your new dress."

Evangeline stopped and looked uncertainly at Jane and blushed. "It's just made over," she said, "it's just. . . ."

"It's cute, Dear," Jane said; and as Evangeline went on Jane nudged her friend in the ribs and the friend smothered a giggle.

Well, that was a good year. Commencement time came, and—along with the newspaper job—I had the task of preparing for finals and all. One thing, I wasn't a student who took part in the class play or anything like that. I was just one of the boys—twenty-fourth in line to get my diploma.

And graduation was bringing an end to my paper-carrying. My father covered a big territory in our part of the state, selling farm equipment; and we were going to move at once to a town seventy miles south. Only because of my finishing the school year had we stayed till graduation.

I had taught another boy my route, always leaving him at the end and walking on out, by myself, to the tree. I didn't really have to go around with him that last day, the day of graduation, but I was going anyway.

At the graduation exercises, held that May afternoon, I wore my brown Sunday suit. My mother was in the audience. It was a heavy day. The girls had on new dresses. But I didn't see her.

I suppose that I did deserve old man Sutton's "Shhh!" as we lined up to march across the stage, but I for the first time in the year forgot my caution, and asked Jane where Evangeline was. She shrugged, and I could see for myself that she was not there.

We marched across the stage; our diplomas were ours; our parents filed out; to the strains of a march on the school organ we trailed to the hall. I unbuttoned my brown suit coat, stuffed the diploma in my pocket, and sidled out of the group and upstairs.

Evangeline's brother was emptying wastebaskets at the far end of the hall. I sauntered toward him and stopped. I didn't know what I wanted to say. Unexpectedly, he solved my problem. Stopping in his work, holding a partly empty wastebasket over the canvas sack he wore over his shoulder, he stared at me, as if almost to say something.

"I noticed that your sister wasn't here," I said. The noise below was dwindling. The hall was quiet, an echoey place; my voice sounded terribly loud. He emptied the rest of the wastebasket and shifted easily. He was a man, in big overalls. He stared at me.

"Evangeline couldn't come," he said. He stopped, looked at me again, and said, "She stole."

"Stole?" I said. "Stole what?"

He shrugged and went toward the next wastebasket, but I followed him.

"She stole the money from her bank—the money she was to use for her graduation dress," he said. He walked stolidly on, and I stopped. He deliberately turned away as he picked up the next wastebasket. But he said something else, half to himself. "You knew her. You talked to her . . . I know." He walked away.

I hurried downstairs and outside. The new carrier would have the papers almost delivered by now; so I ran up the street toward the north. I took a paper from him at the end of the street and told him to go back. I didn't pay any more attention to him.

No one was at the tree, and I turned, for the first time, up the road to the house. I walked over the bridge and on up the narrow, rutty tracks. The house was gray and lopsided. The ground of the yard was packed; nothing grew there. By the back door, the door to which the road led, there was a grayish-white place on the ground where the dishwater had been thrown. A gaunt shepherd dog trotted out growling.

And the door opened suddenly, as if someone had been watching me come up the track. A woman came out—a woman stern-faced, with a shawl over her head and a dark lumpy dress on—came out on the back porch and shouted, "Go 'way, go 'way! We don't want no papers!" She waved violently with one hand, holding the other on her shawl, at her throat. She coughed so hard that she leaned over and put her hand against one of the uprights of the porch. Her face was red. She glanced toward the barn and leaned toward me. "Go 'way!"

Behind me a meadowlark sang. Over all the plains swooped the sky. The land was drawn up somehow toward the horizon.

I stood there, half-defiant, half-ashamed. The dog continued to growl and to pace around me, stiff-legged, his tail down. The windows of the house were all blank, with blinds drawn. I couldn't say anything.

I stood a long time and then, lowering the newspaper I had held out, I stood longer, waiting, without thinking of what to do. The meadowlark bubbled over again, but I turned and walked away, looking back once or twice. The old woman continued to stand, leaning forward, her head out. She glanced at the barn, but didn't call out any more.

My heels dug into the grayish place where the dishwater had been thrown; the dog skulked along behind.

At the bridge, halfway to the road, I stopped and looked back. The dog was lying down again; the porch was empty; and the door was closed. Turning the other way, I looked toward town. Near me stood our ragged little tree—an Osage orange tree it was. It was feebly coming into leaf, green all over the branches, among the sharp thorns. I hadn't wondered before how it grew there, all alone, in the plains country, neglected. Over our pond some ducks came slicing in.

Standing there on the bridge, still holding the folded-boxed-newspaper, that worthless paper, I could see everything. I looked out along the road to town. From the bridge you would see the road going away, to where it went over the rise.

Glancing around, I flipped that last newspaper under the bridge and then bent far over and looked where it had gone. There they were—a pile of boxed newspapers, thrown in a heap, some new, some worn and weathered, by rain, by snow.

41

*"Reach out for someone . . . To communicate is the beginning of understanding."*

AGREE?
DISAGREE?

# The Farm on the Great Plains
## William Stafford

A telephone line goes cold;
birds tread it wherever it goes.
A farm back of a great plain
tugs an end of the line.

I call that farm every year,
ringing it, listening, still;
no one is home at the farm,
the line gives only a hum.

Some year I will ring the line
on a night at last the right one,          10
and with an eye tapered for braille
from the phone on the wall.

I will see the tenant who waits—
the last one left at the place;
through the dark my braille eye
will lovingly touch his face.

"Hello, is Mother at home?"
No one is home today.
"But Father—he should be there."
No one—no one is here.                      20

"But you—are you the one . . .?"
Then the line will be gone
because both ends will be home:
no space, no birds, no farm.

My self will be the plain,
wise as winter is gray,
pure as cold posts go
pacing toward what I know.

42

As you see it, what does the poet "know" (line 28)?

43

# A Way
# of Writing

William Stafford

A writer is not so much someone who has something to say as he is someone who has found a process that will bring about new things he would not have thought of if he had not started to say them. That is, he does not draw on a reservoir; instead, he engages in an activity that brings to him a whole succession of unforeseen stories, poems, essays, plays, laws, philosophies, religions, or—but wait!

Back in school, from the first when I began to try to write things, I felt this richness. One thing would lead to another; the world would give and give. Now, after twenty years or so of trying, I live by that certain richness, an idea hard to pin, difficult to say, and perhaps offensive to some. For there are strange implications in it.

One implication is the importance of just plain receptivity. When I write, I like to have an interval before me when I am not likely to be interrupted. For me, this means usually the early morning, before others are awake. I get pen and paper, take a glance out the window (often it is dark out there), and wait. It is like fishing. But I do not wait very long, for there is always a nibble—and this is where receptivity comes in. To get started I will accept anything that occurs to me. Something always occurs, of course, to any of us. We can't keep from thinking. Maybe I have to settle for an immediate impression: it's cold, or hot, or dark, or bright, or in between! Or—well, the possibilities are endless. If I put down something, that thing will help the next thing come, and I'm off. If I let the process go on, things will occur to me that were not at all in my mind when I started. These things, odd or trivial as they may be, are somehow connected. And if I let them string out, surprising things will happen.

If I let them string out. . . . Along with initial receptivity, then, there is another readiness: I must be willing to fail. If I am to keep on writing, I cannot bother to insist on high standards. I must get into action and not let anything stop me, or even slow me much. By "standards" I do not mean "correctness"—spelling, punctuation, and so on. These details become

44

mechanical for anyone who writes for a while. I am thinking about what many people would consider "important" standards, such matters as social significance, positive values, consistency, etc. I resolutely disregard these. Something better, greater, is happening! I am following a process that leads so wildly and originally into new territory that no judgment can at the moment be made about values, significance, and so on. I am making something new, something that has not been judged before. Later others—and maybe I myself—will make judgments. Now, I am headlong to discover. Any distraction may harm the creating.

So, receptive, careless of failure, I spin out things on the page. And a wonderful freedom comes. If something occurs to me, it is all right to accept it. It has one justification: it occurs to me. No one else can guide me. I must follow my own weak, wandering, diffident impulses.

A strange bonus happens. At times, without my insisting on it, my writings become coherent; the successive elements that occur to me are clearly related. They lead by themselves to new connections. Sometimes the language, even the syllables that happen along, may start a trend. Sometimes the materials alert me to something waiting in my mind, ready for sustained attention. At such times, I allow myself to be eloquent, or intentional, or for great swoops (treacherous! not to be trusted!) reasonable. But I do not insist on any of that; for I know that back of my activity there will be the coherence of my self, and that indulgence of my impulses will bring recurrent patterns and meanings again.

This attitude toward the process of writing creatively suggests a problem for me, in terms of what others say. They talk about "skills" in writing. Without denying that I do have experience, wide reading, automatic orthodoxies and maneuvers of various kinds, I still must insist that I am often baffled about what "skill" has to do with the precious little area of confusion when I do not know what I am going to say and then I find out what I am going to say. That precious interval I am unable to bridge by skill. What can I witness about it? It remains mysterious, just as all of us must feel puzzled about how we are so inventive as to be able to talk along through complexities with our friends, not needing to plan what we are going to say, but never stalled for long in our confident forward progress. Skill? If so, it is the skill we all have, something we must have learned before the age of three or four.

A writer is one who has become accustomed to trusting that grace, or luck, or—skill.

Yet another attitude I find necessary: most of what I write, like most of what I say in casual conversation, will not amount to much. Even I will realize, and even at the time, that it is not negotiable. It will be like practice. In conversation I allow myself random remarks—in fact, as I recall, that is the way I learned to talk—, so in writing I launch many expendable efforts. A result of this free way of writing is that I am not writing for others, mostly;

45

they will not see the product at all unless the activity eventuates in something that later appears to be worthy. My guide is the self, and its adventuring in the language brings about communication.

This process-rather-than-substance view of writing invites a final, dual reflection:

1) Writers may not be special—sensitive or talented in any usual sense. They are simply engaged in sustained use of a language skill we all have. Their "creations" come about through confident reliance on stray impulses that will, with trust, find occasional patterns that are satisfying.

2) But writing itself is one of the great, free human activities. There is scope for individuality, and elation, and discovery, in writing. For the person who follows with trust and forgiveness what occurs to him, the world remains always ready and deep, an inexhaustible environment, with the combined vividness of an actuality and flexibility of a dream. Working back and forth between experience and thought, writers have more than space and time can offer. They have the whole unexplored realm of human vision.

A: So that's how Mr. Stafford does his writing!

B: He doesn't seem to pay much attention to the rules, does he?

A: What "rules"?

46

Here is a page from Mr. Stafford's journal, dated May 25, 1967:

25 May 1967

Yesterday I noticed that the most dishonest words are adverbs. "Tho he did not himself take drugs he sincerely listened to drug takers." "With human beings he was deeply involved, deeply interested, purely related." etc.

Every utterance has a point of balance. If it is solicit — heavy it can never make its way as literature.

Freedom is not following a river. It is deciding now by what happens now. It is living with knowledge that luck makes a difference. No leader is free; no follower is free — the rest of us can be free. Most of the world are living by creeks too odd, chancy, and habit-forming to be worth arguing about by reason.

If you are oppressed, wake up about four in the morning; Most places, you can usually be free some of the time if you wake up before other people.

It is better not to think about chastity at all.

47

# FREEDOM

*William Stafford*

Freedom is not following a river.
Freedom is following a river,
    though, if you want to.
It is deciding now by what happens now.
It is knowing that luck makes a difference.

No leader is free; no follower is free—
    the rest of us can often be free.
Most of the world are living by
creeds too odd, chancy, and habit-forming
    to be worth arguing about by reason.

If you are oppressed, wake up about
four in the morning: most places,
you can usually be free some of the time
    if you wake up before other people.

In Stafford's terms, are you free?

Reprinted by permission of the author. Originally appeared in *New American Review*, Volume 2.

# The Star in the Hills

A star hit in the hills behind our house
up where the grass turns brown touching the sky.

Meteors have hit the world before, but this was near,
and since TV; few saw, but many felt the shock.
The state of California owns that land
(and out from shore three miles), and any stars
that come will be roped off and viewed on week days 8 to 5.

A guard who took the oath of loyalty and denied
any police record told me this:
"If you don't have a police record yet                    10
you could take the oath and get a job
if California should be hit by another star."

"I'd promise to be loyal to California
and to guard any stars that hit it," I said,
"or any place three miles out from shore,
unless the star was bigger than the state—
in which case I'd be loyal to it."

But he said no exceptions were allowed,
and he leaned against the state-owned meteor
so calm and puffed a cork-tip cigarette                    20
that I looked down and traced with my foot in the dust
and thought again and said, "Ok—any star."

*—William Stafford*

From TRAVELING THROUGH THE DARK by William Stafford. Copyright © 1957
by William Stafford. Reprinted by permission of Harper & Row, Publishers, Inc.

3

50

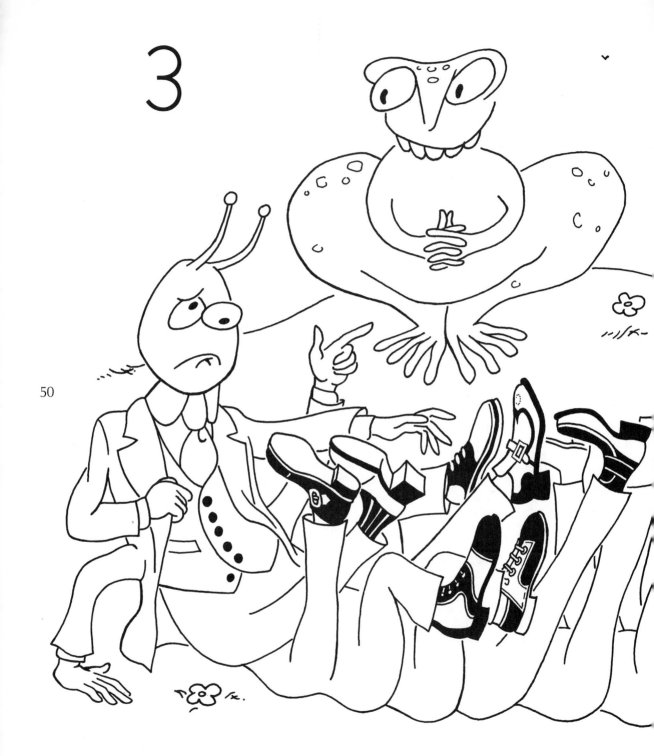

# The Centipede Was Happy . . .

*Anonymous*

The centipede was happy, quite,
Until a toad in fun
Said, "Pray, which leg goes after which?"
This worked his mind to such a pitch,
He lay distracted in a ditch,
Considering how to run.

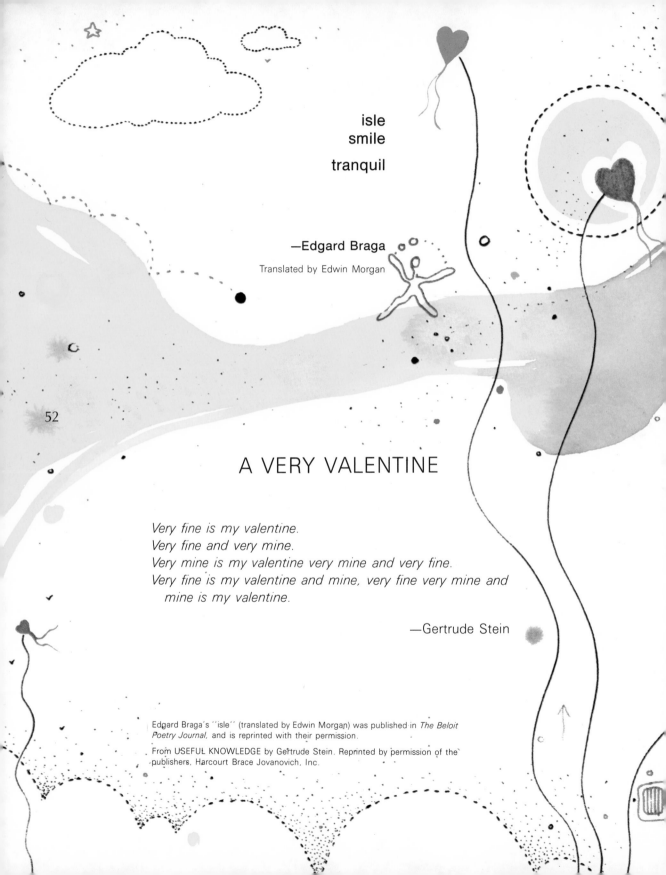

isle

smile

tranquil

—Edgard Braga

Translated by Edwin Morgan

52

# A VERY VALENTINE

*Very fine is my valentine.*
*Very fine and very mine.*
*Very mine is my valentine very mine and very fine.*
*Very fine is my valentine and mine, very fine very mine and*
    *mine is my valentine.*

—Gertrude Stein

Edgard Braga's ''isle'' (translated by Edwin Morgan) was published in *The Beloit Poetry Journal,* and is reprinted with their permission.

From USEFUL KNOWLEDGE by Gertrude Stein. Reprinted by permission of the publishers, Harcourt Brace Jovanovich, Inc.

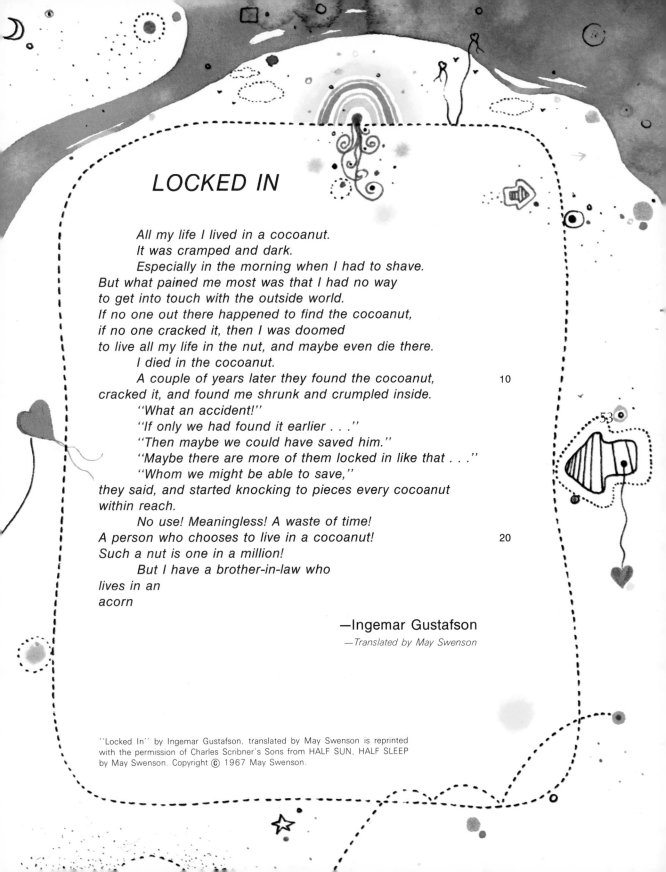

# LOCKED IN

All my life I lived in a cocoanut.
It was cramped and dark.
Especially in the morning when I had to shave.
But what pained me most was that I had no way
to get into touch with the outside world.
If no one out there happened to find the cocoanut,
if no one cracked it, then I was doomed
to live all my life in the nut, and maybe even die there.
I died in the cocoanut.
A couple of years later they found the cocoanut,                    10
cracked it, and found me shrunk and crumpled inside.
"What an accident!"
"If only we had found it earlier . . ."
"Then maybe we could have saved him."
"Maybe there are more of them locked in like that . . ."
"Whom we might be able to save,"
they said, and started knocking to pieces every cocoanut
within reach.
No use! Meaningless! A waste of time!
A person who chooses to live in a cocoanut!                    20
Such a nut is one in a million!
But I have a brother-in-law who
lives in an
acorn

—Ingemar Gustafson
—Translated by May Swenson

# GASTON

*William Saroyan*

They were to eat peaches, as planned, after her nap, and now she sat across from the man who would have been a total stranger except that he was in fact her father. They had been together again (although she couldn't quite remember when they had been together before) for almost a hundred years now, or was it only since day before yesterday? Anyhow, they were together again, and he was kind of funny. First, he had the biggest mustache she had ever seen on anybody, although to her it was not a mustache at all; it was a lot of red and brown hair under his nose and around the ends of his mouth. Second, he wore a blue-and-white striped jersey instead of a shirt and tie, and no coat. His arms were covered with the same hair, only it was a little lighter and thinner. He wore blue slacks, but no shoes and socks. He was barefoot, and so was she, of course.

He was at home. She was with him in his home in Paris, if you could call it a home. He was very old, especially for a young man—thirty-six, he had told her; and she was six, just up from sleep on a very hot afternoon in August.

That morning, on a little walk in the neighborhood, she had seen peaches in a box outside a small store and she had stopped to look at them, so he had bought a kilo.

Now, the peaches were on a large plate on the card table at which they sat.

There were seven of them, but one of them was flawed. It *looked* as good as the others, almost the size of a tennis ball, nice red fading to light green, but where the stem had been there was now a break that went straight down into the heart of the seed.

He placed the biggest and best-looking peach on the small plate in front of the girl, and then took the flawed peach and began to remove the skin. When he had half the skin off the peach he ate that side, neither of them talking, both of them just being there, and not being excited or anything—no plans, that is.

The man held the half-eaten peach in his fingers and looked down into the cavity, into the open seed. The girl looked, too.

While they were looking, two feelers poked out from the cavity. They were attached to a kind of brown knob-head, which followed the feelers, and then two large legs took a strong grip on the edge of the cavity and hoisted some of the rest of whatever it was out of the seed, and stopped there a moment, as if to look around.

The man studied the seed dweller, and so, of course, did the girl.

The creature paused only a fraction of a second, and then continued to come out of the seed, to walk down the eaten side of the peach to wherever it was going.

The girl had never seen anything like it—a whole big thing made out of brown color, a knob-head, feelers, and a great many legs. It was very active, too. Almost businesslike, you might say. The man placed the peach back on the plate. The creature moved off the peach onto the surface of the white plate. There it came to a thoughtful stop.

"Who is it?" the girl said.

"Gaston."

"Where does he live?"

"Well, he *used* to live in this peach seed, but now that the peach has been harvested and sold, and I have eaten half of it, it looks as if he's out of house and home."

"Aren't you going to squash him?"

"No, of course not, why should I?"

"He's a bug. He's *ugh*."

"Not at all. He's Gaston the grand boulevardier."

"Everybody hollers when a bug comes out of an apple, but you don't holler or *anything*."

"Of course not. How would *we* like it if somebody hollered every time we came out of our house?"

"Why *would* they?"

"Precisely. So why should we holler at Gaston?"

"He's not the same as us."

"Well, not exactly, but he's the same as a lot of other occupants of peach seeds. Now, the poor fellow hasn't got a home, and there he is with all that pure design and handsome form, and nowhere to go."

"Handsome?"

"Gaston is just about the handsomest of his kind I've ever seen."

"What's he saying?"

"Well, he's a little confused. Now, inside that house of his he had everything in order. Bed here, porch there, and so forth."

"Show me."

The man picked up the peach, leaving Gaston entirely alone on the white plate. He removed the peeling and ate the rest of the peach.

"Nobody else I know would do that," the girl said. "They'd throw it away."

"I can't imagine why. It's a perfectly good peach."

He opened the seed and placed the two sides not far from Gaston. The girl studied the open halves.

"Is *that* where he lives?"

"It's where he used to live. Gaston is out in the world and on his own now. You can see for yourself how comfortable he was in there. He had everything."

"Now what has he got?"

"Not very much, I'm afraid."

"What's he going to do?"

"What are *we* going to do?"

"Well, we're not going to squash him, that's one thing we're *not* going to do," the girl said.

"What *are* we going to do, then?"

"Put him back?"

"Oh, *that* house is finished."

"Well, he can't live in our house, can he?"

"Not happily."

"Can he live in our house *at all?*"

"Well, he could *try,* I suppose. Don't you want to eat a peach?"

"Only if it's a peach with somebody in the seed."

"Well, see if you can find a peach that has an opening at the top, because if you can, that'll be a peach in which you're likeliest to find somebody."

The girl examined each of the peaches on the big plate.

"They're all shut," she said.

"Well, eat one, then."

"No. I want the same kind that you ate, with somebody in the seed."

"Well, to tell you the truth, the peach I ate would be considered a bad peach, so of course stores don't like to sell them. I was sold that one by mistake, most likely. And so now Gaston is without a home, and we've got six perfect peaches to eat."

"I don't want a perfect peach. I want a peach with people."

"Well, I'll go out and see if I can find one."

"Where will I go?"

56

"You'll go with me, unless you'd rather stay. I'll only be five minutes."

"If the phone rings, what shall I say?"

"I don't think it'll ring, but if it does, say hello and see who it is."

"If it's my mother, what shall I say?"

"Tell her I've gone to get you a bad peach, and anything else you want to tell her."

"If she wants me to go back, what shall I say?"

"Say yes if you want to go back."

"Do you want me to?"

"Of course not, but the important thing is what you want, not what I want."

"Why is *that* the important thing?"

"Because I want you to be where you want to be."

"I want to be here."

"I'll be right back."

He put on socks and shoes, and a jacket, and went out. She watched Gaston trying to find out what to do next. Gaston wandered around the plate, but everything seemed wrong and he didn't know what to do or where to go.

The telephone rang and her mother said she was sending the chauffeur to pick her up because there was a little party for somebody's daughter who was also six, and then tomorrow they would fly back to New York.

"Let me speak to your father," she said.

"He's gone to get a peach."

"*One* peach?"

"One with people."

"You haven't been with your father two days and already you *sound* like him."

"There *are* peaches with people in them. I know. I saw one of them come out."

"A *bug?*"

"Not a bug. Gaston."

"*Who?*"

"Gaston the grand something."

"Somebody else gets a peach with a bug in it, and throws it away, but not him. He makes up a lot of foolishness about it."

"It's not foolishness."

"All right, all right, don't get angry at me about a horrible peach bug of some kind."

"Gaston is right here, just outside his broken house, and I'm not angry at you."

"You'll have a lot of fun at the party."

"OK."

"We'll have fun flying back to New York, too."

"OK."

"Are you glad you saw your father?"

"Of course I am."

"Is he funny?"

"Yes."

"Is he crazy?"

"Yes. I mean, no. He just doesn't holler when he sees a bug crawling out of a peach seed or anything. He just looks at it carefully. But it *is* just a bug, isn't it, *really?*"

"That's all it is."

"And we'll *have* to squash it?"

"That's right. I can't wait to see you, darling. These two days have been like two years to me. Good-bye."

The girl watched Gaston on the plate, and she actually didn't like him. He was all *ugh*, as he had been in the first place. He didn't have a home anymore and he was wandering around on the white plate and he was silly and wrong and ridiculous and useless and all sorts of other things. She cried a little, but only inside, because long ago she had decided she didn't like crying because if you ever started to cry it seemed as if there was so much to cry about you almost couldn't stop, and she didn't like that at all. The open halves of the peach seed were wrong, too. They were ugly or something. They weren't clean.

The man bought a kilo of peaches but found no flawed peaches among them, so he bought another kilo at another store, and this time his luck was better, and there were *two* that were flawed. He hurried back to his flat and let himself in.

His daughter was in her room, in her best dress.

"My mother phoned," she said, "and she's sending the chauffeur for me because there's another birthday party."

"Another?"

"I mean, there's *always* a lot of them in New York."

"Will the chauffeur bring you back?"

"No. We're flying back to New York tomorrow."

"Oh."

"I liked being in your house."

"I liked having you here."

"Why do you live here?"

"This is my home."

"It's nice, but it's a lot different from our home."

"Yes, I suppose it is."

"It's kind of like Gaston's house."

"Where *is* Gaston?"

"I squashed him."

"Really? Why?"

"Everybody squashes bugs and worms."

"Oh. Well. I found you a peach."

"I don't want a peach anymore."

"OK."

He got her dressed, and he was packing her stuff when the chauffeur arrived. He went down the three flights of stairs with his daughter and the chauffeur, and in the street he was about to hug the girl when he decided he had better not. They shook hands instead, as if they were strangers.

He watched the huge car drive off, and then he went around the corner where he took his coffee every morning, feeling a little, he thought, like Gaston on the white plate.

# flowers for algernon

Daniel Keyes

Dr. Strauss says I shud rite down what I think and evrey thing that happins to me from now on. I dont know why but he says its importint so they will see if they will use me. I hope they use me. Miss Kinnian says maybe they can make me smart. I want to be smart. My name is Charlie Gordon. I am 37 years old and 2 weeks ago was my brithday. I have nuthing more to rite now so I will close for today.

I had a test today. I think I faled it. and I think that maybe now they wont use me. What happind is a nice young man was in the room and he had some white cards' with ink spillled all over them. He sed Charlie what do you see on this card. I was very skared even tho I had my rabits foot in my pockit because when I was a kid I always faled tests in school and I spillled ink to.

I told him I saw a inkblot. He said yes and it made me feel good. I thot that was all but when I got up to go he stopped me. He said now sit down Charlie we are not thru yet. Then I dont remember so good but he wantid me to say what was in the ink. I dint see nuthing in the ink but he said there was picturs there other pepul saw some picturs. I coudnt see any picturs. I reely tryed to see. I held the card close up and then far away. Then I said if I had my glases I coud see better I usually only ware my glases in the movies or TV but I said they are in the closit in the hall. I got them. Then I said let me see that card agen I bet Ill find it now.

I tryed hard but I still coudnt find the picturs I only saw the ink. I told him maybe I need new glases. He rote somthing down on a paper and I got skared of faling the test. I told him it was a very nice inkblot with littel points all around the eges. He looked very sad so that wasnt it. I said please let me try agen. Ill get it in a few minits becaus Im not so fast somtimes. Im a slow reeder too in Miss Kinnians class for slow adults but I'm trying very hard.

He gave me a chance with another card that had 2 kinds of ink spilled on it red and blue.

He was very nice and talked slow like Miss Kinnian does and he explaned it to me that it was a *raw shok.* He said pepul see things in the ink. I said show me where. He said think. I told him I think a inkblot but that wasnt rite eather. He said what does it remind you—pretend something. I closd my eyes for a long time to pretend. I told him I pretned a fowntan pen with ink leeking all over a table cloth. Then he got up and went out.

I dont think I passd the *raw shok* test.

Dr Strauss and Dr Nemur say it dont matter about the inkblots. I told them I dint spill the ink on the cards and I coudnt see anything in the ink.

61

They said that maybe they will still use me. I said Miss Kinnian never gave me tests like that one only spelling and reading. They said Miss Kinnian told that I was her bestist pupil in the adult nite scool becaus I tryed the hardist and I reely wantid to lern. They said how come you went to the adult nite scool all by yourself Charlie. How did you find it. I said I askd pepul and sumbody told me where I shud go to lern to read and spell good. They said why did you want to. I told them becaus all my life I wantid to be smart and not dumb. But its very hard to be smart. They said you know it will probly be tempirery. I said yes. Miss Kinnian told me. I dont care if it herts.

Later I had more crazy tests today. The nice lady who gave it me told me the name and I asked her how do you spellit so I can rite it in my progris riport. THEMATIC APPERCEPTION TEST. I dont know the frist 2 words but I know what *test* means. You got to pass it or you get bad marks. This test lookd easy becaus I coud see the picturs. Only this time she dint want me to tell her the picturs. That mixd me up. I said the man yesterday said I shoud tell him what I saw in the ink she said that dont make no difrence. She said make up storys about the pepul in the picturs.

I told her how can you tell storys about pepul you never met. I said why shud I make up lies. I never tell lies any more becaus I always get caut.

She told me this test and the other one the raw-shok was for getting personalty. I laffed so hard. I said how can you get that thing from inkblots and fotos. She got sore and put her picturs away. I dont care. It was sily. I gess I faled that test too.

Later some men in white coats took me to a difernt part of the hospitil and gave me a game to play. It was like a race with a white mouse. They called the mouse Algernon. Algernon was in a box with a lot of twists and turns like all kinds of walls and they gave me a pencil and a paper with lines and lots of boxes. On one side it said START and on the other end it said FINISH. They said it was *amazed* and that Algernon and me had the same *amazed* to do. I dint see how we could have the same *amazed* if Algernon had a box and I had a paper but I dint say nothing. Anyway there wasnt time because the race started.

One of the men had a watch he was trying to hide so I woudnt see it so I tryed not to look and that made me nervus.

Anyway that test made me feel worser than all the others because they did it over 10 times with difernt *amazeds* and Algernon won every time. I dint know that mice were so smart. Maybe thats because Algernon is a white mouse. Maybe white mice are smarter then other mice.

*progris riport 4—Mar 8*

Their going to use me! Im so exited I can hardly v  te. Dr Nemur and Dr Strauss had a argament about it first. Dr Nemur was in the office when Dr Strauss brot me in. Dr Nemur was worryed about using me but

Dr Strauss told him Miss Kinnian rekemmended me the best from all the people who she was teaching. I like Miss Kinnian becaus shes a very smart teacher. And she said Charlie your going to have a second chance. If you volenteer for this experament you mite get smart. They dont know if it will be perminint but theirs a chance. Thats why I said ok even when I was scared because she said it was an operashun. She said dont be scared Charlie you done so much with so little I think you deserv it most of all.

So I got scaird when Dr Nemur and Dr Strauss argud about it. Dr Strauss said I had something that was very good. He said I had a good *motor-vation.* I never even knew I had that. I felt proud when he said that not every body with an eye-q of 68 had that thing. I dont know what it is or where I got it but he said Algernon had it too. Algernons *motor-vation* is the cheese they put in his box. But it cant be that because I didnt eat any cheese this week.

Then he told Dr Nemur something I dint understand so while they were talking I wrote down some of the words.

He said Dr Nemur I know Charlie is not what you had in mind as the first of your new brede of intelek** (coudnt get the word) superman. But most people of his low ment** are host** and uncoop** they are usualy dull apath** and hard to reach. He has a good natcher hes intristed and eager to please.

Dr Nemur said remember he will be the first human beeng ever to have his intelijence trippled by surgicle meens.

Dr Strauss said exakly. Look at how well hes lerned to read and write for his low mentel age its as grate an acheve** as you and I lerning einstines therey of **vity without help. That shows the intenss motor-vation. Its comparat** a tremen** achev** I say we use Charlie.

I dint get all the words and they were talking to fast but it sounded like Dr Strauss was on my side and like the other one wasnt.

Then Dr Nemur nodded he said all right maybe your right. We will use Charlie. When he said that I got so exited I jumped up and shook his hand for being so good to me. I told him thank you doc you wont be sorry for giving me a second chance. And I mean it like I told him. After the operashun Im gonna try to be smart. Im gonna try awful hard.

*progris ript 5—Mar 10*

Im skared. Lots of people who work here and the nurses and the people who gave me the tests came to bring me candy and wish me luck. I hope I have luck. I got my rabits foot and my lucky penny and my horse shoe. Only a black cat crossed me when I was comming to the hospitil. Dr Strauss says dont be supersitis Charlie this is sience. Anyway Im keeping my rabits foot with me.

I asked Dr Strauss if Ill beat Algernon in the race after the operashun and he said maybe. If the operashun works Ill show that mouse I can be as smart as he is. Maybe smarter. Then Ill be abel to read better and spell the words good and know lots of things and be like other people. I want to be smart like other people. If it works perminint they will make everybody smart all over the wurld.

They dint give me anything to eat this morning. I dont know what that eating has to do with getting smart. Im very hungry and Dr Nemur took away my box of candy. That Dr Nemur is a grouch. Dr Strauss says I can have it back after the operashun. You cant eat befor a operashun . . .

### Progress Report 6—Mar 15

The operashun dint hurt. He did it while I was sleeping. They took off the bandijis from my eyes and my head today so I can make a PROGRESS REPORT. Dr Nemur who looked at some of my other ones says I spell PROGRESS wrong and he told me how to spell it and REPORT too. I got to try and remember that.

I have a very bad memary for spelling. Dr Strauss says its ok to tell about all the things that happin to me but he says I shoud tell more about what I feel and what I think. When I told him I dont know how to think he said try. All the time when the bandijis were on my eyes I tryed to think. Nothing happened. I dont know what to think about. Maybe if I ask him he will tell me how I can think now that Im suppose to get smart. What do smart people think about. Fancy things I suppose. I wish I knew some fancy things alredy.

### Progress Report 7—mar 19

Nothing is happining. I had lots of tests and different kinds of races with Algernon. I hate that mouse. He always beats me. Dr Strauss said I got to play those games. And he said some time I got to take those tests over again. Thse inkblots are stupid. And those pictures are stupid too. I like to draw a picture of a man and a woman but I wont make up lies about people.

I got a headache from trying to think so much. I thot Dr Strauss was my frend but he dont help me. He dont tell me what to think or when Ill get smart. Miss Kinnian dint come to see me. I think writing these progress reports are stupid too.

### Progress Report 8—Mar 23

Im going back to work at the factery. They said it was better I shud go back to work but I cant tell anyone what the operashun was for and I have to come to the hospitil for an hour evry night after work. They are gonna pay me mony every month for lerning to be smart.

Im glad Im going back to work because I miss my job and all my frends and all the fun we have there.

Dr Strauss says I shud keep writing things down but I dont have to do it every day just when I think of something or something speshul happins.

He says dont get discoridged because it takes time and it happins slow. He says it took a long time with Algernon before he got 3 times smarter then he was before. Thats why Algernon beats me all the time because he had that operashun too. That makes me feel better. I coud probly do that *amazed* faster than a reglar mouse. Maybe some day Ill beat Algernon. Boy that would be something. So far Algernon looks like he mite be smart perminent.

*Mar 25* (I dont have to write PROGRESS REPORT on top any more just when I hand it in once a week for Dr Nemur to read. I just have to put the date on. That saves time)

We had a lot of fun at the factery today. Joe Carp said hey look where Charlie had his operashun what did they do Charlie put some brains in. I was going to tell him but I remembered Dr Strauss said no. Then Frank Reilly said what did you do Charlie forget your key and open your door the hard way. That made me laff. Their really my friends and they like me.

Sometimes somebody will say hey look at Joe or Frank or George he really pulled a Charlie Gordon. I dont know why they say that but they always laff. This morning Amos Borg who is the 4 man at Donnegans used my name when he shouted at Ernie the office boy. Ernie lost a packige. He said Ernie for god-sake what are you trying to be a Charlie Gordon. I dont understand why he said that. I never lost any packiges.

65

*Mar 28* Dr Strauss came to my room tonight to see why I dint come in like I was suppose to. I told him I dont like to race with Algernon any more. He said I dont have to for a while but I shud come in. He had a present for me only it wasnt a present but just for lend. I thot it was a little television but it wasnt. He said I got to turn it on when I go to sleep. I said your kidding why shud I turn it on when Im going to sleep. Who ever herd of a thing like that. But he said if I want to get smart I got to do what he says. I told him I dint think I was going to get smart and he put his hand on my sholder and said Charlie you dont know it yet but your getting smarter all the time. You wont notice for a while. I think he was just being nice to make me feel good because I dont look any smarter.

Oh yes I almost forgot. I asked him when I can go back to the class at Miss Kinnians school. He said I wont go their. He said that soon Miss Kinnian will come to the hospitil to start and teach me speshul. I was mad at her for not comming to see me when I got the operashun but I like her so maybe we will be frends again.

*Mar 29* That crazy TV kept me up all night. How can I sleep with something yelling crazy things all night in my ears. And the nutty pictures. Wow. I dont know what it says when Im up so how am I going to know when Im sleeping.

Dr Strauss says its ok. He says my brains are lerning when I sleep and that will help me when Miss Kinnian starts my lessons in the hospitl (only I found out it isnt a hospitil its a labatory). I think its all crazy. If you can get smart when your sleeping why do people go to school. That thing I dont think will work. I use to watch the late show and the late late show on TV all the time and it never made me smart. Maybe you have to sleep while you watch it.

Dr Strauss showed me how to keep the TV turned low so now I can sleep. I dont hear a thing. And I still dont understand what it says. A few times I play it over in the morning to find out what I lerned when I was sleeping and I dont think so. Miss Kinnian says Maybe its another langwidge or something. But most times it sounds american. It talks so fast faster then even Miss Gold who was my teacher in 6 grade and I remember she talked so fast I coudnt understand her.

I told Dr Strauss what good is it to get smart in my sleep. I want to be smart when Im awake. He says its the same thing and I have two minds. Theres the *subconscious* and the *conscious* (thats how you spell it). And one dont tell the other one what its doing. They dont even talk to each other. Thats why I dream. And boy have I been having crazy dreams. Wow. Ever since that night TV. The late late late late late show.

I forgot to ask him if it was only me or if everybody had those two minds.

(I just looked up the word in the dictionary Dr Strauss gave me. The word is *subconscious. adj. Of the nature of mental operations yet not present in consciousness; as, subconscious conflict of desires.*) Theres more but I still don't know what it means. This isnt a very good dictionary for dumb people like me.

Anyway the headache is from the party. My frends from the factery Joe Carp and Frank Reilly invited me to go with them to Muggsys Saloon for some drinks. I dont like to drink but they said we will have lots of fun. I had a good time.

Joe Carp said I shoud show the girls how I mop out the toilet in the factory and he got me a mop. I showed them and everyone laffed when I told that Mr Donnegan said I was the best janiter he ever had because I like my job and do it good and never come late or miss a day except for my operashun.

I said Miss Kinnian always said Charlie be proud of your job because you do it good.

Everybody laffed and we had a good time and they gave me lots of drinks and Joe said Charlie is a card when hes potted. I dont know what that means but everybody likes me and we have fun. I cant wait to be smart like my best frends Joe Carp and Frank Reilly.

I dont remember how the party was over but I think I went out to buy a newspaper and coffe for Joe and Frank and when I came back there was no one their. I looked for them all over till late. Then I dont remember so good but I think I got sleepy or sick. A nice cop brot me back home. Thats what my landlady Mrs Flynn says.

But I got a headache and a big lump on my head and black and blue all over. I think maybe I fell but Joe Carp says it was the cop they beat up drunks some times. I don't think so. Miss Kinnian says cops are to help people. Anyway I got a bad headache and Im sick and hurt all over. I don't think Ill drink anymore.

*April 6*  I beat Algernon! I dint even know I beat him until Burt the tester told me. Then the second time I lost because I got so exited I fell off the chair before I finished. But after that I beat him 8 more times. I must be getting smart to beat a smart mouse like Algernon. But I dont *feel* smarter.

I wanted to race Algernon some more but Burt said thats enough for one day. They let me hold him for a minit. Hes not so bad. Hes soft like a ball of cotton. He blinks and when he opens his eyes their black and pink on the eges.

I said can I feed him because I felt bad to beat him and I wanted to be nice and make frends. Burt said no Algernon is a very specshul mouse with an operashun like mine, and he was the first of all the animals to stay smart so long. He told me Algernon is so smart that every day he has to solve a test to get his food. Its a thing like a lock on a door that changes every time Algernon goes in to eat so he has to lern something new to get his food. That made me sad because if he coudnt lern he woud be hungry.

I dont think its right to make you pass a test to eat. How woud Dr Nemur like to have to pass a test every time he wants to eat. I think Ill be frends with Algernon.

*April 9*  Tonight after work Miss Kinnian was at the laboratory. She looked like she was glad to see me but scared. I told her dont worry Miss Kinnian Im not smart yet and she laffed. She said I have confidence in you Charlie the way you struggled so hard to read and right better than all the others. At werst you will have it for a littel wile and your doing somthing for sience.

We are reading a very hard book. I never read such a hard book before. Its called *Robinson Crusoe* about a man who gets merooned on a dessert Iland. Hes smart and figers out all kinds of things so he can have a house and food and hes a good swimmer. Only I feel sorry because hes all alone and has no frends. But I think their must be somebody else on the iland because theres a picture with his funny umbrella looking at footprints. I hope he gets a frend and not be lonly.

*April 10*  Miss Kinnian teaches me to spell better. She says look at a word and close your eyes and say it over and over until you remember. I have lots of truble with *through* that you say *threw* and *enough* and *tough* that you dont say *enew* and *tew*. You got to say *enuff* and *tuff*. Thats how I use to write it before I started to get smart. Im confused but Miss Kinnian says theres no reason in spelling.

*Apr 14*  Finished *Robinson Crusoe*. I want to find out more about what happens to him but Miss Kinnian says thats all there is. *Why*

*Apr 15*  Miss Kinnian says Im lerning fast. She read some of the Progress Reports and she looked at me kind of funny. She says Im a fine person and Ill show them all. I asked her why. She said never mind but I shoudnt feel bad if I find out that everybody isnt nice like I think. She said for a person who god gave so little to you done more then a lot of people with brains they never even used. I said all my frends are smart people but there good. They like me and they never did anything that wasnt nice. Then she got something in her eye and she had to run out to the ladys room.

*Apr 16*  Today, I lerned, the *comma,* this is a comma (,) a period, with a tail, Miss Kinnian, says its important, because, it makes writing, better, she said, sombeody, coud lose, a lot of money, if a comma, isnt, in the, right place, I dont have, any money, and I dont see, how a comma, keeps you, from losing it,

But she says, everybody, uses commas, so Ill use, them too,

*Apr 17*  I used the comma wrong. Its punctuation. Miss Kinnian told me to look up long words in the dictionary to lern to spell them. I said whats the difference if you can read it anyway. She said its part of your education so now on Ill look up all the words Im not sure how to spell. It takes a long time to write that way but I think Im remembering. I only have to look up once and after that I get it right. Anyway thats how come I got the word *punctuation* right. (Its that way in the dictionary). Miss Kinnian says a period is punctuation too, and there are lots of other marks to lern. I told her I thot all the periods had to have tails but she said no.

You got to mix them up, she showed? me" how. to mix! them (up,. and now; I can! mix up all kinds" of punctuation, in! my writing? There, are lots! of rules? to lern; but Im gettin'g them in my head.

One thing I? like about, Dear Miss Kinnian: (thats the way it goes in a business letter if I ever go into business) is she, always gives me' a reason" when—I ask. She's a gen'ius! I wish! I cou'd be smart" like, her;

(Punctuation, is; fun!)

*April 18*  What a dope I am! I didn't even understand what she was talking about. I read the grammar book last night and it explanes the whole thing. Then I saw it was the same way as Miss Kinnian was trying to tell me, but I didn't get it. I got up in the middle of the night, and the whole thing straightened out in my mind.

Miss Kinnian said that the TV working in my sleep helped out. She said I reached a plateau. Thats like the flat top of a hill.

After I figgered out how punctuation worked, I read over all my old Progress Reports from the beginning. Boy, did I have crazy spelling and punctuation! I told Miss Kinnian I ought to go over the pages and fix all the mistakes but she said, "No, Charlie, Dr. Nemur wants them just as they are. That's why he let you keep them after they were photostated, to see your own progress. You're coming along fast, Charlie."

That made me feel good. After the lesson I went down and played with Algernon. We don't race any more.

*April 20*   I feel sick inside. Not sick like for a doctor, but inside my chest it feels empty like getting punched and a heartburn at the same time.

I wasn't going to write about it, but I guess I got to, because it's important. Today was the first time I ever stayed home from work.

Last night Joe Carp and Frank Reilly invited me to a party. There were lots of girls and some men from the factory. I remembered how sick I got last time I drank too much, so I told Joe I didn't want anything to drink. He gave me a plain Coke instead. It tasted funny, but I thought it was just a bad taste in my mouth.

We had a lot of fun for a while. Joe said I should dance with Ellen and she would teach me the steps. I fell a few times and I couldn't understand why because no one else was dancing besides Ellen and me. And all the time I was tripping because somebody's foot was always sticking out.

Then when I got up I saw the look on Joe's face and it gave me a funny feeling in my stomack. "He's a scream," one of the girls said. Everybody was laughing.

Frank said, "I ain't laughed so much since we sent him off for the newspaper that night at Muggsy's and ditched him."

"Look at him. His face is red."

"He's blushing. Charlie is blushing."

"Hey, Ellen, what'd you do to Charlie? I never saw him act like that before."

I didn't know what to do or where to turn. Everyone was looking at me and laughing and I felt naked. I wanted to hide myself. I ran out into the street and I threw up. Then I walked home. It's a funny thing I never knew that Joe and Frank and the others liked to have me around all the time to make fun of me.

Now I know what it means when they say "to pull a Charlie Gordon."

I'm ashamed.

69

## PROGRESS REPORT 11

*April 21*   Still didn't go into the factory. I told Mrs. Flynn my landlady to call and tell Mr. Donnegan I was sick. Mrs. Flynn looks at me very funny lately like she's scared of me.

I think it's a good thing about finding out how everybody laughs at me. I thought about it a lot. It's because I'm so dumb and I don't even know when I'm doing something dumb. People think it's funny when a dumb person can't do things the same way they can.

Anyway, now I know I'm getting smarter every day. I know punctuation and I can spell good. I like to look up all the hard words in the dictionary and I remember them. I'm reading a lot now, and Miss Kinnian says I read very fast. Sometimes I even understand what I'm reading about, and it stays in my mind. There are times when I can close my eyes and think of a page and it all comes back like a picture.

Besides history, geography, and arithmetic, Miss Kinnian said I should start to learn a few foreign languages. Dr. Strauss gave me some more tapes to play while I sleep. I still don't understand how that conscious and unconscious mind works, but Dr. Strauss says not to worry yet. He asked me to promise that when I start learning college subjects next week I wouldn't read any books on psychology—that is, until he gives me permission.

I feel a lot better today, but I guess I'm still a little angry that all the time people were laughing and making fun of me because I wasn't so smart. When I become intelligent like Dr. Strauss says, with three times my I.Q. of 68, then maybe I'll be like everyone else and people will like me and be friendly.

I'm not sure what an I.Q. is. Dr. Nemur said it was something that measured how intelligent you were—like a scale in the drugstore weighs pounds. But Dr. Strauss had a big argument with him and said an I.Q. didn't weigh intelligence at all. He said an I.Q. showed how much intelligence you could get, like the numbers on the outside of a measuring cup. You still had to fill the cup up with stuff.

Then when I asked Burt, who gives me my intelligence tests and works with Algernon, he said that both of them were wrong (only I had to promise not to tell them he said so). Burt says that the I.Q. measures a lot of different things including some of the things you learned already, and it really isn't any good at all.

So I still don't know what I.Q. is except that mine is going to be over 200 soon. I didn't want to say anything, but I don't see how if they don't know *what* it is, or *where* it is—I don't see how they know *how much* of it you've got.

Dr. Nemur says I have to take a *Rorshach Test* tomorrow. I wonder what *that* is.

*April 22* I found out what a *Rorshach* is. It's the test I took before the operation—the one with the inkblots on the pieces of cardboard. The man who gave me the test was the same one.

I was scared to death of those inkblots. I knew he was going to ask me to find the pictures and I knew I wouldn't be able to. I was thinking to myself, if only there was some way of knowing what kind of pictures were hidden there. Maybe there weren't any pictures at all. Maybe it was just a trick to see if I was dumb enough to look for something that wasn't there. Just thinking about that made me sore at him.

"All right, Charlie," he said, "you've seen these cards before, remember?"

"Of course I remember."

The way I said it, he knew I was angry, and he looked surprised. "Yes, of course. Now I want you to look at this one. What might this be? What do you see on this card? People see all sorts of things in these inkblots. Tell me what it might be for you—what it makes you think of."

I was shocked. That wasn't what I had expected him to say at all. "You mean there are no pictures hidden in those inkblots?"

He frowned and took off his glasses. "What?"

"Pictures. Hidden in the inkblots. Last time you told me that everyone could see them and you wanted me to find them too."

He explained to me that the last time he had used almost the exact same words he was using now. I didn't believe it, and I still have the suspicion that he misled me at the time just for the fun of it. Unless—I don't know any more—could I have been *that* feeble-minded?

We went through the cards slowly. One of them looked like a pair of bats tugging at something. Another one looked like two men fencing with swords. I imagined all sorts of things. I guess I got carried away. But I didn't trust him any more, and I kept turning them around and even looking on the back to see if there was anything there I was supposed to catch. While he was making his notes, I peeked out of the corner of my eye to read it. But it was all in code that looked like this:

WF + A   DdF-Ad orig.   WF-A   SF + obj

The test still doesn't make sense to me. It seems to me that anyone could make up lies about things that they didn't really see. How could he know I wasn't making a fool of him by mentioning things that I didn't really imagine? Maybe I'll understand it when Dr. Strauss lets me read up on psychology.

*April 25*   I figured out a new way to line up the machines in the factory, and Mr. Donnegan says it will save him ten thousand dollars a year in labor and increased production. He gave me a twenty-five-dollar bonus.

I wanted to take Joe Carp and Frank Reilly out to lunch to celebrate, but Joe said he had to buy some things for his wife, and Frank said he was meeting his cousin for lunch. I guess it'll take a little time for them to get used to the changes in me. Everybody seems to be frightened of me. When I went over to Amos Borg and tapped him on the shoulder, he jumped up in the air.

People don't talk to me much any more or kid around the way they used to. It makes the job kind of lonely.

*April 27*   I got up the nerve today to ask Miss Kinnian to have dinner with me tomorrow night to celebrate my bonus.

At first she wasn't sure it was right, but I asked Dr. Strauss and he said it was okay. Dr. Strauss and Dr. Nemur don't seem to be getting along so well. They're arguing all the time. This evening when I came in to ask Dr. Strauss about having dinner with Miss Kinnian, I heard them shouting. Dr. Nemur was saying that it was *his* experiment and *his* research, and Dr. Strauss was shouting back that he contributed just as much, because he found me through Miss Kinnian and he performed the operation. Dr. Strauss said that someday thousands of neurosurgeons might be using his technique all over the world.

Dr. Nemur wanted to publish the results of the experiment at the end of this month. Dr. Strauss wanted to wait a while longer to be sure. Dr. Strauss said that Dr. Nemur was more interested in the Chair of Psychology at Princeton than he was in the experiment. Dr. Nemur said that Dr. Strauss was nothing but an opportunist who was trying to ride to glory on *his* coattails.

When I left afterwards, I found myself trembling. I don't know why for sure, but it was as if I'd seen both men clearly for the first time. I remember hearing Burt say that Dr. Nemur had a shrew of a wife who was pushing him all the time to get things published so that he could become famous. Burt said that the dream of her life was to have a big-shot husband.

Was Dr. Strauss really trying to ride on his coattails?

*April 28*  I don't understand why I never noticed how beautiful Miss Kinnian really is. She has brown eyes and feathery brown hair that comes to the top of her neck. She's only thirty-four! I think from the beginning I had the feeling that she was an unreachable genius—and very, very old. Now, every time I see her she grows younger and more lovely.

We had dinner and a long talk. When she said that I was coming along so fast that soon I'd be leaving her behind, I laughed.

"It's true, Charlie. You're already a better reader than I am. You can read a whole page at a glance while I can take in only a few lines at a time. And you remember every single thing you read. I'm lucky if I can recall the main thoughts and the general meaning."

"I don't feel intelligent. There are so many things I don't understand."

She took out a cigarette and I lit it for her. "You've got to be a *little* patient. You're accomplishing in days and weeks what it takes normal people to do in half a lifetime. That's what makes it so amazing. You're like a giant sponge now, soaking things in. Facts, figures, general knowledge. And soon you'll begin to connect them, too. You'll see how the different branches of learning are related. There are many levels, Charlie, like steps on a giant ladder that take you up higher and higher to see more and more of the world around you.

"I can see only a little bit of that, Charlie, and I won't go much higher than I am now, but you'll keep climbing up and up, and see more and more, and each step will open new worlds that you never even knew existed." She frowned. "I hope . . . I just hope to God—"

"What?"

"Never mind, Charles. I just hope I wasn't wrong to advise you to go into this in the first place."

I laughed. "How could that be? It worked, didn't it? Even Algernon is still smart."

We sat there silently for a while and I knew what she was thinking about as she watched me toying with the chain of my rabbit's foot and my keys. I didn't want to think of that possibility any more than elderly people want to think of death. I *knew* that this was only the beginning. I knew what she meant about levels because I'd seen some of them already. The thought of leaving her behind made me sad.

I'm in love with Miss Kinnian.

### PROGRESS REPORT 12

*April 30*  I've quit my job with Donnegan's Plastic Box Company. Mr. Donnegan insisted that it would be better for all concerned if I left. What did I do to make them hate me so?

The first I knew of it was when Mr. Donnegan showed me the petition. Eight hundred and forty names, everyone connected with the factory, except Fanny Girden. Scanning the list quickly, I saw at once that hers was the only missing name. All the rest demanded that I be fired.

Joe Carp and Frank Reilly wouldn't talk to me about it. No one else would either, except Fanny. She was one of the few people I'd known who set her mind to something and believed it no matter what the rest of the world proved, said, or did—and Fanny did not believe that I should have been fired. She had been against the petition on principle and despite the pressure and threats she'd held out.

"Which don't mean to say," she remarked, "that I don't think there's something mighty strange about you, Charlie. Them changes. I don't know. You used to be a good, dependable, ordinary man—not too bright maybe, but honest. Who knows what you done to yourself to get so smart all of a sudden. Like everybody around here's been saying, Charlie, it's not right."

"But how can you say that, Fanny? What's wrong with a man becoming intelligent and wanting to acquire knowledge and understanding of the world around him?"

She stared down at her work and I turned to leave. Without looking at me, she said: "It was evil when Eve listened to the snake and ate from the tree of knowledge. It was evil when she saw that she was naked. If not for that none of us would ever have to grow old and sick, and die."

Once again now I have the feeling of shame burning inside me. This intelligence has driven a wedge between me and all the people I once knew and loved. Before, they laughed at me and despised me for my ignorance and dullness; now, they hate me for my knowledge and understanding. What in God's name do they want of me?

They've driven me out of the factory. Now I'm more alone than ever before . . .

*May 15*   Dr. Strauss is very angry at me for not having written any progress reports in two weeks. He's justified because the lab is now paying me a regular salary. I told him I was too busy thinking and reading. When I pointed out that writing was such a slow process that it made me impatient with my poor handwriting, he suggested that I learn to type. It's much easier to write now because I can type nearly seventy-five words a minute. Dr. Strauss continually reminds me of the need to speak and write simply so that people will be able to understand me.

I'll try to review all the things that happened to me during the last two weeks. Algernon and I were presented to the American Psychological Association sitting in convention with the World Psychological Association last Tuesday. We created quite a sensation. Dr. Nemur and Dr. Strauss were proud of us.

I suspect that Dr. Nemur, who is sixty—ten years older than Dr. Strauss—finds it necessary to see tangible results of his work. Undoubtedly the result of pressure by Mrs. Nemur.

Contrary to my earlier impressions of him, I realize that Dr. Nemur is not at all a genius. He has a very good mind, but it struggles under the specter of self-doubt. He wants people to take him for a genius. Therefore, it is important for him to feel that his work is accepted by the world. I believe that Dr. Nemur was afraid of further delay because he worried that someone else might make a discovery along these lines and take the credit from him.

Dr. Strauss on the other hand might be called a genius, although I feel that his areas of knowledge are too limited. He was educated in the tradition of narrow specialization; the broader aspects of background were neglected far more than necessary—even for a neurosurgeon.

I was shocked to learn that the only ancient languages he could read were Latin, Greek, and Hebrew, and that he knows almost nothing of mathematics beyond the elementary levels of the calculus of variations. When he admitted this to me, I found myself almost annoyed. It was as if he'd hidden this part of himself in order to deceive me, pretending—as do many people I've discovered—to be what he is not. No one I've ever known is what he appears to be on the surface.

Dr. Nemur appears to be uncomfortable around me. Sometimes when I try to talk to him, he just looks at me strangely and turns away. I was angry at first when Dr. Strauss told me I was giving Dr. Nemur an inferiority complex. I thought he was mocking me and I'm oversensitive at being made fun of.

How was I to know that a highly respected psychoexperimentalist like Nemur was unacquainted with Hindustani and Chinese? It's absurd when you consider the work that is being done in India and China today in the very field of his study.

I asked Dr. Strauss how Nemur could refute Rahajamati's attack on his method and results if Nemur couldn't even read them in the first place. That strange look on Dr. Strauss' face can mean only one of two things. Either he doesn't want to tell Nemur what they're saying in India, or else—and this worries me—Dr. Strauss doesn't know either. I must be careful to speak and write clearly and simply so that people won't laugh.

*May 18*  I am very disturbed. I saw Miss Kinnian last night for the first time in over a week. I tried to avoid all discussions of intellectual concepts and to keep the conversation on a simple, everyday level, but she just stared at me blankly and asked me what I meant about the mathematical variance equivalent in Dorbermann's *Fifth Concerto.*

When I tried to explain she stopped me and laughed. I guess I got angry, but I suspect I'm approaching her on the wrong level. No matter what I try to discuss with her, I am unable to communicate. I must review Vrostadt's equations on *Levels of Semantic Progression.* I find that I don't communicate with people much any more. Thank God for books and music and things I can think about. I am alone in my apartment at Mrs. Flynn's boardinghouse most of the time and seldom speak to anyone.

*May 20*  I would not have noticed the new dishwasher, a boy of about sixteen, at the corner diner where I take my evening meals if not for the incident of the broken dishes.

They crashed to the floor, shattering and sending bits of white china under the tables. The boy stood there, dazed and frightened, holding the empty tray in his hand. The whistles and catcalls from the customers (the cries of "hey, there go the profits!" . . . "*Mazeltov!*" . . . and "well, *he* didn't work here very long . . ." which invariably seems to follow the breaking of glass or dishware in a public restaurant) all seemed to confuse him.

When the owner came to see what the excitement was about, the boy cowered as if he expected to be struck and threw up his arms as if to ward off the blow.

"All right! All right, you dope," shouted the owner, "don't just stand there! Get the broom and sweep that mess up. A broom . . . a broom, you idiot! It's in the kitchen. Sweep up all the pieces."

The boy saw that he was not going to be punished. His frightened expression disappeared and he smiled and hummed as he came back with the broom to sweep the floor. A few of the rowdier customers kept up the remarks, amusing themselves at his expense.

"Here, sonny, over here there's a nice piece behind you . . ."

"C'mon, do it again . . ."

"He's not so dumb. It's easier to break 'em than to wash 'em . . ."

As his vacant eyes moved across the crowd of amused onlookers, he slowly mirrored their smiles and finally broke into an uncertain grin at the joke which he obviously did not understand.

I felt sick inside as I looked at his dull, vacuous smile, the wide, bright eyes of a child, uncertain but eager to please. They were laughing at him because he was mentally retarded.

And I had been laughing at him too.

Suddenly, I was furious at myself and all those who were smirking at him. I jumped up and shouted, "Shut up! Leave him alone! It's not his fault he can't understand! He can't help what he is! But for God's sake . . . he's still a human being!"

The room grew silent. I cursed myself for losing control and creating a scene. I tried not to look at the boy as I paid my check and walked out without touching my food. I felt ashamed for both of us.

How strange it is that people of honest feelings and sensibility, who would not take advantage of a man born without arms or legs or eyes—how such people think nothing of abusing a man born with low intelligence. It infuriated me to think that not too long ago I, like this boy, had foolishly played the clown.

And I had almost forgotten.

I'd hidden the picture of the old Charlie Gordon from myself because now that I was intelligent it was something that had to be pushed out of my mind. But today in looking at that boy, for the first time I saw what I had been. *I was just like him!*

Only a short time ago, I learned that people laughed at me. Now I can see that unknowingly I joined with them in laughing at myself. That hurts most of all.

I have often reread my progress reports and seen the illiteracy, the childish naïveté, the mind of low intelligence peering from a dark room, through the keyhole, at the dazzling light outside. I see that even in my dullness I knew that I was inferior, and that other people had something I lacked—something denied me. In my mental blindness, I thought that it was somehow connected with the ability to read and write, and I was sure that if I could get those skills I would automatically have intelligence too.

Even a feeble-minded man wants to be like other men.

A child may not know how to feed itself, or what to eat, yet it knows of hunger.

This then is what I was like, I never knew. Even with my gift of intellectual awareness, I never really knew.

This day was good for me. Seeing the past more clearly, I have decided to use my knowledge and skills to work in the field of increasing human intelligence levels. Who is better equipped for this work? Who else has lived in both worlds? These are my people. Let me use my gift to do something for them.

Tomorrow, I will discuss with Dr. Strauss the manner in which I can work in this area. I may be able to help him work out the problems of widespread use of the technique which was used on me. I have several good ideas of my own.

There is so much that might be done with this technique. If I could be made into a genius, what about thousands of others like myself? What fantastic levels might be achieved by using this technique on normal people? On *geniuses*?

There are so many doors to open. I am impatient to begin.

### PROGRESS REPORT 13

*May 23*  It happened today. Algernon bit me. I visited the lab to see him as I do occasionally, and when I took him out of his cage, he snapped at my hand. I put him back and watched him for a while. He was unusually disturbed and vicious.

*May 24*  Burt, who is in charge of the experimental animals, tells me that Algernon is changing. He is less co-operative; he refuses to run the maze any more; general motivation has decreased. And he hasn't been eating. Everyone is upset about what this may mean.

*May 25*  They've been feeding Algernon, who now refuses to work the shifting-lock problem. Everyone identifies me with Algernon. In a way we're both the first of our kind. They're all pretending that Algernon's behavior is not necessarily significant for me. But it's hard to hide the fact that some of the other animals who were used in this experiment are showing strange behavior.

Dr. Strauss and Dr. Nemur have asked me not to come to the lab any more. I know what they're thinking but I can't accept it. I am going ahead with my plans to carry their research forward. With all due respect to both of these fine scientists, I am well aware of their limitations. If there is an answer, I'll have to find it out for myself. Suddenly, time has become very important to me.

*May 29*  I have been given a lab of my own and permission to go ahead with the research. I'm on to something. Working day and night. I've had a cot moved into the lab. Most of my writing time is spent on the notes which I keep in a separate folder, but from time to time I feel it necessary to put down my moods and my thoughts out of sheer habit.

I find the *calculus of intelligence* to be a fascinating study. Here is the place for the application of all the knowledge I have acquired. In a sense it's the problem I've been concerned with all my life.

*May 31*  Dr. Strauss thinks I'm working too hard. Dr. Nemur says I'm trying to cram a lifetime of research and thought into a few weeks. I know I should rest, but I'm driven on by something inside that won't let me stop.

I've got to find the reason for the sharp regression in Algernon. I've got to know *if* and *when* it will happen to me.

*June 4*

Dear Dr. Strauss:

Under separate cover I am sending you a copy of my report entitled, "The Algernon-Gordon Effect: A Study of Structure and Function of Increased Intelligence," which I would like to have you read and have published.

As you see, my experiments are completed. I have included in my report all of my formulae, as well as mathematical analysis in the appendix. Of course, these should be verified.

Because of its importance to both you and Dr. Nemur (and need I say to myself, too?) I have checked and rechecked my results a dozen times in the hope of finding an error. I am sorry to say the results must stand. Yet for the sake of science, I am grateful for the little bit that I here add to the knowledge of the function of the human mind and of the laws governing the artificial increase of human intelligence.

I recall your once saying to me that an experimental *failure* or the *disproving* of a theory was as important to the advancement of learning as a success would be. I know now that this is true. I am sorry, however, that my own contribution to the field must rest upon the ashes of the work of two men I regard so highly.

Yours truly,
Charles Gordon

encl.: rept.

*June 5* I must not become emotional. The facts and the results of my experiments are clear, and the more sensational aspects of my own rapid climb cannot obscure the fact that the tripling of intelligence by the surgical technique developed by Drs. Strauss and Nemur must be viewed as having little or no practical applicability (at the present time) to the increase of human intelligence.

As I review the records and data on Algernon, I see that although he is still in his physical infancy, he has regressed mentally. Motor activity is impaired; there is a general reduction of glandular activity; there is an accelerated loss of co-ordination.

There are also strong indications of progressive amnesia.

As will be seen by my report, these and other physical and mental deterioration syndromes can be predicted with statistically significant results by the application of my formula.

The surgical stimulus to which we were both subjected has resulted in an intensification and acceleration of all mental processes. The unforeseen development, which I have taken the liberty of calling the *Algernon-Gordon*

*Effect*, is the logical extension of the entire intelligence speed-up. The hypothesis here proven may be described simply in the following terms: Artificially increased intelligence deteriorates at a rate of time directly proportional to the quantity of the increase.

I feel that this, in itself, is an important discovery.

As long as I am able to write, I will continue to record my thoughts in these progress reports. It is one of my few pleasures. However, by all indications, my own mental deterioration will be very rapid.

I have already begun to notice signs of emotional instability and forgetfulness, the first symptoms of the burnout.

*June 10*   Deterioration progressing. I have become absent-minded. Algernon died two days ago. Dissection shows my predictions were right. His brain had decreased in weight and there was a general smoothing out of cerebral convolutions as well as a deepening and broadening of brain fissures.

I guess the same thing is or will soon be happening to me. Now that it's definite, I don't want it to happen.

I put Algernon's body in a cheese box and buried him in the back yard. I cried.

*June 15*   Dr. Strauss came to see me again. I wouldn't open the door and I told him to go away. I want to be left to myself. I have become touchy and irritable. I feel the darkness closing in. It's hard to throw off thoughts of suicide. I keep telling myself how important this introspective journal will be.

It's a strange sensation to pick up a book that you've read and enjoyed just a few months ago and discover that you don't remember it. I remembered how great I thought John Milton was, but when I picked up *Paradise Lost* I couldn't understand it at all. I got so angry I threw the book across the room.

I've got to try to hold on to some of it. Some of the things I've learned. Oh, God, please don't take it all away.

*June 19*   Sometimes, at night, I go out for a walk. Last night I couldn't remember where I lived. A policeman took me home. I have the strange feeling that this has all happened to me before—a long time ago. I keep telling myself I'm the only person in the world who can describe what's happening to me.

*June 21*   Why can't I remember? I've got to fight. I lie in bed for days and I don't know who or where I am. Then it all comes back to me in a flash. Fugues of amnesia. Symptoms of senility—second childhood. I can watch them coming on. It's cruelly logical. I learned so much and so fast. Now my mind is deteriorating rapidly. I won't let it happen. I'll fight it. I can't help thinking of the boy in the restaurant, the blank expression, the silly smile, the people laughing at him. No—please—not that again . . .

*June 22* I'm forgetting things that I learned recently. It seems to be following the classic pattern—the last things learned are the first things forgotten. Or is that the pattern? I'd better look it up again. . . .

I reread my paper on the *Algernon-Gordon Effect* and I get the strange feeling that it was written by someone else. There are parts I don't even understand.

Motor activity impaired. I keep tripping over things, and it becomes increasingly difficult to type.

*June 23* I've given up using the typewriter completely. My coordination is bad. I feel that I'm moving slower and slower. Had a terrible shock today. I picked up a copy of an article I used in my research, Krueger's *Uber psychische Ganzheit,* to see if it would help me understand what I had done. First I thought there was something wrong with my eyes. Then I realized I could no longer read German. I tested myself in other languages. All gone.

*June 30* A week since I dared to write again. It's slipping away like sand through my fingers. Most of the books I have are too hard for me now. I get angry with them because I know that I read and understood them just a few weeks ago.

I keep telling myself I must keep writing these reports so that somebody will know what is happening to me. But it gets harder to form the words and remember spellings. I have to look up even simple words in the dictionary now and it makes me impatient with myself.

Dr. Strauss comes around almost every day, but I told him I wouldn't see or speak to anybody. He feels guilty. They all do. But I don't blame anyone. I knew what might happen. But how it hurts.

*July 7* I don't know where the week went. Todays Sunday I know becuase I can see through my window people going to church. I think I stayed in bed all week but I remember Mrs. Flynn bringing food to me a few times. I keep saying over and over Ive got to do something but then I forget or maybe its just easier not to do what I say Im going to do.

I think of my mother and father a lot these days. I found a picture of them with me taken at a beach. My father has a big ball under his arm and my mother is holding me by the hand. I dont remember them the way they are in the picture. All I remember is my father drunk most of the time and arguing with mom about money.

He never shaved much and he used to scratch my face when he hugged me. My mother said he died but Cousin Miltie said he heard his mom and dad say that my father ran away with another woman. When I asked my mother she slapped my face and said my father was dead. I dont think I ever found out which was true but I don't care much. (He said he was going to take me to see cows on a farm once but he never did. He never kept his promises . . .)

*July 10*  My landlady Mrs Flynn is very worried about me. She says the way I lay around all day and dont do anything I remind her of her son before she threw him out of the house. She said she doesn't like loafers. If Im sick its one thing, but if Im a loafer thats another thing and she wont have it. I told her I think Im sick.

I try to read a little bit every day, mostly stories, but sometimes I have to read the same thing over and over again because I dont know what it means. And its hard to write. I know I should look up all the words in the dictionary but its so hard and Im so tired all the time.

Then I got the idea that I would only use the easy words instead of the long hard ones. That saves time. I put flowers on Algernons grave about once a week. Mrs Flynn thinks Im crazy to put flowers on a mouses grave but I told her that Algernon was special.

*July 14*  Its sunday again. I dont have anything to do to keep me busy now because my television set is broke and I dont have any money to get it fixed. (I think I lost this months check from the lab. I dont remember)

I get awful headaches and asperin doesnt help me much. Mrs Flynn knows Im really sick and she feels very sorry for me. Shes a wonderful woman whenever someone is sick.

*July 22*  Mrs Flynn called a strange doctor to see me. She was afraid I was going to die. I told the doctor I wasnt too sick and that I only forget sometimes. He asked me did I have any friends or relatives and I said no I dont have any. I told him I had a friend called Algernon once but he was a mouse and we used to run races together. He looked at me kind of funny like he thought I was crazy.

He smiled when I told him I used to be a genius. He talked to me like I was a baby and he winked at Mrs Flynn. I got mad and chased him out because he was making fun of me the way they all used to.

*July 24*  I have no more money and Mrs Flynn says I got to go to work somewhere and pay the rent because I haven't paid for over two months. I dont know any work but the job I used to have at Donnegans Plastic Box Company. I dont want to go back there because they all knew me when I was smart and maybe theyll laugh at me. But I dont know what else to do to get money.

*July 25*  I was looking at some of my old progress reports and its very funny but I cant read what I wrote. I can make out some of the words but they dont make sense.

Miss Kinnian came to the door but I said go away I dont want to see you. She cried and I cried too but I wouldnt let her in because I didnt want her to laugh at me. I told her I didn't like her any more. I told her I didnt want to be smart any more. Thats not true. I still love her and I still want to be smart but I had to say that so shed go away. She gave Mrs Flynn money to pay the rent. I dont want that. I got to get a job.

Please . . . please let me not forget how to read and write . . .

*July 27* Mr Donnegan was very nice when I came back and asked him for my old job of janitor. First he was very suspicious but I told him what happened to me then he looked very sad and put his hand on my shoulder and said Charlie Gordon you got guts.

Everybody looked at me when I came downstairs and started working in the toilet sweeping it out like I used to. I told myself Charlie if they make fun of you dont get sore because you remember their not so smart as you once thot they were. And besides they were once your friends and if they laughed at you that doesnt mean anything because they liked you too.

One of the new men who came to work there after I went away made a nasty crack he said hey Charlie I hear your a very smart fella a real quiz kid. Say something intelligent. I felt bad but Joe Carp came over and grabbed him by the shirt and said leave him alone you lousy cracker or Ill break your neck. I didnt expect Joe to take my part so I guess hes really my friend.

Later Frank Reilly came over and said Charlie if anybody bothers you or trys to take advantage you call me or Joe and we will set em straight. I said thanks Frank and I got choked up so I had to turn around and go into the supply room so he wouldn't see me cry. Its good to have friends.

*July 28* I did a dumb thing today I forgot I wasnt in Miss Kinnians class at the adult center any more like I use to be. I went in and sat down in my old seat in the back of the room and she looked at me funny and she said Charles. I dint remember she ever called me that before only Charlie so I said hello Miss Kinnian Im redy for my lesin today only I lost my reader that we was using. She startid to cry and run out of the room and everybody looked at me and I saw they wasnt the same pepul who used to be in my class.

Then all of a suddin I remembered some things about the operashun and me getting smart and I said holy smoke I reely pulled a Charlie Gordon that time. I went away before she came back to the room.

Thats why Im going away from New York for good. I dont want to do nothing like that agen. I dont want Miss Kinnian to feel sorry for me. Evry body feels sorry at the factery and I dont want that eather so Im going someplace where nobody knows that Charlie Gordon was once a genus and now he cant even reed a book or rite good.

Im taking a cuple of books along and even if I cant reed them Ill practise hard and maybe I wont forget every thing I lerned. If I try reel hard maybe Ill be a littel bit smarter then I was before the operashun. I got my rabits foot and my luky penny and maybe they will help me.

If you ever reed this Miss Kinnian dont be sorry for me Im glad I got a second chanse to be smart becaus I lerned a lot of things that I never even new were in this world and Im grateful that I saw it all for a littel bit. I dont know why Im dumb agen or what I did wrong maybe its becaus I dint try hard enuff. But if I try and practis very hard maybe Ill get a littl smarter and know what all the words are. I remember a littel bit how nice I had a feeling with the blue book that has the torn cover when I red it. Thats why Im gonna keep trying to get smart so I can have that feeling agen. Its a good feeling to know things and be smart. I wish I had it rite now if I did I would sit down and reed all the time. Anyway I bet Im the first dumb person in the world who ever found out somthing importent for sience. I remember I did somthing but I dont remember what. So I gess its like I did it for all the dumb pepul like me.

Good-by Miss Kinnian and Dr Strauss and evreybody. And P.S. please tell Dr Nemur not to be such a grouch when pepul laff at him and he woud have more frends. Its easy to make frends if you let pepul laff at you. Im going to have lots of frends where I go.
P.P.S. Please if you get a chanse put some flowrs on Algernons grave in the bak yard . . .


A: The story is sad—and yet, it's sort of heart-warming too.
B: And in places it's funny. But I don't know that I'd put flowers on Algernon's grave.
A: But that's what the story's all about!

83

# 4

## *My Destination*

### *Franz Kafka*

I gave orders for my horse to be brought round from the stable. The servant did not understand me. I myself went to the stable, saddled my horse and mounted. In the distance I heard a bugle call, I asked him what this meant. He knew nothing and had heard nothing. At the gate he stopped me, asking: "Where are you riding to, master?" "I don't know," I said, "only away from here, away from here. Always away from here, only by doing so can I reach my destination." "And so you know your destination?" he asked. "Yes," I answered, "didn't I say so? Away-From-Here, that is my destination." "You have no provisions with you," he said. "I need none," I said, "the journey is so long that I must die of hunger if I don't get anything on the way. No provisions can save me. For it is, fortunately, a truly immense journey."

84

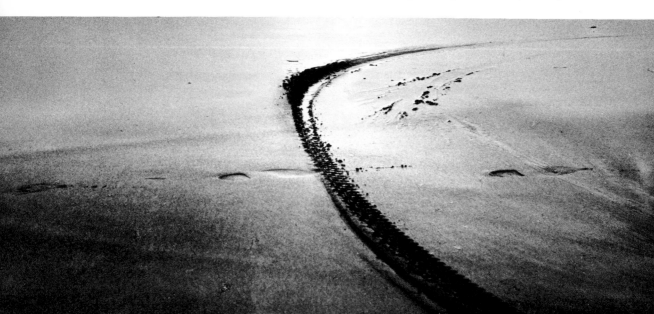

# Chasing After Villa

Abraham Reisin

Pancho Villa (1877–1923) was a Mexican general, rev-
olutionary, and bandit. In 1914, American troops, under
the command of General John J. Pershing, entered
Mexico for the purpose of capturing Villa and stopping
his attacks on Americans and others. They never caught
him!

Where my Benny is, you want to know? Thanks for asking.
Although when you remind me of him, my heart breaks. Imagine—*my*
Benny chasing after Villa! Which Villa! Don't you read the papers?
Really? I mean Villa from Mexico, the one we have to capture "dead or
alive." He's the one my Benny's running after . . .

Two years ago, Benny was working in a shop—when there was
work, that is. Just as often, he wasn't working at all. So he got sick and
tired of both things, working and loafing, because here in America
neither condition is exactly a bed of roses. Working in a shop was too
hard for him. Not because he didn't have the strength—it wasn't that at
all. But he can't stand "walls," my Benny. That's what *he* complained
about. And when he wasn't working, *I* complained—a healthy young
man like him sitting on his father's neck!

So one fine morning he went and enlisted in the army. There's
America for you! Did you ever hear of such a thing back in that
miserable old country—that a young fellow would *volunteer* for the army?
There he would thank God if something was wrong with him—a
whistling in his ears, or varicose veins, or a dozen missing teeth, or
other such lucky defects which the authorities had so much respect for.
My Benny, thank God, did not have any of these things wrong with
him. The only fault he had was whistling. Not his ear, God forbid, but
his mouth. Whenever he used to start whistling in the house, I was
afraid all the spirits in all the forests would come running, as we used
to believe in the old country.

85

"Chasing After Villa" by Abraham Reisin from PUSHCARTS AND DREAMERS,
translated and edited by Max Rosenfeld. Reprinted by permission of the publisher
A. S. Barnes & Company, Inc.

So he went to enlist in the American army. But that's easier said than done. As hard as it was to get *out* of the army back home, that's how hard it is to get *into* the army here. Oh, they'll take you, all right, but first—first your father has to sign a paper.

He comes home one day, my Benny, sticks this paper under my nose and announces that whereas he hates to work in a shop and whereas I won't stand for his loafing, therefore he has made up his mind to join the army. And when he finishes his service in the army, God willing, he will get a job as a policeman on a horse.

Why on a horse, I asked him. Why not a policeman on foot who protects society with both feet on the ground? So Benny explained to me that he has long legs and because he has long legs he wants to join the cavalry and afterwards he can be a mounted policeman and protect society from a height.

Well, I liked it and I didn't like it. I didn't like it that my Benny, who in Russia would probably have been exempted because he is older than my youngest boy by about seven years, should turn out to be a soldier in America. True, he was volunteering, nobody was forcing him, but still, I'd rather he didn't. On the other hand, it wouldn't be so bad to have a son a policeman, especially on a horse. Because if he's on a horse, they won't put him somewhere on Hester Street, but on Fifth Avenue, where the automobiles run all day and the millionaires go for a stroll.

I asked the lawyer from my *landmanschaft.*° What kind of rights will I be entitled to if my son becomes a soldier? And the lawyer told me that in the first place, I would become "almost" a citizen. Which means that if I ever take a trip to Europe, the American government must let me back into this country. Or if I ever wanted to open a saloon, I could get a license easier than somebody else. I would become a sort of relative to Uncle Sam.

I kept changing my mind—yes, no, yes, no—until finally I signed the paper. Which meant that I agreed that my son Benny should be of service to the United States of America. The main thing that convinced me was that I would become a part-citizen, because to become a whole citizen is impossible for me. Not that I haven't been here long enough. I have. And I could have become a citizen three times over, if it wasn't for my mixed-up head. Who has a brain to learn all those things? Just because I have one free day in the week—sometimes Saturday and sometimes Sunday, depending on what shop you work in—should I break my head trying to learn new tricks—like what was the name of the 19th President of the United States?

Of course, if I had only known they would "assign" him to a place that's one jump away from Mexico, and that Pancho Villa would make a

°*LANDMANSCHAFT:* a group of compatriots

revolution and start up with America! That was something I didn't expect! Who can be smart enough to figure all that out in advance? To tell you the truth, I didn't even know that Mexico is a separate country and doesn't belong to our America.

So now things are not so pleasant. I'm sure my Benny is down there in Mexico chasing after Villa, because I haven't received a letter from him for a long time. Before, he used to write me every week and even send me a few dollars from his pay. He gets pretty good wages —15 dollars a month plus room and board. It wouldn't be such a bad job if it weren't for Villa.

One thing my heart tells me. If Villa lets himself be caught it will be my Benny who'll catch him. Benny is a boy who's afraid of nothing! I only hope he captures him alive, because after all, why spill human blood? I don't believe in wars. I ask you, who needs it and what kind of world has it become when even America couldn't manage to get out of this situation—this whatever it is—if it's not a war, it's a hunting expedition . . .

And who has to catch him, Villa I mean? Nobody but my Benny himself, who's been in this country only ten years! I don't say they forced him, you understand, but who knows, if he had had a steady job he might never have thought about the army and I would be able to sleep peacefully. But the way things are, every night I dream about my Benny chasing after him, Villa I mean, and Villa is nobody's fool—he keeps running away.

The other day I went to the movies and they showed a picture about Mexico and how our boys are running things down there. People sit in the movies and beam and applaud Bravo! Bravo! Maybe I'd be just as patriotic as they are if my Benny wasn't down there in the middle of it. But my hands refused to clap—they were too busy wiping the tears from my eyes. One of the soldiers on a horse looked just like my Benny—he was gazing at me sadly as though he regretted the whole thing. I wanted to get a better look but the picture changed to a ship with a big cannon. You should have heard the people cheer! What were they so happy about—that Uncle Sam has a cannon?

Never mind, When *their* sons have to go down there they won't be so tickled about cannons . . . .

# HUSTLING

## Claude Brown

This selection comes from the author's autobiography. *Manchild in the Promised Land*. At fifteen, Claude Brown was arrested for the third time—he was involved in a robbery—and sent back to Warwick, a home for juvenile delinquents.

About a week after Christmas, I was sitting in the cottage that they'd put me in, C3. Al Cohen came in. Mr. Cohen was the superintendent of Warwick, and I had known him before, but only slightly, just to say hello to. I didn't think he really knew me. He used to call me Smiley, since I was always smiling. This time he said, "Hi, Smiley, what are you doin' here?" He looked sort of surprised, because he knew I had gone home.

I just looked up and said, "Hello, Mr. Cohen. Like, I just didn't make it, you know? I had some trouble."

He didn't say anything else. He just left.

I still had my rep at Warwick. Before I left the second time, I was running B1 cottage; I had become the "main man." The cottage parents and the area men thought I was real nice. I knew how to operate up there. I had an extortion game going, but it was a thing that the cats went along with because I didn't allow anybody to bully anybody and that sort of thing. Since I didn't get many visitors from home, I made other guys pay protection fees to me when they received visits or packages from home. I just ran the place, and I kept it quiet. I didn't have to bully anybody—cats knew that I knew how to hit a guy and knock out a tooth or something like that, so I seldom had to hit a cat. My reputation for hurting cats was indisputable. I could run any cottage that I'd been in with an iron hand.

After a few weeks, they told me that my work assignment would be Mr. Cohen's house. One of the nice things about that was that I got to know Mrs. Cohen. She was the nicest lady I'd ever met. She was a real person. I didn't get to know Mr. Cohen too well. I'd see the cat, and he'd talk. I'd see him in the morning when I first came in, before he left, and I'd see him in the afternoon if he came home for lunch. But I didn't really know him. I only got to know Mrs. Cohen, the cook, and the chauffeur.

Mrs. Cohen was always telling me that I could be somebody, that I could go to school and do anything I wanted to, because I had a good head on my shoulders. I thought she was a nice person, but I didn't think she was really seeing me as I was. She'd go on and on, and I'd say, "Yeah, uh-huh, yeah, Mrs. Cohen." I didn't believe it. She would get real excited about it and would start telling me about the great future that lay ahead for me. She tried to get me interested in it, but I couldn't tell her how I really felt about it. Even though I was in the third term, I knew I wasn't going to finish high school. I didn't even know anybody who had finished high school. Cats around my way just didn't do that. It wasn't for me; it was for some other people, that high school business.

She said that I could even go to college if I wanted to. She was nice, but she didn't know what was happening. I couldn't tell her that all cats like me ever did was smoke reefers and steal and fight and maybe eventually get killed. I couldn't tell her that I wasn't going anyplace but to jail or someplace like it. She'd say all these nice things, and I'd try to treat her nice and pretend I believed what she was saying. I couldn't have made her understand that this stuff was impossible for me. Cats who went to college, these were the boys who were in school and playing ball and reading and stuff like that when cats like me were smoking pot and having gang fights and running around with little funky girls. Those other cats were the kind who went to school. Cats like me, they didn't do anything but go to jail.

One time she got Mr. Cohen to talk to me about staying at Warwick, going to high school in the town there until I finished, and then going back to New York after I had gotten my high-school diploma. He just suggested it. He tried to show me that it wasn't being forced on me. I said, "Yeah, Mr. Cohen; like, that's nice," but I think he understood that I wasn't interested in this stuff. He wasn't really going to try too hard, because if I wasn't interested, there was nothing he could do.

All I wanted to do was get back to Harlem. I wanted to get back to Jackie and pot and the streets and stealing. This was my way of life. I couldn't take it for too long when I was there, but this was all I knew. There was nothing else. I wouldn't have known how to stay at Warwick and go to school. I didn't tell him that. When he asked me about staying and going to school, I just said, "Yeah, that would be nice." He saw that I wasn't what you could call excited about it.

One day, Mrs. Cohen gave me a book. It was an autobiography of some woman by the name of Mary McLeod Bethune. When she gave it to me, she said, "Here's something you might like to read." Before that, I had just read pocketbooks. I'd stopped reading comic books, but I was reading the trashy pocketbooks, stuff like *Duke, The Golden Spike,* that kind of nonsense.

I just took it and said, "Yeah, uh-huh." I saw the title on it, but I didn't know who the woman was. I just took it because Mrs. Cohen had given it to me. I said, "Yeah, I'll read it," and I read it because I figured she might ask about it, and I'd have to know something. It wasn't too bad. I felt that I knew something; I knew who Mary McLeod Bethune was, and I figured I probably knew as much about her as anybody else who knew anything about her, after reading a book about her whole life. Anyway, I felt a little smart afterward.

Then Mrs. Cohen gave me other books, usually about people, outstanding people. She gave me a book on Jackie Robinson and on Sugar Ray Robinson. She gave me a book on Einstein and a book on Albert Schweitzer. I read all these books, and I liked them. After a while, I started asking her for books, and I started reading more and more and liking it more and more.

After reading about a lot of these people, I started getting ideas about life. I couldn't talk to the cats in the cottage about the people in the books I was reading. I could talk to them about Jackie Robinson and Sugar Ray Robinson, but everybody knew about them, and there was nothing new to say. But this Einstein was a cat who really seemed to know how to live. He didn't seem to care what people thought about him. Nobody could come up to him and say, "Look, man, like, you're jive," or "You're not down," or any stuff like that. He seemed to be living all by himself; he'd found a way to do what he wanted to in life and just make everybody accept it.

He reminded me a lot of Papanek, somebody who seemed to have a whole lot of control over life and knew what he was going to do and what he wasn't going to do. The cat seemed to really know how to handle these things.

Then I read a book by Albert Schweitzer. He was another fascinating cat. The man knew so much. I really started wanting to know things. I wanted to know things, and I wanted to do things. It made me start thinking about what might happen if I got out of Warwick and didn't go back to Harlem. But I couldn't really see myself not going back to Harlem. I couldn't see myself going anyplace else, because if I didn't go to Harlem, where would I have gone? That was the only place I ever knew.

I kept reading, and I kept enjoying it. Most of the time, I used to just sit around in the cottage reading. I didn't bother with people, and nobody bothered me. This was a way to be in Warwick and not to be there at the same time. I could get lost in a book. Cats would come up and say, "Brown, what you readin'?" and I'd just say, "Man, git . . . away from me, and don't bother me."

July 12, 1953, I went home for good. There was hardly anybody else out. Just about all the people I used to swing with were in jail. They were in Coxsackie, Woodburn, Elmira, those places. The only ones who were left on the street were Bucky and Turk. Tito was in Woodburn, Alley Bush was in Elmira, Dunny was in Woodburn, and Mac was in Coxsackie.

I felt a little bad after I left, because I knew that the Cohens would find out sooner or later that I wasn't the angel that they thought I was. Actually, I would have had to be like a faggot or something to be the nice boy that Mrs. Cohen thought I was. I think Mr. Cohen knew all the time that although I acted nice in the house and did my work, I still had to raise a little bit of hell down at that cottage and keep my reputation or I wouldn't have been able to stay there as his houseboy. Those cats would have had me stealing cigarettes for them. . . . I just had to be good with my hands, and I had to let some people know it sometimes.

I guess Mrs. Cohen learned to live with it if she found out. It didn't matter too much, because I was back on the Harlem scene now. I was sixteen years old, and I knew that I'd never be going back to Warwick. The next stop was Coxsackie, Woodburn, or Elmira. I came back on the street and got ready for it. I started dealing pot. I had all kinds of contacts from Warwick.

Butch, Danny, and Kid were all strung out. They were junkies all the way. They had long habits. Kid had just come out of the Army. Danny had been out all the time. Butch had gone into the

Army to try to get away from his habit, but they had found the needle marks and had thrown him out. Now they were all out there, and they were just junkies. I used to feel sorry for them, especially Danny, because he had tried so hard to keep me off the stuff.

I was hanging out with just Turk from the old crowd. A guy I hadn't known before but had heard about was on the scene. This was Reno, another of Bucky and Mac's brothers. Reno was slick. He was about twenty-one, and he'd just come out of Woodburn when I came out of Warwick for the last time.

He used to kid me about being a better hustler than I was and said he would show me how to make twice the money. He'd heard about me, and we were sort of friends already when we first met. He told me, "If you gon be a hustler, you gon have to learn all the hustlin' tricks." I agreed with him.

When I first came out, I had to get a job in the garment district, because I was on parole, and I had to keep that job for a while to show my parole officer that I was doing good. I kept the job, and I kept dealing pot. I had the best pot in town. Word got around; after a while, I was making a lot of money. I used to always have about two hundred dollars on me. I started buying hundred-dollar suits and thirty-five-dollars shoes and five-dollar ties and dressing real good.

A whole lot of cats in the neighborhood started admiring me, and they wanted to get tight with me; but to me, even though these guys were my age, they were the younger boys. These were good boys who had been in the house for a long time. They were just coming out, and I didn't feel as though they were ready for me, so I couldn't hang out with anybody but Turk.

Turk was a nice cat, but he was slow. He didn't want to make any money, or he didn't know how. He just wasn't down enough. He had come out of the house kind of late, and the older hustlers didn't know him from way back like they knew me. Nobody would do business with him, so he couldn't really get started. I used to give him some money once in a while, but he couldn't really get started in the hustling life. So I just started hanging out with Reno. Reno had said he was going to show me all the hustling tricks.

After a few months, I quit my first job and just dealt pot. I decided I was going to be a hustler. We were going to start from way back, from all the old hustling tricks, and come up to the modern-day stuff. About three months after I'd been out of Warwick, I was going downtown with Reno to learn how to play the Murphy.°

°PLAY THE MURPHY: a kind of "hustle" that seeks to take advantage of tourists and other
   innocents

93

# HOMEBOY

## Malcolm X

*This selection comes from* The Autobiography of Malcolm X.

Most of Roseland's dances were for whites only, and they had white bands only. But the only white band ever to play there at a Negro dance to my recollection, was Charlie Barnet's. The fact is that very few white bands could have satisfied the Negro dancers. But I know that Charlie Barnet's "Cherokee" and his "Redskin Rhumba" drove those Negroes wild. They'd jampack that ballroom, the black girls in way-out silk and satin dresses and shoes, their hair done in all kinds of styles, the men sharp in their zoot suits and crazy conks, and everybody grinning and greased and gassed.

Some of the bandsmen would come up to the men's room at about eight o'clock and get shoeshines before they went to work. Duke Ellington, Count Basie, Lionel Hampton, Cootie Williams, Jimmie Lunceford were just a few of those who sat in my chair. I would really make my shine rag sound like someone had set off Chinese firecrackers. Duke's great alto saxman, Johnny Hodges—he was Shorty's idol—still owes me for a shoeshine I gave him. He was in the chair one night, having a friendly argument with the drummer, Sonny Greer, who was standing there, when I tapped the bottom of his shoes to signal that I was finished. Hodges stepped down, reaching his hand in his pocket to pay me, but then snatched his hand out to gesture, and just forgot me, and walked away. I wouldn't have dared to bother the man who could do what he did with "Daydream" by asking him for fifteen cents.

I remember that I struck up a little shoeshine-stand conversation with Count Basie's great blues singer, Jimmie Rushing. (He's the one famous for "Sent For You Yesterday, Here You Come Today" and things like that.) Rushing's feet, I remember, were big and funny-shaped—not long like most big feet, but they were round and roly-poly like Rushing. Anyhow, he even introduced me to some of the other Basie cats, like Lester Young, Harry Edison, Buddy Tate, Don Byas, Dickie Wells, and Buck Clayton. They'd walk in the rest room later, by themselves.

"Hi, Red." They'd be up there in my chair, and my shine rag was popping to the beat of all of their records, spinning in my head. Musicians never have had, anywhere, a greater shoeshine-boy fan than I was. I would write to Wilfred and Hilda and Philbert and Reginald back in Lansing, trying to describe it.

I never got any decent tips until the middle of the Negro dances, which is when the dancers started feeling good and getting generous. After the white dances, when I helped to clean out the ballroom, we would throw out perhaps a dozen empty liquor bottles. But after the Negro dances, we would have to throw out cartons full of empty fifth bottles—not rotgut, either, but the best brands, and especially Scotch.

During lulls up there in the men's room, sometimes I'd get in five minutes of watching the dancing. The white people danced as though somebody had trained them—left, one, two; right, three, four—the same steps and patterns over and over, as though somebody had wound them up. But those Negroes—nobody in the world could have choreographed the way they did whatever they felt—just grabbing partners, even the white chicks who came to the Negro dances. And my black brethren today may hate me for saying it, but a lot of black girls nearly got run over by some of those Negro males scrambling to get at those white women; you would have thought God had lowered some of his angels. Times have sure changed; if it happened today, those same black girls would go after those Negro men—and the white women, too.

Anyway, some couples were so abandoned—flinging high and wide, improvising steps and movements—that you couldn't believe it. I could feel the beat in my bones, even though I had never danced.

"Showtime!" people would start hollering about the last hour of the dance. Then a couple of dozen really wild couples would stay on the floor, the girls changing to low white sneakers. The band now would really be blasting, and all the other dancers would form a clapping, shouting circle to watch that wild competition as it began, covering only a quarter or so of the ballroom floor. The band, the spectators, and the dancers would be making the Roseland Ballroom feel like a big rocking ship. The spotlight would be turning, pink, yellow, green, and blue, picking up the couples lindy-hopping as if they had gone mad. "Wail, man, wail!" people would be shouting at the band; and it would be wailing, until first one and then another couple just ran out of strength and stumbled off toward the crowd, exhausted and soaked with sweat. Sometimes I would be down there standing inside the door jumping up and down in my gray jacket with the whiskbroom in the pocket, and the manager would have to come and shout at me that I had customers upstairs.

The first liquor I drank, my first cigarettes, even my first reefers, I can't specifically remember. But I know they were all mixed together with my first shooting craps, playing cards, and betting my dollar a day on the numbers, as I started hanging out at night with Shorty and his friends. Shorty's jokes about how country I had been made us all laugh. I still was country, I know now, but it all felt so great because I was accepted. All of us would be in somebody's place, usually one of the girls', and we'd be turning on, the reefers making everybody's head light, or the whisky aglow in our middles. Everybody understood that my head had to stay kinky a while longer, to grow long enough for Shorty to conk it for me. One of these nights, I remarked that I had saved about half enough to get a zoot.

"*Save?*" Shorty couldn't believe it. "Homeboy, you never heard of credit?" He told me he'd call a neighborhood clothing store the first thing in the morning, and that I should be there early.

A salesman, a young Jew, met me when I came in. "You're Shorty's friend?" I said I was; it amazed me—all of Shorty's contacts. The salesman wrote my name on a form, and the Roseland as where I worked, and Ella's address as where I lived. Shorty's name was put down as recommending me. The salesman said, "Shorty's one of our best customers."

I was measured, and the young salesman picked off a rack a zoot suit that was just wild: sky-blue pants thirty inches in the knee and angle-narrowed down to twelve inches at the bottom, and a long coat that pinched my waist and flared out below my knees.

As a gift, the salesman said, the store would give me a narrow leather belt with my initial "L" on it. Then he said I ought to also buy a hat, and I did—blue, with a feather in the four-inch brim. Then the store gave me another present: a long, thick-linked, gold-plated chain that swung down lower than my coat hem. I was sold forever on credit.

When I modeled the zoot for Ella, she took a long look and said, "Well, I guess it had to happen." I took three of those twenty-five-cent sepia-toned, while-you-wait pictures of myself, posed the way "hipsters" wearing their zoots would "cool it"—hat angled, knees drawn close together, feet wide apart, both index fingers jabbed toward the floor. The long coat and swinging chain and the Punjab pants were much more dramatic if you stood that way. One picture I autographed and airmailed to my brothers and sisters in Lansing to let them see how well I was doing. I gave another one to Ella, and the third to Shorty, who was really moved: I could tell by the way he said, "Thanks, homeboy." It was part of our "hip" code not to show that kind of affection.

Shorty soon decided that my hair was finally long enough to be conked. He had promised to school me in how to beat the barber-shops' three- and four-dollar price by making up congolene, and then conking ourselves.

I took the little list of ingredients he had printed out for me, and went to a grocery store, where I got a can of Red Devil lye, two eggs, and two medium-sized white potatoes. Then at a drugstore near the poolroom, I asked for a large jar of vaseline, a large bar of soap, a large-toothed comb and a fine-toothed comb, one of those rubber hoses with a metal spray-head, a rubber apron, and a pair of gloves.

"Going to lay on that first conk?" the drugstore man asked me. I proudly told him, grinning, "Right!"

Shorty paid six dollars a week for a room in his cousin's shabby apartment. His cousin wasn't at home. "It's like the pad's mine, he spends so much time with his woman," Shorty said. "Now, you watch me—"

He peeled the potatoes and thin-sliced them into a quart-sized Mason fruit jar, then started stirring them with a wooden spoon as he gradually poured in a little over half the can of lye. "Never use a metal spoon; the lye will turn it black," he told me.

A jelly-like, starchy-looking glop resulted from the lye and potatoes, and Shorty broke in the two eggs, stirring real fast—his own conk and dark face bent down close. The congolene turned pale-yellowish. "Feel the jar," Shorty said. I cupped my hand against the outside, and snatched it away. "Damn right, it's hot, that's the lye," he said. "So you know it's going to burn when I comb it in—it burns *bad*. But the longer you can stand it, the straighter the hair."

He made me sit down, and he tied the string of the new rubber apron tightly around my neck, and combed up my bush of hair. Then, from the big vaseline jar, he took a handful and massaged it hard all through my hair and into the scalp. He also thickly vaselined my neck, ears and forehead. "When I get to washing out your head, be sure to tell me anywhere you feel any little stinging," Shorty warned me, washing his hands, then pulling on the rubber gloves, and tying on his own rubber apron. "You always got to remember that any congolene left in burns a sore into your head."

The congolene just felt warm when Shorty started combing it in. But then my head caught fire.

I gritted my teeth and tried to pull the sides of the kitchen table together. The comb felt as if it was raking my skin off.

My eyes watered, my nose was running. I couldn't stand it any longer; I bolted to the washbasin. I was cursing Shorty with every name I could think of when he got the spray going and started soap-lathering my head.

He lathered and spray-rinsed, lathered and spray-rinsed, maybe ten or twelve times, each time gradually closing the hot-water faucet, until the rinse was cold, and that helped some.

"You feel any stinging spots?"

97

"No," I managed to say. My knees were trembling.

"Sit back down, then. I think we got it all out okay."

The flame came back as Shorty, with a thick towel, started drying my head, rubbing hard. "*Easy,* man, *easy!*" I kept shouting.

"The first time's always worst. You get used to it better before long. You took it real good, homeboy. You got a good conk."

When Shorty let me stand up and see in the mirror, my hair hung down in limp, damp strings. My scalp still flamed, but not as badly; I could bear it. He draped the towel around my shoulders, over my rubber apron, and began again vaselining my hair.

I could feel him combing, straight back, first the big comb, then the fine-toothed one.

Then, he was using a razor, very delicately, on the back of my neck. Then, finally, shaping the sideburns.

My first view in the mirror blotted out the hurting. I'd seen some pretty conks, but when it's the first time, on your *own* head, the transformation, after the lifetime of kinks, is staggering.

The mirror reflected Shorty behind me. We both were grinning and sweating. And on top of my head was this thick, smooth sheen of shining red hair—real red—as straight as any white man's.

How ridiculous I was! Stupid enough to stand there simply lost in admiration of my hair now looking "white," reflected in the mirror in Shorty's room. I vowed that I'd never again be without a conk, and I never was for many years.

This was my first really big step toward self-degradation: when I endured all of that pain, literally burning my flesh with lye, in order to cook my natural hair until it was limp, to have it look like a white man's hair. I had joined that multitude of Negro men and women in America who are brainwashed into believing that the black people are "inferior"—and white people "superior"—that they will even violate and mutilate their God-created bodies to try to look "pretty" by white standards.

Look around today, in every small town and big city, from two-bit catfish and soda-pop joints into the "integrated" lobby of the Waldorf-Astoria, and you'll see conks on black men. And you'll see black women wearing these green and pink and purple and red and platinum-blonde wigs. They're all more ridiculous than a slapstick comedy. It makes you wonder if the Negro has completely lost his sense of identity, lost touch with himself.

You'll see the conk worn by many, many so-called "upper class" Negroes, and, as much as I hate to say it about them, on all too many Negro entertainers. One of the reasons that I've especially admired some of them, like Lionel Hampton and Sidney Poitier, among others, is that they have kept their natural hair and fought to the top. I admire any Negro man who has never had himself conked, or who has had the sense to get rid of it—as I finally did.

I don't know which kind of self-defacing conk is the greater shame—the one you'll see on the heads of the black so-called "middle class" and "upper class," who ought to know better, or the one you'll see on the heads of the poorest, most downtrodden, ignorant black men. I mean the legal-minimum-wage ghetto-dwelling kind of Negro, as I was when I got my first one. It's generally among these poor fools that you'll see a black kerchief over the man's head, like Aunt Jemima; he's trying to make his conk last longer, between trips to the barbershop. Only for special occasions is this kerchief-protected conk exposed—to show off how "sharp" and "hip" its owner is. The ironic thing is that I have never heard any woman, white or black, express any admiration for a conk. Of course, any white woman with a black man isn't thinking about his hair. But I don't see how on earth a black woman with any race pride could walk down the street with any black man wearing a conk—the emblem of his shame that he is black.

To my own shame, when I say all of this I'm talking first of all about myself—because you can't show me any Negro who ever conked more faithfully than I did. I'm speaking from personal experience when I say of any black man who conks today, or any white-wigged black woman, that if they gave the brains in their heads just half as much attention as they do their hair, they would be a thousand times better off.

# The Murder of Two Men by a Young Kid
# Wearing Lemon-colored Gloves

*Kenneth Patchen*

Wait.

        Wait.

    Wait.

Wait. Wait.

Wait.

          Wait.

      W a i t .

  Wait.

     Wait.

         Wait.

     Wait.

      Wait.

*Wait.*

   NOW.

# A Visit to Newgate   *Charles Dickens*

"The force of habit" is a trite phrase in everybody's mouth; and it is not a little remarkable that those who use it most as applied to others, unconsciously afford in their own persons singular examples of the power which habit and custom exercise over the minds of men, and of the little reflection they are apt to bestow on subjects with which every day's experience has rendered them familiar. If Bedlam could be suddenly removed like another Aladdin's palace, and set down on the space now occupied by Newgate, scarcely one man out of a hundred, whose road to business every morning lies through Newgate-street or the Old Bailey, would pass the building without bestowing a hasty glance on its small, grated windows, and a transient thought at least upon the condition of the unhappy beings immured in its dismal cells; and yet these same men, day by day, and hour by hour, pass and repass this gloomy depository of the guilt and misery of London, in one perpetual stream of life and bustle, utterly unmindful of the throng of wretched creatures pent up within it—nay not even knowing, or if they do, not heeding the fact, that as they pass one particular angle of the massive wall with a light laugh or a merry whistle, they stand within one yard of a fellow-creature, bound and helpless, whose hours are numbered, from whom the last feeble ray of hope has fled forever, and whose miserable career will shortly terminate in a violent and shameful death. Contact with death even in its least terrible shape is solemn and appalling. How much more awful is it to reflect on this near vicinity to the dying—to men in full health and vigor, in the flower of youth or the prime of life, with all their faculties and perceptions as acute and perfect as your own; but dying, nevertheless—dying as surely—with the hand of death imprinted upon them as indelibly—as if mortal disease had wasted their frames to shadows, and loathsome corruption had already begun!

It was with some such thoughts as these that we determined not many weeks since to visit the interior of Newgate—in an amateur capacity, of course; and, having carried our intention into effect, we proceed to lay its results before our readers, in the hope—founded more upon the nature of the subject, than on any presumptuous confidence in our own descriptive powers—that this paper may not be found wholly devoid of interest. We have only to premise, that we do not intend to fatigue the reader with any statistical accounts of the prison: they will be found at length in numerous reports of numerous committees, and a variety of authorities of equal weight. We took no notes, made no memoranda, measured none of the yards, ascertained the exact number of inches

101

"A Visit to Newgate" from SKETCHES BY BOZ by Charles Dickens, published by Oxford University Press, London.

in no particular room; are unable even to report of how many apartments the gaol is composed.

We saw the prison, and saw the prisoners; and what we did see, and what we thought, we will tell at once in our own way.

Having delivered our credentials to the servant who answered our knock at the door of the governor's house, we were ushered into the "office"; a little room, on the right-hand side as you enter, with two windows looking into the Old Bailey, fitted up like an ordinary attorney's office, or merchant's counting-house, with the usual fixtures—a wainscoted partition, a shelf or two, a desk, a couple of stools, a pair of clerks, an almanack, a clock, and a few maps. After a little delay, occasioned by sending into the interior of the prison for the chaperon whose duty it was to conduct us, that functionary arrived; a respectable-looking man of about two or three and fifty, in a broad-brimmed hat, and full suit of black, who, but for his keys, would have looked quite as much like a clergyman as a turnkey: we were quite disappointed; he had not even top-boots on. Following our conductor by a door opposite to that at which we had entered, we arrived at a small room, without any other furniture than a little desk, with a book for visitors' autographs, and a shelf, on which were a few boxes for papers, and casts of the heads and faces of the two notorious murderers, Bishop and Williams; the former, in particular, exhibiting a style of head and set of features, which would have afforded sufficient moral grounds for his instant execution at any time, even had there been no other evidence against him. Leaving this room

also by an opposite door, we found ourself in the lodge which opens on the Old Bailey, one side of which is plentifully garnished with a choice collection of heavy sets of irons, including those worn by the redoubtable Jack Sheppard—genuine; and those *said* to have been graced by the sturdy limbs of the no less celebrated Dick Turpin—doubtful. From this lodge a heavy oaken gate, bound with iron, studded with nails of the same material, and guarded by another turnkey, opens on a few steps, if we remember right, which terminate in a narrow and dismal stone passage, running parallel with the Old Bailey, and leading to the different yards, through a number of tortuous and intricate windings, guarded in their turn by huge gates and gratings, whose appearance is sufficient to dispel at once the slightest hope of escape that any new comer may have entertained; and the very recollection of which, on eventually traversing the place again, involves one in a maze of confusion.

It is necessary to explain here, that the buildings in the prison or in other words the different wards—form a square, of which the four sides abut respectively on the Old Bailey, the old College of Physicians (now forming a part of Newgate-market), the Sessions-house, and Newgate-street. The intermediate space is divided into several paved yards, in which the prisoners take such air and exercise as can be had in such a place. These yards, with the exception of that in which prisoners under sentence of death are confined (of which we shall presently give a more detailed description), run parallel with Newgate-street, and consequently from the Old Bailey, as it were, to Newgate-market. The women's side is in the right

Vincent Van Gogh. *Prisoners' Rounds*. The Pushkin Museum.

wing of the prison nearest the Sessions-house; and as we were introduced into this part of the building first, we will adopt the same order, and introduce our readers to it also.

Turning to the right, then, down the passage to which we just now adverted, omitting any mention of intervening gates—for if we noticed every gate that was unlocked for us to pass through, and locked again as soon as we had passed, we should require a gate at every comma—we came to a door composed of thick bars of wood, through which were discernible, passing to and fro in a narrow yard, some twenty women, the majority of whom, however, as soon as they were aware of the presence of strangers, retreated to their wards. One side of this yard is railed off at a considerable distance, and formed into a kind of iron cage, about five feet ten inches in height, roofed at the top, and defended in front by iron bars, from which the friends of the female prisoners communicate with them. In one corner of this singular-looking den was a yellow, haggard, decrepit old woman, in a tattered gown that had once been black, and the remains of an old straw bonnet, with faded ribbon of the same hue, in earnest conversation with a young girl—a prisoner of course—of about two-and-twenty. It is impossible to imagine a more poverty-stricken object, or a creature so borne down in soul and body, by excess of misery and destitution. The girl was a good-looking robust female, with a profusion of hair streaming about in the wind—for she had no bonnet on—and a man's silk pocket-handkerchief was loosely thrown over a most ample pair of shoulders. The old woman was talking in that low, stifled tone of voice which

tells so forcibly of mental anguish; and every now and then burst into an irrepressible sharp, abrupt cry of grief, the most distressing sound that human ears can hear. The girl was perfectly unmoved. Hardened beyond all hope of redemption, she listened doggedly to her mother's entreaties, whatever they were: and, beyond inquiring after "Jem," and eagerly catching at the few halfpence her miserable parent had brought her, took no more apparent interest in the conversation than the most unconcerned spectators. God knows there were enough of them in the persons of the other prisoners in the yard, who were no more concerned by what was passing before their eyes, and within their hearing, than if they were blind and deaf. Why should they be? Inside the prison, and out, such scenes were too familiar to them, to excite even a passing thought, unless of ridicule or contempt for the display of feelings which they had long since forgotten, and lost all sympathy for.

A little farther on, a squalid-looking woman in a slovenly, thick-bordered cap, with her arms muffled up in a large red shawl, the fringed ends of which straggled nearly to the bottom of a dirty white apron, was communicating some instructions to *her* visitor—her daughter evidently. The girl was thinly clad, and shaking with the cold. Some ordinary word of recognition passed between her and her mother when she appeared at the grating, but neither hope, condolence, regret, nor affection was expressed on either side. The mother whispered her instructions, and the girl received them with her pinched-up, half-starved features twisted into an expression of careful cunning. It was some scheme for the woman's defense that she was disclosing; and a sullen smile came over the girl's face for an instant, as if she were pleased, not so much at the probability of her mother's liberation, as at the chance of her "getting off" in spite of her prosecutors. The dialogue was soon concluded; and with the same careless indifference with which they had approached each other, the mother turned towards the inner end of the yard, and the girl to the gate at which she had entered.

The girl belonged to a class—unhappily but too extensive—the very existence of which should make men's hearts bleed. Barely past her childhood, it required but a glance to discover that she was one of those children born and bred in poverty and vice, who have never known what childhood is; who have never been taught to love and court a parent's smile, or to dread a parent's frown. The thousand nameless endearments of childhood, its gaiety and its innocence, are alike unknown to them. They have entered at once upon the stern realities and miseries of life, and to their better nature it is almost hopeless to appeal in aftertimes, by any of the references which will awaken, if it be only for a moment, some good feeling in ordinary bosoms, however corrupt they may have become. Talk to them of parental solicitude, the happy days of childhood, and the merry games of infancy! Tell them of hunger and the streets, beggary and stripes, the gin-shop, the station-house, and the pawnbroker's, and they will understand you.

Two or three women were standing at different parts of the grating conversing with their friends, but a very large proportion of the prisoners appeared to have no friends at all, beyond such of their old companions as might happen to be within the walls. So, passing hastily down the yard, and pausing only for an instant to notice the little incidents we have just recorded, we were conducted up a clean and well-lighted flight of stone stairs to one of the wards. There are several in this part of the building, but a description of one is a description of the whole.

It was a spacious, bare, white-washed apartment, lighted, of course, by windows looking into the interior of the prison, but far more light and airy than one could reasonably expect to find in such a situation. There was a large fire with a deal table before it, round which ten or a dozen women were seated on wooden forms at dinner. Along both sides of the room ran a shelf; and below it, at regular intervals, a row of large hooks were fixed in the wall, on each of which was hung the sleeping mat of a prisoner; her rug and blanket being folded up, and placed on the shelf above. At night these mats are placed on the floor, each beneath the hook on which it hangs during the day; and the ward is thus made to answer the purposes both of a dayroom and sleeping apartment. Over the fireplace was a large sheet of pasteboard, on which were displayed a variety of texts from Scripture, which were also scattered about the room in scraps about the size and shape of the copy-slips which are used in schools. On the table was a sufficient provision of a kind of stewed beef and brown bread, in pewter dishes, which are kept perfectly bright and displayed on shelves in great order and regularity when they are not in use.

The women rose hastily on our entrance and retired in a hurried manner to either side of the fireplace. They were all cleanly—many of them decently—attired, and there was nothing peculiar either in their appearance or demeanor. One or two resumed the needlework which they had probably laid aside at the commencement of their meal, others gazed at the visitors with listless curiosity, and a few retired behind their companions to the very end of the room, as if desirous to avoid even the casual observation of the strangers. Some old Irish women, both in this and other wards, to whom the thing was no novelty, appeared perfectly indifferent to our presence, and remained standing close to the seats from which they had just risen; but the general feeling among the females seemed to be one of uneasiness during the period of our stay among them, which was very brief. Not a word was uttered during the time of our remaining, unless indeed by the wardswoman in reply to some question which we put to the turnkey who accompanied us. In every ward on the female side a wardswoman is appointed to preserve order, and a similar regulation is adopted among the males. The wardsmen and wardswomen are all prisoners, selected for good conduct. They alone are allowed the privilege of sleeping on bedsteads, a small stump bedstead being placed in every ward for that purpose. On both sides of the gaol is a small receiving-room to which prisoners are conducted on their first reception, and whence they cannot be removed until they have been examined by the surgeon of the prison.°

Retracing our steps to the dismal passage in which we found ourselves at first (and which, by-the-bye, contains three or four dark cells for the accom-

°The regulations of the prison relative to the confinement of prisoners during the day, their sleeping at night, their taking their meals, and other matters of gaol economy have been all altered—greatly for the better—since this sketch was written.

106

modation of refractory prisoners), we were led through a narrow yard to the "school"—a portion of the prison set apart for boys under fourteen years of age. In a tolerable-sized room, in which were writing-materials and some copy-books, was the schoolmaster, with a couple of his pupils; the remainder having been fetched from an adjoining apartment, the whole were drawn up in line for our inspection. There were fourteen of them in all, some with shoes, some without; some in pinafores without jackets, others in jackets without pinafores, and one in scarce anything at all. The whole number, without an exception we believe, had been committed for trial on charges of pocket-picking; and fourteen such villanous little faces we never beheld. There was not one redeeming feature among them—not a glance of honesty—not a wink expressive of anything but the gallows and the hulks, in the whole collection. As to anything like shame or contrition, that was entirely out of the question. They were evidently quite gratified at being thought worth the trouble of looking at; their idea appeared to be that we had come to see Newgate as a grand affair, and that they were an indispensable part of the show: and every boy as he "fell in" to the line, actually seemed as pleased and important as if he had done something excessively meritorious in getting there at all. We never looked upon a more disagreeable sight, because we never saw fourteen such hopeless and irreclaimable wretches before.

On either side of the schoolyard is a yard for men, in one of which—that towards Newgate-street—prisoners of the more respectable class are confined. Of the other we have little description to offer, as the different wards necessarily partake of the same character. They are provided, like the wards on the women's side, with mats and rugs, which are disposed of in the same manner during the day; and the only very striking difference between their appearance and that of the wards inhabited by the females, is the utter absence of any employment whatever. Huddled together upon two opposite forms, by the fireside, sit twenty men perhaps; here a boy in livery, there a man in a rough greatcoat and top-boots; further on, a desperate-looking fellow in his shirt sleeves, with an old Scotch cap upon his shaggy head; near him again, a tall ruffian, in a smock-frock, and next to him a miserable being of distressed appearance, with his head resting on his hand;—but all alike in one respect, all idle and listless: when they do leave the fire, sauntering moodily about, lounging in the window, or leaning against the wall, vacantly swinging their bodies to and fro. With the exception of a man reading an old newspaper in two or three instances, this was the case in every ward we entered.

The only communication these men have with their friends is through two close iron gratings, with an intermediate space of about a yard in width between the two, so that nothing can be handed across, nor can the prisoner have any communication by touch with the person who visits him. The married men have a separate grating, at which to see their wives, but its construction is the same.

The prison chapel is situated at the back of the governor's house, the latter having no windows looking into the interior of the prison. Whether the associations connected with the place— the knowledge that here a portion of the burial service is, on some dreadful occasions, performed over the quick and not upon the dead—cast over it a still more gloomy and somber air than art has imparted to it, we know not, but its appearance is very striking. There is something in a silent and deserted place of worship highly solemn and impressive at any time; and the very dissimilarity of this one from any we have been accustomed to, only enhances the impression. The meanness of its appointments—the bare and scanty pulpit, with the paltry painted pillars on either side—the women's gallery with its great heavy curtain, the men's with its unpainted benches and dingy front—the tottering little table at the altar, with the commandments on the wall above it, scarcely legible through lack of paint, and dust and damp—so unlike the rich velvet and gilding, the stately marble and polished wood of a modern church—are the more striking from their powerful contrast. There is one object, too, which rivets the attention and fascinates the gaze, and from which we may turn disgusted and horror-stricken in vain, for the recollection of it will haunt us, waking and sleeping, for months afterwards. Immediately below the reading desk, on the floor of the chapel, and forming the most conspicuous object in its little area, is *the condemned pew;* a huge black pen, in which the wretched men, who are singled out for death, are placed, on the Sunday preceding their execution, in sight of all their fellow-prisoners, from many of whom they may have been separated but a week before, to hear prayers for their own souls, to join in the responses of their own burial service, and to listen to an address, warning their recent companions to take example by their fate, and urging themselves, while there is yet time—nearly four-and-twenty hours—to "turn, and flee from the wrath to come!" Imagine what have been the feelings of the men whom that fearful pew has enclosed, and of whom, between the gallows and the knife, no mortal remnant may now remain; think of the hopeless clinging to life to the last, and the wild despair, far exceeding in anguish the felon's death itself, by which they have heard the certainty of their speedy transmission to another world, with all their crimes upon their heads, rung into their ears by the officiating clergyman!

At one time—and at no distant period either—the coffins of the men about to be executed, were placed in that pew, upon the seat by their side, during the whole service. It may seem incredible, but it is strictly true. Let us hope that the increased spirit of civilization and humanity which abolished this frightful and degrading custom may extend itself to other usages equally barbarous; usages which have not even the plea of utility in their defense, as every year's experience has shown them to be more and more inefficacious.

Leaving the chapel, descending to the passage so frequently alluded to, and crossing the yard before noticed as being allotted to prisoners of a more respectable description than the generality of men confined here, the visitor arrives at a thick iron gate of great size and strength. Having been admitted through it by the turnkey on duty, he turns sharp round to the left, and pauses before another gate; and, having passed this last barrier, he stands in the most terrible part of this gloomy building—the condemned ward.

The press yard, well known by name to newspaper readers, from its frequent mention (formerly thank God!) in accounts of executions, is at the corner of the building, and next to the ordinary's house, in Newgate-street: running from Newgate-street, towards the center of the prison, parallel with Newgate-market. It is a long, narrow court of which a portion of the wall in Newgate-street forms one end, and the gate the other. At the upper end, on the left-hand—that is, adjoining the wall in Newgate-street—is a cistern of water, and at the bottom a double grating (of which the gate itself forms a part) similar to that before described. Through these grates the prisoners are allowed to see their friends, a turnkey always remaining in the vacant space between, during the whole interview. Immediately on the right as you enter, is a building containing the pressroom, dayroom, and cells; the yard is on every side surrounded by lofty walls guarded by *chevaux de frise;* and the whole is under the constant inspection of vigilant and experienced turnkeys.

In the first apartment into which we were conducted—which was at the top of a staircase, and immediately over the pressroom—were five-and-twenty or thirty prisoners, all under sentence of death, awaiting the result of the Recorder's report—men of all ages and appearances, from a hardened old offender with swarthy face and grizzly beard of three days' growth, to a handsome boy, not fourteen years old, of singularly youthful appearance even for that age, who had been condemned for burglary. There was nothing remarkable in the appearance of these prisoners. One or two decently-dressed men were brooding with a dejected air over the fire; several little groups of two or three had been engaged in conversation at the upper end of the room, or in the windows; and the remainder were crowded round a young man seated at a table, who appeared to be engaged in teaching the younger ones to write. The room was large, airy, and clean. There was very little anxiety or mental suffering depicted in the countenance of any of the men; they had all been sentenced to death, it is true, and the Recorder's report had not yet been made; but we question whether there was a man among them, notwithstanding, who did not *know* that although he had undergone the ceremony, it never was intended that his life should be sacrificed. On the table lay a Testament, but there were no signs of its having been in recent use.

In the pressroom below were three men, the nature of whose offence rendered it necessary to separate them, even from their companions in guilt. It is a long, somber room, with two windows sunk into the stone wall, and here the wretched men are pinioned on the morning of their execution, before moving towards the scaffold. The fate of one of these men was uncertain; some mitigatory circumstances having come to light since his trial, which had been humanely represented in the proper quarter. The other two had nothing to expect from the mercy of the Crown; their doom was sealed; no plea could be urged in extenuation of their crime, and they well knew that for them there was no hope in this world. "The two short ones," the turnkey whispered, "were dead men."

The man to whom we have alluded as entertaining some hopes of escape was lounging at the greatest distance he could place between himself and his companions, in the window nearest the door. He was probably aware of our approach, and had assumed an air of courageous indifference; his face was purposely averted towards the window, and he stirred not an inch while we were present. The other two men were at the upper end of the room. One of them, who was imperfectly seen in the dim light, had his back towards us, and was stooping over the fire with his right arm on the mantelpiece, and his head sunk upon it. The other was leaning on the sill of the farthest window. The light fell full upon him and communicated to his pale, haggard face and disordered hair, an appearance which, at that distance, was perfectly ghastly. His cheek rested upon his hand; and, with his face a little raised, and his eyes widely staring before him, he seemed to be unconsciously intent on counting the chinks in the opposite wall. We passed this room again afterwards. The first man was pacing up and down the court with a firm military step—he had been a soldier in the foot-guards—and a cloth cap jauntily thrown on one side of the head. He bowed respectfully to our conductor, and the salute was returned. The other two still remained in the positions we have described, and were motionless as statues.°

A few paces up the yard, and forming a continuation of the building, in which are the two rooms we have just quitted, lie the condemned cells. The entrance is by a narrow and obscure staircase leading to a dark passage, in which a charcoal stove casts a lurid

°These two men were executed shortly afterwards. The other was respited during his Majesty's pleasure.

tint over the objects in its immediate vicinity, and diffuses something like warmth around. From the left-hand side of this passage, the massive door of every cell on the story opens, and from it alone can they be approached. There are three of these passages, and three of these ranges of cells one above the other, but in size, furniture, and appearance, they are all precisely alike. Prior to the Recorder's report being made, all the prisoners under sentence of death are removed from the day-room at five o'clock in the afternoon, and locked up in these cells where they are allowed a candle until ten o'clock, and here they remain until seven next morning. When the warrant for a prisoner's execution arrives, he is immediately removed to the cells and confined in one of them until he leaves it for the scaffold. He is at liberty to walk in the yard, but both in his walks and in his cell, he is constantly attended by a turnkey who never leaves him on any pretense whatever.

We entered the first cell. It was a stone dungeon, eight feet long by six wide, with a bench at the further end, under which were a common horse rug, a Bible, and prayer book. An iron candlestick was fixed into the wall at the side; and a small high window in the back admitted as much air and light as could struggle in between a double row of heavy, crossed iron bars. It contained no other furniture of any description.

Conceive the situation of a man, spending his last night on earth in this cell. Buoyed up with some vague and undefined hope of reprieve, he knew not why—indulging in some wild and visionary idea of escaping, he knew not how—hour after hour of the three pre-

ceding days allowed him for preparation has fled with a speed which no man living would deem possible, for none but this dying man can know. He has wearied his friends with entreaties, exhausted the attendants with importunities, neglected in his feverish restlessness the timely warnings of his spiritual consoler; and now that the illusion is at last dispelled, now that eternity is before him and guilt behind, now that his fears of death amount almost to madness, and an overwhelming sense of his helpless, hopeless state rushes upon him, he is lost and stupified, and has neither thoughts to turn to, nor power to call upon the Almighty Being, from whom alone he can seek mercy and forgiveness, and before whom his repentance can alone avail.

Hours have glided by, and still he sits upon the same stone bench with folded arms, heedless alike of the fast decreasing time before him, and the urgent entreaties of the good man at his side. The feeble light is wasting gradually, and the deathlike stillness of the street without, broken only by the rumbling of some passing vehicle which echoes mournfully through the empty yards, warns him that the night is waning fast away. The deep bell of St. Paul's strikes—one! He heard it; it has roused him. Seven hours left! He paces the narrow limits of his cell with rapid strides, cold drops of terror starting on his forehead, and every muscle of his frame quivering with agony. Seven hours! He suffers himself to be led to his seat, mechanically takes the Bible which is placed in his hand, and tries to read and listen. No: his thoughts will wander. The book is torn and soiled by use—and how like the book he read his lessons in at school just forty years ago!

110

He has never bestowed a thought upon it since he left it as a child: and yet the place, the time, the room—nay, the very boys he played with, crowd as vividly before him as if they were scenes of yesterday; and some forgotten phrase, some childish word of kindness, rings in his ears like the echo of one uttered but a minute since. The deep voice of the clergyman recalls him to himself. He is reading from the sacred book its solemn promises of pardon for repentance, and its awful denunciation of obdurate men. He falls upon his knees and clasps his hands to pray. Hush! what sound was that? He starts upon his feet. It cannot be two yet. Hark! Two quarters have struck;—the third—the fourth. It is! Six hours left. Tell him not of repentance. Six hours' repentance for eight times six years of guilt and sin! He buries his face in his hands, and throws himself on the bench.

Worn with watching and excitement, he sleeps, and the same unsettled state of mind pursues him in his dreams. An insupportable load is taken from his breast; he is walking with his wife in a pleasant field, with the blue sky above them, and a fresh and boundless prospect on every side—how different from the stone walls of Newgate! She is looking—not as she did when he saw her for the last time in that dreadful place, but as she used to when he loved her—long, long ago, before misery and ill-treatment had altered her looks, and vice had changed his nature, and she is leaning upon his arm, and looking up into his face with tenderness and affection—and he does *not* strike her now, nor rudely shake her

from him. And oh! how glad he is to tell her all he had forgotten in that last hurried interview, and to fall on his knees before her and fervently beseech her pardon for all the unkindness and cruelty that wasted her form and broke her heart! The scene suddenly changes. He is on his trial again: there are the judge and jury, and prosecutors, and witnesses, just as they were before. How full the court is—what a sea of heads—with a gallows, too, and a scaffold—and how all those people stare at *him!* Verdict, "Guilty." No matter; he will escape.

The night is dark and cold, the gates have been left open, and in an instant he is in the street, flying from the scene of his imprisonment like the wind. The streets are cleared, the open fields are gained, and the broad wide country lies before him. Onward he dashes in the midst of darkness, over hedge and ditch, through mud and pool, bounding from spot to spot with a speed and lightness, astonishing even to himself. At length he pauses: he must be safe from pursuit now; he will stretch himself on that bank and sleep till sunrise.

A period of unconsciousness succeeds. He wakes cold and wretched; the dull grey light of morning is stealing into the cell, and falls upon the form of the attendant turnkey. Confused by his dreams, he starts from his uneasy bed in momentary uncertainty. It is but momentary. Every object in that narrow cell is too frightfully real to admit of doubt or mistake. He is the condemned felon again, guilty and despairing; and in two hours more he is a corpse.

111

The art on these pages is a
representation of the work of
two art students, who are also inmates
at the Norfolk Correctional Institution
of Massachusetts.

# My Dungeon Shook

*Letter to My Nephew*
*on the One Hundredth Anniversary*
*of the Emancipation*

James Baldwin

Dear James:

I have begun this letter five times and torn it up five times.
I keep seeing your face, which is also the face of your father and my
brother. Like him, you are tough, dark, vulnerable, moody—with a
very definite tendency to sound truculent because you want no one
to think you are soft. You may be like your grandfather in this,
I don't know, but certainly both you and your father resemble him
very much physically. Well, he is dead, he never saw you, and he
had a terrible life; he was defeated long before he died because, at
the bottom of his heart, he really believed what white people said
about him. This is one of the reasons that he became so holy. I am
sure that your father has told you something about all that. Neither
you nor your father exhibit any tendency towards holiness: you really
*are* of another era, part of what happened when the Negro left the
land and came into what the late E. Franklin Frazier called "the cities
of destruction." You can only be destroyed by believing that you
really are what the white world calls a *nigger*. I tell you this because
I love you, and please don't you ever forget it.

I have known both of you all your lives, have carried your
Daddy in my arms and on my shoulders, kissed and spanked him
and watched him learn to walk. I don't know if you've known
anybody from that far back; if you've loved anybody that long, first
as an infant, then as a child, then as a man, you gain a strange
perspective on time and human pain and effort. Other people cannot
see what I see whenever I look into your father's face, for behind
your father's face as it is today are all those other faces which were
his. Let him laugh and I see a cellar your father does not remember
and a house he does not remember and I hear in his present

laughter his laughter as a child. Let him curse and I remember him falling down the cellar steps, and howling, and I remember, with pain, his tears, which my hand or your grandmother's so easily wiped away. But no one's hand can wipe away those tears he sheds invisibly today, which one hears in his laughter and in his speech and in his songs. I know what the world has done to my brother and how narrowly he has survived it. And I know, which is much worse, and this is the crime of which I accuse my country and my countrymen, and for which neither I nor time nor history will ever forgive them, that they have destroyed and are destroying hundreds of thousands of lives and do not know it and do not want to know it. One can be, indeed one must strive to become, tough and philosophical concerning destruction and death, for this is what most of mankind has been best at since we have heard of man. (But remember: *most* of mankind is not *all* of mankind.) But it is not permissible that the authors of devastation should also be innocent. It is the innocence which constitutes the crime.

Now, my dear namesake, these innocent and well-meaning people, your countrymen, have caused you to be born under conditions not very far removed from those described for us by Charles Dickens in the London of more than a hundred years ago. (I hear the chorus of the innocents screaming, "No! This is not true! How *bitter* you are!"—but I am writing this letter to *you,* to try to tell you something about how to handle *them,* for most of them do not yet really know that you exist. I *know* the conditions under which you were born, for I was there. Your countrymen were *not* there, and haven't made it yet. Your grandmother was also there, and no one has ever accused her of being bitter. I suggest that the innocents check with her. She isn't hard to find. Your countrymen don't know that *she* exists, either, though she has been working for them all their lives.)

Well, you were born, here you came, something like fifteen years ago; and though your father and mother and grandmother, looking about the streets through which they were carrying you, staring at the walls into which they brought you, had every reason to be heavyhearted, yet they were not. For here you were, Big James, named for me—you were a big baby, I was not—here you were; to be loved. To be loved, baby, hard, at once, and forever, to strengthen you against the loveless world. Remember that: I know how black it looks today, for you. It looked bad that day, too, yes, we were trembling. We have not stopped trembling yet, but if we had not loved each other none of us would have survived. And now you must survive because we love you, and for the sake of your children and your children's children.

This innocent country set you down in a ghetto in which, in fact, it intended that you should perish. Let me spell out precisely what I mean by that, for the heart of the matter is here, and the root of my dispute with my country. You were born where you were born and faced the future that you faced because you were black and *for no other reason*. The limits of your ambition were, thus, expected to be set forever. You were born into a society which spelled out with brutal clarity, and in as many ways as possible, that you were a worthless human being. You were not expected to aspire to excellence: you were expected to make peace with mediocrity. Wherever you have turned, James, in your short time on this earth, you have been told where you could go and what you could do (and *how* you could do it) and where you could live and whom you could marry. I know your countrymen do not agree with me about this, and I hear them saying, "You exaggerate." They do not know Harlem, and I do. So do you. Take no one's word for anything, including mine—but trust your experience. Know whence you came. If you know whence you came, there is really no limit to where you can go. The details and symbols of your life have been deliberately constructed to make you believe what white people say about you. Please try to remember that what they believe, as well as what they do and cause you to endure, does not testify to your inferiority but to their inhumanity and fear. Please try to be clear, dear James, through the storm which rages about your youthful head today, about the reality which lies behind the words *acceptance* and *integration*. There is no reason for you to try to become like white people and there is no basis whatever for their impertinent assumption that *they* must accept *you*. The really terrible thing, old buddy, is that *you* must accept *them*. And I mean that very seriously. You must accept them and accept them with love. For these innocent people have no other hope. They are, in effect, still trapped in a history which they do not understand; and until they understand it, they cannot be released from it. They have had to believe for many years, and for innumerable reasons, that black men are inferior to white men. Many of them, indeed, know better, but, as you will discover, people find it very difficult to act on what they know. To act is to be committed, and to be committed is to be in danger. In this case, the danger, in the minds of most white Americans, is the loss of their identity. Try to imagine how you would feel if you woke up one morning to find the sun shining and all the stars aflame. You would be frightened because it is out of the order of nature. Any upheaval in the universe is terrifying because it so profoundly attacks one's sense of one's own reality. Well, the black man has functioned in the white man's world as a fixed star, as an immovable pillar: and

116

as he moves out of his place, heaven and earth are shaken to their foundations. You, don't be afraid. I said that it was intended that you should perish in the ghetto, perish by never being allowed to go behind the white man's definitions, by never being allowed to spell your proper name. You have, and many of us have, defeated this intention; and, by a terrible law, a terrible paradox, those innocents who believed that your imprisonment made them safe are losing their grasp of reality. But these men are your brothers—your lost, younger brothers. And if the word *integration* means anything, this is what it means: that we, with love, shall force our brothers to see themselves as they are, to cease fleeing from reality and begin to change it. For this is your home, my friend, do not be driven from it; great men have done great things here, and will again, and we can make America what America must become. It will be hard, James, but you come from sturdy, peasant stock, men who picked cotton and dammed rivers and built railroads, and, in the teeth of the most terrifying odds, achieved an unassailable and monumental dignity. You come from a long line of great poets, some of the greatest poets since Homer. One of them said, *The very time I thought I was lost, My dungeon shook and my chains fell off.*

You know, and I know, that the country is celebrating one hundred years of freedom one hundred years too soon. We cannot be free until they are free. God bless you, James, and Godspeed.

Your uncle,
James

# 5

## ESCAPE

I never hear the word ''escape''
Without a quicker blood,
A sudden expectation,
A flying attitude.

I never hear of prisons broad
By soldiers battered down,
But I tug childish at my bars,—
Only to fail again!

—Emily Dickinson

# SINGING DINAH'S SONG

Frank London Brown

A Gypsy woman once told me. She said: "Son, beware of the song that will not leave you."

But then I've never liked Gypsy women no way, which is why I was so shook when my buddy Daddy-o did his number the other day. I mean his natural number.

You see, I work at Electronic Masters, Incorporated, and well, we don't make much at this joint although if you know how to talk to the man you might work up to a dollar and a half an hour.

Me, I work on a punch press. This thing cuts steel sheets and molds them into shells for radio and television speakers. Sometimes when I'm in some juice joint listening to Dinah Washington and trying to get myself together, I get to thinking about all that noise that that big ugly punch press makes, and me sweating and scuffing, trying to make my rates, and man I get eeevil!

This buddy of mine though, he really went for Dinah Washington; and even though his machine would bang and scream all over the place and all those high-speed drills would whine and cry like a bunch of sanctified soprano church-singers, this fool would be in the middle of all that commotion just singing Dinah Washington's songs to beat the band. One day I went up and asked this fool what in the world was he singing about; and he looked at me and tucked his thumbs behind his shirt collar and said: "Baby, I'm singing Dinah's songs. Ain't that broad mellow?"

Well, I . . . Really, all I could say was: "Uh, why yes."

And *I* went back to *my* ma*chine.*

It was one of those real hot days when it happened: about ten-thirty in the morning. I was sweating already. Me and that big ugly scoundrel punch press. Tussling. Lord, I was *so* beat. I felt like singing Dinah's songs myself. I had even started thinking in rhythm with those presses banging down on that steel: sh-bang boom bop! Sh, bang boom bop, sh'bang boom bop. Then all of a sudden:

In walks Daddy-o!

My good buddy. Sharp? You'd better believe it: dark blue single breast, a white on white shirt, and a black and yellow rep tie! Shoes shining like new money. And that pearl gray hat kinda pulled down over one eye. I mean to tell you, that Negro was sharp.

I was way behind on my quota because, you see, fooling around with those machines is *not* no play thing. You just get tired sometimes and fall behind. But I just *had* to slow down to look at my boy.

James, that was his real name. We call him Daddy-o because he's so—I don't know; there just ain't no other name would fit him. Daddy-o's a long, tall, dark cat with hard eyes and a chin that looks like the back end of a brick. Got great big arms and a voice like ten lions. Actually, sometimes Daddy-o scares you.

He walked straight to his machine. Didn't punch his time card or nothing. I called him: "Hey, Daddy-o, you must have had a good one last night. What's happening?"

Do you know that Negro didn't open his mouth?

"Hey, Daddy-o, how come you come strolling in here at ten-thirty? We start at seven-thirty around this place!"

Still no answer.

So this cat walks over to his machine and looks it up and down and turns around and heads straight for the big boss's office. Well, naturally I think Daddy-o's getting ready to quit, so I kind of peeps around my machine so that I can see him better.

He walked to the big boss's office and stopped in front of the door and lit a cigarette smack-dab underneath the "No Smoking" sign. Then he turned around like he had changed his mind about quitting and headed back to his machine. Well, I just started back to work. After all it's none of my business if a man wants to work in his dark blue suit and a white on white shirt with his hat on.

By this time Charlie walked up just as Daddy-o started to stick his hand into the back of the machine.

Charlie liked to busted a blood vessel. "Hey, what the hell are you doing? You want to 'lectrocute yourself?"

Now I don't blame Charlie for hollering. Daddy-o knows that you can get killed sticking your hand in the back of a machine. Everybody in the plant knows that.

Daddy-o acted like he didn't hear Charlie, and he kept right on reaching into the hole. Charlie ran up and snatched Daddy-o's hand back. Daddy-o straightened up, reared back and filled his chest with a thousand pounds of air: one foot behind him and both of those oversized fists doubled up. Charlie cleared his throat and started feeling around in his smock like he was looking for something, which I don't think he was.

Pretty soon Mr. Grobber, the big boss, walked up. One of the other foremen came up and then a couple of set-up men from another department. They all stood around Daddy-o and he just stood there cool, smoking one of those long filter-tips. He started to smile, like he was bashful. But whenever anyone went near the machine, he filled up with more air and got those big ham-fists ready.

Well after all, Daddy-o was my buddy and I couldn't just let all those folks surround him without doing *some*thing, so I turned my machine off and walked over to where they were crowding around him.

"Daddy-o, what's the matter, huh? You mad at somebody, Daddy-o?"

Mr. Grobber said: "James, if you don't feel well, why don't you just go home and come in tomorrow?"

All Daddy-o did was to look slowly around the plant. He looked at each one of us. A lot of the people in the shop stopped working and were looking back at him. Others just kept on working. But he looked at them, kind of smiling, like he had a feeling for each and every one of them.

Then quick like a minute, he spread his legs out, and stretched his arms in front of the machine like it was all he had in this world.

I tried once again to talk to him.

"Aww come on, Daddy-o. Don't be that way."

That Negro's nose started twitching. Then he tried to talk but his breath was short like he had been running or something.

"Ain't nobody getting this machine. I own this machine, baby. This is mine. Ten years! On this machine. Baby, this belongs to me."

"I know it do, Daddy-o. I *know* it do."

Charlie Wicowycz got mad hearing him say that, so he said, "Damn," and started into Daddy-o. Daddy-o's eyes got big and he drew his arm back and kind of stood on his toes and let out a holler like, like I don't know what.

"Doonnnn't you *touch* this machiiinnneeeee!"

Naturally Charlie stopped, then he started to snicker and play like he was tickled except his face was as white as a fish belly. I thought I would try, so I touched Daddy-o's arm. It was hard like brick. I let his arm go.

"Daddy-o man, I know how you feel. Let me call your wife so she can come and get you. You'll be all right tomorrow. What's your phone number, Daddy-o? I'll call your wife for you, hear?"

His eyes started twitching and he started blinking like he was trying to keep from crying. Still he was smiling that little baby-faced smile.

"Daddy-o, listen to me. Man, *I* ain't trying to do nothing to you. Give me your number and your wife will know what to do."

122

His lips started trembling. Big grown man, standing there with his lips trembling. He opened his mouth. His whole chin started trembling as he started to speak: "Drexel."

I said: "Okay, Drexel. Now Drexel what?"

"Drexel."

"Drexel what else, Daddy-o?"

"Drexel seven-two-three."

"Seven-two-three. What else Daddy-o? Man, I'm trying to help you. I'm going to call your wife. She'll be here in a few minutes. Drexel seven-two-three-what else? What is the rest of your phone number. Daddy-o! I'm talkin' to you!"

"Eight-eight-eight-eight-nine."

"Drexel seven-two-three-eight-nine? That it, Daddy-o?"

Mr. Grobber started walking around scratching his stomach. He stopped in front of Charlie Wicowycz. "Call the police, Charlie."

Charles left.

The other foremen went back to their departments. The setup men followed them. Mr. Grobber, seeing that he was being left alone with Daddy-o, went back to his office.

Daddy-o just stood there smiling.

I ran to the office and called the number he had given me. Daddy-o's wife wasn't home, but a little girl who said that she was Daddy-o's "Babygirl" answered and said that she would tell her mother as soon as she came home from work.

When I walked out of the office, the police were there. I thought about the time I had to wait three hours for the police to get to my house the time somebody broke in and took every stitch I had. One of the cops, a big mean-looking something with ice-water eyes, moved in on Daddy-o with his club out and Daddy-o just shuffled his feet, doubled up his fists and waited for him.

I started talking up for my boy.

"Officer, please don't hurt him. He's just sick. He won't do no harm."

"Who are you? Stay outa."

I tried to explain to him. "Look, Officer, just let me talk to him. I . . . I'm his friend."

"All right. Talk to him. Tell him to get into the wagon."

I touched Daddy-o's arm again. He moved it away, still smiling. I said: "Man, Daddy-o, come on now. Come on, go with me. I know how it is. I *know* how it is."

He still had that smile. I swear I could have cried.

I started walking, pulling his arm a bit.

"Come on, Daddy-o."

He came along easy, still smiling, and walking with a kind of strut. Looking at each and every one of us like we were his best

123

friends. When we got to the door, he stopped and looked back at his machine. Still smiling. When we got outside, I led him right up to the wagon. The back door was open and it was *dark* in there. Some dusty light scooted through a little window at the back of the wagon that had a wire grating in it. It didn't look very nice in there. I turned to Daddy-o.

"Come on, Daddy-o. The man said you should get in. Ain't nothing going to git you, Daddy-o. Come on, man. Get in."

I felt like anybody's stoolie.

"Come on, get in."

He started moving with me, then he stopped and looked back at the plant. One of the officers touched his arm. And that's when he did his natural number.

He braced his arms against the door. And started to scream to bust his lungs: "That *is* my machine. I *own*. Me and *this* machine is *blood* kin. Don't *none* of you somitches touch it. You *heah?* You, you *heah?*"

The water-eyed policeman started to agree with Daddy-o.

"Sure kid. You *know* it. Lotsa machines. You got lots of 'em."

Daddy-o turned to look at him at the same time his partner gave him a shove. The water-eyed policeman shoved him too. Daddy-o swung at him and missed. When he did that, the water-eyed policeman chunked him right behind the ear and Daddy-o fell back into the wagon. Both policemen grabbed his feet and pushed him past the door and the water-eye slammed it.

They jumped in and started to drive away. Daddy-o was up again and at the window. He was hollering, and his voice got mixed up with the trucks and cars that went by. I watched the wagon huff out of sight and I went back into the plant.

Inside, I got to thinking about how sharp Daddy-o was. I was real proud of that. I caught sight of Daddy-o's machine. You know that thing didn't look right without Daddy-o working on it?

I got to thinking about my machine and how I know that big ugly thing better than I know most live people. Seemed funny to think that it wasn't really mine. It sure *seemed* like mine.

Ol' Daddy-o was sure crazy about Dinah Washington. Last few days that's all he sang: her songs. Like he was singing in place of crying; like being in the plant *made* him sing those songs and like finally the good buddy couldn't sing hard enough to keep up the dues on his machine and then . . . Really.

You know what? Looking around there thinking about Daddy-o and all, I caught myself singing a song that had been floating around in my head.

It goes: "I got bad news, baby, and you're the first to know."

That's one of Dinah Washington's songs.

124

# Three Brown Girls Singing

*M. Carl Holman*

In the ribs of an ugly school building
Three rapt faces
Fuse one pure sound in a shaft of April light:
Three girls, choir robes over their arms, in a stairwell singing
Compose the irrelevancies of a halting typewriter,
Chalk dust and orange peel,
A French class drilling,
Into a shimmering column of flawed perfection;
Lasting as long
As their fresh, self-wondering voices climb to security;          10
Outlasting
The childbed death of one,
The alto's divorce,
The disease-raddled face of the third
Whose honey brown skin
Glows now in a nimbus of dust motes,
But will be as estranged
As that faceless and voiceless typist
Who, unknown and unknowing, enters the limpid column,
Joins chalk, French verbs, the acrid perfume of oranges,          20
To mark the periphery
Of what shall be saved from calendars and decay.

125

What is "saved from calendars and decay"?

# Me and the Mule

*Langston Hughes*

My old mule,
He's got a grin on his face.
He's been a mule so long
He's forgot about his race.

I'm like that old mule—
Black—and don't give a damn!
You got to take me
Like I am.

# THE BEAN EATERS

## Gwendolyn Brooks

They eat beans mostly, this old yellow pair.
Dinner is a casual affair.
Plain chipware on a plain and creaking wood,
Tin flatware.

Two who are Mostly Good.
Two who have lived their day,
But keep on putting on their clothes
And putting things away.

And remembering . . .
Remembering, with twinklings and twinges,
As they lean over the beans in their rented back room that
       is full of beads and receipts and dolls and cloths,
       tobacco crumbs, vases and fringes.

Who *are* the bean eaters?

# BRONZEVILLE MAN WITH A BELT IN THE BACK

*Gwendolyn Brooks*

In such an armor he may rise and raid
The dark cave after midnight, unafraid,
And slice the shadows with his able sword
Of good broad nonchalance, hashing them down.

And come out and accept the gasping crowd,
Shake off the praises with an airiness.
And, searching, see love shining in an eye,
But never smile.

In such an armor he cannot be slain.

129

Why, in your opinion, doesn't the Bronzeville man ever smile?
What kind of armor does he wear?
And where do you think Bronzeville is?

# THE OPENED ORDER

## Ilse Aichinger

*Translated by Eric Mosbacher*

No instructions had come from headquarters for a long time, and it looked as if they were going to stay there for the winter. In the fields all around, the last berries were falling from the bushes and rotting in the moss. Sentries sat forlornly in the treetops and watched the falling shadows. The enemy lay beyond the river and did not attack. Instead the shadows grew longer every evening, and every morning the mist clung more stubbornly to the hollows. Among the young volunteers of the defending army there were some who resented this kind of warfare, and they had made up their minds to attack, if need be without orders, before the snow came.

When therefore one of them was ordered one morning to take a message to headquarters, he had an uncomfortable feeling of foreboding. Careless though they seemed in other matters, he knew that they would stand no nonsense in the event of mutiny. Some questions that were put to him after he had delivered his message almost reminded him of an interrogation, and increased his uneasiness.

He found it all the more surprising therefore when, after a long wait, he was given an order in a sealed envelope, with instructions to get back to his unit with it before nightfall.

He was told to take the shorter way, which was shown him on the map and, to his displeasure, a man was detailed to go with him. Through the open window he could see the beginning of the road he had to take. After crossing the clearing it disappeared wantonly between the hazel bushes. He was warned again to take extreme care, and then set off.

It was soon after midday. Clouds drifted across the sun and grazing cattle wandered over the grass and vanished unconcernedly into the thickets. The road was bad, and in places almost impassable because of encroachment by undergrowth. As soon as the driver put on a little speed, branches started hitting them in the face. The forest seemed to be waiting for the wood gatherers, and the river down below, when they caught glimpses of it from time to time through a clearing, seemed totally unconcerned. On the crests felled timber gleamed in the midday sun. Nothing in nature showed any awareness of the proximity of a frontier.

Every now and again they merged from between the tree trunks into open fields, which gave them a better view and also enabled a better view to be had of them; they crossed them as quickly as possible. The driver bounced the vehicle over the roots of trees, and every now and then glanced back at the man with the order, as if to make sure that his load was all right. This made him angry and convinced him of his superiors' mistrust.

What had his message contained? He had heard that early that morning one of the distant posts had observed movement on the other side of the river, but such rumors were continually in circulation, and it was possible that they were invented by the staff to keep the troops quiet. But it was equally possible that sending him to deliver the message had been a subterfuge, and that the confidence shown in him was sheer dissimulation. If his message had contained something unexpected, it would emerge from the contents of the order that he was taking back. He said to himself that it would be better to find out what it said now, while they were traveling in an area under enemy observation. When he was asked why he had broken the seal he could give some explanation on these lines. He felt the envelope in his pocket and fingered the seal. In the failing light the itch to open it mounted like a fever within him.

To gain time he asked the driver to change places with him. Driving calmed him. They had been driving through the woods for hours. In places the track was covered with rubble where obstacles had been built, and from this it was evident that they were nearing their destination. This proximity filled the man with indifference; perhaps it would prevent him from breaking the seal. He drove on calmly and confidently. At a spot where the track suddenly curved and plunged downwards in a suicidal manner, they escaped without harm, but immediately afterwards the vehicle came to a halt in the middle of a mud patch. The engine had failed, and the cries of the birds made the quiet deeper than ever. Ferns grew all around. They dragged the vehicle out of the mud. The driver set about finding out the cause of the trouble. While he was lying underneath the vehicle, the man hesitated no further, but broke open the envelope, scarcely bothering even to preserve the seal. He leant over the vehicle and read the order, which said that he was to be shot.

He managed to put it back in his breast-pocket before the driver scrambled out and announced that everything was now in order. He asked whether he should drive on. Yes, he should. While he bent over the starting-handle the man wondered whether to shoot him now or while he was driving. He had no doubt now that his driver was an escort.

The track broadened out, as if it repented of its sudden plunge downwards, and started gently mounting. "The soul of a suicide, carried by angels," the man quoted to himself. But the angels had been taking a soul

131

to judgment, and the supposedly innocent act had turned out to be a guilty one. It had been action without orders. What surprised him was the trouble that was being taken with him.

In the falling darkness he could make out the other man's outline in front of him, the silhouette of his head and shoulders—an unquestioningness of outline that was denied to him. The sharp outlines of consciousness dissolve in the dark.

The driver turned and said: "We shall have a quiet night." This sounded like the sheerest irony. But their closeness to their destination seemed to make him talkative, and he went on, without waiting for an answer: "That is, if we get there safely!" The man took his revolver from its holster. It was so dark in the wood that one might have supposed that night had already fallen. "When I was a boy," the driver said, "I used to have to walk home from school through the woods. When it was dark I always used to sing!"

They reached the last clearing unexpectedly quickly. He decided to kill the driver as soon as they had crossed it, because there the wood grew thick again, before it opened out on reaching the burned-out hamlet where his unit lay. But this clearing was bigger than the others, and the river gleamed from a closer distance. A web of moonlight lay over the fields, which stretched all the way to the crest. The track was rutted by the wheels of oxcarts. In the moonlight the dry ruts looked like the inside of a death-mask; to anyone looking down across the clearing towards the river the earth bore the impression of an alien face.

The man rested his revolver on his knees. When the first shot rang out, he had the impression that he had fired prematurely, against his will. But if his companion had been hit, his ghost must have had great presence of mind, because it accelerated and drove on. It took a relatively long time to discover that it was not the driver but he himself who had been hit. His arm sagged, and he dropped his revolver. More shots rang out before they reached the cover of the wood again, but they all missed.

The ghost in front turned his cheerful face towards him. "We were lucky to get across," he said. "That field was under observation." "Stop!" the man exclaimed. "Not here," the driver answered. "We had better go a little deeper into the wood." "I've been hit," the man said in desperation. The driver drove on a little way without looking round, and then stopped. He managed to stanch the flow of blood and tie up the wound. Then he said the only comforting thing he could think of. "We're nearly there," he said. A wounded man condemned to death, the man said to himself. "Wait!" he said aloud. "Is anything else the matter?" the driver said impatiently. "The order," the man said, and felt in his breast-pocket. At the moment of his deepest despair he had read its contents in a new light. The order said the bearer was to be shot, but mentioned no names. "Take it," he said, "my coat is covered in blood." If his companion refused to take it, it would put the matter beyond doubt. After a moment's silence he felt the envelope being taken from his hand. "All right," said the driver.

The last half-hour passed in silence. Time and distance had turned into wolves devouring each other. Sheep are protected in the heavenly pastures, but the latter turned out to be a place of execution.

The unit was quartered in a hamlet of five farmhouses, of which three had been burned out in earlier skirmishes. The ease with which they could make out the undamaged houses made it clear that the virginity of the evening had not yet yielded to night. The place was surrounded by forest, the grass had been trampled down, and vehicles and guns were standing about. Barbed wire marked off the area from the surrounding forest.

When the sentry asked him his business, the driver said he had a wounded man with him, and had brought an order. They drove round the area. While the wounded man tried to sit up he thought to himself that this place was no more of a goal than any other place in the wide world. They were all to be regarded as points of departure rather than of arrival. He heard a voice asking: "Is he conscious?" and kept his eyes shut. It was important to gain time.

He had found new strength and new weapons to facilitate his flight before anything else happened. When they lifted him out of the vehicle he hung limply in their arms.

They carried him into one of the houses across a yard in the middle of which was a well. Two dogs snuffled about him. The wound hurt. They laid him on a bench in a room on the ground floor. The windows were open, and there was no light. "You look after him," the driver said, "I mustn't lose any more time."

The man expected them to come and dress his wound, but when he cautiously opened his eyes he found himself alone. Perhaps they had gone to fetch the first-aid kit. There was a lively coming and going in the house, the sound of voices and footsteps and doors being slammed. But all this contained its own peculiar hush and increased the surrounding silence, just as the shrieking of the birds had done. What is all this about? the man said to himself and, after a few more minutes in which no one appeared, he started considering the possibility of immediate flight. A number of rifles were in the room. He would tell the sentry he had been ordered back to headquarters with another message. He had the necessary papers. If he did so soon, nobody would know for certain.

He tried to sit up, but was surprised to find how great was the weakness which he thought he had been shamming. Impatiently he put his feet down and tried to get up, but found that he could not stand. He sat down again, and stubbornly tried a second time. In doing so he tore open the emergency dressing that the driver had put on his wound, and it started bleeding again. It opened with the vehemence of a hidden wish. He felt that blood seeping through his shirt and wetting the wood of the bench on which he had sunk back. Through the window he saw the sky over the white-washed farmhouse wall. He heard the noise of hooves; the horses were being put back in their stable. There was more activity in the house than ever; it grew noisier and noisier; something unexpected must have happened. He pulled himself up to the window, but collapsed again, and he called out, but no one heard. He had been forgotten.

As he lay there the revolt seething inside him yielded to a desperate cheerfulness. It struck him that bleeding to death was like escaping through a bolted door, by-passing all the sentries. The room, which was illuminated only by the reflection of the opposite wall as if by snowlight, revealed itself as circumstance; and was not solitude the purest kind of circumstance, and was not the flowing of blood action? As he had wished for action for its own sake, and not for the sake of his country's defense, the sentence that was being fulfilled on him was right. As he was sick of inaction on the frontier, it meant release.

Shots rang out in the distance. He opened his eyes and remembered. Handing the order to the driver had been stupid and useless. While he lay here bleeding to death, they were leading the man to execution among the debris of the burnt-out farmhouses. Perhaps they had already bound his eyes, and only his mouth was still half-open with surprise, and they were presenting, aiming, and . . .

When he came round he felt that his wound had been dressed. He thought it an unnecessary service carried out by the angels for a man who had bled to death, an act of mercy performed too late. "So we meet again!" he said to the driver, who was bending over him. Only when he noticed that an officer from the staff was standing at the foot of his bed did he realize with horror that he was not dead.

"The order!" he said. "What happened to the order?"

"It was damaged by the round that hit you," the officer answered, "but it was still legible."

"I should have delivered it myself," he said.

"We got here just in time," the driver interrupted. "The enemy has started a general assault."

"It was the news we were waiting for," the officer remarked as he turned to go. At the door he turned again and, just for the sake of saying something, added:

"It's just as well you didn't know the wording of the message. We had an extraordinary code-phrase for the beginning of the operation!"

A: The soldier certainly brought suffering on himself when he opened that order, didn't he?

B: Yes, and it served him right for not following his instructions.

# BABII YAR

## Yevgeny Yevtushenko

*Translated by George Reavey*

In 1941, the Germans killed more than 100,000 Russian Jews in a massacre outside the city of Kiev. The method of execution was simple: The Jews were lined up at the edge of a ravine, 100 at a time, and machine-gunned to death. The bodies were then thrown into the ravine and covered with some dirt. Babii Yar is the name of the area in which this atrocity occurred.

No monument stands over Babii Yar.
A drop sheer as a crude gravestone.
I am afraid.
       Today I am as old in years
as all the Jewish people.
Now I seem to be
       a Jew
Here I plod through ancient Egypt.
Here I perish crucified, on the cross,
and to this day I bear the scars of nails.      10
I seem to be
       Dreyfus.°
The Philistine
       is both informer and judge.
I am behind bars.
       Beset on every side.
Hounded,
     spat on,
       slandered.
Squealing, dainty ladies in flounced Brussels lace    20
stick their parasols into my face.
I seem to be then
       a young boy in Byelostok.°

°DREYFUS: a Jewish officer in the French army; unjustly accused of treason, convicted, and sent to Devil's Island

°BYELOSTOK: a town on the Russian-Polish border formerly populated largely by Jews

135

Blood runs, spilling over the floors.
The bar-room rabble-rousers
give off a stench of vodka and onion.
A boot kicks me aside, helpless.
In vain I plead with these pogrom bullies.
While they jeer and shout,
                    "Beat the Yids. Save Russia!"        30
some grain-marketeer beats up my mother.
O my Russian people!
              I know
          you
are international to the core.
But those with unclean hands
have often made a jingle of your purest name.
I know the goodness of my land.
How vile these antisemites—
                 without a qualm        40
they pompously called themselves
"The Union of the Russian People"!
I seem to be
        Anne Frank°
transparent
        as a branch in April.
And I love.
        And have no need of phrases.
My need
        is that we gaze into each other.        50
How little we can see
          or smell!
We are denied the leaves,
          we are denied the sky.
Yet we can do so much—
          tenderly
embrace each other in a darkened room.
They're coming here?
          Be not afraid. Those are the booming
sounds of spring:        60
          spring is coming here.
Come then to me.
        Quick, give me your lips.

137

°ANNE FRANK: a young Jewish girl who, together with her family, hid from the
   Nazis in the attic of a friend's house in Amsterdam in the 1940's

Are they smashing down the door?
                              No, it's the ice cracking . . .
The wild grasses rustle over Babii Yar.
The trees look ominous,
                    like judges.
Here all things scream silently,
                              and, baring my head,                    70
I slowly feel myself
                    turning gray.
And I myself
            am one massive, soundless scream
above the thousand thousand buried here.
I am
      each old man
                    here shot dead.
I am
      every child                                                     80
                    here shot dead.
Nothing in me
            shall ever forget!
The "Internationale," let it
                        thunder
when the last antisemite on earth
is buried forever.
In my blood there is no Jewish blood.
In their callous rage, all antisemites
must hate me now as a Jew.                                            90
For that reason
            I am a true Russian!

138

# WHEN THE WAR IS OVER

W. S. Merwin

When the war is over
We will be proud of course the air will be
Good for breathing at last
The water will have been improved the salmon
And the silence of heaven will migrate more perfectly
The dead will think the living are worth it we will know
Who we are
And we will all enlist again

# plato told. . .

e. e. cummings

plato told

him:he couldn't
believe it(jesus

told him;he
wouldn't believe
it)lao

tsze
certainly told
him,and general
(yes

mam)
sherman;
and even
(believe it
or

not)you
told him:i told
him;we told him
(he didn't believe it,no

sir)it took
a nipponized bit of
the old sixth

avenue
el;in the top of his head:to tell

him

What *did* everybody tell him?

**6**

Satchell Paige was a star pitcher
in the Negro baseball league at the
same time that Babe Ruth and Lou Gehrig
were playing in the then segregated major leagues.
It wasn't until Paige was about forty that he became
a strike-out artist in the majors.

# To Satch

*Samuel Allen*

Sometimes I feel like I will never stop
Just go on forever
Till one fine morning
I'll reach up and grab me a hand fulla stars
Swing out my long lean leg
And whip three hot strikes burning down the heavens
And look over at God and say
How about that!

From SOON, ONE MORNING, Edited by Herbert Hill, 1963. Reprinted by permission of the author.

# The Origin of Baseball

Kenneth Patchen

Someone had been walking in and out
Of the world without coming
To much decision about anything.
The sun seemed too hot most of the time.
There weren't enough birds around
And the hills had a silly look
When he got on top of one.
The girls in heaven, however, thought
Nothing of asking to see his watch
Like you would want someone to tell          10
A joke—"Time," they'd say, "what's
That mean—time?", laughing with the edges
Of their white mouths, like a flutter of paper
In a madhouse. And he'd stumble over
General Sherman or Elizabeth B.
Browning, muttering, "Can't you keep
Your big wings out of the aisle?" But down
Again, there'd be millions of people without
Enough to eat and men with guns just
Standing there shooting each other.          20

So he wanted to throw something
And he picked up a baseball.

# An Unusual Look at Things

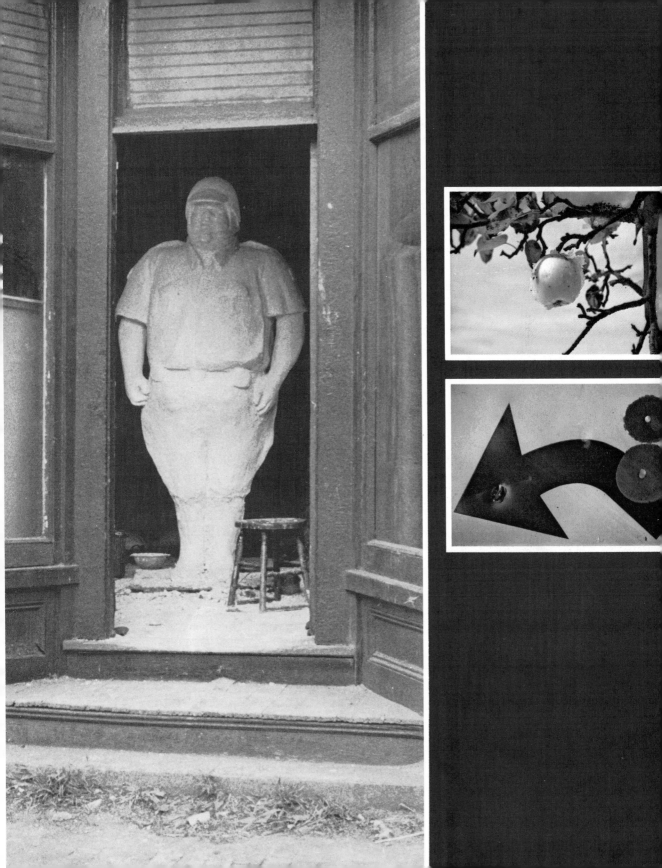

# in Just-/spring . . .

*e. e. cummings*

in Just-
spring     when the world is mud-
luscious the little
lame balloonman

whistles     far     and wee

and eddieandbill come
running from marbles and
piracies and it's
spring

when the world is puddle-wonderful     10

the queer
old balloonman whistles
far     and     wee
and bettyandisbel come dancing

from hop-scotch and jump-rope and
it's
spring
and
        the

                goat-footed     20

balloonMan     whistles
far
and
wee

146

# VERNAL SENTIMENT

Though the crocuses poke up their heads in the usual places,
The frog scum appear on the pond with the same froth of green,
And boys moon at girls with last year's fatuous faces,
I never am bored, however familiar the scene.

When from under the barn the cat brings a similar litter—
Two yellow and black, and one that looks in between—
Though it all happened before, I cannot grow bitter:
I rejoice in the spring, as though no spring had been.

147

—Theodore Roethke

# from THE SONG OF SOLOMON

2: 9–17

*My* beloved is like a roe or a young hart: behold, he standeth behind our wall, he looketh forth at the windows, shewing himself through the lattice.

*My* beloved spake, and said unto me, "Rise up, my love, my fair one, and come away.

*For*, lo, the winter is past, the rain is over and gone;

*The* flowers appear on the earth; the time of the singing of birds is come, and the voice of the turtle is heard in our land;

*The* fig tree putteth forth her green figs, and the vines with the tender grape give a good smell. Arise, my love, my fair one, and come away."

*O* my dove, that art in the clefts of the rock, in the secret places of the stairs, let me see thy countenance, let me hear thy voice; for sweet is thy voice, and thy countenance is comely.

*Take* us the foxes, the little foxes, that spoil the vines: for our vines have tender grapes.

*My* beloved is mine, and I am his: he feedeth among the lilies.

*Until* the day break, and the shadows flee away, turn, my beloved, and be thou like a roe or a young hart upon the mountains of Bether.

# In a Garden

Gertrude Stein

## Characters

LUCY WILLOW
PHILIP HALL
KIT RACOON

*Scene: A garden with a bench.*

LUCY WILLOW:   I am thinking how to be a queen, I am not thinking about how to be a princess, I am thinking about how to be a queen. I am thinking not about being Lucy Willow but how to be a queen.

> *Philip Hall on one side and Kit Racoon on the other each carrying a battle-axe come behind and listen.*

LUCY WILLOW:   It would be lovely to be a queen, I must be a queen, I will be a queen.

> *Philip Hall and Kit Racoon rush forward each one on a side and they fall on their knees and they stretch out their hands and they both say:*   Be a queen, be a queen be my queen.

LUCY WILLOW:   What do you mean. I am a queen but not your queen, you (*pointing at Philip Hall*) you are Philip Hall and that is all, how can you be a king, but I (*she gives a sigh*) I am a queen oh it is so lovely to be a queen.

PHILIP HALL (*jumping to his feet*):   I am a king and how can I tell I can tell because when I hit my chest I ring like a bell, that is what happens when you are a king, (*and then falling on his knees*) oh queen be a queen be my queen.

KIT RACOON (*jumping to his feet he had been murmuring*):   Be a queen be my queen. I am a king and I do not have to change my name I can be a king all the same I am Kit Racoon the first, all you have to do is to be the first and then you are a king, listen to me I am king Kit Racoon the first (*and falling on his knees*) and you are my queen, be a queen be my queen.

LUCY WILLOW:   You both say you are a king but that does not prove anything, now I know I am a queen, and it is lovely to be a queen, and I must be a queen I will be a queen, I am a queen, but you two you just say you are a king, that does not prove anything.

> *Philip Hall jumps to his feet Kit Racoon continues kneeling murmuring:*   be a queen be my queen.

PHILIP HALL:   Aha you say you are a queen, aha, but where is your crown, look at me (*and out of his pocket he takes a gold crown°*) aha, I am a king I have a crown (*putting it on his head*) I am a king but you you a queen where is your crown, Aha.

LUCY WILLOW (*shrinking back terrified*):   Oh perhaps I am no queen perhaps I am only Lucy Willow lovely Lucy Willow but no queen (*and then drawing herself up proudly*) crown or no crown I know I am a queen.

KIT RACOON (*jumps to his feet*):   Aha you a queen, look at me Kit Racoon the first and a crown (*he takes a gold crown out of his pocket and puts it on his head*) Kit Racoon the first and every inch a king with his crown (*and then falling on his knees*) but all the same be a queen dear be my queen.

PHILIP HALL (*on his knees too with a crown on his head*):   Lovely queen be a queen be my queen.

LUCY WILLOW (*perplexed*):   I am a queen I know I am a queen I have no crown but I know I am a queen but how can I be your queen, I am only one queen and you are two kings because you each have a crown, what can I do I can only frown (*and she frowns*).

> *Both the kings jump up and seize their battle-axes.*

PHILIP HALL:   I will kill him and then there will only be one king, and I will be that king and you will be a queen my queen. I will fight like anything and

°CROWN: a gold English coin, worth about a dollar, or is it a *regular* crown?

(*handing her his gold crown*) here is my gold crown hold it so that it will not get torn.

*Lucy Willow takes the crown and holds it lovingly.*

KIT RACOON (*flourishing his axe*):   Wait and see Kit Racoon the first can kill like lightning, all he has to do is to hit another king with his axe and that other king will be dead like anything. Here queen here is my crown, do not let it fall down.

> *The two kings begin to fight and they fight hard with their axes and they are both killed and as they are dying they stretch out their hands to her and cry:   As I die be my queen be a queen be my queen (and they both die).*

LUCY WILLOW (*slowly looking at the two crowns in her hand*):   It is lovely to be a queen, I must be a queen, I am a queen, I can tell by feeling, I am a queen and it is lovely to be a queen (*and she slowly crowns herself with the double crown while the curtain falls*).

# AFTERNOON OF A PAWNBROKER

*Kenneth Fearing*

Still they bring me diamonds, diamonds, always diamonds,
Why don't they pledge something else for a change, if they
        must have loans, other than those diamond clasps
        and diamond rings,
Rubies, sapphires, emeralds, pearls,
Ermine wraps, silks and satins, solid gold watches and silver
        plate and violins two hundred years old,
And then again diamonds, diamonds, the neighborhood dia-
        monds I have seen so many times before, and shall
        see so many times again?                      10

Still I remember the strange afternoon (it was a season of
        extraordinary days and nights) when the first of the
        strange customers appeared,
And he waited, politely, while Mrs. Nunzio redeemed her
        furs, then he stepped to the counter and he laid
        down a thing that looked like a trumpet,
In fact, it was a trumpet, not mounted with diamonds, not
        plated with gold or even silver, and I started to say:
        "We can't use trumpets—"
But a light was in his eyes,                      20
And after he was gone, I had the trumpet. And I stored it
        away. And the name on my books was Gabriel.

It should be made clear my accounts are always open to the
        police, I have nothing to conceal,
I belong, myself, to the Sounder Business Principles League,
Have two married daughters, one of them in Brooklyn, the
        other in Cleveland,
And nothing like this had ever happened before.
How can I account for my lapse of mind?
All I can say is, it did not seem strange. Not at the time. Not    30
        in that neighborhood. And not in that year.

And the next to appear was a man with a soft, persuasive
     voice,
And a kindly face, and the most honest eyes I have ever seen,
     and ears like arrows, and a pointed beard,
And what he said, after Mrs. Case had pledged her diamond
     ring and gone, I cannot now entirely recall,
But when he went away I found I had an apple. An apple,
     just an apple.
"It's been bitten," I remember that I tried to argue. But he     40
     smiled, and said in his quiet voice: "Yes, but only
     once."
And the strangest thing is, it did not seem strange. Not
     strange at all.

And still those names are on my books.
And still I see listed, side by side, those incongruous, and
     not very sound securities:
(1) Aladdin's lamp (I must have been mad), (1) Pandora's
     box, (1) Magic carpet,
(1) Fountain of youth (in good condition), (1) Holy Grail,     50
     (1) Invisible man (the only article never redeemed,
     and I cannot locate him), and others, others, many
     others,
And still I recall how my storage vaults hummed and
     crackled, from time to time, or sounded with music,
     or shot forth flame,
And I wonder, still, that the season did not seem one of
     unusual wonder, not even different—not at the time.

And still I think, at intervals, why didn't I, when the chance
     was mine, drink just once from that Fountain of     60
     youth?
Why didn't I open that box of Pandora?
And what if Mr. Gabriel, who redeemed his pledge and went
     away, should some day decide to blow on his
     trumpet?
Just one short blast, in the middle of some busy afternoon?

But here comes Mr. Barrington, to pawn his Stradivarius.
And here comes Mrs. Case, to redeem her diamond ring.

153

# The Country of the Blind

*H. G. Wells*

Three hundred miles and more from Chimborazo, one hundred from the snows of Cotopaxi, in the wildest wastes of Ecuador's Andes, there lies that mysterious mountain valley, cut off from the world of men, the Country of the Blind. Long years ago that valley lay so far open to the world that men might come at last through frightful gorges and over an icy pass into its equable meadows; and thither indeed men came, a family or so of Peruvian half-breeds fleeing from the lust and tyranny of an evil Spanish ruler. Then came the stupendous outbreak of Mindobamba, when it was night in Quito for seventeen days, and the water was boiling at Yaguachi and all the fish floating dying even as far as Guayaquil; everywhere along the Pacific slopes there were landslips and swift thawings and sudden floods, and one whole side of the old Arauca crest slipped and came down in thunder, and cut off the Country of the Blind forever from the exploring feet of men. But one of these early settlers had chanced to be on the hither side of the gorges when the world had so terribly shaken itself, and he perforce had to forget his wife and his child and all the friends and possessions he had left up there, and start life over again in the lower world. He started it again but ill, blindness overtook him, and he died of punishment in the mines; but the story he told begot a legend that lingers along the length of the Cordilleras of the Andes to this day.

He told of his reason for venturing back from that vastness, into which he had first been carried lashed to a llama, beside a vast bale of gear, when he was a child. The valley, he said, had in it all that the heart of man could desire—sweet water, pasture, an even climate, slopes of rich brown soil with tangles of a shrub that bore an excellent fruit, and on one side great hanging forests of pine that held the avalanches high. Far overhead, on three sides, vast cliffs of grey-green rock were capped by cliffs of ice; but the glacier stream came not to them but flowed away by the farther slopes, and only now and then huge ice masses fell on the valley side. In this valley it neither rained nor snowed, but the abundant springs gave a rich green pasture, that irrigation would spread over all the valley space. The settlers did well indeed there. Their beasts did well and multiplied, and but one thing marred their happiness. Yet it was enough to mar it greatly. A strange disease had come upon them, and had made all the children born to them there—and indeed, several older children also—blind. It was to seek some charm or antidote against this plague of blindness that he had with fatigue and danger and difficulty returned down the gorge. In those days, in such cases, men did not think of germs and infections but of sins; and it seemed to him that the reason of this affliction must lie in the negligence of these priestless immigrants to set up a shrine so soon as they entered the valley. He wanted a shrine—a handsome, cheap, effectual shrine—to be erected in the valley; he wanted relics and such-like potent things of faith, blessed objects and mysterious medals and prayers. In his wallet he had a bar of native silver for which he would not account; he insisted there was none in the valley with something of the insistence of an inexpert liar. They had all clubbed their money and ornaments together, having little need for such treasure up there, he said, to buy them holy help against their ill. I figure this dim-eyed young mountaineer, sunburnt, gaunt, and anxious, hat-brim clutched feverishly, a man all unused to the ways of the lower world, telling this story to some keen-eyed, attentive priest before the great convulsion; I can picture him presently seeking to return with pious and infallible remedies against that trouble, and the infinite dismay with which he must have faced the tumbled vastness where the gorge had once come out. But the rest of his story of mischances is lost to me, save that I know of his evil death after several years. Poor stray from that remoteness! The stream that had once made the gorge now bursts from the mouth of a rocky cave, and the legend his poor, ill-told story set going developed into the legend of a race of blind men somewhere "over there" one may still hear today.

And amidst the little population of that now isolated and forgotten valley the disease ran its course. The old became groping and purblind, the young saw but dimly, and the children that were born to them saw never at all. But life was very easy in that snow-rimmed basin, lost to all the world, with neither thorns nor briars, with no evil insects nor any beasts save the gentle breed of llamas they had lugged and thrust and followed up the beds of the shrunken rivers in the gorges up which they had come. The seeing had become purblind so gradually that they scarcely noted their loss. They guided the sightless youngsters hither and thither until they knew the whole valley marvelously, and when at last sight died out among them the race lived on. They had even time to adapt themselves to the blind control of fire, which they made carefully in stoves of stone. They were a simple strain of people at the first, unlettered, only slightly touched with the Spanish civilization, but with something of a tradition of the arts of old Peru and of its lost philosophy. Generation followed generation. They forgot many things; they devised many things. Their tradition of the greater world they came from became mythical in color and uncertain. In all things save sight they were strong and able; and presently the chance of birth and heredity sent one who had an original mind and who could talk and persuade among them, and then afterwards another. These two passed, leaving their effects, and the little community grew in numbers and in understanding, and met and settled social and economic problems that arose. Generation followed generation. There came a time when a child was born who was fifteen generations from that ancestor who went out of the valley with a bar of silver to seek God's aid, and who never returned. Thereabouts it chanced that a man came into this community from the outer world. And this is the story of that man.

He was a mountaineer from the country near Quito, a man who had been down to the sea and had seen the world, a reader of books in an original way, an acute and enterprising man, and he was taken on by a party of Englishmen who had come out to Ecuador to climb mountains, to replace one of their three Swiss guides who had fallen ill. He climbed here and he climbed there, and then came the attempt on Parascotopetl, the Matterhorn of the Andes, in which he was lost to the outer world. The story of the accident has been written a dozen times. Pointer's narrative is the best. He tells how the party worked their difficult and almost vertical way up to the very foot of the last and greatest precipice, and how they built a night shelter amidst the snow upon a little shelf of rock, and, with a touch of real dramatic power, how presently they found Núñez had gone from them. They shouted, and there was no reply; shouted and whistled, and for the rest of that night they slept no more.

As the morning broke they saw the traces of his fall. It seems impossible he could have uttered a sound. He had slipped eastward towards the unknown side of the mountain; far below he had struck a steep slope of snow, and ploughed his way down it in the midst of a snow avalanche. His track went straight to the edge of a frightful precipice, and beyond that everything was hidden. Far, far below, and hazy with distance, they could see trees rising out of a narrow, shut-in valley—the lost Country of the Blind. But they did not know it was the lost Country of the Blind, nor distinguish it in any way from any other narrow streak of upland valley. Unnerved by this disaster, they abandoned their attempt in the afternoon, and Pointer was called away to the war before he could make another attack. To this day Parascotopetl lifts an unconquered crest, and Pointer's shelter crumbles unvisited amidst the snows.

And the man who fell survived.

At the end of the slope he fell a thousand feet, and came down in the midst of a cloud of snow upon a snow slope even steeper than the one above. Down this he was whirled, stunned and insensible, but without a bone broken in his body; and then at last came to gentler slopes, and at last rolled out and lay still, buried amidst a softening heap of the white masses that had accompanied and saved him. He came to himself with a dim fancy that he was ill in bed; then realized his position with a mountaineer's intelligence, and worked himself loose, and after a rest or so, out until he saw the stars. He rested flat upon his chest for a space, wondering where he was and what had happened to him. He explored his limbs, and discovered that several of his buttons were gone and his coat turned over his head. His knife had gone from his pocket and his hat was lost, though he had tied it under his chin. He recalled that he had been looking for loose stones to raise his piece of the shelter wall. His ice-axe had disappeared.

He decided he must have fallen, and looked up to see, exaggerated by the ghastly light of the rising moon, the tremendous flight he had taken. For a while he lay, gazing blankly at that vast pale cliff towering above, rising moment by moment out of a subsiding tide of darkness. Its phantasmal mysterious beauty held him for a space, and then he was seized with a paroxysm of sobbing laughter. . . .

After a great interval of time he became aware that he was near the lower edge of the snow. Below, down what was now a moonlit and practicable slope, he saw the dark and broken appearance of rock-strewn turf. He struggled to his feet, aching in every joint and limb, got down painfully from the heaped loose snow about him, went downward until he was on the turf, and there dropped rather than lay beside a boulder, drank deep from the flask in his inner pocket, and instantly fell asleep. . . .

He was awakened by the singing of birds in the trees far below.

He sat up and perceived he was on a little alp at the foot of a vast precipice, that was grooved by the gully down which he and his snow had come. Over against him another wall of rock reared itself against the sky. The gorge between these precipices ran east and west and was full of the morning sunlight, which lit to the westward the mass of fallen mountain that closed the descending gorge. Below him it seemed there was a precipice equally steep, but behind the snow in the gully he found a sort of chimney-cleft dripping with snow-water which a desperate man might venture. He found it easier than it seemed, and came at last to another desolate alp, and then after a rock climb of no particular difficulty to a steep slope of trees. He took his bearings and turned his face up the gorge, for he saw it opened out above upon green meadows, among which he now glimpsed quite distinctly a cluster of stone huts of unfamiliar fashion. At times his progress was like clambering along the face of a wall, and after a time the rising sun ceased to strike along the gorge, the voices of the singing birds died away, and the air grew cold and dark about him. But the distant valley with its houses was all the brighter for that. He came presently to talus, and among the rocks he noted—for he was an observant man—an unfamiliar fern that seemed to clutch out of the crevices with intense green hands. He picked a frond or so and gnawed its stalk and found it helpful.

About midday he came at last out of the throat of the gorge into the plain and the sunlight. He was stiff and weary; he sat down in the shadow of a rock, filled up his flask with water from a spring and drank it down, and remained for a time resting before he went on to the houses.

They were very strange to his eyes, and indeed the whole aspect of that valley became, as he regarded it, queerer and more unfamiliar. The greater part of its surface was lush green meadow, starred with many beautiful flowers, irrigated with extraordinary care, and bearing evidence of systematic cropping piece by piece. High up and ringing the valley about was a wall, and what appeared to be a circumferential water-channel, from which the little trickles of water that fed the meadow plants came, and on the higher slopes above this flocks of llamas cropped the scanty herbage. Sheds, apparently shelters or feeding places for the llamas, stood against the boundary wall here and there. The irrigation streams ran together into a main channel down the center of the valley, and this was enclosed on either side by a wall breast high. This gave a singularly urban quality to this secluded place, a quality that was greatly enhanced by the fact that a number of paths paved with black and white stones, and each with a curious little curb at the side, ran hither and thither in an orderly manner. The houses of the central village were quite unlike the casual and higgledy-piggledy agglomeration of the mountain villages he knew; they stood in a continuous row on either side of a central street of astonishing cleanness; here and there their parti-colored façade was pierced by a door, and not a solitary window broke their even frontage. They were parti-colored with extraordinary irregularity; smeared with a sort of plaster that was sometimes grey, sometimes drab, sometimes slate-colored or dark brown; and it was the sight of this wild plastering first brought the word "blind" into the thoughts of the explorer. "The good man who did that," he thought, "must have been as blind as a bat."

He descended a steep place, and so came to the wall and channel that ran about the valley, near where the latter spouted out its surplus contents into the deeps of the gorge in a thin and wavering thread of cascade. He could now see a number of men and women resting on piled heaps of grass, as if taking a siesta, in the remoter part of the meadow, and nearer the village a number of recumbent children, and then nearer at hand three men carrying pails on yokes along a little path that ran from the encircling wall towards the houses. These latter were clad in garments of llama cloth and boots and belts of leather, and they wore caps of cloth with back and ear flaps. They followed one another in single file, walking slowly and yawning as they walked, like men who have been up all night. There was something so reassuringly prosperous and respectable in their bearing that after a moment's hesitation Núñez stood forward as conspicuously as possible upon his rock, and gave vent to a mighty shout that echoed round the valley.

The three men stopped, and moved their heads as though they were looking about them. They turned their faces this way and that, and Núñez gesticulated with freedom. But they did not appear to see him for all his gestures, and after a time, directing themselves towards the mountains far away to the right, they shouted as if in answer. Núñez bawled again, and then once more, and as he gestured ineffectually the word "blind" came up to the top of his thoughts. "The fools must be blind," he said.

When at last, after much shouting and wrath, Núñez crossed the stream by a little bridge, came through a gate in the wall, and approached them, he was sure that they were blind. He was sure that this was the Country of the Blind of which the legends told. Conviction had sprung upon him, and a sense of great and rather enviable adventure. The three stood side by side, not looking at him, but with their ears directed towards him, judging him by his unfamiliar steps. They stood close together like men a little afraid, and he could see their eyelids closed and sunken, as though the very balls beneath had shrunken away. There was an expression near awe on their faces.

"A man," one said, in hardly recognizable Spanish—"a man it is—a man or a spirit—coming down from the rocks."

But Núñez advanced with the confident steps of a youth who enters upon life. All the old stories of the lost valley and the Country of the Blind had come back to his mind, and through his thoughts ran this old proverb, as if it were a refrain—

"In the Country of the Blind the One-eyed Man is King."

"In the Country of the Blind the One-eyed Man is King."

And very civilly he gave them greeting. He talked to them and used his eyes.

"Where does he come from, brother Pedro?" asked one.

"Down out of the rocks."

"Over the mountains I come," said Núñez, "out of the country beyond there—where men can see. From near Bogotá, where there are a hundred thousands of people, and where the city passes out of sight."

"Sight?" muttered Pedro. "Sight?"

"He comes," said the second blind man, "out of the rocks."

The cloth of their coats Núñez saw was curiously fashioned, each with a different sort of stitching.

They startled him by a simultaneous movement towards him, each with a hand outstretched. He stepped back from the advance of these spread fingers.

"Come hither," said the third blind man, following his motion and clutching him neatly.

And they held Núñez and felt him over, saying no word further until they had done so.

"Carefully," he cried, with a finger in his eye, and found they thought that organ, with its fluttering lids, a queer thing in him. They went over it again.

"A strange creature, Correa," said the one called Pedro. "Feel the coarseness of his hair. Like a llama's hair."

"Rough he is as the rocks that begot him," said Correa, investigating Núñez's unshaven chin with a soft and slightly moist hand. "Perhaps he will grow finer." Núñez struggled a little under their examination, but they gripped him firm.

"Carefully," he said again.

"He speaks," said the third man. "Certainly he is a man."

"Ugh!" said Pedro, at the roughness of his coat.

"*Out* of the world. Over mountains and glaciers; right over above there, halfway to the sun. Out of the great big world that goes down, twelve days' journey to the sea."

They scarcely seemed to heed him. "Our fathers have told us men may be made by the forces of Nature," said Correa. "It is the warmth of things and moisture, and rottenness—rottenness."

"Let us lead him to the elders," said Pedro.

"Shout first," said Correa, "lest the children be afraid. This is a marvelous occasion."

So they shouted, and Pedro went first and took Núñez by the hand to lead him to the houses.

He drew his hand away. "I can see," he said.

"See?" said Correa.

"Yes, see," said Núñez, turning towards him, and stumbled against Pedro's pail.

"His senses are still imperfect," said the third blind man. "He stumbles, and talks unmeaning words. Lead him by the hand."

"As you will," said Núñez, and was led along, laughing.

It seemed they knew nothing of sight.

Well, all in good time he would teach them.

He heard people shouting, and saw a number of figures gathering together in the middle roadway of the village.

He found it taxed his nerve and patience more than he had anticipated, that first encounter with the population of the Country of the Blind. The place seemed larger as he drew near to it, and the smeared plasterings queerer, and a crowd of children and men and women (the women and girls, he was pleased to note, had some of them quite sweet faces, for all that their eyes were shut and sunken) came about him, holding on to him, touching him with soft, sensitive hands, smelling at him, and listening at every word he spoke. Some of the maidens and children, however, kept aloof as if afraid, and indeed his voice seemed coarse and rude beside their softer notes. They mobbed him. His three guides kept close to him with an effect of proprietorship, and said again and again, "A wild man out of the rocks."

"Bogotá," he said. "Bogotá. Over the mountain crests."

"A wild man—using wild words," said Pedro. "Did you hear that— Bogotá? His mind is hardly formed yet. He has only the beginnings of speech."

A little boy nipped his hand. "Bogotá!" he said mockingly.

"Ay! A city to your village, I come from the great world—where men have eyes and see."

"His name's Bogotá," they said.

"He stumbled," said Correa, "stumbled twice as we came hither."

"Bring him to the elders."

And they thrust him suddenly through a doorway into a room as black as pitch, save at the end there faintly glowed a fire. The crowd closed in behind him and shut out all but the faintest glimmer of day, and before he could arrest himself he had fallen headlong over the feet of a seated man. His arm, out-flung, struck the face of someone else as he went down; he felt the soft impact of features and heard a cry of anger, and for a moment he struggled against a number of hands that clutched him. It was a one-sided fight. An inkling of the situation came to him, and he lay quiet.

"I fell down," he said; "I couldn't see in this pitchy darkness."

There was a pause as if the unseen persons about him tried to understand his words. Then the voice of Correa said: "He is but newly formed. He stumbles as he walks and mingles words that mean nothing with his speech."

Others also said things about him that he heard or understood imperfectly.

"May I sit up?" he asked, in a pause. "I will not struggle against you again."

They consulted and let him rise.

The voice of an older man began to question him, and Núñez found himself trying to explain the great world out of which he had fallen, and the sky and mountains and sight and such-like marvels, to these elders who sat in darkness in the Country of the Blind. And they would believe and understand nothing whatever he told them, a thing quite outside his expectation. They would not even understand many of his words. For fourteen generations these people had been blind and cut off from all the seeing world; the names for all the things of sight had faded and changed; the story of the outer world was faded and changed to a child's story; and they had ceased to concern themselves with anything beyond the rocky slopes above their circling wall. Blind men of genius had arisen among them and questioned the shreds of belief and tradition they had brought with them from their seeing days, and had dismissed all these things as idle fancies, and replaced them with new and saner explanations. Much of their imagination had shriveled with their eyes, and they had made for themselves new imaginations with their ever more sensitive ears and finger-tips. Slowly Núñez realized this; that his expectation of wonder and reverence at his origin and his gifts was not to be borne out; and after his poor attempt to explain sight to them had been set aside as the confused version of a new-made being describing the marvels of his incoherent sensations, he subsided, a little dashed, into listening to their instruction. And the eldest of the blind men explained to him life and philosophy and religion, how that the world (meaning their valley) had been first an empty hollow in the rocks, and then had come, first, inanimate things without the gift of touch, and llamas and a few other creatures that had little sense, and then men, and at last angels, whom one could hear singing and making fluttering sounds, but whom no one could touch at all, which puzzled Núñez greatly until he thought of the birds.

He went on to tell Núñez how this time had been divided into the warm and the cold, which are the blind equivalents of day and night, and how it was good to sleep in the warm and work during the cold, so that now, but for his advent, the whole town of the blind would have been asleep. He said Núñez must have been specially created to learn and serve the wisdom they had acquired, and for that all his mental incoherency and stumbling behavior he must have courage and do his best to learn, and at that all the people in the doorway murmured encouragingly. He said the night—for the blind call their day night—was now far gone, and it behooved everyone to go back to sleep. He asked Núñez if he knew how to sleep, and Núñez said he did, but that before sleep he wanted food.

They brought him food—llama's milk in a bowl, and rough salted bread—and led him into a lonely place to eat out of their hearing, and afterwards to slumber until the chill of the mountain evening roused them to begin their day again. But Núñez slumbered not at all.

Instead, he sat up in the place where they had left him, resting his limbs and turning the unanticipated circumstances of his arrival over and over in his mind.

Every now and then he laughed, sometimes with amusement, and sometimes with indignation.

"Unformed mind!" he said. "Got no senses yet! They little know they've been insulting their heaven-sent king and master. I see I must bring them to reason. Let me think—let me think."

He was still thinking when the sun set.

Núñez had an eye for all beautiful things, and it seemed to him that the glow upon the snowfields and glaciers that rose about the valley on every side was the most beautiful thing he had ever seen. His eyes went from that inaccessible glory to the village and irrigated fields, fast sinking into the twilight, and suddenly a wave of emotion took him, and he thanked God from the bottom of his heart that the power of sight had been given him.

He heard a voice calling to him from out of the village.

"Ya ho there, Bogotá! Come hither!"

At that he stood up smiling. He would show these people once and for all what sight would do for a man. They would seek him, but not find him.

"You move not, Bogotá," said the voice.

He laughed noiselessly, and made two stealthy steps aside from the path.

"Trample not on the grass, Bogotá; that is not allowed."

Núñez had scarcely heard the sound he made himself. He stopped, amazed.

The owner of the voice came running up the piebald path towards him.

He stepped back into the pathway. "Here I am," he said.

"Why did you not come when I called you?" said the blind man. "Must you be led like a child? Cannot you hear the path as you walk?"

Núñez laughed. "I can see it," he said.

"There is no such word as *see*," said the blind man, after a pause. "Cease this folly, and follow the sound of my feet."

Núñez followed, a little annoyed.

"My time will come," he said.

"You'll learn," the blind man answered. "There is much to learn in the world."

"Has no one told you, 'In the Country of the Blind the One-eyed Man is King'?"

"What is blind?" asked the blind man carelessly over his shoulder.

Four days passed, and the fifth found the King of the Blind still incognito, as a clumsy and useless stranger among his subjects.

It was, he found, much more difficult to proclaim himself than he had supposed, and in the meantime, while he meditated his *coup d'état,* he did what he was told and learned the manners and customs of the Country of the Blind. He found working and going about at night a particularly irksome thing, and he decided that that should be the first thing he would change.

They led a simple, laborious life, these people, with all the elements of virtue and happiness, as these things can be understood by men. They toiled, but not oppressively; they had food and clothing sufficient for their needs; they had days and seasons of rest; they made much of music and singing, and there was love among them, and little children.

It was marvelous with what confidence and precision they went about their ordered world. Everything, you see, had been made to fit their needs; each of the radiating paths of the valley area had a constant angle to the others, and was distinguished by a special notch upon its curbing; all obstacles and irregularities of path or meadow had long since been cleared away; all their methods and procedure arose naturally from their special needs. Their senses had become marvelously acute; they could hear and judge the slightest gesture of a man a dozen paces away—could hear the very beating of his heart. Intonation had long replaced expression with them, and touches gesture, and their work with hoe and spade and fork was as free and confident as garden work can be. Their sense of smell was extraordinarily fine; they could distinguish individual differences as readily as a dog can, and they went about the tending of the llamas, who lived among the rocks above and came to the wall for food and shelter, with ease and confidence. It was only when at last Núñez sought to assert himself that he found how easy and confident their movements could be.

He rebelled only after he had tried persuasion.

He tried at first on several occasions to tell them of sight. "Look you here, you people," he said. "There are things you do not understand in me."

Once or twice one or two of them attended to him; they sat with faces downcast and ears turned intelligently towards him, and he did his best to tell them what it was to see. Among his hearers was a girl, with eyelids less red and sunken than the others, so that one could almost fancy she was hiding eyes, whom especially he hoped to persuade. He spoke of the beauties of sight, of watching the mountains, of the sky and the sunrise, and they heard him with amused incredulity that presently became condemnatory. They told him there were indeed no mountains at all, but that the end of the rocks where the llamas grazed was indeed the end of the world; thence sprang a cavernous roof of the universe, from which the dew and the avalanches fell; and when he maintained stoutly the world had neither end nor roof such as they supposed, they said his thoughts were wicked. So far as he could describe sky and clouds and stars to them it seemed to them a hideous void, a terrible blankness in the place of the smooth roof to things in which they believed—it was an article of faith with them that the cavern roof was exquisitely smooth to the touch. He saw that in some manner he shocked them, and gave up that aspect of the matter altogether, and tried to show them the practical value of sight. One morning he saw Pedro in the path called Seventeen and coming towards the central houses, but still too far off for hearing or scent, and he told them as much. "In a little while," he prophesied, "Pedro will be here." An old man remarked that Pedro had no business on Path Seventeen, and then, as if in confirmation, that individual as he drew near turned and went transversely into Path Ten, and so back with nimble paces towards the outer wall. They mocked Núñez when Pedro did not arrive, and afterwards, when he asked Pedro questions to clear his character, Pedro denied and outfaced him, and was afterwards hostile to him.

Then he induced them to let him go a long way up the sloping meadows towards the wall with one complacent individual, and to him he promised to describe all that happened among the houses. He noted certain goings and comings, but the things that really seemed to signify to these people happened inside of or behind the windowless houses—the only things they took note of to test him by—and of these he could see or tell nothing; and it was after the failure of this attempt, and the ridicule they could not repress, that he resorted to force. He thought of seizing a spade and suddenly smiting one or two of them to earth, and so in fair combat showing the advantage of eyes. He went so far with that resolution as to seize his spade, and then he discovered a new thing about himself, and that was that it was impossible for him to hit a blind man in cold blood.

He hesitated, and found them all aware that he snatched up the spade. They stood alert, with their heads on one side, and bent ears towards him for what he would do next.

"Put that spade down," said one, and he felt a sort of helpless horror. He came near obedience.

Then he thrust one backwards against a house wall, and fled past him and out of the village.

He went athwart one of their meadows, leaving a track of trampled grass behind his feet, and presently sat down by the side of one of their ways. He felt something of the buoyancy that comes to all men in the beginning of a fight, but more perplexity. He began to realize that you cannot even fight happily with creatures who stand upon a different mental basis to yourself. Far away he saw a number of men carrying spades and sticks come out of the street of houses, and advance in a spreading line along the several paths towards him. They advanced slowly, speaking frequently to one another, and ever and again the whole cordon would halt and sniff the air and listen.

The first time they did this Núñez laughed. But afterwards he did not laugh.

One struck his trail in the meadow grass, and came stooping and feeling his way along it.

For five minutes he watched the slow extension of the cordon, and then his vague disposition to do something forthwith became frantic. He stood up, went a pace or so towards the circumferential wall, turned, and went back a little way. There they all stood in a crescent, still and listening. He also stood still, gripping his spade very tightly in both hands. Should he charge them?

The pulse in his ears ran into the rhythm of "In the Country of the Blind the One-eyed Man is King!"

Should he charge them?

He looked back at the high and unclimbable wall behind—unclimbable because of its smooth plastering, but withal pierced with many little doors, and at the approaching line of seekers. Behind these, others were now coming out of the street of houses.

Should he charge them?

"Bogotá!" called one. "Bogotá! where are you?"

He gripped his spade still tighter, and advanced down the meadows towards the place of habitations, and directly he moved they converged upon him. "I'll hit them if they touch me," he swore: "by Heaven, I will. I'll hit." He called aloud, "Look here, I'm going to do what I like in this valley. Do you hear? I'm going to do what I like and go where I like!"

They were moving in upon him quickly, groping, yet moving rapidly. It was like playing blind man's buff, with everyone blindfolded except one. "Get hold of him!" cried one. He found himself in the arc of a loose curve of pursuers. He felt suddenly he must be active and resolute.

"You don't understand," he cried in a voice that was meant to be great and resolute, and which broke. "You are blind, and I can see. Leave me alone!"

"Bogotá! Put down that spade, and come off the grass!"

The last order, grotesque in its urban familiarity, produced a gust of anger.

"I'll hurt you," he said, sobbing with emotion. "By Heaven, I'll hurt you. Leave me alone!"

He began to run, not knowing clearly where to run. He ran from the nearest blind man, because it was a horror to hit him. He stopped, and then made a dash to escape from their closing ranks. He made for where a gap was wide, and the men on either side, with a quick perception of the approach of his paces, rushed in on one another. He sprang forward, and then saw he must be caught, and *swish!* the spade had struck. He felt the soft thud of hand and arm, and the man was down with a yell of pain, and he was through.

166

Through! And then he was close to the street of houses again, and blind men, whirling spades and stakes, were running with a sort of reasoned swiftness hither and thither.

He heard steps behind him just in time, and found a tall man rushing forward and swiping at the sound of him. He lost his nerve, hurled his spade a yard wide at his antagonist, and whirled about and fled, fairly yelling as he dodged another.

He was panic-stricken. He ran furiously to and fro, dodging when there was no need to dodge, and in his anxiety to see on every side of him at once, stumbling. For a moment he was down and they heard his fall. Far away in the circumferential wall a little doorway looked like heaven, and he set off in a wild rush for it. He did not even look round at his pursuers until it was gained, and he had stumbled across the bridge, clambered a little way among the rocks, to the surprise and dismay of a young llama, who went leaping out of sight, and lay down sobbing for breath.

And so his *coup d'état* came to an end.

He stayed outside the wall of the valley of the Blind for two nights and days without food or shelter, and meditated upon the unexpected. During these meditations he repeated very frequently and always with a profounder note of derision the exploded proverb: "In the Country of the Blind the One-Eyed Man is King." He thought chiefly of ways of fighting and conquering these people, and it grew clear that for him no practicable way was possible. He had no weapons, and now it would be hard to get one.

The canker of civilization had got to him even in Bogotá, and he could not find it in himself to go down and assassinate a blind man. Of course, if he did that, he might then dictate terms on the threat of assassinating them all. But—sooner or later he must sleep! . . .

He tried also to find food among the pine trees, to be comfortable under pine boughs while the frost fell at night, and—with less confidence—to catch a llama by artifice in order to try to kill it—perhaps by hammering it with a stone—and so finally, perhaps, to eat some of it. But the llamas had a doubt of him and regarded him with distrustful brown eyes, and spat when he drew near. Fear came on him the second day and fits of shivering. Finally he crawled down to the wall of the Country of the Blind and tried to make terms. He crawled along by the stream, shouting, until two blind men came out to the gate and talked to him.

"I was mad," he said. "But I was only newly made."

They said that was better.

He told them he was wiser now, and repented of all he had done.

Then he wept without intention, for he was very weak and ill now, and they took that as a favorable sign.

They asked him if he still thought he could *"see."*

"No," he said. "That was folly. The word means nothing—less than nothing!"

They asked him what was overhead.

"About ten times ten the height of a man there is a roof above the world—of rock—and very, very smooth." . . . He burst again into hysterical tears. "Before you ask me any more, give me some food or I shall die."

He expected dire punishments, but these blind people were capable of toleration. They regarded his rebellion as but one more proof of his general idiocy and inferiority; and after they had whipped him they appointed him to do the simplest and heaviest work they had for anyone to do, and he, seeing no other way of living, did submissively what he was told.

He was ill for some days, and they nursed him kindly. That refined his submission. But they insisted on his lying in the dark, and that was a great misery. And blind philosophers came and talked to him of the wicked levity of his mind, and reproved him so impressively for his doubts about the lid of rock that covered their cosmic casserole that he almost doubted whether indeed he was not the victim of hallucination in not seeing it overhead.

So Núñez became a citizen of the Country of the Blind, and these people ceased to be a generalized people and became individualities and familiar to him, while the world beyond the mountains became more and more remote and unreal. There was Yacob, his master, a kindly man when not annoyed; there was Pedro, Yacob's nephew; and there was Medina-saroté, who was the youngest daughter of Yacob. She was little esteemed in the world of the Blind, because she had a clear-cut face, and lacked that satisfying, glossy smoothness that is the blind man's ideal of feminine beauty; but Núñez thought her beautiful at first, and presently the most beautiful thing in the whole creation. Her closed eyelids were not sunken and red after the common way of the valley, but lay as though they might open again at any moment; and she had long eyelashes, which were considered a grave disfigurement. And her voice was strong, and did not satisfy the acute hearing of the valley swains. So that she had no lover.

There came a time when Núñez thought that, could he win her, he would be resigned to live in the valley for all the rest of his days.

He watched her; he sought opportunities of doing her little services, and presently he found that she observed him. Once at a rest-day gathering they sat side by side in the dim starlight, and the music was sweet. His hand came upon hers and he dared to clasp it. Then very tenderly she returned his pressure. And one day, as they were at their meal in the darkness, he felt her hand very softly seeking him, and as it chanced the fire leaped then and he saw the tenderness of her face.

He sought to speak to her.

He went to her one day when she was sitting in the summer moonlight spinning. The light made her a thing of silver and mystery. He sat down at her feet and told her he loved her, and told her how beautiful she seemed to him. He had a lover's voice, he spoke with a tender reverence that came near to awe, and she had never before been touched by adoration. She made him no definite answer, but it was clear his words pleased her.

After that he talked to her whenever he could take an opportunity. The valley became the world for him, and the world beyond the mountains where men lived in sunlight seemed no more than a fairy tale he would some day pour into her ears. Very tentatively and timidly he spoke to her of sight.

Sight seemed to her the most poetical of fancies, and she listened to his description of the stars and the mountains and her own sweet white-lit beauty as though it was a guilty indulgence. She did not believe, she could only half understand, but she was mysteriously delighted, and it seemed to him that she completely understood.

His love lost its awe and took courage. Presently he was for demanding her of Yacob and the elders in marriage, but she became fearful and delayed. And it was one of the elder sisters who first told Yacob that Medina-saroté and Núñez were in love.

There was from the first very great opposition to the marriage of Núñez and Medina-saroté; not so much because they valued her as because they held him as a being apart, an idiot, incompetent thing below the permissible level of a man. Her sisters opposed it bitterly as bringing discredit on them all; and old Yacob, though he had formed a sort of liking for his clumsy, obedient serf, shook his head and said the thing could not be. The young men were all angry at the idea of corrupting the race, and one went so far as to revile and strike Núñez. He struck back. Then for the first time he found an advantage in seeing, even by twilight, and after that fight was over no one was disposed to raise a hand against him. But they still found his marriage impossible.

Old Yacob had a tenderness for his last little daughter, and was grieved to have her weep upon his shoulder.

"You see, my dear, he's an idiot. He has delusions; he can't do anything right."

"I know," wept Medina-saroté. "But he's better than he was. He's getting better. And he's strong, dear father, and kind—stronger and kinder than any other man in the world. And he loves me—and, Father, I love him."

Old Yacob was greatly distressed to find her inconsolable, and, besides—what made it more distressing—he liked Núñez for many things. So he went and sat in the windowless council chamber with the other elders and watched the trend of the talk, and said, at the proper time, "He's better than he was. Very likely, some day, we shall find him as sane as ourselves."

Then afterwards one of the elders, who thought deeply, had an idea. He was the great doctor among these people, their medicine man, and he had a very philosophical and inventive mind, and the idea of curing Núñez of his peculiarities appealed to him. One day when Yacob was present he returned to the topic of Núñez.

"I have examined Bogotá," he said, "and the case is clearer to me. I think very probably he might be cured."

"That is what I have always hoped," said old Yacob.

"His brain is affected," said the blind doctor.

The elders murmured assent.

"Now, *what* affects it?"

"Ah!" said old Yacob.

"*This*," said the doctor, answering his own question. "Those queer things that are called the eyes, and which exist to make an agreeable soft depression in the face, are diseased, in the case of Bogotá, in such a way as to affect his brain. They are greatly distended, he has eyelashes, and his eyelids move, and consequently his brain is in a state of constant irritation and distraction."

"Yes?" said old Yacob. "Yes?"

"And I think I may say with reasonable certainty that, in order to cure him completely, all that we need do is a simple and easy surgical operation— namely, to remove these irritant bodies."

"And then he will be sane?"

"Then he will be perfectly sane, and a quite admirable citizen."

"Thank Heaven for science!" said old Yacob, and went forth at once to tell Núñez of his happy hopes.

But Núñez's manner of receiving the good news struck him as being cold and disappointing.

"One might think," he said, "from the tone you take, that you did not care for my daughter."

It was Medina-saroté who persuaded Núñez to face the blind surgeons.

"*You* do not want me," he said, "to lose my gift of sight?"

She shook her head.

"My world is sight."

Her head drooped lower.

"There are the beautiful things, the beautiful little things—the flowers, the lichens among the rocks, the lightness and softness on a piece of fur, the far sky with its drifting down of clouds, the sunsets and the stars. And there is *you*. For you alone it is good to have sight, to see your sweet, serene face, your kindly lips, your dear, beautiful hands folded together. . . . It is these eyes of mine you won, these eyes that hold me to you, that these idiots seek. Instead, I must touch you, hear you, and never see you again. I must come under that roof of rock and stone and darkness, that horrible roof under which your imagination stoops. . . . No; you would not have me do that?"

A disagreeable doubt had arisen in him. He stopped, and left the thing a question.

"I wish," she said, "sometimes——" She paused.

"Yes?" said he, a little apprehensively.

"I wish sometimes—you would not talk like that."

"Like what?"

"I know it's pretty—it's your imagination. I love it, but *now*——"

He felt cold. *"Now?"* he said faintly.

She sat still.

"You mean—you think—I should be better, better perhaps——"

He was realizing things very swiftly. He felt anger, indeed, anger at the dull course of fate, but also sympathy for her lack of understanding—a sympathy near akin to pity.

*"Dear,"* he said, and he could see by her whiteness how intensely her spirit pressed against the things she could not say. He put his arms about her, he kissed her ear, and they sat for a time in silence.

"If I were to consent to this?" he said at last, in a voice that was very gentle.

She flung her arms about him, weeping wildly. "Oh, if you would," she sobbed, "if only you would!"

For a week before the operation that was to raise him from his servitude and inferiority to the level of a blind citizen, Núñez knew nothing of sleep, and all through the warm sunlit hours, while the others slumbered happily, he sat brooding or wandered aimlessly, trying to bring his mind to bear on his dilemma. He had given his answer, he had given his consent, and still he was not sure. And at last work time was over, the sun rose in splendor over the golden crests, and his last day of vision began for him. He had a few minutes with Medina-saroté before she went apart to sleep.

"Tomorrow," he said, "I shall see no more."

"Dear heart!" she answered, and pressed his hands with all her strength.

"They will hurt you but little," she said; "and you are going through this pain—you are going through it, dear lover, for *me*. . . . Dear, if a woman's heart and life can do it, I will repay you. My dearest one, my dearest with the tender voice, I will repay."

He was drenched in pity for himself and her.

He held her in his arms, and pressed his lips to hers, and looked on her sweet face for the last time. "Good-bye!" he whispered at that dear sight, "good-bye!"

And then in silence he turned away from her.

She could hear his slow retreating footsteps, and something in the rhythm of them threw her into a passion of weeping.

He had fully meant to go to a lonely place where the meadows were beautiful with white narcissus, and there remain until the hour of his sacrifice should come, but as he went he lifted up his eyes and saw the morning, the morning like an angel in golden armor, marching down the steeps. . . .

171

It seemed to him that before this splendor he, and this blind world in the valley, and his love, and all, were no more than a pit of sin.

He did not turn aside as he had meant to do, but went on, and passed through the wall of the circumference and out upon the rocks, and his eyes were always upon the sunlit ice and snow.

He saw their infinite beauty, and his imagination soared over them to the things beyond he was now to resign for ever.

He thought of that great free world he was parted from, the world that was his own, and he had a vision of those further slopes, distance beyond distance, with Bogotá, a place of multitudinous stirring beauty, a glory by day, a luminous mystery by night, a place of palaces and fountains and statues and white houses, lying beautifully in the middle distance. He thought how for a day or so one might come down through passes, drawing ever nearer and nearer to its busy streets and ways. He thought of the river journey, day by day, from great Bogotá to the still vaster world beyond, through towns and villages, forest and desert places, the rushing river day by day, until its banks receded and the big steamers came splashing by, and one had reached the sea—the limitless sea, with its thousand islands, its thousands of islands, and its ships seen dimly far away in their incessant journeyings round and about that greater world. And there, unpent by mountains, one saw the sky—the sky, not such a disc as one saw it here, but an arch of immeasurable blue, a deep of deeps in which the circling stars were floating. . . .

His eyes scrutinized the great curtain of the mountains with a keener inquiry.

For example, if one went so, up that gully and to that chimney there, then one might come out high among those stunted pines that ran round in a sort of shelf and rose still higher and higher as it passed above the gorge. And then? That talus might be managed. Thence perhaps a climb might be found to take him up to the precipice that came below the snow; and if that chimney failed, then another farther to the east might serve his purpose better. And then? Then one would be out upon the amber-lit snow there, and halfway up to the crest of those beautiful desolations.

He glanced back at the village, then turned right round and regarded it steadfastly.

He thought of Medina-saroté, and she had become small and remote.

He turned again towards the mountain wall, down which the day had come to him.

Then very circumspectly he began to climb.

When sunset came he was no longer climbing, but he was far and high. He had been higher, but he was still very high. His clothes were torn, his limbs were blood stained, he was bruised in many places, but he lay as if he were at his ease, and there was a smile on his face.

From where he rested the valley seemed as if it were in a pit and nearly a mile below. Already it was dim with haze and shadow, though the mountain summits around him were things of light and fire. The mountain summits around him were things of light and fire, and the little details of the rocks near at hand were drenched with subtle beauty—a vein of green mineral piercing the grey, the flash of crystal faces here and there, a minute, minutely beautiful orange lichen close beside his face. There were deep mysterious shadows in the gorge, blue deepening into purple, and purple into a luminous darkness, and overhead was the illimitable vastness of the sky. But he heeded these things no longer, but lay quite inactive there, smiling as if he were satisfied merely to have escaped from the valley of the Blind in which he had thought to be King.

The glow of the sunset passed, and the night came, and still he lay peacefully contented under the cold stars.

A: I wonder whether Núñez shouldn't have submitted to the operation after all. He had found someone who loved him, and the valley was a pleasant place to live.

B: That's crazy. When you can see what life is really like, how can you settle for a life of ignorance?

C: They weren't ignorant. They were just blind.

B: Well, blind or ignorant, I'd still like to know why they were able to push him around so easily. But I think I know how frustrated he felt. I sometimes get the feeling that I'm living in a country of the blind. Don't you?

In the desert
I saw a creature, naked, bestial,
Who, squatting upon the ground,
Held his heart in his hands,
And ate of it.
I said, "Is it good, friend?"
"It is bitter—bitter," he answered;
"But I like it
Because it is bitter,
And because it is my heart."

# from The Black Riders

### Stephen Crane

Once there came a man
Who said,
"Range me all men of the world in rows."
And instantly
There was terrific clamor among the people
Against being ranged in rows.
There was a loud quarrel, world-wide.
It endured for ages;
And blood was shed
By those who would not stand in rows,
And by those who pined to stand in rows.
Eventually, the man went to death, weeping.
And those who stayed in bloody scuffle
Knew not the great simplicity.

In a lonely place,
I encountered a sage
Who sat, all still,
Regarding a newspaper.
He accosted me:
"Sir, what is this?"
Then I saw that I was greater,
Ay, greater than this sage.
I answered him at once,
"Old, old man, it is the wisdom of the age."
The sage looked upon me with admiration.

From THE COLLECTED POEMS OF STEPHEN CRANE published by Alfred
A. Knopf, Inc.

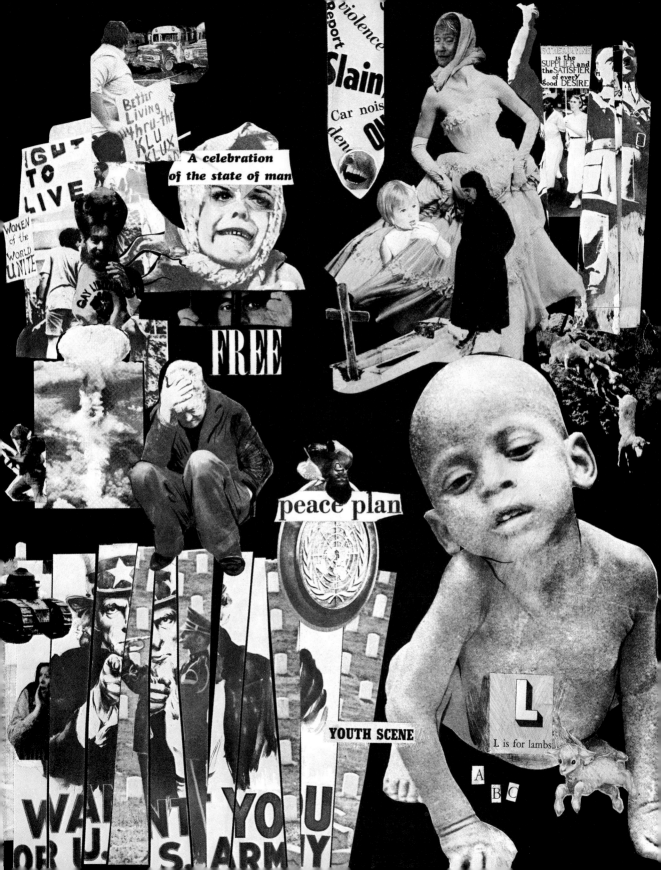

# PUPPETS

*The marionettes*
*Are carved of wood.*
*Endowed with life*
*When the strings are pulled,*
*They look,*
*With their wrinkled skin*
*And thin white hair,*
*Like real old men;*

*But, when the play is over*
*And the scene is changed,*
*They lie lifeless,*
*Without movement, without breath.*

*So man is born,*
*And passes like a puppet*
*Through the dream-play*
*We call life. .*

—Ming Huang

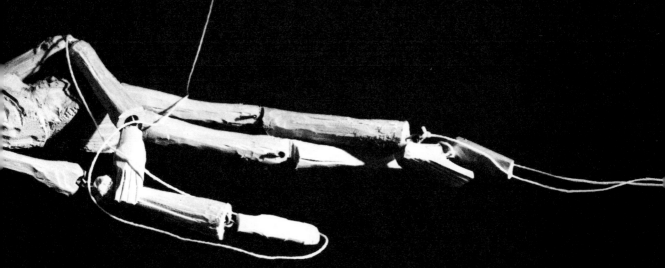

# LITTLE MOON OF ALBAN

*A play for television*

James Costigan

## Characters

| | | |
|---|---|---|
| BRIGID MARY | FATHER CURRAN | SISTER MARTHA KEVIN |
| KENNETH BOYD | SISTER SERVANT | SISTER BARBARA |
| DR. CLIVE | BOY SINGER | NEWSMAN |
| DENNIS WALSH | PATCH KEEGAN | ENGLISH SOLDIERS |
| SHELAGH MANGAN | ENGLISH OFFICER | SISTER THERESA |
| | BLIND MAN | OTHERS |

# ACT ONE

FADE IN:  *A small square in Dublin. Evening. The year 1919.*
*Solemn façades of decaying Georgian houses. The yellow light of*
*street lamps glowing through translucent leaves of trees. The camera*
*holds on a shot high above the square. A flute begins to play a*
*mournful tune. An occasional passerby moves resolutely beneath the*
*streetlights, first fleeing his shadow, then pursuing it. In the gutter*
*beneath one of the lamps stand two wretchedly dressed men, one*
*old and blind, the other a sickly-looking youth. The old man plays*
*dreamily on a kind of tin flute. The other clutches his upturned cap*
*in his hands and sings in a high, sweet voice.*

BOY (*singing*):  "Come all you loyal heroes, wherever that you be. Don't hire
with any master till you know what your work will be."

*The camera moves down to a close shot of the two men. During the*
*following, a window is heard to open in a house directly above them.*
*The young man then looks up and directs the end of the quatrain*
*in that direction.*

BOY:  "For you must rise up early, from the clear daylight till dawn, or I'm afraid
you'll never be able to plow the rocks of Bawn."

*A coin is thrown from the window. The boy's eyes follow its descent.*
*He bends to retrieve it from the gutter. Camera follows the turn of*
*his head as he again looks up at the window.*
CUT TO:  *A bleakly furnished room. Patch Keegan stands at the win-*
*dow, looking down. Dennis Walsh stands beside the window, his back*
*pressed against the wall. They wear caps and mufflers and threadbare*
*jackets. A calendar from a Dublin granary hangs behind Dennis.*
*October 1919.*

DENNIS:  What's he doing?

PATCH:  He's looking this way.

DENNIS:  Does he recognize the coin?

PATCH:  I think so.

DENNIS:  Is he giving a signal or what is he doing at all?

PATCH:  He's saying something to the blind piper. He's going to sing again.

DENNIS:  That'll be the signal then.

CUT TO: *The singer and the piper.*
*As the old man plays, the boy begins to improvise a lyric in Gaelic.*

BOY:
Ar woreen shteevne
Ar woreen shteevne,
Rightful, rightful,
Tiddy fol-day . . .

CUT TO: *The room. Dennis and Patch as before.*

PATCH: He's singing in the Irish. Get over close, Dennis, and tell me what he's saying.

*Dennis crouches by the window, listening to the song drifting up from below.*

DENNIS: "In Steeven's Lane, in Steeven's Lane, in the place you know . . ." What place is that, Patch?

PATCH: Listen—listen! What does he say now?

DENNIS: "When the church bells are striking nine, a fire will, uh . . . (*Pressed for an equivalent*)—burst out . . . in Dublin. Rightful, rightful, tiddy fol—"

PATCH: Never mind the tiddy fol-day! What's the rest of it?

DENNIS (*listening*): "Tell your two friends to be there, too. It will all be as was planned before. It will be a great night in Dublin."

*From below comes the singer's voice repeating: "Rightful, rightful . . ." ending abruptly. Patch starts nervously.*

PATCH: Why did he stop?

DENNIS: Patch, there's some sort of motor thing coming into the square.

PATCH: What do you mean, "motor thing"?

DENNIS: I can't make it out; it's not—oh, Lord, there's another one! It's them armored cycles and they looking like an armada with a gun in every mitt.

CUT TO: *A high shot, looking down into the square. Two armored motorcycles with side cars have pulled into the square. Two men alight from the side cars, one an officer, the other armed with a small machine gun. They walk across the square toward the two street musicians.*
CUT TO: *A close shot of the musicians' faces, both frightened, both awaiting the enemy with dignity and composure. The boy begins to*

180

*sing in a defiant voice, and the old man picks up the tune on his flute. The song continues through the ensuing action.*

BOY (*singing*):   "Bold Robert Emmet, the darling of Erin, Bold Robert Emmet will die with a smile. 'Farewell, companions, both loyal and daring—I'll lay down my life for the Emerald Isle!'"

> CUT TO:   *The room. Dennis watching the spectacle in the street with impotent anger.*

DENNIS:   They're going to take them in. Patch, why is he singing that song now? Inflammatory songs are forbidden. They'll give him an extra year for that.

> *The song ends. Silence in the little room. A pause.*

PATCH:   That'll be an end to his singing. Bless you, Phinny, me boy, it was a daft thing but it was a gorgeous gesture.

DENNIS:   They're herding them toward the cycles.

PATCH:   The old beggar, too? (*He starts toward the window.*) Ah, leave him be, why can't you? He's no harm to anyone, you dirty oul' . . . (*He snaps suddenly back from the window, flattening himself against the wall.*) Judas priest, they saw me!

DENNIS (*falling to his knees below the window*):   Are you sure?

PATCH:   The minute I stuck me gob out, one of them looked 'round. We're in for it now, Dennis lad.

> *He takes a small automatic pistol from his pocket, kisses it.*
> CUT TO:   *A high shot above the square. The two Englishmen have stopped and one of them is pointing toward a third-story window and talking excitedly to the other, his superior, who turns and goes quickly toward the cycles where his men wait.*
> CUT TO:   *The room. Dennis and Patch on either side of window.*

DENNIS:   It's a great and glorious sight you'd be fighting them off with that, and they carrying a slough of carbines and a tommy gun.

PATCH:   We've no choice.

DENNIS:   We have. The flat in the back of this building opens out onto a roof.

PATCH:   Let's go then!

DENNIS:   There's nobody home this time of day. We'll have to bust the door open.

181

*They start out of the room.*
CUT TO: *A shot of the square. The senior officer has taken a mega-phone from the side car and approached the building. He stops and calls in a loud metallic voice.*

OFFICER: You men up there! Hullo, you men up there! Whatever your business, I order you to show yourselves. If you have firearms, throw them down. Come out peacefully. We are armed and we are prepared for any eventuality!

CUT TO: *The doorway leading from the room to the hall. Dennis and Patch hesitate, looking back toward the window.*

PATCH: Whisht, he's a long-winded oul' yahoo, ain't he?

OFFICER's VOICE (*offstage*): I invite you to make yourselves known to us!

PATCH: That's kind of you, me darlin', but we'll have to decline your invitation, and I hope you won't be thinking too bad of us. Go on, Dennis.

*They make their way down a narrow, dimly lit corridor.*

DENNIS: Patch, I want to go with you tonight.

PATCH: You can't. I told you. The plan was made weeks ago, just so many boys. You'd be in the way.

DENNIS: Please, Patch, I want to do something useful.

PATCH: You have, lad, you have. Which door is it?

DENNIS: The one at the end there. I'm coming with you.

PATCH: You *are* not. Didn't you tell me Brigid Mary's expecting you for supper? We'll split up when we reach the alley. It's safer, one by one.

DENNIS: Patch . . .

PATCH (*trying the door*): Come on now—put your shoulder to it. One, two, three!

*Both throw their weight against the door. The molding shatters. The door flies open, spilling them into the darkened flat.*
CUT TO: *The square. The officer is delegating his men, one to circle to the right, one to the left, the other to rush the building, crouching as he himself does, guns poised, suddenly breaking into a run. The camera catches the energy of this move, one of the men in extreme close-up suddenly bursting away in a straight, diminishing line. A violent crescendo of music behind this.*

182

CUT TO:   *Close shot of a door. Dennis throws himself against it, panting feverishly, beating on it with both fists. Music out abruptly.*
CUT TO:   *The kitchen of the Mangan apartment. Brigid Mary, a young girl with a thin, attractive face and long, straight hair, stands over a table in the center of the room, squeezing rosettes from a pastry tube onto a cake which bears the legend: "Happy Birthday to Dennis." Her mother, Shelagh Mangan, stands at the stove stirring a thick stew. She starts at the knocking, drops the ladle, turns.*

SHELAGH:   Mother in heaven, what's that now?

BRIGID MARY:   It must be Dennis. (*She starts out.*)

SHELAGH:   Tell him will he be so good as to spare the door, if he don't mind.

*Camera follows Brigid Mary as she crosses through the living-dining room to the front door. She opens it. Dennis pushes quickly past her, slamming the door behind him.*

BRIGID MARY (*alarmed*):   What's wrong?

*He falls back against the door, too winded to reply, still panting heavily. Mrs. Mangan calls from the kitchen.*

SHELAGH:   Spare the door, won't you, Dennis? (*They both look toward the kitchen.*) Brigid Mary, is it Dennis? Is anything wrong? I'll come out if you don't answer me!

*Dennis shakes his head, indicating that he doesn't want Shelagh to see him like this.*

BRIGID MARY (*calling*):   No, Mama! Stay where you are. It's all right! (*To Dennis*) Go in the parlor.

*Dennis turns and stumbles toward the parlor end of the room. Brigid Mary crosses through the dining portion toward the kitchen, intercepting her mother in the kitchen door.*

SHELAGH:   Is it Dennis?

BRIGID MARY:   Yes. Don't let the chicken scorch. (*Gently she guides her mother back into the kitchen.*)

SHELAGH:   I didn't hear a word out of the two of yous. What's wrong?

BRIGID MARY:   Nothing. Dennis wants a glass of water.

SHELAGH:   Are you quarreling?

BRIGID MARY: No, Mama. (*She draws a glass of water.*)

SHELAGH: Is that all he wants? There's a drop of Paddy behind the flour canister.

BRIGID MARY: Maybe that's a good idea. (*She takes a small whisky bottle from a cupboard.*)

SHELAGH: Sure, it's his birthday, isn't it? Take a glass for yourself and another for me and we'll drink his good health. That's a tough old bird in the pot. A bit of whisky will make it more palatable.

BRIGID MARY (*obeying*): You're a bad woman, Shelagh Mangan.

SHELAGH: Go on. That makes two of us.

> *Brigid Mary crosses through the dining alcove into the parlor. She stops as she sees Dennis at a window, looking furtively through a crack in the blind at the street below. She crosses in behind him.*

BRIGID MARY: Happy birthday.

> *Startled, Dennis turns nervously, his hand snapping away from the blind.*

BRIGID MARY: Are they gone?

DENNIS: I can't see anyone.

> *Brigid Mary sets bottle and glasses on a table.*

BRIGID MARY: What have you done? Have you blown up another barracks? Have you killed somebody?

DENNIS: Shut up, Brig. I haven't done nothing.

BRIGID MARY: "I haven't done *nothing*." You ignorant boy, why do I bother with you?

DENNIS: I haven't done *anything*, Brig, I swear.

BRIGID MARY: Then what is it you're going to do? You're up to something. They're not chasing you around because they fancy the look of your retreating backside.

DENNIS: I was with Patch Keegan. They recognized him. His picture's on a circular.

BRIGID MARY: And what were you doing with Patch Keegan—planning a picnic in Stephen's Green?

DENNIS: There's mighty fires kindling, Brig, that's all I can tell you.

BRIGID MARY:   Oh, you great bleeding eejit! Why do you run with those hot-heads? Do you *want* to die—is that it? Because if you do, I'll kill you with my two hands . . .

DENNIS (*overlapping*):   Brig, shut up. She'll hear you.

*With this he seizes her wrists as she raises her hands as if to strike him. Shelagh enters, removing her apron, and sees them thus intimately engaged.*

SHELAGH:   Ah, that's nice to see yous holding hands, children. Don't be embarrassed. Good evening, Dennis.

DENNIS:   Good evening, Mrs. Mangan.

SHELAGH:   What's wrong with you? You look peaked.

DENNIS:   I feel all right.

SHELAGH:   All right isn't worth much. The graveyards are full of people with fine feelings and chalky faces. You spend too much time in classrooms and libraries. Has Dennis had his drink, Brigid Mary?

BRIGID MARY:   Not yet, Mama.

SHELAGH:   Well, pour, girl, pour. Sit down, Dennis. (*They sit. She pats her hair coquettishly.*) How're things at the university?

DENNIS:   It's not a time I relish. The final examinations are coming on next week. I'm sitting again for the degree I went to the wall on last year, you know.

SHELAGH (*raising the glass Brigid Mary has given her*):   Well, now here's to better luck and a passing grade.

BRIGID MARY:   With honors.

SHELAGH:   Don't you drink, Dennis. We're toasting you. Slainte! (*After a sip*) Now you.

DENNIS:   I drink to the two ladies of me heart.

SHELAGH:   He's laying it on.

DENNIS:   To Shelagh . . .

SHELAGH:   The cheek of him.

DENNIS:   And to Brigid Mary, who is as fickle as the wind and as sharp as the rain . . .

BRIGID MARY:   Get out.

DENNIS (*simply*):   . . . and who I love—*whom* I love—with a great, clumsy, ungrammatical devotion. There now.

185

*He drinks, takes a cigarette from a crumpled pack.*

SHELAGH:  Isn't he a grand one to blather?

*Brigid Mary is staring fixedly at Dennis.*

BRIGID MARY:  Take the cigarette out of your mouth.

DENNIS:  Can't I smoke, Mrs. Mangan?

SHELAGH:  It's your birthday. Set fire to the house if you like.

BRIGID MARY:  Take the cigarette out of your gob, Dennis.

DENNIS:  Why?

BRIGID MARY:  I want to kiss you.

SHELAGH:  Oh, the hussy! She doesn't get that from me.

> *Dennis takes the cigarette from his mouth, accepting Brigid Mary's kiss.*

SHELAGH (*rising*):  I'm going to put the supper on the table. I can only think she's destroyed with hunger and it's debauched her entirely.

> *She goes out toward the kitchen, leaving Dennis and Brigid Mary smiling after her. When they look at each other their faces go soft with love.*

BRIGID MARY:  I don't know what I see in you, and you the great fool of the world—the way you'd be breaking my heart . . .

DENNIS:  Sshh.

BRIGID MARY:  Put your arms around me, Dennis Walsh.

DENNIS:  Funny old Brig.

BRIGID MARY:  Fickle as the wind, it it?

DENNIS:  Yes. Blow cool, girl, blow gentle.

BRIGID MARY:  You're my wind and my rain—and sun and stars. I'm jealous of you. I don't want you to have any cause but me.

DENNIS:  And where does a man go to enlist?

BRIGID MARY:  Right here. (*She takes his face in her hands.*) Right here.

> *They kiss.*

186

DISSOLVE TO: *The dinner table. Focus on Shelagh at the head of the table, prodding the remains of her stew with a fork.*

SHELAGH: There now, you stringy old cock-a-doodle-doo, I've done with you. Did you ever taste anything as tough as the hide of it? Spring chicken, says the butcher. Milkfed, says he. Spring of what year? I'd like to know. Milk of *magnesia*-fed, by the taste of it.

*Another shot to include Dennis. Brigid Mary is not in her place. Finished, Dennis puts napkin to mouth sedately.*

DENNIS: My bit was lovely, Mrs. Mangan.

SHELAGH: You're polite to say so, God forgive you. (*Calls toward kitchen*) Brigid Mary, we're ready now!

BRIGID MARY (*offstage*): Just coming, Mama!

DENNIS: What's she up to?

SHELAGH: I'm sworn to secrecy. But whatever you think of it, in heaven's name, praise it—praise it to the skies. It took her five hours and six precious egg whites to bake it, and I'm afraid I knocked it flat slamming the oven door.

BRIGID MARY (*offstage*): All right now. Here I come!

187

CUT TO: *The arch as Brigid Mary enters carrying a cake blazing with candles. As she sets it on the table, the camera discerns that it is a rather small, concave affair. Still, Shelagh gasps appreciatively, and Dennis smiles his gratitude.*

SHELAGH: Ah, it's a handsome cake and a fragrant cake! Isn't it a lovely cake, Dennis?

DENNIS: It is so. It's massive. Thank you, Brig.

*Brigid Mary takes the plates from the others' places, sets them on the sideboard, bringing dessert plates in their stead.*

SHELAGH: The little package there is for you. Is it there?

*Dennis picks up a tiny wad of tissue and ribbon from the table.*

DENNIS: You shouldn't have bought me anything.

SHELAGH: We didn't. We had it already.

BRIGID MARY: Mama. (*To Dennis*) Blow out the candles first. Make a wish.

*Dennis thinks for a moment, then blows out all but one candle.*

SHELAGH:   Aw . . .

*A pause. Dennis looks up at Brigid Mary. She wets her forefinger, snuffs out the candle.*

BRIGID MARY:   Open your gift. It's better than a wish.

DENNIS (*opening it*):   It's a medal. St. Brigid.

BRIGID MARY (*nods*):   She'll look after you for me. You won't need any wishes coming true with her in your hand.

SHELAGH:   It was blessed by Pope Pius the Tenth in the Vatican in Rome. Old Father Guffy brought it back to Brigid Mary for her first Holy Communion.

DENNIS:   It's a grand thing surely. I'll be carrying it to mine.

*Brigid Mary begins cutting and serving the cake.*

SHELAGH:   When do you go up, Dennis?

DENNIS:   Well, I finish my instructions on Friday week. I'm to be baptized that evening. Confession's on Saturday afternoon, and I go to Communion Sunday morning at eight-o'clock Mass.

BRIGID MARY:   And we'll be married in St. John's on the following Sunday, and that'll be an end to his philandering and his wild ways.

SHELAGH:   Wild, is it? I hope he's not that. I know you're not, Dennis. (*To Brigid Mary*) The cake is lovely and light, my dear. (*To Dennis*) Praise be, you're not like these young bloods that do be meeting in dark places in the dead of night while their mothers and wives lie on their beds with no sleep in them at all and a great trembling fear on them.

BRIGID MARY:   Now, Mama . . .

SHELAGH:   And what's the good of it?

DENNIS:   The boys must think there's some good in it, Mrs. Mangan.

SHELAGH:   Don't tell me about the boys, my dear. I'm asking what's the good of it now, with everyone saying Mr. O'Neill will have us a truce negotiated by summer and a free Ireland sure to follow?

DENNIS:   That's all talk in the air.

SHELAGH:   Don't say that, Dennis. Don't say that. I'm putting my faith in the Mayor and the old men and I'm praying the young will trust them patiently. Because it's peace that's coming to us at long last, and what's the good,

I'm asking, for any boy to be spilling out his life in some street skirmish between now and summer?

*Dennis looks from Mrs. Mangan to Brigid Mary, who has been staring at him. He speaks to her quietly.*

DENNIS: Are you watching the time?

BRIGID MARY: It was half-seven by the kitchen clock when I fetched the cake.

DENNIS: We'd better get a move on. Father Curran expects us at eight-fifteen.

SHELAGH: Don't ever tell me about the boys, Dennis.

BRIGID MARY: Ah, give over, Mama.

SHELAGH: I've a son lost and a husband and that's all the boys I had to give. Matthew was one of the first to fall on the post-office steps on Easter Monday. Colm was with De Valera at Boland's Bakery in Grand Canal Street. He was caught in a grenade attack and burned alive.

BRIGID MARY: Dennis knows all that, Mama. Why do you . . . ?

SHELAGH (*overlapping*): I'm only saying I'm glad you've found yourself a quiet, *sensible* boy who wouldn't be breaking your heart with a foolish and useless death now that the troubles are nearly behind us. What did Matt and Colm die for if you should be keening at your bridegroom's wake and the banns hardly published?

BRIGID MARY: Mama, we're going along now and have our talk with Father Curran. Leave the dishes till I get back. Come on, Dennis.

*They rise, Dennis hesitates, embarrassed by Shelagh's behavior.*

DENNIS: Good night now.

SHELAGH: It's a shocking and a shameful waste of Father Curran's precious time, I'm thinking, if Dennis should be dying before he's fully converted to the faith. No mother to mourn you, Dennis. That's a pity for you and a blessing for her.

DENNIS: I'll not be doing anything foolish, Mrs. Mangan.

SHELAGH: No, no, I know you won't. Don't mind me. I'm rambling. I shouldn't have had that whisky before supper. I'm not used to it.

DENNIS: It was a grand feed. I feel like I've had a fine birthday party. Thank you.

SHELAGH: Go on with you, you blatherskite. And see that you get her in at a respectable hour.

189

DENNIS: I will. Good night.

BRIGID MARY: Good night, Mama.

SHELAGH: Ta ta.

*The young people go out. The camera moves across the debris on the table to a close shot of Shelagh. Visible on the sideboard behind her are framed photographs of two men, one middle-aged, the other in his early twenties. She speaks with quiet familiarity, looking into space before her.*

SHELAGH: Sure, it's a grand bunch of liars you are, the lot of yous. Where are you off to, Matt? It's nothing, Shelagh, only the boys are holing up in the post office and I'll be joining them there. Is it safe, Matt? Safe as your own two arms, me heart. Colm, where are you going and why do you carry the gun? It's a precaution only, Mama. I'm off to the bakery and I'll be home for supper.

*She sits staring blankly before her, immobile, expressionless. The smiling photographs beam from their metal frames.*
*DISSOLVE TO: Thomas Street. Night. The steps and façade of St. John the Baptist Church on one side, the hill sloping away on the other. The church door stands open, faint light shining from within. Brigid Mary, her scarf drawn over her head, comes out, followed by Dennis and Father Curran.*

BRIGID MARY: Good night, Father.

FATHER CURRAN: Good night, Brigid Mary. Dennis, I'll see you at catechism tomorrow.

DENNIS: Yes, Father. And I'll know *all* the answers tomorrow, I promise.

FATHER CURRAN: I'll fetch you a terrible clout and you don't. Straight home now, the two of yous. The streets aren't safe for walking these nights.

DENNIS: Good night, Father.

FATHER CURRAN: Good night.

*The priest goes back into the church and closes the door behind him, reducing the light in the street. Dennis and Brigid Mary begin walking, she taking her scarf down, looping it about her throat.*

BRIGID MARY: It's turned a bit raw.

DENNIS: You're not cold, are you?

BRIGID MARY:   No, no, it's nice.

*Dennis stops, looks off down the hill.*

DENNIS:   Brig, look down there.

BRIGID MARY:   What is it?

DENNIS:   Down there through Bridgefoot Street. You can see the river.

BRIGID MARY:   That's a glorious discovery. (*Teasing*) Dennis Columbus.

DENNIS:   No, but I never noticed it before. It's a curious thing how you'll pass a place every day of your life and not be noticing there's some special beauty about it. Do you think that Robert Emmet could see the river from the scaffold?

BRIGID MARY:   I don't know where it stood.

*Dennis walks out into the street.*

DENNIS:   They say it was about here. (*Standing tiptoe*) No, I guess not.

BRIGID MARY:   Well, who knows if there were buildings there to block the view a hundred years ago—more than a hundred?

DENNIS:   If I were higher I could see it. Do you suppose that maybe the last thing Emmet saw from the end of his rope was the River Liffey coasting by indifferently down there?

BRIGID MARY:   Leave your old patriots in peace now. Come on.

DENNIS:   Old. He was scarcely as old as I am the morning they led him out here to die.

*The church bells begin striking the hour of nine.*

BRIGID MARY:   Dennis, come.

*Dennis looks off down the hill, quotes.*

DENNIS:   "I have burnt out my lamp of life. I have parted with everything that was dear to me in this life for my country's cause. I am going to my cold and silent grave. I am ready to die. Since no man defends me, let no man write my epitaph. But when my country takes her place among the nations of the earth, then shall my character be vindicated. Then let my epitaph be written."

*Moved, Brigid Mary goes close, puts her arms around him.*

191

DENNIS:  Those were great times, Brig.

BRIGID MARY:  And these are dangerous ones. You heard what Father said. Walk me home now like a good little convert.

> *Arm in arm, they turn and start along the street toward the sidewalk. They stop short at the sound of feet running wildly toward them. As they turn back, three men come hurtling around the corner beyond the church. One of them carries a wooden case of ammunition. Another has in his arms five carbine rifles. The third is Patch Keegan, carrying two small Thompson guns.*

PATCH (*shouting as he runs*):  Get off the street! Get that woman off the street!

DENNIS:  Patch! Patch Keegan!

PATCH:  Is it you, Dennis? (*Shouting the others on*) Go on, boys, cut through High Street. (*To Dennis*) We've cracked open an ammunition depot. They're on our tail. Are you with us, lad?

BRIGID MARY:  Dennis, no!

> *He turns to her, and in one swift moment the street lamp reveals the persuasion of each to the other, neither yielding.*

DENNIS (*to Patch*):  I'm with you.

> *He seizes Brigid Mary's arm and propels her toward the church.*

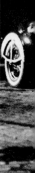

BRIGID MARY:   Dennis, in the name of God, they've done the thing. You're not in it.

DENNIS:   I should have been. Stay in the church till this blows over.

*He turns away from her at the church steps, toward Patch.*

PATCH:   Come on, if you're coming! Take this!

*He flings one of the guns. Dennis catches it.*

BRIGID MARY:   No, please!

*Patch runs off in the direction the others took. Dennis hurries after them, reaches the center of the street, at which moment a British military cycle careens around the corner beyond the church. Instinctively, Dennis turns toward it, the gun clutched in both hands.*

BRIGID MARY:   Dennis!

*A machine gun flares from the cycle. Dennis crumples.*
CUT TO:   *A close shot of Brigid Mary's face. The cycle's headlight flashes across, illuminating horror, and the roar of the cycle's motor passes and fades.*

193

BRIGID MARY:   Jesus, Mary, and Joseph...Jesus, Mary, and Joseph...Jesus, Mary, and Joseph...

*She remains rigid for a moment, then begins moving toward him without a will, spastically, muscles and nerves warring insanely. Dennis raises himself to his knees as she reaches him, clutching his belly, a widening pool of blood beneath him.*

DENNIS:   Let me get up. Don't grab onto me, Brig.

*The church door opens behind them, light pouring out. Father Curran comes down the steps toward them.*

DENNIS:   Did they get the gun?

FATHER CURRAN:   Dennis . . . (*Seeing the boy's wounds*) Oh, merciful God! Get him inside, Brigid Mary, get him inside. Take his other arm.

*Stationing themselves on either side, they conduct Dennis toward the church, slowly and painfully.*

DENNIS:   Are you angry with me, Brig? Father, are you angry?

FATHER CURRAN:   No one is angry, son. Be careful of the step.

*They help him up the stairs.*

DENNIS:   Easy! Easy . . . I'm all smashed inside. I'm like a Christmas pudding. I'm leaking badly.

BRIGID MARY:   Don't talk, Dennis.

*They lead him through the church door into a small chapel to one side of the vestibule. A benign and placid Christ looks down from behind a bank of votive candles.*

DENNIS:   Brigid Mary's angry. "Since no man defends me, let no man write my epitaph." I can't go any further.

FATHER CURRAN:   Just to the little room beside the altar, Dennis? There's a soft couch there. You can lie down while I fetch a doctor.

DENNIS:   I don't want to lie down. I won't get up again. Let you be stopping here.

BRIGID MARY:   Dennis, *try.*

DENNIS:   I don't want a doctor. Don't leave me, Father. I won't be here when you get back.

BRIGID MARY: He can lie on the pew there, Father.

DENNIS:   No . . . I'm fine.

*He slumps forward, almost out of their grasp.*

BRIGID MARY:   Dennis!

DENNIS:   I'm all right. Let me down easy. I'll kneel here for a bit.

*Gently they lower him into a kneeling position before the altar. He looks up at the small statue.*

DENNIS:   Oh, my sweet Christ, I am gravely wounded.

BRIGID MARY:   I've got to get help.

DENNIS:   Don't go, Brig! Please! (*Urgently*) Father, I want to be baptized. Can you do that for me, Father?

FATHER CURRAN:   Yes, Dennis, yes. I'll get the holy water.

*Father Curran goes quickly out toward the rear. Brigid Mary kneels beside Dennis.*

DENNIS:   Brig, make a lap, where I can put my head down. (*Weakly, whimsically*) Lady, may I lie in your lap?

*She sits on the floor beside him. He lowers himself sideways, placing his head in her lap but remaining in a cramped position. She takes off her scarf, slips it inside his jacket, vainly trying to stanch the bleeding. He winces, groans.*

BRIGID MARY:   I'm sorry. How can I help you? Is it a terrible pain?

DENNIS:   It'll do. It'll do.

BRIGID MARY:   I wish it were in my mouth. I wish I'd the pain on my tongue for every cruel or wicked thing I've said to you.

DENNIS:   Shhh. Blow gentle.

*Brigid Mary bends low over him, striking her breast.*

BRIGID MARY:   Through my fault, through my fault, through my most grievous fault . . .

DENNIS:   It's queer you look from down here, Brig. I can see your two nostrils but I can't see your eyes.

195

*Suddenly, desperately, he clings to her. Alarmed, she cries out.*

BRIGID MARY: Dennis!

DENNIS: My life is running out the holes! Don't let me go! Hold on! Hold on, damn you!

BRIGID MARY (*pressing him close, she turns her face, tear-streaked, to Christ's statue*): Lamb of God, who takest away the sins of the world, spare us, O Lord! Lamb of God, who takest away the sins of the world, graciously hear us, O Lord! Lamb of God, who takest away the sins of the world, have mercy on . . .

> *Something, some almost imperceptible movement of Dennis', arrests her. She looks down at him, knowing at once that the life has left his body. With all her strength she draws him to her, burying her face in his throat, stifling the scream that wrenches her whole being. Very softly and unobtrusively, music begins here—the voices of women keening in Gaelic. Father Curran returns carrying a small white china stoup with a cruciform top. He stops when he sees what has happened, sadly holds the stoup to his chest.*

196

FATHER CURRAN: That'll be all right. He *wanted* to be baptized, and that's the important thing after all. Baptism of desire, they call it. The holy water and the prayer is only part of it. God knows the wish that he had in the heart of him.

*Brigid Mary raises her head a little, attempting to extricate the hand that is caught in Dennis' death grasp. As she pries open his hand, she sees the little medal in his palm. Father Curran watches her as she raises it, studies it with fascination, then extends it to him.*

BRIGID MARY:   I gave him this. I said, "She'll look after you for me."

*Suddenly, she violently flings the medal onto the floor at the priest's feet. The music ends abruptly.*

FATHER CURRAN:   Brigid Mary!

BRIGID MARY:   Leave it lie there! It was no good to him and it's no good to anyone living. Oh, my sweet boy, my beautiful Dennis, my life, my joy, I want you back again!

FATHER CURRAN:   Stop it now.

BRIGID MARY:   There's nothing without you. I told you that. I'll tell them all. No wind, no rain, no sun or stars, nor anything lovely on the face of the earth and you not here. Take back your holy water, Father! Put it back in the stoup for the women will be coming to kneel in their men's blood, the way they'll be praying to your gentle God. I keened and cried and prayed for a father killed and a brother, too, but I'll come no more to your deaf God, your bitter little God of death and grief. For see what He's given me in the end of all.

FATHER CURRAN:   Ah, Brigid Mary, you're that crazed with grief yourself you don't know what you're saying at all.

BRIGID MARY:   Don't I though? Look at me, Father! Look what I'm holding here. This great, sweet lump of a boy came to your God for my sake, for love of me, came knocking at the church door with his cap in his hand. He was the loveliest thing I ever had and I gave him gladly to your God, the way he gladly gave himself. Is this the way a boy like that is received in God's house?

FATHER CURRAN:   Don't speak to me of my God, Brigid Mary Mangan. He's your God and the God of all of us, and who are you to question His will?

BRIGID MARY:   Question Him? I don't question Him. I might have so when Da died with half his face blasted off him or when Colm was burned alive. I'm past questioning now. I deny Him.

FATHER CURRAN:   God forgive you. Shut your mouth now at once, and when you've control of yourself again, pray for forgiveness.

*Brigid Mary slips out from under Dennis' body, rises defiantly.*

BRIGID MARY:   I will not shut up. I will say it again and again, in any place whatever, to anyone who will listen. I deny Him!

FATHER CURRAN:   Go out from this holy place then.

*Brigid Mary turns and addresses the statue, in a wild, increasing voice.*

BRIGID MARY:   I deny Him. I deny Him!

*She begins stamping out the candles with the palms of her hands, tearing them awry with her fingers, striking the votive jars from their racks.*

BRIGID MARY:   No more candles! Guns! Guns that spit and roar! The world is on fire! This is too tame!

FATHER CURRAN:   Stop! Stop! You're defiling the house of the Lord!

BRIGID MARY:   There is no God! There is only fire! Fire!

*As she stretches to smash the upper level of candles nearest the feet of the statue, Father Curran rushes forward, grabs her, struggles with her, pulls her around and finally, despairing of subduing her, strikes her violently in the face, once, twice, three times, shocking them both terribly. Brigid Mary's hysteria subsides. She stands at last docile, defeated, tears still staining her face, now childlike and bloated. With a groan of remorse, the priest sinks to his knees.*

198

FATHER CURRAN:   What have you made me do? Oh, merciful Heaven!

*Brigid Mary turns up the palms of her hands like a little girl showing cleanliness. The palms of both are sooted and badly burned. Father Curran takes them gently in his own.*

BRIGID MARY:   I hurt myself. (*Quietly, barely able to speak*) It was his birthday.

*The priest looks up at her compassionately, deeply shaken, his eyes full of tears. When she speaks again, her voice is a drowning cry from far off.*

BRIGID MARY:   Help me, Father.

FATHER BURRAN:   I will.

BRIGID MARY:   Help me.

FATHER CURRAN:   I will. I will.

BRIGID MARY:   Oh, please—somebody—help . . . help . . .

*Her eyes close against the tide.*
*Fade out.*

199

# ACT TWO

FADE IN:   *The square seen in the first scene of Act I. Evening. The street lamps are lit. Over the scene comes the gentle tenor voice of the boy, singing:*

BOY'S VOICE:   "She is far from the land where her young hero sleeps, and lovers around her sighing."

*Camera moves down into the square as Father Curran and Shelagh come along the pavement. They turn in at the door of an old Georgian house. Father Curran rings the bell.*

BOY'S VOICE:   "But sadly she turns from their gaze and weeps, for her heart in his grave is lying."

*The door opens. A Catholic Sister in a blue habit and winglike white headdress admits them. As the door closes, the camera holds on the engraved brass plate affixed to it which reads: "Saint Vincent de Paul Chapter House."*

DISSOLVE TO:   *A small, bare room with a low ceiling and an arched window, its mahogany frame stark against the plaster walls. Brigid Mary sits in a straight-back chair between the narrow bed and the window. Her hands are folded in her lap. She stares before her, her face a mask concealing emotion, a mask as stark as the room itself. The voice of the singer is heard humming softly in the background, ending with a knock at the door. It opens, and Father Curran lets himself in.*

FATHER CURRAN:   Is it all right?

BRIGID MARY:   Yes, come in, Father.

*The priest enters, closing the door behind him.*

FATHER CURRAN:   How are you the day, child?

BRIGID MARY:   Fine.

FATHER CURRAN:   How are your hands?

BRIGID MARY:   Sister took the bandages off this morning. The blisters are all healed. (*She holds up her hands.*)

FATHER CURRAN:   They look like new. Why are you sitting here in the dark? (*He moves to light a lamp beside the bed.*)

BRIGID MARY:   I didn't notice the day go. Is it night again? So soon? (*She rises, goes to the window, opens it.*)

FATHER CURRAN:   It is. A fine one with a slip of a moon.

> CUT TO:   *A close shot of Brigid Mary at the window, looking up at the sky. The melody of "She Is Far from the Land" is heard gently in the background, played on a single harp. A pause before Brigid Mary speaks.*

BRIGID MARY:   Little moon, little moon of Alban.

FATHER CURRAN:   What?

BRIGID MARY:   I was thinking of some words from a play that Dennis and I were reading together once. *Deirdre of the Sorrows.*

FATHER CURRAN:   Ah, yes.

BRIGID MARY:   Her young man is killed, and she left standing beside his open grave, and she says, "I see the trees naked and bare, and the moon shining. Little moon, little moon of Alban, it's lonesome you'll be this night, and tomorrow night, and long nights after, and you pacing the woods beyond Glen Laoi, looking every place for Deirdre and Naisi, the two lovers who slept so sweetly with each other." And then she presses the knife into her heart and falls herself into the grave.

FATHER CURRAN:   Brigid Mary . . . (*Pause. She is lost in reverie.*) Your mother is here.

BRIGID MARY (*not quite hearing, turns to him*): I'm sorry, Father. What . . . ?

FATHER CURRAN:   I brought your mother with me. She's waiting outside. She wants to see you.

BRIGID MARY:   She wants to take me home. I won't go. I can't go.

FATHER CURRAN: Hear what she has to say. Talk to her.

BRIGID MARY:   We've talked every day since I made up my mind to stay here with the Sisters. She doesn't . . .

> *She stops short as Shelagh enters, wearing a shapeless woolen coat and a plain hat that cannot contain all the vagrant wisps of her hair. She stops inside the door. She and Brigid Mary stand looking at each other, the recent anger and anguish preventing them from any display of affection. A pause.*

BRIGID MARY:   Hello, Mama.

SHELAGH:   I've come to fetch you home.

*Brigid Mary looks to Father Curran.*

FATHER CURRAN: Maybe I'd best wait outside.

BRIGID MARY: No, don't go, Father Curran. Please. I don't want to quarrel any more, Mama.

SHELAGH: That makes two of us. So get your things together and come on with me.

BRIGID MARY: I can't. I can't go back to that house. If I've any hope of life, it's here. I can't live without hope, Mama. I can't live with the dead.

SHELAGH: I have lived with them.

BRIGID MARY: I'm not you. You don't know what I was like the night Father brought me here. If I hadn't burned my hands, if he hadn't brought me here to let the Sisters care for them, if he'd let me go my way, I swear to you I would have thrown myself into the river. I would have died somehow that night. I would have found the men who shot Dennis and tormented them into killing me, too. When the Sisters saw what state I was in, they knew it was more than my poor hands wanted tending, and they took me in. Not half an hour before, I had renounced God, and here He was, taking me back and nursing me where I had wounded Him. I have to stay here, Mama. It's what I have to do.

SHELAGH (*to Father Curran*): Is that what they mean by a "calling," Father? If I burn me two hands and a nun treats them, do I become a nun? Is that all there is to it?

FATHER CURRAN: No, and I don't think it was that way with Brigid Mary.

SHELAGH: I always prayed that one of my children might enter the Church. But not if the persuasion hasn't come from up above. Am I right, Father?

FATHER CURRAN: My dear, if Brigid Mary wants to join these Sisters here, it's between her and God. You and me don't enter into it.

SHELAGH (*to Brigid Mary*): Did God speak to you? With this holy man and your mother as witnesses, tell the truth now. Did God speak to you?

BRIGID MARY: No.

SHELAGH: There!

BRIGID MARY: But I spoke to Him.

SHELAGH: You did what?

BRIGID MARY: It was as if I spoke to Him, and He listened. If I thought He had called to me, I'd be entering a convent and spending my life in a quiet place where nothing could interfere between His voice and me. But I called to *Him*, Father, and that's the next best thing, isn't it?

202

FATHER CURRAN:   I suppose it is.

BRIGID MARY:   That's why I want to be one of the Daughters of Charity here, working with the sick and the poor the way they do, working with children. Because they're not nuns, but they are Sisters who do God's work, and my life is a call, not a calling.

>*A pause. Shelagh sighs wearily, sits on the edge of the bed, her tasseled mesh bag clutched in her lap.*

SHELAGH:   There's no reasoning with her. Do what you will, and God help you.

>*Brigid Mary crosses, kneels beside her.*

BRIGID MARY:   Give me your blessing, Mama.

SHELAGH:   I can't.

BRIGID MARY:   Please.

SHELAGH:   No, by all that's holy. I can't. I'm your mother, and I know you. Don't you think I would give my life to see a daughter of mine take the veil, herself cloistered in beauty, and I kneeling to kiss the hem of her robe? How can I give you over to live and work among these dedicated Sisters? What good will you be to them at all, and half your heart buried in Glasnevin Cemetery?

BRIGID MARY:   Mama, don't . . .

SHELAGH:   Grief is your persuasion. Fear is holding you here.

BRIGID MARY:   No!

SHELAGH:   Come on away out of this, then.

BRIGID MARY:   I've told you and told you—there's nothing for me out there.

SHELAGH:   That's no reason. Nobody comes this way because there's nothing out there. Only because, to them, everything is here. They walk through these doors serenely, with a great pride to them. They're not running. They are not running away from life, from love, from a man who might be holding you in his two arms one minute and lying dead the next.

FATHER CURRAN:   Mrs. Mangan . . .

BRIGID MARY:   Stop it, Mama, stop it!

SHELAGH:   I'm through talking. I won't open me mush again.

BRIGID MARY (*on her knees, embracing her mother desperately, weeping*): Mama, don't scold me any more. We have to say goodbye! I love you so! I love you.

SHELAGH (*softening at her child's touch*):   Ah, what a bad girl it is . . .

> *There is a sharp rap at the door, and it opens abruptly. The Sister servant enters, a middle-aged woman with a serene face. Shelagh quickly puts Brigid Mary from her.*

SHELAGH:   Let me go now. Let go.

> *Brigid Mary rises, trying to conceal her tears from the Sister servant.*

SISTER SERVANT:   Oh, I'm sorry. Brigid Mary, the new postulants are gathering for prayers and meditation. I thought you might want to join them. It's time you began.

BRIGID MARY: Yes, Sister. Yes, I would so.

SISTER SERVANT:   Come along, then. (*She smiles and nods to Father Curran, looks at Shelagh.*) This is your mother, is it? She looks like you.

SHELAGH (*rising*):   Good evening, Sister.

SISTER SERVANT:   God is grateful to you for this good, strong girl, Mrs. Mangan. She will be useful to Him in His work.

SHELAGH (*looking at Brigid Mary*):   I'll pray that she will.

SISTER SERVANT (*starts out, turns*):   Are you coming with *me*, Brigid Mary?

> *Brigid Mary crosses, turns to look at her mother uncertainly.*

BRIGID MARY:   Mama . . . ?

SHELAGH:   Go on if you're going.

> *Brigid Mary looks at Father Curran, turns, goes out, followed by the Sister servant. The room is quiet when they have gone. Neither the old woman nor the priest speaks for a moment. The camera moves in to a close shot of Shelagh.*

SHELAGH:   They're all gone now, one way or another. It's the war. You sit listening for a footstep on the landing, and all you can hear is the dust settling in the empty cup on the pantry shelf. And no smell of them in the rooms, only the smell of camphor under the closet door where their coats are hanging stiff and silent.

FATHER CURRAN:   Let you be moving up to your sister's place in Meath. You'll not be lonely the nights.

SHELAGH:   It doesn't matter, Father. It's all one to me now. I've nothing more to give to God or Ireland.

DISSOLVE TO: *The corridor. Several young women (Sisters Millikin, Barbara, and Theresa among them) wearing the seminary bonnet and shawl move along the corridor toward and past the camera, all carrying prayerbooks. Others are seen to pass in the opposite direction. Chapel bells ring out in the background. A moment after the last of them has passed, we see Brigid Mary, similarly dressed, at the far end of the corridor. She walks toward the camera, ever more slowly, hesitating before the statue of the Blessed Virgin on its pedestal. She looks about to assure herself that no one is watching. Then she kneels before the statue and blesses herself. After a brief, silent prayer, she reaches into her blouse and brings out the little St. Brigid medal. Holding it in her upturned hand, she looks up into the face of the Madonna and begins to pray for a blessing.*

BRIGID MARY: Hail Mary, full of grace, the Lord is with thee. Blessed art thou amongst women, and blessed is the fruit of thy womb, Jesus . . .

*She continues to pray in silence, her lips moving rapidly. An ominous rumble of music replaces her voice.*

SUPERIMPOSE: *A shot of British soldiers careening toward the camera on motorcycles, Thompson guns spitting fire.*
CUT TO: *Close shot of guns.*
FADE OUT: *The shot of Brigid Mary. Over the shot of the gun muzzles,*
SUPERIMPOSE: *A shot of several young rebels running toward the camera, stopping at a fixed point, looking about as if the enemy were surrounding them.*
FADE OUT: *The shot of guns. Over the shot of rebels,*
SUPERIMPOSE: *A close-up of the senior English officer shouting commands. We do not hear his voice, only the increasing roar of battle—guns and distant explosions. As the shot of the officer fades, one of the rebels (Patch Keegan) draws the pin from a hand grenade. Over this action,* SUPERIMPOSE: *The figure of Brigid Mary as before, her head bowed in prayer. As Patch pulls back to heave the grenade, she raises her face in fear, clutching the holy medal over her breast. Patch throws the grenade.*
QUICK FADE: *The shot of Patch over the shot of Brigid Mary.*
SUPERIMPOSE: *A shot of the grenade exploding in limbo. Explosive sound coupled with percussive music. Brigid Mary claps her hands over her ears. Flames and smoke billow where the grenade went off, seeming to envelop her. As she lowers her head in anguish,*
FADE OUT *the shot of fire. Music and sound go with it. New music creeps in, something tranquil and votary. Brigid Mary is kneeling, facing the camera. Shoot, as if from the vantage of the statue. A slant*

*cathedral light falls across Brigid Mary in the darkness. The Sister servant appears behind her.*

SISTER SERVANT:   Sister Mangan . . . (*No answer*) Sister Mangan . . .

BRIGID MARY (*raising her face*):   Yes, Sister?

SISTER SERVANT:   Will you not come and pray with the others?

BRIGID MARY:   I would, Sister, but they always seem to be finished before I've properly begun.

SISTER SERVANT:   I see. You're creating a private atmosphere of austerity for yourself, is that it?

*Brigid Mary rises, starts to protest.*

BRIGID MARY:   Ah, Sister . . .

SISTER SERVANT:   Now hold on. I want to say something to you. You are too hard on Brigid Mary Mangan.

BRIGID MARY:   Too hard?

SISTER SERVANT:   We don't make our own terms of expiation. We have priests for that. It's through them we communicate our confession and our penance to the Heavenly Father. None of us has the right to sit in judgment on herself.

BRIGID MARY:   No, but we have to question ourselves, don't we, Sister? We have to be *sure* of ourselves.

SISTER SERVANT:   Don't you remember what St. Vincent de Paul said to the first Daughters of Charity there in Paris? "Just think," he said, "when God chose you there were plenty of other people in the world. And yet He chose *you*." (*Brigid Mary averts her gaze.*) Slow down, Sister. You've another whole year before you take your vows. God is in no hurry. Go on now and join your Sisters before the Blessed Sacrament.

*She starts to turn and proceed along the corridor.*

BRIGID MARY:   Sister . . .

SISTER SERVANT (*stops*):   Yes, Sister Mangan?

BRIGID MARY:   If any of us didn't belong here . . .

SISTER SERVANT:   What?

BRIGID MARY:   If any of us were wrong for this life, God would surely be weeding them out in the year ahead, wouldn't He?

SISTER SERVANT (*hesitates, then*):   Why ever not?

> *She goes, leaving Brigid Mary staring after her. Brigid Mary turns her gaze up to the statue above her. The music swells.*
> DISSOLVE TO:   *The street outside the chapter house's front door. Focus very tight on the grimy face of a ragged newsman, his mouth open wide as he calls:*

NEWSMAN:   Paper! Evening paper! Get your paper here! *Times! Press! Independent!*

> *The camera pulls back just far enough to include the paper which he holds flush against his chest, front page exposed. The headline reads: "Violence Mounts. Bloody Hand-to-Hand Fighting in the South." The camera pushes in to see the date, "May 27, 1920."*
> DISSOLVE TO:   *Another newspaper which reads "June 26, 1921." The camera pulls back to reveal the headline "Peace Looms! Lloyd George Invites De Valera to London." The final paper holds, filling the screen. Over this, music assisting the transition,* SUPERIMPOSE:   *The establishing shot of the following scene, then* FADE OUT *newspaper.*
> *A hallway in the chapter house. The Sister servant and Sister Millikin (later called Sister Martha Kevin) stand side by side as a group of seminarists pass along on either side of them, toward and past the camera. An organ sounds climactically in background.*

SISTER MILLIKIN:   It was a beautiful service, Sister. I kept thinking, This is the last time I'll be hearing Mass as Sister Millikin. Tomorrow I'll be Sister Martha Kevin.

SISTER SERVANT:   Have you tried on your habit yet?

SISTER MILLIKIN (*shaking her head*):   I'm half afraid to. The lot of us have thought of nothing else for eighteen months. (*Excitedly*) And now . . .

SISTER SERVANT (*smiling*):   I know.

SISTER MILLIKIN:   Will you come along to me, Sister, and see that I've put it on properly?

SISTER SERVANT:   I will surely. Go along with you now.

> *Sister Millikin exits in the direction of her room. The Sister servant turns toward the door beside her. It is slightly ajar. She pushes it open, and we see Brigid Mary, standing with her back to the door and to the Sister servant. She has put on her habit and is making a final adjustment in the cornette.*

SISTER SERVANT:   Sister Brigid Mary . . .

*Brigid Mary turns, her eyes wide with excitement. Nervously her hands fall away from their task, flutter a moment about the starched dickey, then clasp desperately at her waist. Her eyes search her superior's face for some sign of encouragement or disapproval.*

SISTER SERVANT:   Your sleeves, Sister. Turn back your sleeves. Like mine, you see?

*Brigid Mary makes a cuff on each sleeve, again looks up hopefully. Pause.*

SISTER SERVANT:   That's better. Yes. (*She nods her head.*) Yes.

BRIGID MARY (*suddenly, impetuously*):   Does it look all right?

SISTER SERVANT (*alarmed by the outburst, covering her ears facetiously*):   Blessed saints!

BRIGID MARY:   Sister . . . does it? I can't tell. You're my looking glass, Sister. I'm trying to see myself in you. I've no other way of knowing at all if I look all right.

SISTER SERVANT:   You look beautiful.

BRIGID MARY (*very modestly*):   Oh, no. I was never even pretty.

SISTER SERVANT:   You're beautiful now. God thinks so.

BRIGID MARY:   You think He's pleased? He's brought me along so patiently, and now here I am. Oh, He must have wanted me this way, mustn't He, Sister? He must have remembered that I have a green finger with children, and said to Himself, "This girl will be all right when she's settled into a country orphanage, somewhere away from the fighting and killing, a place where—"

SISTER SERVANT (*interrupting*):   Sister!

BRIGID MARY (*a pause; contritely*):   My mouth ran away with me.

SISTER SERVANT (*with difficulty*):   The fact is that during your training here you've shown a special aptitude for hospital work.

BRIGID MARY (*anticipating disappointment*):   Oh . . .

SISTER SERVANT:   I'm sorry, I had no choice, you see. As many Sisters as are proficient nurses are needed at once in the hospital there in Adelaide Road. If I'd any option to exempt a Sister from this duty, believe me, child, I'd send you elsewhere—anywhere.

BRIGID MARY:   Why *me*, Sister? I don't . . . (*She shrugs.*)

SISTER SERVANT: It's not one of *our* hospitals. It's a hospital for the English, and most of them wounded fighting our boys.

BRIGID MARY (*a little gasp*): Ah . . .

SISTER SERVANT: They're desperate for nurses. The Visitatrix said she told them the Daughters of Charity work mainly among the poor, and the English doctor-in-charge there says to her: "Sister, these wounded boys are very poor. An Englishman on Irish soil is without friends, and that is a great poverty."

BRIGID MARY: Did you think I wouldn't go, Sister?

SISTER SERVANT: Oh, I know you'll go wherever you're stationed. I was only thinking because of the losses you endured in the world, if I'd had the chance to ask only one exemption—

BRIGID MARY: Please don't, Sister. You shame me. I know you're saying that out of kindness. But I'm a Daughter of *Charity* now.

> *The Sister servant looks at her for a long moment. A flow of affection passes between them. The older woman reaches up and straightens Brigid Mary's headdress. Then she moves to the door, turns back, speaks briskly, authoritatively.*

SISTER SERVANT: I'll be expecting you in the refectory in twenty minutes. There'll be a car to take you to Adelaide Road. Make your kit as meager as possible. Pack only essential things. Leave this room as you found it. Twenty minutes, mind now.

BRIGID MARY: Yes, Sister.

> *The Sister servant goes out. As Brigid Mary turns toward the crucifix hanging on the wall above her bed, the camera moves in to a close shot of her face.*

BRIGID MARY: God, give me strength. Cleanse me of rancor. I want to be worthy. I do so want to be.

> DISSOLVE TO: *The hospital reception hall. An English soldier mounts guard near the doorway, pacing to and fro. As he crosses, we see Sister Martha Kevin on duty at the reception desk, making notations on a chart by the light of a kerosene lamp. Sister Theresa approaches, carrying a lamp.*

SISTER THERESA: Good evening, Sister.

SISTER MARTHA KEVIN: Good evening, Sister.

SISTER THERESA:   Have you heard the glorious news?

SISTER MARTHA KEVIN:   I have, God be praised. Do you think it might have anything to do with the electric lights going on the blink?

SISTER THERESA:   I don't know, I'm sure, but wouldn't it happen that Dr. Clive'd be in the midst of an emergency operation when they went out?

SISTER MARTHA KEVIN:   Holy Mother, whatever did he do?

SISTER THERESA:   Went right on as cool as you please with Sister Angelica striking match after match until enough lamps had been gathered up to make a proper light.

SISTER MARTHA KEVIN:   And was it a success? The operation?

SISTER THERESA:   It's not over yet.

> *Brigid Mary crosses the room, wearing the white habit of the hospital Sister, carrying a lantern.*

SISTER MARTHA KEVIN:   Sister Brigid Mary, have you a minute to listen to some wonderful news?

BRIGID MARY:   I've no time to linger. I must see that a bed's prepared for him that's in surgery. Save it till I come back.

SISTER MARTHA KEVIN:   I will, Sister. (*With an informed smile, to Sister Theresa*) It'll keep.

> *Sister Theresa smiles in return.*
> CUT TO:   *Brigid Mary as she passes along the corridor, stops before a numbered door. Voices are heard within—husky whispering, then coarse laughter, then precipitate quiet as Brigid Mary opens the door and the man in the first bed speaks.*
> CUT TO:   *A hospital room. It is rectangular, with a large casement window in the wall opposite the door. There are six beds in the room, three on either side of the passage from door to window, their heads flush against the long side walls, their feet extended out to the passage. The only illumination in the room is moonlight falling through a tree outside the window and throwing mottled patterns over beds and floor. Only the four beds nearest the door are occupied. The two that stand opposite each other near the window are empty. As Brigid Mary makes her way along the passage, the men call to her in English accents of varying degrees of refinement. The camera moves along before her, isolating each of the men as Brigid Mary speaks to him.*

FIRST BED:   Ease off now, chaps, ease off. It's the lady with the lamp.

BRIGID MARY:  Why aren't you asleep, Corporal?

FIRST BED:  I thought I *was,* Sister. I thought I was dreaming and you was the ghost of Florence Nightingale come to collect the bedpans.

BRIGID MARY:  Aren't you the limit now? Close your eyes.

SECOND BED:  Don't mind him, Sister. He don't mean nothing by it.

BRIGID MARY:  Double negative, Sergeant Peale. I seem to remember saying good night to you more than an hour ago.

SECOND BED:  Well, I . . .

BRIGID MARY:  *Good night,* Sergeant.

> The patient in bed number three snaps his head away surreptitiously as Brigid Mary approaches, closing his eyes.

THIRD BED:  Good night, Sister.

FOURTH BED:  I can't say good night, Sister. I'm asleep.

> Brigid Mary shakes her head as she places her lamp beside one of the empty beds, at the end of the passage.

THIRD BED:  Sister . . . ?

BRIGID MARY:  Sshhh!

> She turns down the bed, smoothing sheets and fluffing the pillow. She then crosses to the window and opens it. As she stands looking out, Sister Barbara, one of the young women from the chapter house, comes up behind her. When she speaks, Brigid Mary starts.

SISTER BARBARA:  Sister . . . ?

BRIGID MARY:  Oh! (*She turns, smiles.*) I'm sorry, Sister Barbara. Something in the air has put me on the pig's back tonight.

SISTER BARBARA:  They're bringing the new patient along from surgery.

BRIGID MARY:  I'm ready for him. (*Turning again toward the window, her face puzzled*) It's such a queer night. Something's on fire out there. There's a red glow on the edge of the town.

SISTER BARBARA:  That's bonfires. They're lighting them all over Dublin. Didn't you hear the bells ringing?

BRIGID MARY:  I didn't.

SISTER BARBARA: I didn't either. Sister Martha Kevin told me just now as I passed the desk. It's over. It's ended.

BRIGID MARY: What's over? What're you talking about?

SISTER BARBARA: The troubles. (*Brigid Mary gasps.*) The announcement came from the Lord Mayor's office at noon today. A cease-fire has been signed in London. There'll be no more fighting or killing.

BRIGID MARY: Thank God! (*She turns toward the window, eyes full of tears, and whispers.*) Oh, Dennis . . . Dennis . . .

SISTER BARBARA: They're coming now. (*She moves to the empty bed and turns the covers down to the very foot.*) It's a great pity surely that this one should have been shot down, and neither him nor them that did it knowing the awful business was finished and they'd no quarrel with one another.

> As Brigid Mary moves to her side, two orderlies come in bearing Lieutenant Kenneth Boyd on a stretcher. Dr. Clive, an old man, rumpled and fatigued, still in his operating gown, walks behind them.

DR. CLIVE: Give us a hand here, Sister.

> Sister Barbara helps them to place the patient in the bed. Brigid Mary draws the bedclothes over him. As she arranges his pillow, we see his face clearly for the first time, from her angle. It is a young, handsome face, innocent but for the slightly cynical line of the mouth. The forehead and curly hair are wet with perspiration. In repose, it is a child's face, eminently vulnerable.

BRIGID MARY: How young he is.

DR. CLIVE: Are you on duty here, Sister?

BRIGID MARY: Yes, Doctor.

DR. CLIVE: I want someone to watch over him all night long. If there's any change for the worse—any complication whatever—I'm to be called at once.

BRIGID MARY: I understand.

DR. CLIVE: Should he go off quietly in his sleep—well, don't wake me. If I've botched this one, I don't . . . Damn those lights! I beg your pardon, Sister. I'm worn out, you know. Good night.

BRIGID MARY: Good night, Doctor.

SISTER BARBARA: Good night, Doctor.

DR. CLIVE: Good night.

*He follows the orderlies off. Sister Barbara turns to Brigid Mary, who is still staring down at her patient.*

SISTER BARBARA:   It'd break your heart, wouldn't it? Face like a cherub in a painting.

*Brigid Mary answers with a characteristic little gasp, pulls a straight-back chair to the bedside, sits, folds her hands in her lap, eyes still fixed on the young man in the bed.*

SISTER BARBARA:   You're due to be relieved soon, aren't you, Sister?

BRIGID MARY:   I'm not tired. I've been so tense and thorny all evening, it'll be good for me to sit quiet once and not be tossing in bed.

SISTER BARBARA:   Can I bring you anything?

BRIGID MARY:   No, thank you, Sister.

*Sister Barbara exits. Brigid Mary takes a cloth from the bedside table, dampens it from a water carafe, then gently bathes the patient's face. One hand carefully and delicately brushes the hair back from his forehead.*
*On a close shot of Brigid Mary's face, DISSOLVE TO:   A close shot of Kenneth's face, illuminated by early-morning light. The camera moves back to include Brigid Mary. Dawn creases the sky outside the window behind her. Brigid Mary's eyes have closed for a minute. They open suddenly, instantaneously solicitous of her patient's welfare. She leans a little forward, scrutinizing his face. As she reaches out a hand to feel his forehead, his eyes open. Her hand stops, caught in the young man's gaze, then is withdrawn. His eyes follow it to Brigid Mary's face.*

213

BRIGID MARY:   Good morning, Lieutenant.

*The eyes close painfully.*

KENNETH:   I thought I'd dreamed it. I've been awake behind my eyes for several minutes, but I was afraid to open them. I kept thinking, Oh, let me be back in the barracks! (*He opens his eyes, looks at her.*) Why did I have to see *you* first thing? One could only suppose one had died and gone not to heaven but to some bizarre masquerade. Do you have any idea how terrifying it is to know you've been shot in the belly and then cut open and sewed up again and suddenly to awake and see that haggard, anxious face and that absurd headdress looming over one? You look like some sort of great carnivorous bird.

BRIGID MARY: I'm sorry. I didn't mean to frighten you.

*A pause. He considers.*

KENNETH: I'm not in pain. I don't feel anything down there. Why is that? Am I paralyzed?

BRIGID MARY: No, no, you're fine. Why should you be wanting to feel pain?

KENNETH: I don't *want* to feel pain. I'm terrified of pain. I'm so terrified at this moment I don't dare move for fear of starting it all over again, the way it was in the lorry right after it happened. I thought I'd bleed to death. (*He turns his head to one side.*) Where are the others? Reynolds and Powys, where are they? Are they in those beds? I can't see their faces. (*He looks back at Brigid Mary, reads the answer in her face.*) Dead?

BRIGID MARY: Yes.

KENNETH: The lot of them?

BRIGID MARY: Yes.

KENNETH (*bitterly*): We were unarmed.

BRIGID MARY: I know. Lie easy now.

214

KENNETH: We were on a routine mission. We'd been confined to barracks because of the possibility of a truce. I was ordered to take a small detail down to Blackrock to pick up a stalled lorry full of supplies. We were ambushed on the road.

BRIGID MARY: Don't be thinking about it.

KENNETH: Those gangsters attacked us from behind.

BRIGID MARY: Now, they were not gangsters.

KENNETH: My men hadn't a chance. They were picked off by snipers before they could surrender.

BRIGID MARY: It's a terrible thing surely. But they've been taught to fear and suspect the Tans. They've been themselves surprised and ambushed so often their good control is gone—some valor go with it.

KENNETH (*interrupting*): We are not Black and Tans, as you call them. We are military. We wear the uniform of His Majesty's Army. We were viciously attacked by civilian hoodlums.

BRIGID MARY: I tell you they are not hoodlums and they are not gangsters. They are soldiers like yourself, though maybe their uniforms are not much for regulation.

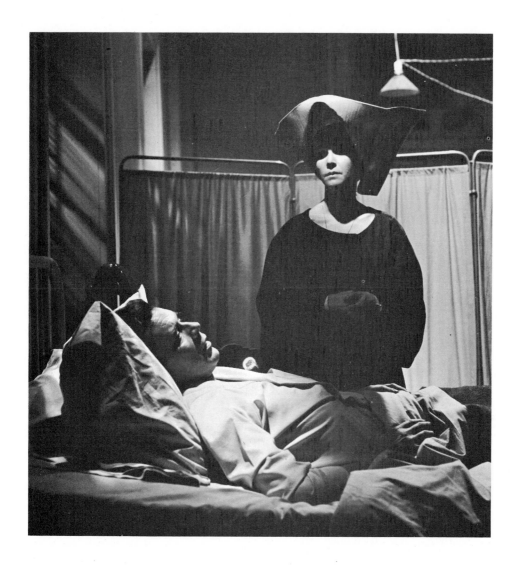

KENNETH:  What the devil are you talking about? How dare you defend them to me? What sort is this? Is this a British hospital?

BRIGID MARY:  It is a hospital under British supervision.

KENNETH:  And is it part of your function to remind every Englishman carted in here how fortunate he is to have been wounded by one of your fine Irish patriots?

BRIGID MARY:  That's all I want, that you think of them as patriots and not what you said.

KENNETH (*suddenly violent*):   Listen, my men are dead!

BRIGID MARY (*retorting in kind*):   My men are dead, too!

*A pause. Brigid Mary places a hand over her mouth.*

KENNETH:   What does *that* mean?

*Brigid Mary turns away, toward the window. The anger in her face subsides.*

BRIGID MARY:   Why are you and I fighting? It's all over. I can still see the smoke of bonfires in the town. The truce was declared at noon yesterday.

KENNETH:   At noon? It was almost sunset when we . . . (*He begins to laugh weakly, ironically.*) Then I'm a peacetime casualty—(*He winces in sudden sharp pain.*) Uh! . . . Well, I'm not paralyzed.

BRIGID MARY (*turning*):   Are you in pain? (*He nods.*) Is it bad?

KENNETH:   It'll do.

*A close-up of Brigid Mary's face as the memory of the words suffuses it.*

BRIGID MARY:   What?

KENNETH:   I said, it'll do.

BRIGID MARY:   I'll fetch the doctor.

KENNETH:   Wait a minute. Is he Irish, too?

BRIGID MARY (*defiantly*):   No, he's not. And if he were, what of it? Do you think he'd skimp his duty on that account? What sort of dishonorable hypocrites do you take us for?

KENNETH:   How angry you are. How unlike the white Sisters one hears about. You're all cut up inside, too, aren't you? They may have made a truce out there, sitting in stuffy rooms with long, political faces, but it's not over for us, is it? Is it?

*Brigid Mary hesitates, looking at him, her hand stealing to grasp the rosary at her waist. In a close shot, we see her stark face impaled on his penetrating stare. With an effort, she turns and starts out of the room.*
*CUT TO:  Close shot of Kenneth's face, concentration surmounting pain, as he watches her go.*
*FADE OUT.*

# ACT THREE

FADE IN:  *The hospital room. Early evening. Focus on the patient in bed number one, sitting up, strumming the guitar that lies in his lap and singing. The patient in the next bed lies listening, and those from beds number two and four sit on the ends of beds one and three, wearing bathrobes, and joining in the chorus of the song.*

FIRST BED (*singing*):  "Oh, have you heard the news, my Johnny?"

CHORUS:  "One more day."

FIRST BED:  "We're homeward bound tomorrow."

CHORUS:  "One more day! Only one more . . ."

*Bed number two signals them to keep their voices down, nodding toward the far end of the room. As they look toward that end, we see a white fabric screen set around Kenneth's bed. The singing becomes quiet, continuing behind the ensuing action.*

CHORUS:  ". . . day, my Johnny, one more day. Oh, rock and row me over, one more day."

CUT TO:  *A shot of the activity behind the screen. Dr. Clive bends over Kenneth, moving a stethoscope over his bare chest. Sister Brigid Mary stands watching the doctor. When she looks at Kenneth, his eyes meet hers and he smiles slightly.*

KENNETH:  Hear what they're singing? I call that overconfident. They confuse truce with treaty.

*The doctor stands up with a grunt, pulls the stethoscope from his ears, sighs.*

KENNETH:  You're a marvelous doctor, you know it? You grunt and sigh like some pessimistic Cassandra. That's called "cheering the patient up," I suppose.

DR. CLIVE:  Did I grunt? I'm sorry. I'm tired.

KENNETH:  You're always tired. Do you know what I think?

*As Brigid Mary moves to button his pajama top, he brushes her hands away.*

KENNETH: Don't do that. I'm not entirely helpless. (*To the doctor*) I think it's something quite remote from work or long hours that fatigues you. I think it's death. You've seen too much of it. Just the thought of it wears you out.

DR. CLIVE: Oh, now, Lieutenant . . .

KENNETH: No, I'm right. (*Indicating Brigid Mary*) She feels it, too, though she never says anything. She's always hovering about like a curious white cat, watching me, wondering when I'll spew out my life and what it will be like when I do. Wondering if she can catch it in a basin.

DR. CLIVE: Ignore him, Sister. He's trying to shock us.

*Beyond the screen, the song changes to: "Oh, soldier, soldier, will you marry me? With your musket, fife and drum . . ."*

KENNETH: Poor conspirators. She's fighting for my spirit and you're fighting for my body, and you're both losing. Small wonder you look wretched and gray. On that side of the screen they're getting better. Two of them can move about now and wear hideous dressing gowns. They can all sing, though not very pleasantly. They're your successes. But it doesn't compensate for the awful failure on this side of the screen, does it? (*To doctor*) She despairs of finding a *heart* in me, let alone an immortal soul. And when you put that preposterous little object against my chest, all you can hear is the metallic ticking of a child's five-shilling watch that has momentarily outrun its broken spring.

DR. CLIVE (*dryly*): You're in far better condition than you think.

KENNETH: Ha! Marvelous. Thank you, Doctor. You couldn't have said anything more incisively reassuring. I am so very fond of chestnuts.

*Amused, Dr. Clive smiles at Brigid Mary.*

DR. CLIVE: You just relax and leave the rest to Sister Brigid Mary and me. Getting you well is our job. Eh, Sister?

BRIGID MARY: Yes, Doctor.

DR. CLIVE: As for the others moving about, I see no reason why you can't have a turn in the garden while the afternoons are still pleasant. Sister will arrange for a rolling chair tomorrow, eh?

BRIGID MARY: I will, Doctor.

DR. CLIVE: I'll look in on you again in the morning.

*Brigid Mary accompanies him to the edge of the screen. When he is out of Kenneth's line of vision, he turns to her, shakes his head despairingly, turns and walks, stoop-shouldered, out of the room. Brigid Mary turns to Kenneth. They stare at each other for a moment. Her manner has a new composure in it. One senses that she may now aspire to serenity. Their voices muted, the patients sing "Keep the Home Fires Burning." Brigid Mary goes to the window, which is ajar, and pushes it open wide, looking up and breathing deeply. A long pause, filled with gentle, wistful song.*

KENNETH:   What color is the evening, Sister?

BRIGID MARY:   What color?

KENNETH:   Yes. I can't really see from here.

BRIGID MARY:   Well, it's blue. It's what you might call Mediterranean blue, the way it is in the south of France, with the lights coming on along the Riviera and the sea and the sky all one color.

KENNETH:   I say, you never cease to amaze me. When were you on the Riviera? What sort of nun *are* you?

BRIGID MARY:   I told you, I'm not a nun. I'm a Daughter of Charity. And I've never been any place except to the National Gallery of Art. I used to go there with . . . a friend of mine.

KENNETH:   You hesitated then. Who was this friend? I'm terribly jealous. Male or female?

BRIGID MARY:   It was a boy I knew.

KENNETH:   A chum? Or was he . . . ?

BRIGID MARY (*overlapping*):   They had a painting in the Gallery that we liked. It was called "Twilight on the Promenade des Anglais." That's in Nice there in the south of France. It was all in this marvelous shade of blue.

KENNETH:   Tell me . . . (*He coughs dryly.*) . . . why you say . . .

*He falters, his voice breaks off. He closes his eyes for a moment, trying to get his breath. Concerned, Brigid Mary crosses to his side.*

BRIGID MARY:   No more talking now. You're tired out. You must try to sleep.

KENNETH:   No, please. Sit down. I'm all right.

*Brigid Mary pulls the chair close, switches on the little lamp beside the bed, sits.*

BRIGID MARY:   Is that in your eyes?

KENNETH:   No. Now what did I want to ask you? Oh, yes. Why do you say you're not a nun? You look like a nun. So very sanctimonious.

BRIGID MARY:   Now . . .

KENNETH:   I don't mean that. I mean pious. All nuns look very pious and mysterious.

BRIGID MARY:   Mysterious? Go on.

KENNETH:   They are to me. I don't believe in anything they represent and yet I never fail to leap up and offer one my seat in a tram or a bus. Why is that? It must be the medieval costume. You do *dress* like a nun.

BRIGID MARY:   Yes, but St. Vincent de Paul didn't want his daughters to be nuns, because when you say "nun" you're talking about a cloister, but we have to go everywhere. St. Vincent says, "Your convents are the houses of the sick. Your cell is a hired room. Your chapel, the parish church. Your cloister, the streets of the city. Your enclosure, obedience. Your grille, the fear of God. Your veil, holy modesty."

KENNETH:   It sounds rather like punitive duty in the Army. You do the dirty work.

220

BRIGID MARY:   Our work is to look after the material and the spiritual needs of the poor.

KENNETH:   Ah, but I'm rich, you see. I have an enormous annuity. I'm very rich.

BRIGID MARY:   You're poor in spirit, though, aren't you, Lieutenant?

KENNETH:   Am I? I believe that's a stock phrase you have for people who don't think the way you do.

BRIGID MARY:   St. Vincent tells us to humble ourselves and to ask God incessantly for the ability to pray.

KENNETH:   How monotonous for God.

*From beyond the screen the voices sing "Greensleeves." They listen separately, then their eyes meet, and for a moment they are together.*

BRIGID MARY:   You must sleep.

*She starts to rise.*

KENNETH:   One moment. When you ask your God for prayer, does He grant it?

BRIGID MARY:   Yes.

KENNETH:   Always?

BRIGID MARY:   If I'm worthy.

KENNETH:   "If I'm worthy." How degrading!

BRIGID MARY:   You've such a way with words, you must know the difference between humility and degradation.

KENNETH:   Oh, please don't bore me with your tired catechismal epigrams. That's no answer.

BRIGID MARY:   Are you asking me for answers, Lieutenant? What is it you're looking for?

KENNETH:   Nothing. I'm not looking for anything. Not any more. Don't irritate me now. I'm supposed to be sick, remember?

BRIGID MARY:   I'm sorry. Try to sleep. I'll shush the others.

KENNETH:   And you? Will you go to your antiseptic little cell and pray?

BRIGID MARY:   I will go to my room and pray.

KENNETH:   For what? What is there to pray for?

BRIGID MARY:   For many things. For you.

KENNETH:   For me? (*He laughs, shakes his head.*) You'd do better to pray for poor Bertie there. Pray that some miracle will persuade him to sing on key.

BRIGID MARY (*rising*):   Shall I leave the light burning?

KENNETH:   No, thank you. I'm not afraid of the dark.

*Brigid Mary turns off the lamp. A gentle light from outside the window makes deep shadows in the corner of the room.*

KENNETH:   I like the dark. I'm very nasute. That means "having an acute sense of smell." In the dark, one's nostrils are more important than one's eyes. I can smell the garden outside, and I can smell the starch in the cloth of your gown. Will you pull my covers up, please?

*Brigid Mary pulls the covers up to his chin. She feels his warm cheeks and forehead with one hand.*

KENNETH:   How cool your hand is. How very gentle. When I was a little boy, my mother became ill and I was allowed to have a playmate come and spend the night with me. After my nanny put out the light and left us alone, we talked. I remember Dickie asked me to define God for him. I was eight years old. I said, "God is round. He has no sharp corners. He is soft as snow and sweet as honey. God is taller and wider and deeper than anything else. He is very gentle and kind." Later that night, my mother

221

died in the room below mine, screaming with pain and fear. We lay listening all night long until she was quiet at last.

BRIGID MARY (*moved, speaks with difficulty*):   Sometimes . . .

KENNETH:   No more epigrams, please. If you're going to preach to me about God moving in strange ways, His wonders to perform, I'd rather you said nothing at all. I can't see your face, but I know there are tears in your eyes.

BRIGID MARY:   You can smell them, I suppose?

KENNETH:   I'm the one who makes bad jokes. Here's one for you. I'm going to need one of your charming needles. It's started again, in my stomach. It's getting worse.

> *Brigid Mary switches on the lamp, wiping her eyes with her hands, quickly preparing a syringe. She peels back his sleeve, sterilizes the inside of the elbow. He stares at her fixedly while she plumbs for a vein, trying not to wince.*

KENNETH:   I tell you once and for all I am bitterly opposed to everything you represent. Religion—religion is a fantasy invented to assuage the human animal's fear of death. But I don't fear death, you see. Only pain. You're hurting me, you know.

> *Brigid Mary, unnerved by her inability to locate the vein, perspiring and vexed, speaks sharply and emotionally as she goes on trying.*

BRIGID MARY:   Be quiet. I tell you once and for all to keep your mouth closed. You are hurting *me*, too.

> *She bites her lip and presses the needle deeper.*
> DISSOLVE TO:   *The garden which extends from the rear of the hospital. It is small, with several ash trees and one large linden, gravel paths and patches of grass. The surrounding stone wall is banked with shrubs. The camera follows Sister Barbara as she pushes a patient in a wheelchair along the path toward the hospital door. Just short of the door, they encounter Sister Brigid Mary coming out.*

BRIGID MARY:   Going in?

SISTER BARBARA:   Yes, Sister. We felt a bit of a snap in the air. I'm afraid the summer has almost passed us by.

> *The camera goes with Brigid Mary as she crosses the garden. Kenneth sits in a wheelchair, a blanket around his legs, beneath the linden tree at the farthest remove from the hospital door. Sunlight, falling*

*through the leaves, mottles his face. It is more sallow than before, shadows underlining the eyes. His whole manner is frailer, less flinty. His hands rest on a newspaper in his lap. His tone, at first, is rather petulant.*

BRIGID MARY:   Why did you move into the shade? Let me wheel you into the sunshine. It's a pity to waste—

KENNETH (*overlapping*):   Don't. I don't want my face in the light. I can't bear the others looking at me as they pass and thinking: Poor old chap, the worms are at him already and he's not quite dead yet.

BRIGID MARY:   I'll leave you straight away and you talk like that.

KENNETH:   I'll yell the place down if you do. You've been gone half an hour as it is. You said ten minutes. You promised.

BRIGID MARY:   Now listen, I've other patients to be looking after. I'm not your private nurse.

KENNETH (*pause*):   Was that necessary? Don't imagine for a moment that I'm not constantly reminding myself I'm no more to you than a scrofulous old man or a sick child might be. I am a case. Nothing more.

BRIGID MARY:   Ah, I don't know what to say to you. You *are* a child. You are a great baby and I've no patience with you at all, God forgive me. Why will you do nothing to make my time with you a little easier?

KENNETH:   That's your conscience, not me. You're terrified of my dying and it makes you doubt the things you say you believe in. It's unjust. It's unjust, and you hate it as much as I do.

BRIGID MARY:   Why do you torment me? What do you want of me? Only tell me so I can help you.

*Kenneth cannot meet the direct entreaty of her eyes. He looks away.*

BRIGID MARY:   Don't look away. I want to understand you.

KENNETH:   No, you want to understand the phenomenon, this shockingly ill-mannered dancer who goes on waltzing after the music has stopped. I must say I can't blame you for being fascinated. Everyone is. Every morning the others come and peek round the screen to see if I'm still breathing. Like you, they pretend an interest in me, but it's really the ancient spectacle of prolonged death that attracts them.

BRIGID MARY:   Why don't you die then, Lieutenant?

*Kenneth looks at her, astonished.*

223

KENNETH:   How cruel of you to say that.

BRIGID MARY:   I am talking with God's righteous anger now. I don't know how to be kind to you any more. You won't let me. Why won't you die, I'm asking? Is it because you can't, knowing you haven't made your peace with God Almighty?

KENNETH:   Made my peace? You mean the way Dennis did?

BRIGID MARY (*with a little gasp*):   Ah, let you not be throwing that back in my face. Don't make me regret telling you about him.

KENNETH:   I can be cruel, too, you see. I've had a long matriculation in cruelty.

BRIGID MARY:   I'm not equal to it. I'll take you inside.

KENNETH:   No, not just yet please. We'll talk about something else. Small talk. (*Looking at the sky*) The days are drawing in, aren't they?

BRIGID MARY:   It'll be autumn before the week has crawled over the garden wall.

KENNETH:   And still no treaty. It says here there's an Irish delegation going to London next month.

BRIGID MARY:   Well, that'll be it then. Mr. De Valera and Mr. Lloyd George will have you all home in England for Christmas.

KENNETH:   You can't wait, can you? Never mind. You'll be rid of me long before Christmas.

> *He unclenches one hand, holds it up. A yellow leaf lies in his palm.*

BRIGID MARY:   What's that now?

KENNETH:   A leaf. It fell into my lap while I was sitting here. (*Looks up into the tree*) What will it be like in the cold earth, I wonder, when all these leaves are lying on my grave? Will you come where I'm buried in the winter and say your beads for me as you do for Dennis?

BRIGID MARY:   Ah, don't.

KENNETH:   I lied to you, you know. I *do* fear death. I fear it most awfully. You're wrong to think I don't want to believe in anything. I want to—but I can't. I did believe once. Death wasn't the end of everything then. If only I could believe again . . .

BRIGID MARY:   You can. You can.

KENNETH:   Tell me how.

BRIGID MARY:   I've tried. You don't want to listen; you want to argue. I'm not a theologian. I can't recite canonical law. I'm not clever enough to answer you. That would take a Bishop or a Cardinal. I can only answer what I feel.

KENNETH: That's why you're the only one who can help me.

BRIGID MARY: Is it I?

KENNETH: I want to believe as you do. As a child does. Oh, Sister, help me. You're my last hope in the world. Help me.

> *He has seized both her hands, desperately. Now he bends his head and presses them to his face.*

BRIGID MARY: I will. I will if I can.

KENNETH: You must. Don't you see? I need your certainty now. I need your strength.

> *In a close shot of Brigid Mary, we see the perplexed brow, the mouth that strains but says nothing.*
> DISSOLVE TO: *The reception hall. Night. An electric lamp burns on Sister Martha Kevin's desk. Sister Barbara comes in hurriedly from the direction of surgery, whispers urgently to Sister Martha Kevin, then goes out by the same exit. Sister Martha Kevin rises and walks quickly toward the camera, then past it into the corridor. The camera moves behind her down the hallway to a door. She stops, knocks twice, opens the door.*
> CUT TO: *Inside the room. It is almost identical to the one Brigid Mary had in the chapter house. Beside the bed, Brigid Mary kneels beneath a crucifix, praying by candlelight. She ends her prayer, makes the sign of the Cross, turns to Sister Martha Kevin.*

SISTER MARTHA KEVIN: Come along, Sister. You're needed.

BRIGID MARY: What is it, Sister?

SISTER MARTHA KEVIN: It's Lieutenant Kenneth Boyd. He suddenly started to hemorrhage. They're preparing him for surgery. He's asking to see you. Quickly now.

> *She exits. Brigid Mary turns back to the crucifix.*

BRIGID MARY: Heavenly Father, help me to help this boy. I am not strong or certain. I am weak and tortured with doubt. Oh, not of You. Of myself. If I am ever to be worthy, speak to me now.

> CUT TO: *An anteroom off the surgical theater. Kenneth lies under a bright light on a rolling table, a sheet drawn over him to his shoulders, which are bare. The circles beneath his eyes are black gashes*

*now in a face chiseled from meager white stone. His eyes are wide, the pupils dilated. Sister Barbara stands beside him, speaking gently, comfortingly through the babble of incoherent mumbling that comes from his barely moving lips.*

SISTER BARBARA:  Now . . . now . . . it's all right . . . rest . . . sshh . . .

*Brigid Mary comes through the door leading from the hall. Sister Barbara crosses to meet her.*

SISTER BARBARA:  They're almost ready in there. He's had a lot of drug. I don't think he's making very good sense.

KENNETH:  I heard that. For shame, Sister Barbara.

*Sister Barbara looks abashed, exits into the surgical theater. Brigid Mary crosses to Kenneth's side. He turns his head slightly. They look at each other for a long moment. Kenneth is short of breath throughout this, speaking in broken sentences.*

KENNETH:  Actually I make *very* good sense—every now and then. I was asking her about the Daughters of Charity. She says you renew your vows every year and that every twenty-fifth of March you're free to leave the—what do you call it?—community.

BRIGID MARY:  On Lady Day—that's right. But very few ever leave.

KENNETH:  The point is, you can do so if you wish—if you feel you don't belong here, if you feel that some other life would be more—consistent with God's wishes for you?

BRIGID MARY:  Yes.

KENNETH:  Now why did I ask that? Uh . . . listen. How did Dennis decide to—you know—so that he could marry you?

BRIGID MARY:  You mean, embrace my faith?

KENNETH (*nods*):  When did it happen?

BRIGID MARY:  Oh, he thought about it for a long time. And then one day we climbed up on the Hill of Howth together. The sun was shining and the sky was vast and blue and everywhere clear it seemed—when all of a sudden I saw the loveliest and most mysterious thing I'd ever seen. There was a single dark cloud way out over Dublin Bay toward Dun Loaghaire. It had a glow of sunlight round it like a halo, and rain was falling from it, pocketing the sea underneath. It was like something you'd see in a cathedral. I said to Dennis, "Look there what God is doing." Dennis started to say, "Brig, I believe . . ." but his voice trailed off. We didn't talk again for a long while, and then he told me what was on his mind.

KENNETH:   I have no hilltop. I have a naked light bulb in an empty room and there is nothing miraculous in nature for us to see. But I want to tell you I believe with all my heart that if you and I had met a long time ago, in some other place, in a different world, perhaps, we would have loved each other and we would have defied the universe to spend our lives together. I can say this to you now because in a very few minutes I shall be dead.

BRIGID MARY:   You won't.

KENNETH:   I shall. They know it in there, the doctors. This is merely routine for them.

BRIGID MARY:   Is it yourself, of so little faith, being so credulous of doctors? I tell you, you will not die.

KENNETH:   I can almost believe you when you say it that way.

BRIGID MARY:   You will believe.

KENNETH:   I want to. Oh, God, I want to.

BRIGID MARY:   What did you say?

KENNETH:   I said, Oh, God . . .

BRIGID MARY:   Say it again.

KENNETH:   Oh, God!

BRIGID MARY:   Again.

KENNETH:   God, God!

BRIGID MARY:   Keep saying it.

KENNETH:   I want to live!

BRIGID MARY:   Keep talking to Him. He hears you. He remembers when you were a little boy and you talked to Him.

KENNETH:   I don't remember any prayers.

BRIGID MARY:   You don't need any.

> Sister Barbara comes in, followed by an attendant. Together, they begin wheeling Kenneth toward Surgery. Brigid Mary moves along beside him.

BRIGID MARY:   Everything you say to Him now is a prayer.

KENNETH:   Bend down. (*Brigid Mary leans close.*) I want to know—what color is your hair?

*Sister Barbara signals for Brigid Mary to stop short of the swinging doors.*

SISTER BARBARA:  I'm sorry, Sister.

*They push the table through the doors. Kenneth calls out.*

KENNETH:  What color?

BRIGID MARY:  Brown. Light brown. Kenneth!

*The doors swing closed, and she is alone in the room. She falls to her knees, bends her head in prayer.*
SUPERIMPOSE:  *The wooden clock in the foyer, its moon-faced pendulum clacking ominously.*
FADE OUT:  *The shot of Brigid Mary. Hold on the clock for a moment, then* SUPERIMPOSE:  *Close shot of Dr. Clive's hands, stripping off a pair of rubber gloves.*
FADE OUT:  *Shot of the clock. Camera moves back, goes with Dr. Clive as he passes through the swinging doors into the anteroom, pulling off his surgical mask. Brigid Mary moves to encounter him in a close shot.*

228

BRIGID MARY:  Dr. Clive . . .?

DR. CLIVE (*shaking his head*):  It was an impractical hope from the beginning, a certain reluctance to acknowledge futility. One does this sort of thing because one wants to say afterward, "At least, I tried." We stood there like confounded children, cursing our teachers for failing to give us the answer to the question in his flesh.

BRIGID MARY:  Is he dead?

DR. CLIVE:  He will be—imminently. I doubt he'll regain consciousness. If he should survive the night it would be . . . (*He shrugs.*)

BRIGID MARY:  A miracle?

*He looks at her for a moment, then smiles sadly.*

DR. CLIVE:  I vow I sometimes think that nursing schools should be restricted to atheists and fatalists. Go in, Sister. They need you in there.

*He starts out toward the hall. Brigid Mary turns and goes through the swinging doors.*
DISSOLVE TO:  *The hospital room. Night. Focus on the little lamp beside Kenneth's bed. The camera moves down to reveal his face in*

*repose, eyes closed. The camera pulls back. Brigid Mary sits beside the bed, watching.*

DISSOLVE TO: *The same scene from another angle. Dawn. The first morning light glows outside the window. Brigid Mary looks toward the window, then back at Kenneth. In a close shot, we see his lips part, move slightly. Brigid Mary leans forward, feels his face, rises, starts quickly out of the room.*

*On a shot of her retreating figure,* DISSOLVE TO: *Kenneth's bed. Dr. Clive bends over him, testing his pulse. When he straightens up, he looks across the bed to Brigid Mary, raises his brows in a gesture that concedes a slight improvement. With that for fuel, an anxious hope flares in Brigid Mary's face.*

DISSOLVE TO: *The other patients. Gathered about the bed of number one, they are all looking toward the screen at the far end of the room. Number one idly plucks a chord on his guitar. The others quickly silence him. He looks sheepish, then speaks sarcastically, in a whisper.*

FIRST BED: Tell me, is one permitted to breathe?

SECOND BED: Shut up, Bertie, 'e's only 'anging on by 'is shoelace.

FIRST BED: Is he conscious?

FOURTH BED: I don't think so. Not yet.

THIRD BED: Old Clive says it's the damnedest thing he's ever seen, the way the kid's fighting back.

SECOND BED: Still 'e don't think 'e'll pull through, *does* 'e?

FIRST BED: Poor ol' man.

SECOND BED: Mmm.

> CUT TO: *A shot, from their angle, of the white screen.*
> DISSOLVE TO: *Kenneth's bed. Brigid Mary is bending over him, fluffing his pillow. As she gently raises his head and places it under, he opens his eyes. She gasps. He smiles weakly. His voice is small and tentative.*

KENNETH: You have a funny little habit, do you know it? (*Brigid Mary presses her hands over her mouth in relief.*) It annoyed me terribly at first. Now I love it. You draw your breath in a priggish little gasp. I believe it's rather common in elderly maiden ladies and shopkeepers.

BRIGID MARY: Ah, you were always a grand one to talk!

KENNETH: I talk too much, don't I? (*Sleepily*) I just wanted to wake up long enough to tell you that your God and I are settling a lot of things between us. I knew you'd be sitting there with that worried little face. I couldn't have borne it if you hadn't been.

229

BRIGID MARY:   I know.

KENNETH:   What day is it?

BRIGID MARY:   Wednesday.

KENNETH:   Have I been away for two whole days?

BRIGID MARY:   Almost. It's been a very long time.

KENNETH:   Did you miss me?

BRIGID MARY:   I did.

KENNETH:   I *am* sorry. I sha'n't stay so long this time. (*Closing his eyes*) You won't go away, will you?

BRIGID MARY:   I'll be right here.

KENNETH:   Yes. Did I tell you—I love brown hair. And, oh, yes . . . (*He opens his eyes.*) I'm not going to die. (*He closes them again.*)

> *Close-up of Brigid Mary. She bows her head into her hands, weeping silently. Then a close-up of Kenneth, sleeping peacefully. Behind this shot, the soft strumming of the guitar and a voice humming "One More Day."*
> DISSOLVE TO:   *The corridor. The doctor and Brigid Mary walk along, the camera moving before them.*

DR. CLIVE:   I don't want to say anything that might compromise my reputation as a cynic. Let it be set down merely that the patient made a most remarkable and unlooked-for recovery.

> *He nods his head, providing his own affirmation.*

BRIGID MARY:   You *do* think he'll get well then?

DR. CLIVE:   At this rate, I don't see how he can avoid it. It was a very contrary thing for him to do.

BRIGID MARY:   Ah, you're a great bluff, aren't you?

DR. CLIVE (*with mock indignation*):   Oh, I say!

BRIGID MARY:   You're as thrilled as I am.

DR. CLIVE:   Thrilled? I'm astonished. I'm stupefied.

> *Brigid Mary hesitates before her door. He stops, turns to her.*

DR. CLIVE:   What was it that saved him, Sister? No, I don't want to know. I want to go home. I want to plant an English garden and finish my days contemplating the miracle of nasturtium and ranunculus. I can't cope with *anything* any more, neither failure nor success. Do stop looking at me that way.

BRIGID MARY:   What way was I looking at you?

DR. CLIVE:   So—I don't know—radiant. Where will you go when all this is cleared up? Are you headed for martyrdom? I'm very ignorant about the . . . *degrees*—of what you people feel and strive for. Tell me the truth. I'll believe you, whatever you say. I'm quite gullible. Are you a saint?

BRIGID MARY:   A saint? Oh, glory be, I'm only a girl who speaks to God.

*Sister Barbara approaches from the opposite direction.*

DR. CLIVE:   I see.

SISTER BARBARA:   Doctor, can you come?

DR. CLIVE:   Excuse me.

*He continues down the corridor. Brigid Mary goes into her room, closes the door behind her, leans back against it, closes her eyes almost in ecstasy.*

231

BRIGID MARY:   And sometimes . . . He answers.

DISSOLVE TO:   *The hospital room. Focus on a calendar hanging near bed number one. A hand comes into the shot and makes a heavy crayon circle around the date: January 7, 1922. The camera moves back. Bertie of the first bed has made the mark. The others crowd about him, whooping with joy and relief. They throw their arms about one another, ruffling one another's hair. Vociferously they begin to sing "Pack Up Your Troubles in Your Old Kit Bag and Smile, Smile, Smile." One of them begins to dance while the others press round, clapping their hands in rhythm and singing.*
CUT TO:   *The garden. Focus on Kenneth's wheelchair. It is empty. The blanket lies on the seat.*
CUT TO: *A shot of Kenneth, sitting on the bench that circles the linden tree. Brigid Mary stands beside him as he reads from the front page of a newspaper. Her face glows in the cold air. She has achieved serenity. The trees are bare now. Kenneth wears a heavy coat and a muffler, Brigid Mary a cloak over her habit. Both look toward the windows, listening to the laughter and singing within.*

KENNETH:   Good heavens, you'd think England had won her independence from Ireland, the way they're carrying on, wouldn't you?

BRIGID MARY:  Finish reading.

KENNETH:  Where was I? Ah . . . (*Reads*) "Mr. Diar . . ."

(*He hesitates over the pronunciation.*)

BRIGID MARY:  Diarmuid.

KENNETH:  "Mr. Diarmuid O'Hegarty then began the roll call. There was complete silence in the room at Earlsfort Terrace, save for the answers, which were given in Irish. When it was over, Mr. . . ." (*Hesitates, spells*) E-o-i-n.

BRIGID MARY:  Eoin.

KENNETH:  "Mr. Eoin MacNeill arose and read the results. Sixty-four in favor, fifty-seven opposed. The treaty had been approved by seven votes."

*They look at each other, sharing relief. Kenneth lays the paper aside. Together, they listen for a moment to the jubilation inside. Then, mustering all his courage, Kenneth looks at Brigid Mary, smiles, rises.*

BRIGID MARY:  Careful now—not too much all at once.

KENNETH:  I'm all right. Sit down.

BRIGID MARY:  I don't want to.

KENNETH:  Please.

BRIGID MARY:  Well . . . (*Uncertainly, she sits.*) You look so solemn. Is anything the matter?

KENNETH:  No, it's just that I have something rather important I want to do. Are you quite comfortable there?

BRIGID MARY:  Yes.

KENNETH:  Good. Now I'm going to say a lot of things that have to be said. I ask you to hear me through without interrupting.

BRIGID MARY:  What on earth . . . ?

KENNETH:  Ah-ah. Just listen. (*Indicating the paper*) You know what this news means. All British troops will be withdrawn from the Free State immediately. This place will be closed up very quickly. We'll be shipped home and you'll go on to a new assignment.

BRIGID MARY:  Don't let's think about that now. We—

KENNETH:  You're interrupting. Now . . . (*Nervously, as the topic becomes more critical*) I'll probably be held in military hospital in England for a few weeks' convalescence—tests and things, you know—and then discharged. It will be late February or early March by that time. I shall go home to my family in Bognor. Does that name frighten you? It does most people. Actually it's a very charming little village on the sea—near Chichester. That's worse, isn't it? Don't mind the names. It's beautiful there. You'd love it. Now this is the crucial part. I know that March twenty-fifth is the day you either renew your vows or leave the community. I wasn't delirious when I went into Surgery, you see. I want you to understand that I sincerely believe your place in this life is with me, as my wife. (*Speaking quickly, as Brigid Mary makes a move to interrupt*) No, please, I'm not quite finished. I believe that's why God spared me. You must feel something like that, too. Otherwise, why? I'm fully prepared now to do exactly as Dennis did, to be converted to your faith. Oh, I know what a difficult decision it would be for you. That's why I don't want you to answer now. I won't say anything more except that beginning March twenty-fifth I shall meet every train that comes to Bognor. There now. I think I had better sit down.

> *He sits beside her. For a long moment they do not look at each other but sit staring before them. Then Kenneth turns to study her in profile. She is too moved to speak. Finally she turns her face to him. He smiles limply at her and she tries to force a smile that will not come. She lowers her eyes and speaks in a throttled voice.*

233

BRIGID MARY:  My heart is full to bursting. I'm trying to think what to say to you.

KENNETH:  I told you—don't say anything.

BRIGID MARY:  I must. I must . . . (*She looks at him directly.*) the way you'll be meeting all those trains, and I not on *one* of them.

> *A stunned pause.*

KENNETH (*mechanically*):  Didn't I tell you not to talk?

BRIGID MARY:  And let you go on from this with maybe and perhaps for companions? I can't do that.

KENNETH:  Well, you mustn't give me no, you mustn't say irrevocably never, when you haven't thought about it. When you're not sure.

BRIGID MARY:  Ah, but I've thought of nothing else since the night you were given back to me. I *am* sure. For the very first time, I am sure of myself and the way I must go, and I've you to thank for it.

KENNETH:  I don't want your gratitude. I didn't survive hell and agony to be thanked and patted on the head for accepting Jesus Christ as my Saviour. How can you sit there and talk about the night I was given back to you? You don't want me.

BRIGID MARY:   I do. I want you for Him.

KENNETH:   I don't know Him. Not really. Not yet. He only spoke to me through you.

BRIGID MARY:   And it was through you that *I* heard Him for the first time. I'd been listening with my ears only, for such a long while. And then yourself came, and you talking such a great storm of words till I'd no ears left in the night when I was alone with Him and making a novena that you'd be spared. I think now that must have been the first time I ever listened with my heart. Oh, what things I heard then! No words. Just things. For the first time I understood what it meant to be doing God's work out of love and not out of fear. In the beginning I was only a Sister by sufferance. Every day I thought, Today God will give me the sack. And now He's given me a promotion instead. He's made me a Sister in truth. I can never forsake Him now.

KENNETH (*bitterly*):   But you can forsake *me* quite easily, can't you, without the least bit of remorse? "The Daughters of Mercy have no charity and the Daughters of Charity have no mercy."

*A pause. Brigid Mary speaks softly and meaningfully.*

BRIGID MARY:   I have lived most of my life in grief and mourning. I'm no stranger to remorse. As long as I draw breath, no matter how much joy I find in work and prayer, there won't be a day goes by that I won't think of you,

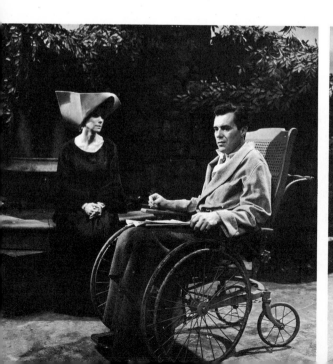

that I won't miss you, never a day that's not somehow changed because you're not there to share it. The girl I was before I put on this habit would have loved you the way a young girl loves in a summer frock with flowers in her hair, if it had been left to her. It wasn't. But no matter where I go from this place, I can't leave that girl behind entirely.

KENNETH: I wish I had died. You should have let me die.

BRIGID MARY: That's child's talk. It's no good pretending from this on that you're not a man and equal to the trouble will be coming your way. I know you are. I'm not worried about you any more.

KENNETH: No, that's obvious. Why don't you leave me? I wish you would.

BRIGID MARY: Don't be like that. We must be very careful not to hurt each other now. We must be very jealous of the little time we have left together. (*She rises.*) Let me wheel you inside. It's too cold out here.

KENNETH: Do go away. I'm quite serious. I can't look at you.

BRIGID MARY: I won't leave you out here like this.

KENNETH (*angrily*): For pity's sake, get away from me! I'm not in your care any more. Go in to your other charges. Go on! Spread the word. You have the knack of making it digestible. Put it in their liver salts; they'll never taste it!

235

BRIGID MARY: Do you know what you're doing to me?

KENNETH: I told you to go! Why don't you go?

BRIGID MARY (*in despair*):   I'll send Sister Barbara to help you in.

> *She turns and goes quickly into the hospital. Kenneth turns desperately, sees that she has gone, presses his eyes so tightly closed that the hot tears squeeze painfully from beneath his lids. He bites the knuckles of one hand to stifle the sobbing in his throat.*
> DISSOLVE TO:   *The hospital room. It stands ready for total evacuation. The bedclothes have been stripped from the beds. The patients are all making last-minute adjustments in their uniforms, adding the last odds and ends to their kit bags, folding their mattresses in half. One of them removes the tacks from photographs of his family, stripping them from the wall. Bertie of the first bed lays his guitar in readiness on the bed springs. All wear heavy coats and put on caps during the scene. Kenneth is at his bed, slowly transferring comb, toothbrush, etc., from the bedside table to his kit bag. Sister Martha Kevin comes in from the corridor.*

SISTER MARTHA KEVIN:   The lorry is here, gentlemen, the lorry is here!

FIRST BED:   Come on, boys, 'op it, 'op it.

SISTER MARTHA KEVIN:   The officer has asked that you assemble at the front door.

SECOND BED:   You tell 'im we'd be delighted, Sister.

FIRST BED:   What about *your* lorry, Sister? You can't stay on after we go. There'd be nobody for you to bully.

SISTER MARTHA KEVIN:   Shame on you, Corporal. The Sisters will be leaving directly all the patients are out the door. We'll be on our way ourselves before you reach the bottom of the road. Come along now, gentlemen. (*She goes out.*)

THIRD BED:   Time, gentlemen, time—if you please.

FIRST BED:   First ruddy pub I was ever glad to get 'eaved out of. (*Hefting his gear to his shoulder*) Off we go, lads.

> *Brigid Mary enters. She now wears the blue habit. They turn to greet her as she passes along the aisle, all calling, "Good morning, Sister."*

BRIGID MARY:   Good morning. Are you all ready to go?

> *She stops as she reaches the center of the room, looking toward Kenneth. He raises his head as he hears her voice. Their eyes meet. We see their faces, first his, then hers, in extreme close-up.*

FOURTH BED (*off-scene*):   All ready, Sister.

*She hesitates only an instant, then turns back to them.*

BRIGID MARY:   You haven't forgotten anything now? Is there anything I can do for any of you?

FIRST BED:   You can kiss the Blarney Stone for us when you see it.

BRIGID MARY:   I will and gladly if I ever get down Cork way.

THIRD BED:   And keep the home fires burning and all that, Sister, you know. (*Embarrassed*) You know what I mean.

BRIGID MARY:   Yes, I know.

FOURTH BED:   He means keep up the good work and all that.

BRIGID MARY:   Yes, thank you, Sergeant.

> *They all stand in a row, rather stupidly, not knowing quite how to take leave of her. Brigid Mary looks from one face to another. When she comes to number two, he speaks haltingly.*

SECOND BED:   Uh . . . Sister, is it all right—that is, uh, are you allowed to shake 'ands with Protestants?

BRIGID MARY (*smiles*):   I bathed you for nearly six months, Sergeant Peale. I don't think shaking you by the hand is liable to corrupt me.

237

> *The others laugh. Second bed blushes, steps forward sheepishly, shakes her hand.*

SECOND BED:   Goodbye, Sister.

BRIGID MARY:   Goodbye, Sergeant.

> *The others follow suit, each passing out into the corridor after he has briefly shaken her hand.*

FOURTH BED:   Goodbye, Sister.

BRIGID MARY:   Goodbye.

THIRD BED:   Goodbye, Sister.

BRIGID MARY:   Goodbye.

FIRST BED:   Give 'em hell, Sister.

BRIGID MARY:   I shall try to do the opposite of that, Corporal. Godspeed. I hope you learned some Irish songs while you were here.

*He grins, sings in a spirited voice, affecting a brogue, to the tune of "The Rocks of Bawn."*

FIRST BED:  "My curse attend you, Sweeney, you have me nearly robbed . . ." (*He salutes and goes out, still singing and marching with a jaunty, strutting step.*) "You're sittin' by the fireside with your *duidin* in your gob . . ."

*Brigid Mary watches him go. The room, as his singing fades, grows very quiet. Slowly, Brigid Mary turns to face Kenneth. There is a long pause.*

KENNETH:  I behaved very badly the other day. I'm sorry. I apologize.

BRIGID MARY:  Ah, no, please—it's all right.

KENNETH:  I was full of resentment and . . . anger. I wanted to strike out at you. I wanted to hurt you back. That was childish. I don't feel like that any more. I'm not angry or resentful any more. I suppose if I'm honest I must admit I still feel a bit envious. That's funny, isn't it? Perhaps I never loved you at all. Perhaps it was only envy. Because you have something . . . extraordinary. I haven't anything like that. Of course I hadn't anything before, either, but the point is that now I *want* something and I won't stop looking until I find it. You see, you *have* worked a change in me. Now you can write me off as one of your successes. One of your first.

BRIGID MARY:  Kenneth, please.

KENNETH:  I'm still trying to hurt you a little. I can't seem to stop. I have no excuse now except that I have to say goodbye to you and I don't know how. I can't.

BRIGID MARY:  Oh, Ken . . .

KENNETH:  Will you say goodbye to *me*?

*Brigid Mary looks at him for a moment, then lowers her head.*

KENNETH:  Well, Sister?

*She raises her face to him. Her eyes well with tears.*

KENNETH:  Oh, God, I never meant to make you weep. (*Very simply*) I do love you so terribly.

BRIGID MARY:  Dear Kenneth . . .

KENNETH:  You keep saying my name. This is like some awful dream. I can't . . . (*He breaks off, touches his hand to his head confusedly.*) I feel I have something vitally important to tell you, and I can't think what it is. I shall never see you again. I mustn't leave it unsaid. (*She is too moved to help him. He smiles wryly.*) What a time for *me* to run out of *words*. (*He picks up his bag.*) I'm going now. I don't want to shake hands or anything of that sort. But you must know that in my heart, I kiss your mouth most humbly and gratefully.

> *He looks at her a moment longer, then goes quickly past her and out of the room. Brigid Mary stands rigidly looking at the place where he has stood, not turning. Then she looks down, sees that he has failed to turn his mattress. Slowly she bends and doubles it over toward the head of the bed. As she straightens up, Sister Martha Kevin appears in the doorway behind her.*

SISTER MARTHA KEVIN:   Are they all out?

BRIGID MARY:   All out.

> *Looking from right to left, inspecting cursorily, Sister Martha Kevin crosses down the aisle toward the window.*

SISTER MARTHA KEVIN:   Will you see that everything is in order in this room, Sister?

BRIGID MARY:   I will, yes.

SISTER MARTHA KEVIN:   There's a car waiting will take us back to the chapter house.

BRIGID MARY:   I'll be along in a moment, so.

> *The window is ajar. Sister Martha Kevin closes it, looks up.*

SISTER MARTHA KEVIN:   Will you look at that now? (*Brigid Mary remains motionless.*) It's scarcely onto half-four, and there's a little moon there in the afternoon sky. (*Brigid Mary lifts a surprised, nostalgic face.*) Is it any word you've had of your new assignment, Sister?

BRIGID MARY:   No, not yet. I'm hoping . . . to work with children.

SISTER MARTHA KEVIN:   You won't forget to see the shutters are closed?

BRIGID MARY:   No, Sister.

> *Sister Martha Kevin moves on down the corridor, out of sight. Brigid Mary crosses to the window, opens it. A cold wind tosses her cornette as she reaches outside to draw the louvered shutters closed. She looks up at the sky, at the premature moon. She then shuts the window.*

239

*Light filters through the panels of the shutters, falling at an almost horizontal angle into the room. Brigid Mary turns and we see the room from her angle, dim and deserted, regimented beds and rolled mattresses standing like sentinels. The calendar on the wall hangs lopsided, still showing the date, January 7, 1922, circled in red. The voice of the boy at the beginning is heard singing off-scene.*

BOY'S VOICE:   "Come all you loyal heroes, wherever that you be. Don't hire with any master till you know what your work will be."

*The camera holds as Brigid Mary begins walking toward the door. The camera moves up as her diminishing figure passes out through the open door.*

BOY'S VOICE:   "For you must rise up early, from the clear daylight till dawn, or I'm afraid you'll never be able to plow the rocks of Bawn."

FADE OUT.

A: I thought the play was sad, but it left me with a good feeling. I'm not sure I know why.

B: Well, I'm not sure that I agree entirely with Brigid Mary's decision.

# HOPE

*Emily Dickinson*

Hope is the thing with feathers
That perches in the soul,
And sings the tune without the words,
And never stops at all,

And sweetest in the gale is heard;
And sore must be the storm
That could abash the little bird
That kept so many warm.

I've heard it in the chillest land,
And on the strangest sea;
Yet, never, in extremity,
It asked a crumb of me.

242

# THE FROST

## Tzu Yeh

*Young man,*
*Seize every minute*
*Of your time.*
*The days fly by;*
*Ere long you too*
*Will grow old.*

*If you believe me not,*
*See there, in the courtyard,*
*How the frost*
*Glitters white and cold and cruel*
*On the grass*
*That once was green.*

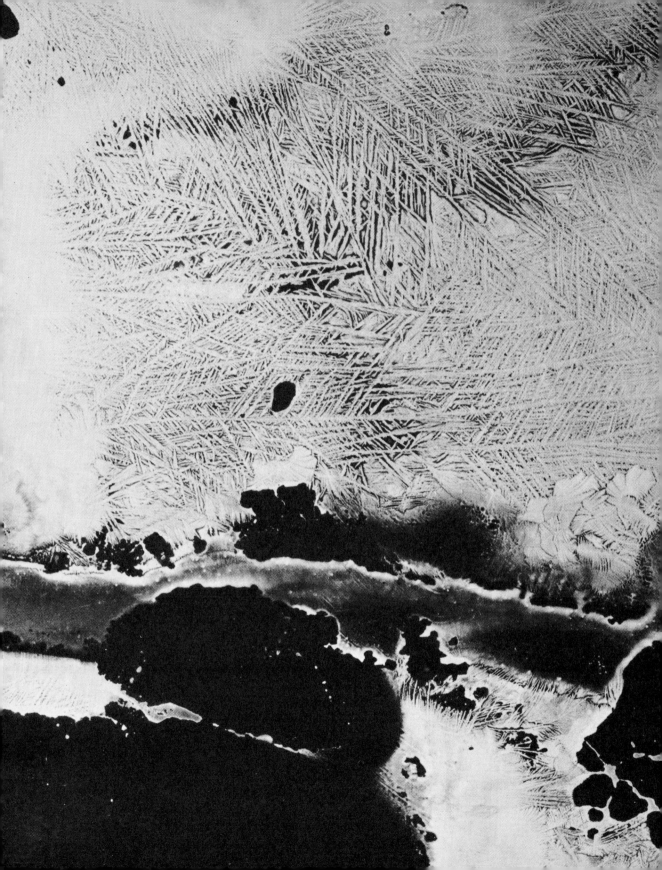

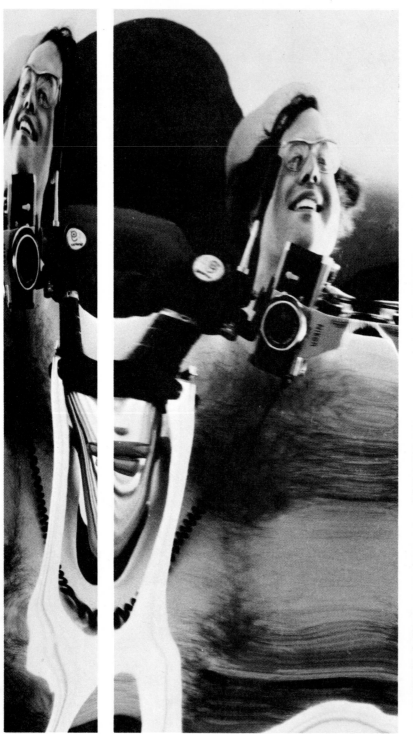

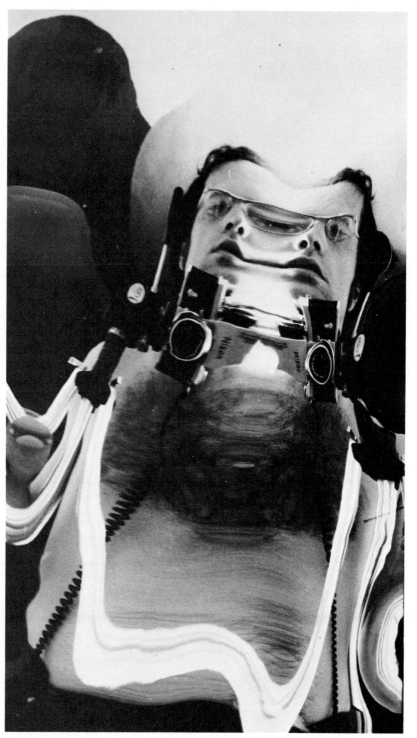

8

# The Hut of the Man Alone

### *Donald Hall*

Jerome had lived alone for thirty years.
Last winter, hunting in a freezing spell,
We found him huddled frozen at his well,
Bent double at the rocky lip of it,
As if he stared for something through the tears
That hardened on his beard and looked like sweat.

We took him home. What was it that we sensed?
I hacked the lock to open the black hut
The man alone had managed to keep shut.
I felt, of course, like some damned interferer.
The winter sun bent in, and caught against
The shattered pieces of a wall of mirror.

246

# earl

Andrew Glaze

*He was twenty. He was half crazy.*
*With his head like a half-baffled chocolate easter egg,*
*there he was painting my house in Birmingham Alabama*
*doing things backwards,*
*painting from the bottom up*
*so the new paint from above*
*ran down on the new paint below,*
*putting turpentine in the water colors.*
*He always jumped from the back-porch roof*
*to the ground—fourteen feet.*                          10
*—I used to be a paratrooper, said Earl—*
*I came down in the war with Russia*
*shooting a submachine gun around me in circles,*
*nobody had a chance to get a bead on me—*
*I shot them first. They thought*
*I was the holy, iron-assed, frosted bird.*
*I won the war—*

*The top of the house was fifty feet in the air.*
*The ladder was forty.*
*Earl fastened the ladder to the gutter.*                20
*He nailed a two by four with wooden cleats*
*to the top of the ladder.*
*He nailed a paintbrush to a broom.*
*He climbed and sat up on the top of them all.*
*He looked like a man just out of a fountain spray*
*of white paint. He waved the paintbrush*
*over his head like a banner on top of the broom.*
*He yelled out over the roofs of Birmingham Alabama*
*—look at me up here—*
*Look at me! Anybody want to argue?—*                    30

247

248

# The Death of the Hired Man

*Robert Frost*

Mary sat musing on the lamp flame at the table,
Waiting for Warren. When she heard his step,
She ran on tiptoe down the darkened passage
To meet him in the doorway with the news
And put him on his guard. "Silas is back."
She pushed him outward with her through the door
And shut it after her. "Be kind," she said.
She took the market things from Warren's arms
And set them on the porch, then drew him down
To sit beside her on the wooden steps.                    10

"When was I ever anything but kind to him?
But I'll not have the fellow back," he said.
"I told him so last haying, didn't I?
'If he left then,' I said, 'that ended it.'
What good is he? Who else will harbor him
At his age for the little he can do?
What help he is there's no depending on.
Off he goes always when I need him most.
He thinks he ought to earn a little pay,
Enough at least to buy tobacco with,                      20
So he won't have to 'beg and be beholden.'
'All right,' I say, 'I can't afford to pay
Any fixed wages, though I wish I could.'
'Someone else can.' 'Then someone else will have to.'
I shouldn't mind his bettering himself
If that was what it was. You can be certain,
When he begins like that, there's someone at him
Trying to coax him off with pocket money—
In haying time, when any help is scarce.
In winter he comes back to us. I'm done."                 30

From THE POETRY OF ROBERT FROST edited by Edward Connery Lathem.
Copyright 1930, 1939, © 1969 by Holt, Rinehart and Winston, Inc. Copyright
© 1958 by Robert Frost. Copyright © 1967 by Lesley Frost Ballantine. Reprinted
by permission of Holt, Rinehart and Winston, Inc., the Estate of Robert Frost,
and Jonathan Cape Ltd.

"Sh! not so loud: he'll hear you," Mary said.

"I want him to: he'll have to soon or late."

"He's worn out. He's asleep beside the stove.
When I came up from Rowe's I found him here,
Huddled against the barn door fast asleep,
A miserable sight, and frightening, too—
You needn't smile—I didn't recognize him—
I wasn't looking for him—and he's changed.
Wait till you see."

     "Where did you say he'd been?"    40

"He didn't say. I dragged him to the house,
And gave him tea, and tried to make him smoke.
I tried to make him talk about his travels.
Nothing would do: he just kept nodding off."

"What did he say? Did he say anything?"

"But little."

    "Anything? Mary, confess
He said he'd come to ditch the meadow for me."

"Warren!"

     "But did he? I just want to know."    50

"Of course he did. What would you have him say?
Surely you wouldn't grudge the poor old man
Some humble way to save his self-respect.
He added, if you really care to know,
He meant to clear the upper pasture, too.
That sounds like something you have heard before?
Warren, I wish you could have heard the way
He jumbled everything. I stopped to look
Two or three times—he made me feel so queer—
To see if he was talking in his sleep.    60
He ran on Harold Wilson—you remember—
The boy you had in haying four years since.
He's finished school, and teaching in his college.
Silas declares you'll have to get him back.

He says they two will make a team for work:
Between them they will lay this farm as smooth!
The way he mixed that in with other things.
He thinks young Wilson a likely lad, though daft
On education—you know how they fought
All through July under the blazing sun,                    70
Silas up on the cart to build the load,
Harold along beside to pitch it on."

"Yes, I took care to keep well out of earshot."

"Well, those days trouble Silas like a dream.
You wouldn't think they would. How some things linger!
Harold's young college boy's assurance piqued him.
After so many years he still keeps finding
Good arguments he sees he might have used.
I sympathize. I know just how it feels
To think of the right thing to say too late.          80
Harold's associated in his mind with Latin.
He asked me what I thought of Harold's saying
He studied Latin like the violin
Because he liked it—that an argument!
He said he couldn't make the boy believe
He could find water with a hazel prong—
Which showed how much good school had ever done him.
He wanted to go over that. But most of all
He thinks if he could have another chance
To teach him how to build a load of hay—"          90

"I know, that's Silas' one accomplishment.
He bundles every forkful in its place,
And tags and numbers it for future reference,
So he can find and easily dislodge it
In the unloading. Silas does that well.
He takes it out in bunches like big birds' nests.
You never see him standing on the hay
He's trying to lift, straining to lift himself."

"He thinks if he could teach him that, he'd be
Some good perhaps to someone in the world.          100
He hates to see a boy the fool of books.
Poor Silas, so concerned for other folk,
And nothing to look backward to with pride,
And nothing to look forward to with hope,
So now and never any different."

251

Part of a moon was falling down the west,
Dragging the whole sky with it to the hills.
Its light poured softly in her lap. She saw
And spread her apron to it. She put out her hand
Among the harplike morning-glory strings,                          110
Taut with the dew from garden bed to eaves,
As if she played unheard the tenderness
That wrought on him beside her in the night.
"Warren," she said, "he has come home to die:
You needn't be afraid he'll leave you this time."

"Home," he mocked gently.

                              "Yes, what else but home?
It all depends on what you mean by home.
Of course he's nothing to us, any more
Than was the hound that came a stranger to us                      120
Out of the woods, worn out upon the trail."

"Home is the place where, when you have to go there,
They have to take you in."

                              "I should have called it
Something you somehow haven't to deserve."

Warren leaned out and took a step or two,
Picked up a little stick, and brought it back
And broke it in his hand and tossed it by.
"Silas has better claim on us, you think,
Than on his brother? Thirteen little miles                          130
As the road winds would bring him to his door.
Silas has walked that far no doubt today.
Why didn't he go there? His brother's rich,
A somebody—director in the bank."

"He never told us that."

                              "We know it though."

"I think his brother ought to help, of course.
I'll see to that if there is need. He ought of right
To take him in, and might be willing to—
He may be better than appearances.                                  140
But have some pity on Silas. Do you think
If he'd had any pride in claiming kin
Or anything he looked for from his brother,
He'd keep so still about him all this time?"

"I wonder what's between them."

"I can tell you.
Silas is what he is—we wouldn't mind him—
But just the kind that kinsfolk can't abide.
He never did a thing so very bad.
He don't know why he isn't quite as good                          150
As anyone. He won't be made ashamed
To please his brother, worthless though he is."

"*I* can't think Si ever hurt anyone."

"No, but he hurt my heart the way he lay
And rolled his old head on that sharp-edged chair back.
He wouldn't let me put him on the lounge.
You must go in and see what you can do.
I made the bed up for him there tonight.
You'll be surprised at him—how much he's broken.
His working days are done; I'm sure of it."                        160

"I'd not be in a hurry to say that."

"I haven't been. Go, look, see for yourself.
But, Warren, please remember how it is:
He's come to help you ditch the meadow.
He has a plan. You mustn't laugh at him.
He may not speak of it, and then he may.
I'll sit and see if that small sailing cloud
Will hit or miss the moon."

                         It hit the moon.
Then there were three, making a dim row,                           170
The moon, the little silver cloud, and she.

Warren returned—too soon, it seemed to her,
Slipped to her side, caught up her hand and waited.

"Warren?" she questioned.

                    "Dead," was all he answered.

253

# it really must/be Nice . . .

## e. e. cummings

*it really must*
*be Nice, never to*

*have no imagination)or never*
*never to wonder about guys you used to(and them*
*slim hot queens with dam next to nothing*

*on)tangoing*
*(while a feller tries*
*to hold down the fifty bucks per*
*job with one foot and rock a*

254

*cradle with the other)it Must be*  10
*nice never to have no doubts about why you*
*put the ring*
*on(and watching her*
*face grow old and tired to which*

*you're married and hands get red washing*
*things and dishes)and to never, never really wonder i*
*mean about the smell*
*of babies and how you*

*know the dam rent's going to and everything and never, never*
*Never to stand at no window*
*because i can't sleep(smoking sawdust*  20

*cigarettes in the*
*middle of the night*

# The Good Samaritan

*from St. Luke 10: 25–36*

And, behold, a certain lawyer stood up, and tempted him, saying, "Master, what shall I do to inherit eternal life?"

He said unto him, "What is written in the law? How readest thou?"

And he answering said, "Thou shalt love the Lord thy God with all thy heart, and with all thy soul, and with all thy strength, and with all thy mind; and thy neighbor as thyself."

And he said unto him, "Thou hast answered right; this do, and thou shalt live."

But he, willing to justify himself, said unto Jesus, "And who is my neighbor?"

And Jesus answering said, "A certain man went down from Jerusalem to Jericho, and fell among thieves, which stripped him of his raiment, and wounded him, and departed, leaving him half dead.

And by chance there came down a certain priest that way: and when he saw him, he passed by on the other side.

And likewise a Levite, when he was at the place, came and looked on him, and passed by on the other side.

But a certain Samaritan, as he journeyed, came where he was: and when he saw him, he had compassion on him.

And went to him, and bound up his wounds, pouring in oil and wine, and set him on his own beast, and brought him to an inn, and took care of him.

And on the morrow when he departed, he took out two pence and gave them to the host, and said unto him, 'Take care of him; and whatsoever thou spendest more, when I come again, I will repay thee.'

Which now of these three, thinkest thou, was neighbor unto him that fell among the thieves?"

# The Accident

Jesse Stuart

"How would you like to go for a ride with your Aunt Effie and me?" Uncle Jad said. "It's a nice Sunday afternoon and we won't have many more such days before snow falls."

Uncle Jad Higgins ran the Ranceburg Men's Clothing Store in Ranceburg. He had inherited this store from his father, and there was a sign above the door which read: SEVENTY-SEVEN YEARS IN BUSINESS. The Higginses were without posterity, and I was Uncle Jad's sister's son; it was understood that I would take over the store someday after Uncle Jad retired or was deceased. Since my father was a farmer, Uncle Jad had invited me to live with him and Aunt Effie while learning the business from A to Z, and of course I couldn't let an opportunity like that pass. Naturally, if Uncle Jad asked me to do something, I did it. If he wanted me to take a drive with him and Aunt Effie on a sunny fall afternoon, I went along. I'd seen enough of the Lantern County hills to do me a lifetime, but if they wanted me with them, then that was all right with me.

"It's a nice idea to take a drive, Uncle Jad," I said. "You are so right. We won't have many more afternoons as pretty and as sunny as this one."

"Yes, and your Aunt Effie and I have seen more seasons—winters, springs, summers, autumns—than we will ever see again," he said. "The years take their toll. But it's always nice just to get out and drive around."

"You want me to drive so you and Aunt Effie can relax and look at the countryside?" I asked.

"No, Tom, I'd rather have my own hands on the steering wheel," he said. "You know I have faith in you. But this is just my nature. I've never had a wreck in my life. And I've been driving since I was sixteen."

Aunt Effie came into the room dressed like she was going to church. Aunt Effie was a big woman, with twinkling blue eyes. She was always smiling and she always had something to say. She dressed in the latest style, wearing big hats and dresses with frills and laces. No wonder Uncle Jad and Aunt Effie were considered the best-dressed couple in Lantern County. They spent a lot of money for clothes, and took plenty of time getting properly dressed for an occasion. Uncle Jad warned me about wearing the right clothes when I took over his store after he was gone. He said I'd be selling men's clothes, and young men would be watching what I wore, so I'd have to be a living example of the well-dressed man. Uncle Jad was himself a living example of the well-dressed man in Lantern County.

Uncle Jad was not tall, and he was big around the middle and little

256

on each end, which made him hard to fit, but he wore the kind of clothes that made him look good. He wore small hats with broad brims, and pinstripe suits to give him height. On this particular fall Sunday afternoon he wore a pair of gloves, not because he'd need them in the car, but just to accent the positive. He never missed a trick when it came to wearing clothes or selling them. He wouldn't wear a pair of shoes out of his own house onto the porch unless they were shined.

"Effie, you look real well," Uncle Jad said. "You look real nice in that blue suit and that white blouse with the lace collar. It's most appropriate for early winter wear."

"Well, Poppie, *you* look wonderful," she complimented him. "Yes, I've got the most handsome man in Lantern County." She pulled him over to her and kissed him. She was always very affectionate with Uncle Jad.

Well, they were telling each other the truth with their compliments, I thought as they walked toward the garage. I got ahead of them and raised the garage door. Then Uncle Jad opened the car door for Aunt Effie and, after she got in, pushed the door shut gently behind her. Then he walked around to the other side, got in, started the engine, and backed the car out. He waited for me to pull the garage door back down and get in the back seat. This was our regular routine.

"Well, which way shall we go, Mother?" he asked Aunt Effie.

"Let's drive up Kinney Creek Valley and over to Taysville," she replied quickly. Aunt Effie always knew where she wanted to go. All Uncle Jad

had to do, if he was undecided, was to ask. She could soon make a decision.

"Then up Kinney Valley and over to Taysville we will go," Uncle Jad said.

"The valley will be beautiful this time of year," I said. "I am glad, Aunt Effie, that you have chosen this route. There'll still be autumn leaves on many of the oaks."

"You are so right," Aunt Effie said.

Uncle Jad drove slowly and carefully down the street. When he came to the railway crossing at the edge of Ranceburg, he stopped and looked carefully this way and that, though he could see for a mile either up or down the tracks.

"It always pays to be careful," he said. "Never had a wreck or hit a person. I can certainly boast of my record."

"I've not been driving very long, Uncle Jad," I said. "But I've never hit a person or had a wreck either."

"You're a careful young man, Tom," he said. "That is why I'm turning everything over to you someday. You're a lot like my father and me. By looks and by nature you could well have been my son!"

"Thank you, Uncle Jad," I said.

"I've got security in life," he said. "Mother and I could live to the end of our days without my working anymore. Mother and I have had a good life. We go to our church, vote for our party, belong to a few organizations. We are somebody in Ranceburg now, and remember, Tom, it *pays* in this life to be somebody. So be a somebody when your Aunt Effie and I are no longer around. Marry a nice woman. Drive a nice car and wear good clothes. Make your life a safe adventure."

We were in Kinney Valley now. There had been a few killing frosts, and the grass on the pasture fields was brown, but the oaks in the wooded areas were still filled with multicolored leaves. As we passed farmhouse after farmhouse, Uncle Jad called out the name of the man who lived there, and told how many sons he had and if they traded at the store. Uncle Jad also mentioned which men he had to ask for cash, and which could be trusted to buy now and pay later.

There were green areas on the Kinney Valley bottoms where winter wheat had been sown. When the wind swept through the valley, the wheat bent and rose up again after the wind had passed. The sun was bright, and when a crow flew over, though we didn't always see the crow, we could tell where he was flying by his shadow on the brown grass of the fields.

"Life is just so wonderful, Poppie," Aunt Effie said with enthusiasm. And she put her arm around Uncle Jad's neck, pulled him over, and kissed his cheek.

"Do be careful, Mother," Uncle Jad said. "You could cause me to have my first wreck." Actually, he liked for her to do him this way. He was just pretending that it could be dangerous.

"Yes, I have a fine automobile, fine store, fine home, prettiest wife in Ranceburg," Uncle Jad said. "When a man gets old enough to have security and enjoy life, the tragedy is he's about old enough to die and leave this world. Not a very pleasant thought, but how true it is!"

If life could shape up for me, I thought, like it had shaped up for Uncle Jad and Aunt Effie, then I'd be a happy man. They had everything they wanted. They had security. And they would go to the end of their days like this!

"Look out, Poppie!" Aunt Effie screamed, and covered her face with her hands. Uncle Jad slammed on the brakes. The car skidded, tires squealed, and there was a thud. I saw a man fly up and hit a tree.

"Where did he come from?" Uncle Jad said. "I didn't see him until he was in front of the car."

"I saw just as you hit him!" I shouted.

258

"I wonder if I killed him," Uncle Jad said. His face was extremely white. He had lost that redness of color that made his cheeks pink. He sat with his hands on the steering wheel, looking out of the car at the man who lay at the foot of a large oak close to the highway.

"Oh, Poppie!" Aunt Effie wailed. She kept her hands over her face. "We bragged too soon! Life has been too good. We couldn't go on until the end with all this good fortune we have been having."

"He's not dead," Uncle Jad said. "He's trying to raise his head up to see what has happened. He's looking at the car. The poor fellow is looking at me! He's looking at me and trying to smile."

When Uncle Jad got out of the car, I got out with him.

"I never saw you," Uncle Jad told the man. "I'm sorry. How bad are you hurt?"

"I don't know," he answered softly. "Lift me upon my feet."

Uncle Jad got on one side and I got on the other, and we lifted him up. The man put his arms around our shoulders.

"See if you can bear your weight," Uncle Jad said.

The man tried one foot and then the other, and took two steps.

"Thank God!" Uncle Jad said. "No broken legs."

"It knocked the wind from me," the man said. "It jarred me to my foundations!"

Well, I knew that the big car had done that much and more too. The man had hit the side of the tree about six feet up and then fallen to the ground in a crumpled mass of humanity. Such a lick should have killed him outright.

"And what's your name?" Uncle Jad asked.

"Mort Simmons." He sighed softly. "I'm John Simmons' boy."

He was a less-than-average-sized man who looked like he weighed about one hundred and thirty pounds. He was wearing a work shirt and jeans, and brush-scarred brogan shoes without socks. His face was unshaven, with a growth of stubbly black beard.

"And where do you live?" Uncle Jad asked.

"On Shelf's Fork of Kinney."

"I thought I knew about everybody in Lantern County," Uncle Jad said, "but I'm sorry to say I don't know you or your father. Have you ever traded in my store in Ranceburg?"

"No, but I will in the future," the man replied.

"Poppie, let's take him to Doctor Raike and have him checked," Aunt Effie said.

"Not a bad idea, Mother," Uncle Jad said, and sighed.

We helped Mort Simmons to the car. When we took his arms from around our shoulders, he stood up all right, and although we helped him to get on the rear seat, I think he could have done it by himself.

"I feel much better," he said.

"What about going back to Ranceburg with us and letting Doctor Raike see you before we take you home?" Uncle Jad asked him.

"That will be all right," He said. "Yes, I'd like to go see how bad I'm hurt."

"You watch over him now, Tom," Uncle Jad told me. "If he gets dizzy he might just pitch over! Watch him!"

"I will, Uncle Jad," I said as I got in the car. "Don't you worry!"

"No, I've got a lot to worry about now," he said.

Aunt Effie, who couldn't stand much excitement, was trembling like a leaf on a November oak. Uncle Jad was still pale, and his hands shook so on the steering wheel that the car swerved back and forth. But there was very little traffic on the country roads this time of year, and we made it safely back to Dr. Raike's office in Ranceburg.

"I'm glad you are here, Doctor Raike," Uncle Jad said. "I hit this man and knocked him upon the side of an oak tree. I never saw him until my car hit him. Seems like he just came up out of the ground. Mort Simmons. You ever have him for a patient before?"

"Can't say that I have," Dr. Raike said. "No, I don't know that name Simmons in Lantern County."

Dr. Raike, who was almost as old as my Uncle Jad, was a little man with blue eyes and a kind face. He had once had golden blond hair, but time had turned it white.

"I'm John Simmons' boy, and we live on Shelf's Fork of Kinney Valley," Mort Simmons said.

"Well, I wouldn't know all the people who live on Kinney Valley anymore," Dr. Raike said. "Now, let me see about you."

Dr. Raike went over Mort Simmons' head and arms and legs. Then he had Mort strip off his shirt so that his back could be examined.

"You've been shaken up," Dr. Raike said, "and you've got a lot of minor bruises. But you don't have any broken bones. I can release you, all right."

"Doc, how much do I owe you?" Uncle Jad asked.

"Not anything, Jad," Dr. Raike said. "Glad to do it. I hope everything will be all right for you."

"Thank you, Doc," Uncle Jad said, with a worried look.

Mort Simmons walked out of the office under his own power, though he limped and moved his legs very stiffly, and Uncle Jad wasn't as nervous on the drive back to Kinney Valley as he had been when he drove Mort in to Ranceburg. He had more self-composure.

"Let me out here," Mort Simmons said at last. "You can't drive up Shelf's Fork. The road is too bad. I don't want you to hurt your fine car."

"Sure you can make it all right?" Uncle Jad asked. "I'll try to take you on. I don't mind hurting my car."

"I can make it," Mort Simmons said. "Thank you for taking me to the doctor, and thank you for bringing me back."

"I'm so sorry this happened," Uncle Jad said. "I truly am."

Mort Simmons smiled and walked up a narrow little slit of a road alongside a small stream. Uncle Jad drove back toward Ranceburg.

"Well, Mother, our pleasant Sunday afternoon didn't turn out too well," he said. "It seems like I've dreamed what has happened! But when I wake up in the morning, I'll know it *did* happen. We might be sued for everything we have.

We might not have any more security in this life."

"See John as soon as we get back," Aunt Effie said.

"John Lovell is a good lawyer," Uncle Jad said. "I'm glad we have him."

He asked Aunt Effie and me if either of us had seen where Mort Simmons came from at the time of the accident, and we said we never saw him until he was in front of the car and it was making contact with his body.

"I'd just climbed a rise," Uncle Jad said. "I wasn't going fast. If I had been going fast, he wouldn't have known what struck him. I am a lucky man."

"It's worked out for the best," Aunt Effie said. "I believe what is to be will be."

That evening Uncle Jad told John Lovell what had happened and how it had happened. John Lovell said that one bit of luck Uncle Jad would have if he were sued was that he would have two witnesses while Mort Simmons would only have himself. Uncle Jad told John Lovell how pleasant the man was and about his good manners. He told how Mort Simmons had been thankful for being taken to Dr. Raike and examined, and for being brought back to the Shelf's Fork road that led to his home. But John Lovell admonished Uncle Jad that Mort Simmons might nevertheless be thinking he had a good chance to sue, for everybody in Lantern Valley was pretty sure Uncle Jad had plenty of money.

When Uncle Jad came back from the lawyer's house, he told Aunt Effie about how he had been warned, and that night he was so worried he had to take medicine to put himself to sleep. The next morning he said to Aunt Effie, "Mother, yesterday is still a bad dream."

"I can't believe it either," she said. "But all three of us know that it *did* happen."

After breakfast Uncle Jad and I walked to the store, only two blocks away. We always opened at seven to catch the early morning trade of men on their way to work. It didn't seem like anything special was going to happen that day, but that afternoon I looked out of the office at the back of the store and saw Mort Simmons looking at some shirts. "See what he wants," Uncle Jad said when I told him. "I'll stay out of the way. I think I know what he wants. He wants to know more about this business before he sues me."

I went out to Mort Simmons and said with a smile, "Good afternoon." He smiled and said, "Howdy." Then he said, "I've come for some work shirts. We've been working in the tobacco, and I've got glue from the tobacco on all my shirts. I want a couple of clean shirts to go against my body. But I can't pay you until tomorrow. Our tobacco sells today in Taysville, and Pa will fetch the money home. So I'll pay you tomorrow, if that will be all right?"

"It will be all right," I said.

I knew Uncle Jad was in the back listening, and I knew he wouldn't want me to contrary Mort Simmons. I hoped I was doing things the right way, and decided that I would make the debt good if it didn't get paid.

I showed Mort Simmons all the work shirts we had, and he ended up buying two, size fifteen with a thirty-two-inch sleeve length. He smiled when he left, and I smiled and thanked him for purchasing in this store. When Mort Simmons was gone, Uncle Jad came out of the little office where he had kept himself hidden.

"You played it just right," he said. "You are a good diplomat, Tom! I feel sure he's going to sue, but it doesn't hurt to soften him up. We've let him know how friendly we are. We have built our business here because the people know we are friendly and reliable. We serve the public! And this will be the first time a Higgins has ever been sued. My father before me, Abraham Higgins, was never sued. And I have never been sued."

"I can't figure that man out," I said.

"Well, I can't either," Uncle Jad said. "But I don't think he will be back to pay for the shirts. I think this is the last time we will see him before he sues me. The friendly man that looks at you and smiles and asks some little favor, that is the man who will sue you quicker than you can bat your eye."

At home that evening we told Aunt Effie what had happened, and Aunt Effie, who had always been good at judging people, said she didn't know what to think. She said she was puzzled.

The next day went along very quietly until the early afternoon. I was restacking some shirts when I turned around, and there stood Mort Simmons again. I looked back and saw Uncle Jad scurrying into his office.

"Pa is here with me," Mort Simmons said. "And four of my brothers have come too."

I thought I was going to sink through the floor! His father and his brothers! They had come for Uncle Jad and me! It ran through my mind that this was the way with the people who lived among the high hills and in the deep hollows. Do something to one, even if it is an accident, and his blood kin will never stop harassing you as long as you live. Uncle Jad and I were in a lot of trouble!

"We've come to get some orders filled," Mort Simmons said. "It's shoe and clothes time before real winter sets in."

"All right," I said.

"Come and meet Mr. John Simmons, my pa, and my four brothers," he said.

I said hello to the five big men standing over by the door. And then I filled the biggest order I had ever filled for one family since I came to work in Uncle Jad's store. They took two pairs of shoes each; they took socks, underwear, handkerchiefs, work pants, work shirts and Sunday shirts. And all five brothers picked out suits. I handed out almost five hundred dollars' worth of clothes and shoes, and I was sure there would be no mention of paying till Mort Simmons got through suing Uncle Jad.

After they had everything, John Simmons said to me, "Where is your uncle? I would like to see him."

Here it comes, I thought. I knew that Uncle Jad couldn't run from trouble. He would have to meet this Simmons family and tell them he had an attorney to represent him. They would have to consult his attorney. Or his attorney could talk to them.

I went back to the office and told Uncle Jad that John Simmons and his sons were asking for him, and that they had ordered almost five hundred dollars' worth of merchandise. Uncle Jad's face lost its color just like it had when his car hit Mort Simmons and flung him upon the side of the big oak.

"Guess I'll have to go and face them," he said. "You with me, Tom?"

"Of course," I said.

We went back to where the Simmonses were standing with bundles of merchandise in their arms, and more bundles around them on the floor. Uncle Jad was shaking. His lips were twitching nervously, and he kept jerking his head.

"Mr. Higgins, I wanted to meet you," John Simmons said. "You are a fine man. That's the reason my son Mort was in here yesterday. And that's why I brought my other sons here today to get new Sunday suits and winter clothes and shoes."

"Thank you, Mr. Simmons," Uncle Jad stammered. He couldn't understand why he was being called a fine man.

"We've got our tobacco money now," John Simmons said. "No charging anything. Here is what we owe you, including the cost of those shirts Mort bought yesterday."

Uncle Jad and I stood there, so surprised we couldn't speak, and John Simmons handed over the money, every cent. "As I have said, Mr.

Higgins," he said, "we know from what happened last Sunday that you are a fine man."

"Last Sunday? You mean the accident?" Uncle Jad was still stammering.

"It was not the kind of accident you mean," John Simmons corrected. "You see, my son Mort has a fault. He's as absentminded as can be, never thinks what he's doing or looks where he is going. I have warned him many times about that fault, but he keeps walking out in front of cars, and he tells me he just can't think why it's so hard for him to remember not to do it. He will be marked by a car one of these days."

Uncle Jad was beginning to recover himself. Color was coming back into his face.

"You see, Mr. Higgins," John Simmons said, "my son Mort has been struck by cars half a dozen times, and you're the only man who ever picked him up, took him to the doctor, and was even nice enough to fetch him back toward his home. I just want you to know that his mother and I appreciate what you did. And buying from you is a good way to thank you. We will be back to your store and trade with you from now on. Thank you."

Uncle Jad and I shook hands with all the Simmonses, and they smiled and we smiled. I have known my Uncle Jad since I was a little boy big enough to remember anything. And I never saw him so happy as he was right then, though he still had a puzzled look on his face.

263

A: You see, there still are some considerate people in the world.

B: But are there enough?

264

*John Updike*

In walks these three girls in nothing but bathing suits. I'm in the
third checkout slot, with my back to the door, so I don't see them until
they're over by the bread. The one that caught my eye first was the one
in the plaid green two-piece. She was a chunky kid, with a good tan
and a sweet broad soft-looking can with those two crescents of white
just under it, where the sun never seems to hit, at the top of the backs
of her legs. I stood there with my hand on a box of HiHo crackers
trying to remember if I rang it up or not. I ring it up again and the
customer starts giving me hell. She's one of these cash-register-watchers,
a witch about fifty with rouge on her cheekbones and no eyebrows, and
I know it made her day to trip me up. She'd been watching cash
registers for fifty years and probably never seen a mistake before.

By the time I got her feathers smoothed and her goodies into a
bag, she gives me a little snort in passing—if she'd been born at the

right time they would have burned her over in Salem—by the time I get her on her way the girls had circled around the bread and were coming back, without a pushcart, back my way along the counters, in the aisle between the checkouts and the Special bins. They didn't even have shoes on. There was this chunky one, with the two-piece—it was bright green and the seams on the bra were still sharp and her belly was still pretty pale so I guessed she just got it (the suit)—there was this one, with one of those chubby berry-faces, the lips all bunched together under her nose, this one, and a tall one, with black hair that hadn't quite frizzed right, and one of these sunburns right across under the eyes, and a chin that was too long—you know, the kind of girl other girls think is very "striking" and "attractive" but never quite makes it, as they very well know, which is why they like her so much—and then the third one, that wasn't quite so tall. She was the queen. She kind of led them, the other two peeking around and making their shoulders round. She didn't look around, not this queen, she just walked straight on slowly, on these long white prima-donna legs. She came down a little hard on her heels, as if she didn't walk in her bare feet that much, putting down her heels and then letting the weight move along to her toes as if she was testing the floor with every step, putting a little deliberate extra action into it. You never know for sure how girls' minds work (do you really think it's a mind in there or just a little buzz like a bee in a glass jar?) but you got the idea she had talked the other two into coming in here with her, and now she was showing them how to do it, walk slow and hold yourself straight.

She had on a kind of dirty-pink—beige maybe, I don't know—bathing suit with a little nubble all over it and, what got me, the straps were down. They were off her shoulders looped loose around the cool tops of her arms, and I guess as a result the suit had slipped a little on her, so all around the top of the cloth there was this shining rim. If it hadn't been there you wouldn't have known there could have been anything whiter than those shoulders. With the straps pushed off, there was nothing between the top of the suit and the top of her head except just *her*, this clean bare plane of the top of her chest down from the shoulder bones like a dented sheet of metal tilted in the light. I mean, it was more than pretty.

She had sort of oaky hair that the sun and salt had bleached, done up in a bun that was unraveling, and a kind of prim face. Walking into the A & P with your straps down, I suppose it's the only kind of face you *can* have. She held her head so high her neck, coming up out of those white shoulders, looked kind of stretched, but I didn't mind. The longer her neck was, the more of her there was.

She must have felt in the corner of her eye me and over my shoulder Stokesie in the second slot watching, but she didn't tip.

Not this queen. She kept her eyes moving across the racks, and stopped, and turned so slow it made my stomach rub the inside of my apron, and buzzed to the other two, who kind of huddled against her for relief, and then they all three of them went up the cat-and-dog-food-breakfast-cereal-macaroni-rice-raisins-seasonings-spreads-spaghetti-soft-drinks-crackers-and-cookies aisle. From the third slot I look straight up this aisle to the meat counter, and I watched them all the way. The fat one with the tan sort of fumbled with the cookies, but on second thought she put the package back. The sheep pushing their carts down the aisle—the girls were walking against the usual traffic (not that we have one-way signs or anything)—were pretty hilarious. You could see them, when Queenie's white shoulders dawned on them, kind of jerk, or hop, or hiccup, but their eyes snapped back to their own baskets and on they pushed. I bet you could set off dynamite in an A & P and the people would by and large keep reaching and checking oatmeal off their lists and muttering "Let me see, there was a third thing, began with A, asparagus, no, ah, yes, applesauce!" or whatever it is they do mutter. But there was no doubt, this jiggled them. A few houseslaves in pin curlers even looked around after pushing their carts past to make sure what they had seen was correct.

You know, it's one thing to have a girl in a bathing suit down on the beach, where what with the glare nobody can look at each other much anyway, and another thing in the cool of the A & P, under the fluorescent lights, against all those stacked packages, with her feet paddling along naked over our checkerboard green-and-cream rubber-tile floor.

"Oh Daddy," Stokesie said beside me. "I feel so faint."

"Darling," I said. "Hold me tight." Stokesie's married, with two babies chalked up on his fuselage already, but as far as I can tell that's the only difference. He's twenty-two, and I was nineteen this April.

"Is it done?" he asks, the responsible married man finding his voice. I forgot to say he thinks he's going to be manager some sunny day, maybe in 1990 when it's called the Great Alexandrov and Petrooshki Tea Company or something.

What he meant was, our town is five miles from a beach, with a big summer colony out on the Point, but we're right in the middle of town, and the women generally put on a shirt or shorts or something before they get out of the car into the street. And anyway these are usually women with six children and varicose veins mapping their legs and nobody, including them, could care less. As I say, we're right in the middle of town, and if you stand at our front doors you can see two banks and the Congregational church and the newspaper store and three real-estate offices and about twenty-seven old freeloaders tearing up Central Street because the sewer broke again. It's not as if we're on the

Cape; we're north of Boston and there's people in this town haven't seen the ocean for twenty years.

The girls had reached the meat counter and were asking McMahon something. He pointed, they pointed, and they shuffled out of sight behind a pyramid of Diet Delight peaches. All that was left for us to see was old McMahon patting his mouth and looking after them sizing up their joints. Poor kids, I began to feel sorry for them, they couldn't help it.

Now here comes the sad part of the story, at least my family says it's sad, but I don't think it's so sad myself. The store's pretty empty, it being Thursday afternoon, so there was nothing much to do except lean on the register and wait for the girls to show up again. The whole store was like a pinball machine and I didn't know which tunnel they'd come out of. After a while they come around out of the far aisle, around the light bulbs, records at discount of the Caribbean Six or Tony Martin Sings or some such gunk you wonder they waste the wax on, sixpacks of candy bars, and plastic toys done up in cellophane that fall apart when a kid looks at them anyway. Around they come, Queenie still leading the way, and holding a little gray jar in her hand. Slots Three through Seven are unmanned and I could see her wondering between Stokes and me, but Stokesie with his usual luck draws an old party in baggy gray pants who stumbles up with four giant cans of pineapple juice (what do these bums *do* with all that pineapple juice? I've often asked myself) so the girls come to me. Queenie puts down the jar and I take it into my fingers icy cold. Kingfish Fancy Herring Snacks in Pure Sour Cream: 49¢. Now her hands are empty, not a ring or a bracelet, bare as God made them, and I wonder where the money's coming from. Still with that prim look she lifts a folded dollar bill out of the hollow at the center of her nubbled pink top. The jar went heavy in my hand. Really, I thought that was so cute.

Then everybody's luck begins to run out. Lengel comes in from haggling with a truck full of cabbages on the lot and is about to scuttle into that door marked MANAGER behind which he hides all day when the girls touch his eye. Lengel's pretty dreary, teaches Sunday school and the rest, but he doesn't miss that much. He comes over and says, "Girls, this isn't the beach."

Queenie blushes, though maybe it's just a brush of sunburn I was noticing for the first time, now that she was so close. "My mother asked me to pick up a jar of herring snacks." Her voice kind of startled me, the way voices do when you see the people first, coming out so flat and dumb yet kind of tony, too, the way it ticked over "pick up" and "snacks." All of a sudden I slid right down her voice into her living room. Her father and the other men were standing around in ice-cream coats and bow ties and the women were in sandals picking up herring snacks on toothpicks off a big glass plate and they were all holding drinks the color of water with olives and sprigs of mint in them. When my parents have somebody over they get lemonade and if it's a real racy affair Schlitz in tall glasses with "They'll Do It Every Time" cartoons stenciled on.

"That's all right," Lengel said. "But this isn't the beach." His repeating this struck me as funny, as if it had just occurred to him, and he had been thinking all these years the A & P was a great big dune and he was the head lifeguard. He didn't like my smiling—as I say he doesn't miss much—but he concentrates on giving the girls that sad Sunday-school-superintendent stare.

Queenie's blush is no sunburn now, and the plump one in plaid, that I liked better from the back—a really sweet can—pipes up, "We weren't doing any shopping. We just came in for the one thing."

"That makes no difference," Lengel tells her, and I could see from the way his eyes went that he hadn't noticed she was wearing a two-piece before. "We want you decently dressed when you come in here."

"We *are* decent," Queenie says suddenly, her lower lip pushing, getting sore now that she remembers her place, a place from which the crowd that runs the A & P must look pretty crummy. Fancy Herring Snacks flashed in her very blue eyes.

"Girls, I don't want to argue with you. After this come in here with your shoulders covered. It's our policy." He turns his back. That's policy for you. Policy is what the kingpins want. What the others want is juvenile delinquency.

All this while, the customers had been showing up with their carts but, you know, sheep, seeing a scene, they had all bunched up on Stokesie, who shook open a paper bag as gently as peeling a peach, not wanting to miss a word. I could feel in the silence everybody getting nervous, most of all Lengel, who asks me, "Sammy, have you rung up their purchase?"

I thought and said "No" but it wasn't about that I was thinking. I go through the punches, 4, 9, GROC, TOT—it's more complicated than you think, and after you do it often enough, it begins to make a little song, that you hear words to, in my case "Hello (*bing*) there, you (*gung*) hap-py pee-pul (*splat*)!"—the *splat* being the drawer flying out. I uncrease the bill, tenderly as you may imagine, it just having come from between the two smoothest scoops of vanilla I had ever known were there, and pass a half and a penny into her narrow pink palm, and nestle the herrings in a bag and twist its neck and hand it over, all the time thinking.

The girls, and who'd blame them, are in a hurry to get out, so I say "I quit" to Lengel quick enough for them to hear, hoping they'll stop and watch me, their unsuspected hero. They keep right on going, into the electric eye; the door flies open and they flicker across the lot to their car, Queenie and Plaid and Big Tall Goony-Goony (not that as raw material she was so bad), leaving me with Lengel and a kink in his eyebrow.

"Did you say something, Sammy?"

"I said I quit."

"I thought you did."

"You didn't have to embarrass them."

"It was they who were embarrassing us."

I started to say something that came out "Fiddle-de-doo." It's a saying of my grandmother's, and I know she would have been pleased.

"I don't think you know what you're saying," Lengel said.

"I know you don't," I said. "But I do." I pull the bow at the back of my apron and start shrugging it off my shoulders. A couple customers that had been heading for my slot begin to knock against each other, like scared pigs in a chute.

Lengel sighs and begins to look very patient and old and gray. He's been a friend of my parents for years. "Sammy, you don't want to do this to your Mom and Dad," he tells me. It's true, I don't. But it seems to me that once you begin a gesture it's fatal not to go through with it. I fold the apron, "Sammy" stitched in red on the pocket, and put it on the counter, and drop the bow tie on top of it. The bow tie is theirs, if you've ever wondered. "You'll feel this for the rest of your life," Lengel says, and I know that's true, too, but remembering how he made that pretty girl blush makes me so scrunchy inside I punch the No Sale tab and the machine whirs "pee-pul" and the drawer splats out. One advantage to this scene taking place in summer, I can follow this up with a clean exit, there's no fumbling around getting your coat and galoshes, I just saunter into the electric eye in my white shirt that my mother ironed the night before, and the door heaves itself open, and outside the sunshine is skating around on the asphalt.

I look around for my girls, but they're gone, of course. There wasn't anybody but some young married screaming with her children about some candy they didn't get by the door of a powder-blue Falcon station wagon. Looking back in the big windows, over the bags of peat moss and aluminum lawn furniture stacked on the pavement, I could see Lengel in my place in the slot, checking the sheep through. His face was dark gray and his back stiff, as if he'd just had an injection of iron, and my stomach kind of fell as I felt how hard the world was going to be to me hereafter.

269

A: I think Sammy did exactly the right thing when he quit his job.

B: Are you kidding? What good did it do him or anybody else?

# You Can't Tell a Man by the Song He Sings

*Philip Roth*

It was in a freshman high school class called "Occupations" that, fifteen years ago, I first met the ex-con, Alberto Pelagutti. The first week my new classmates and I were given "a battery of tests" designed to reveal our skills, deficiencies, tendencies, and psyches. At the end of the week, Mr. Russo, the Occupations teacher, would add the skills, subtract the deficiencies, and tell us what jobs best suited our talents; it was all mysterious but scientific. I remember we first took a "Preference Test": "Which would you prefer to do, this, that, or the other thing . . ." Albie Pelagutti sat one seat behind me and to my left, and while this first day of high school I strolled happily through the test, examining ancient fossils here, defending criminals there, Albie, like the inside of Vesuvius, rose, fell, pitched, tossed, and swelled in his chair. When he finally made a decision, he made it. You could hear his pencil drive the *x* into the column opposite the activity in which he thought it wisest to prefer to engage. His agony reinforced the legend that had preceded him: he was seventeen; had just left Jamesburg Reformatory; this was his third high school, his third freshman year; but now—I heard another *x* driven home—he had decided "to go straight."

Halfway through the hour Mr. Russo left the room. "I'm going for a drink," he said. Russo was forever at pains to let us know what a square-shooter he was and that, unlike other teachers we might have had, he would not go out the front door of the classroom to sneak around to the back door and observe how responsible we were. And sure enough, when he returned after going for a drink, his lips were wet; when he came from the men's room, you could smell the soap on his hands. "Take your time, boys," he said, and the door swung shut behind him.

His black wingtipped shoes beat down the marble corridor and five thick fingers dug into my shoulder. I turned around; it was Pelagutti. "What?" I said. "Number twenty-six," Pelagutti said, "What's the answer?" I gave him the truth: "Anything." Pelagutti rose halfway over his desk and glared at me. He was a hippopotamus, big, black, and smelly; his short sleeves squeezed tight around his monstrous arms as though they were taking his own blood pressure—which at that moment was sky-bound: "What's the answer!" Menaced, I flipped back three pages in my question booklet and reread number twenty-six. "Which would you prefer to do: (1) Attend a World Trade Convention. (2) Pick cherries. (3) Stay with and read to a sick friend. (4) Tinker with automobile engines." I looked blank-faced back to Albie, and shrugged my shoulders. "It doesn't matter—there's no right answer. Anything." He almost rocketed out of his seat. "Don't give me that crap! What's the answer!" Strange heads popped up all over the room—thin-eyed glances, hissing lips, shaming grins—and I realized that any minute Russo, wet-lipped, might come back and my first day in high school I would be caught cheating. I looked again at number twenty-six; then back to Albie; and then propelled—as I always was towards him—by anger, pity, fear, love, vengeance, and an instinct for irony that was at the time delicate as a mallet, I whispered, "Stay and read to a sick friend." The volcano subsided, and Albie and I had met.

We became friends. He remained at my elbow throughout the testing, then throughout lunch, then after school. I learned that Albie, as a youth, had done all the things I, under direction, had not: he had eaten hamburgers in strange diners; he had gone out after cold showers, wet-haired, into winter weather; he had been cruel to animals; he had trafficked with whores; he had stolen, he had been caught, and he had paid. But now he told me, as I unwrapped my lunch in the candy store across from school, "Now, I'm through crappin' around. I'm gettin' an education. I'm gonna—" and I think he picked up the figure from a movie musical he had seen the previous afternoon while the rest of us were in English class—

"I'm gonna put my best foot forward." The following week when Russo read the results of the testing it appeared that Albie's feet were not only moving forward but finding strange, wonderful paths. Russo sat at his desk, piles of tests stacked before him like ammunition, charts and diagrams mounted huge on either side, and delivered our destinies. Albie and I were going to be lawyers.

Of all that Albie confessed to me that first week, one fact in particular fastened on my brain: I soon forgot the town in Sicily where he was born; the occupation of his father (he either made ice or delivered it); the year and model of the cars he had stolen. I did not forget though that Albie had apparently been the star of the Jamesburg Reformatory baseball team. When I was selected by the gym teacher, Mr. Hopper, to captain one of my gym class's softball teams (we played softball until the World Series was over, then switched to touch football), I knew that I had to get Pelagutti on my side. With those arms he could hit the ball a mile.

The day teams were to be selected Albie shuffled back and forth at my side, while in the locker room I changed into my gym uniform—jockstrap, khaki-colored shorts, T-shirt, sweat socks, and sneakers. Albie had already changed: beneath his khaki gym shorts he did not wear a support but retained his lavender undershorts; they hung down three inches below the outer shorts and looked like a long fancy hem. Instead of a T-shirt he wore a sleeveless undershirt; and beneath his high, tar-black sneakers he wore thin black silk socks with slender arrows embroidered up the sides. Naked he might, like some centuries-dead ancestor, have tossed lions to their death in the Collosseum; the outfit, though I didn't tell him, detracted from his dignity.

As we left the locker room and padded through the dark basement corridor and up onto the sunny September playing field, he talked continually, "I didn't play sports when I was a kid, but I played at Jamesburg and baseball came to me like nothing." I nodded my head. "What you think of Pete Reiser?" he asked. "He's a pretty good man," I said. "What you think of Tommy Henrich?" "I don't know," I answered, "he's dependable, I guess." As a Dodger fan I preferred Reiser to the Yankees' Henrich; and besides, my tastes have always been a bit baroque, and Reiser, who repeatedly bounced off outfield walls to save the day for Brooklyn, had won a special trophy in the Cooperstown of my heart. "Yeh," Albie said, "I like all them Yankees."

I didn't have a chance to ask Albie what he meant by that, for Mr. Hopper, bronzed, smiling, erect, was flipping a coin; I looked up, saw the glint in the sun, and I was calling "heads." It landed tails and the other captain had first choice. My heart flopped over when he looked at Albie's arms, but calmed when he passed on and chose first a tall, lean, first-baseman type. Immediately I said, "I'll take Pelagutti." You don't very often see smiles like the one that crossed Albie Pelagutti's face that moment: you would think I had paroled him from a life sentence.

The game began. I played shortstop—left-handed—and batted second; Albie was in center field and, at his wish, batted fourth. Their first man grounded out, me to the first baseman. The next batter hit a high, lofty fly ball to center field. The moment I saw Albie move after it I knew Tommy Henrich and Pete Reiser were only names to him; all he knew about baseball he'd boned up on the night before. While the ball hung in the air, Albie jumped up and down beneath it, his arms raised upward directly above his head; his wrists were glued together, and his two hands flapped open and closed like a butterfly's wings, begging the ball toward them.

"C'mon," he was screaming to the sky, "c'mon you bastard . . ." And his legs bicycle-pumped up and down, up and down. I hope the moment of my death does not take as long as it did for that damn ball to drop. It hung, it hung, Albie cavorting beneath like a Holy Roller. And then it landed, smack into Albie's chest. The runner was rounding second and heading for third while Albie twirled all around, looking, his arms down now, stretched out, as though he were playing ring-around-a-rosy with two invisible children. "Behind you, Pelagutti!" I screamed. He stopped moving. "What?" he called back to me. I ran halfway out to center field. "Behind you—relay it!" And then, as the runner rounded third, I had to stand there defining "relay" to him.

At the end of the first half of the first inning we came to bat behind, 8-0—eight home runs, all relayed in too late by Pelagutti.

Out of a masochistic delight I must describe Albie at the plate: first, he *faced* the pitcher; then, when he swung at the ball—and he did, at every one—it was not to the side but down, as though he were driving a peg into the ground. Don't ask if he was right-handed or left-handed. I don't know.

While we changed out of our gym uniforms I was silent. I boiled as I watched Pelagutti from the corner of my eye. He kicked off those crazy black sneakers and pulled his pink gaucho shirt on over his undershirt—there was still a red spot above the U front of the undershirt where the first fly ball had hit him. Without removing his gym shorts he stuck his feet into his gray trousers—I watched as he hoisted the trousers over the red splotches where ground balls had banged off his shins, past the red splotches where pitched balls had smacked his knee caps and thighs.

Finally I spoke. "Damn you, Pelagutti, you wouldn't know Pete Reiser if you fell over him!" He was stuffing his sneakers into his locker; he didn't answer. I was talking to his mountainous pink shirt back. "Where do you come off telling me you played for that prison team?" He mumbled something. "What?" I said. "I did," he grumbled. . . . He turned and, black-eyed, glared at me: "I did!" "That must've been some team!" I said. We did not speak as we left the locker room. As we passed the gym office on our way up to Occupations, Mr. Hopper looked up from his desk and winked at me. Then he motioned his head at Pelagutti to indicate that he knew I'd picked a lemon, but how could I have expected a bum like Pelagutti to be an All-American boy in the first place? Then Mr. Hopper turned his sun-lamped head back to his desk.

"Now," I said to Pelagutti as we turned at the second floor landing, "now I'm stuck with you for the rest of the term." He shuffled ahead of me without answering; his oxlike behind should have had a tail on it to flick the flies away—it infuriated me. "You goddamn liar!" I said.

He spun around as fast as an ox can. "You ain't stuck with nobody." We were at the top of the landing headed into the locker-lined corridor; the kids who were piling up the stairs behind stopped, listened. "No you ain't, you snot-ass!" And I saw five hairy knuckles coming right at my mouth. I moved but not in time, and heard a crash inside the bridge of my nose. I felt my hips dip back, my legs and head come forward, and, curved like the letter c, I was swept fifteen feet backward before I felt cold marble beneath the palms of my hands. Just then I looked up to see Mr. Russo's black wingtipped shoes enter the room. I'm almost sure he had seen Albie blast me but I'll never know. Nobody, including Albie and myself, ever mentioned it again. Perhaps it had been a mistake for me to call Albie a liar, but if he had starred at baseball, it was in some league I did not know.

By way of contrast I want to introduce Duke Scarpa, another ex-con who was with us that year. Neither Albie nor the Duke, incidentally, was a typical member of my high school community. Both lived at the other end of Newark, "down neck," and they had reached us only after the Board of Education had tried Albie at two other schools and the Duke at four. The Board hoped finally, like Marx, that the higher culture would absorb the lower.

Albie and Duke had no particular use for each other; where Albie had made up his mind to go straight, one always felt that the Duke, in his oily quietness, his boneless grace, was planning a job. Yet, though affection never lived between them, Duke wandered after Albie and me, aware, I suspect, that if Albie despised him it was because he was able to read his soul—and that such an associate was easier to abide than one who despises you because he does not know your soul at all. Where Albie was a hippopotamus, an ox, Duke was reptilian. Me? I don't know; it is easy to spot the animal in one's fellows.

During lunch hour, the Duke and I used to spar with each other in the hall outside the cafeteria. He did not know a hook from a jab and disliked having his dark skin roughened or his hair mussed; but he so delighted in moving, bobbing, coiling, and uncoiling, that I think he would have paid for the privilege of playing the serpent with me. He hypnotized me, the Duke; he pulled some slimy string inside me—where Albie Pelagutti sought and stretched a deeper and, I think, a nobler cord.

But I make Albie sound like peaches-and-cream. Let me tell you what he and I did to Mr. Russo.

Russo believed in his battery of tests as his immigrant parents (and Albie's, and maybe Albie himself) believed in papal infallibility. If the tests said Albie was going to be a lawyer, then he was going to be a lawyer. As for Albie's past, it seemed only to increase Russo's devotion to the prophecy: he approached Albie with salvation in his eyes. In September, then, he gave Albie a biography to read, the life of Oliver Wendell Holmes; during October, once a week, he had the poor fellow speak impromptu before the class; in November he had him write a report on the Constitution, which I wrote; and then in December, he sent Albie and me (and two others who displayed a legal bent) to the Essex County Court House where we could see "real lawyers in action."

It was a cold, windy morning and as we flicked our cigarettes at the Lincoln statue on the courtyard plaza, and started up the long flight of white cement steps, Albie suddenly did an about-face and headed back across the plaza and out to Market Street. I called to him but he shouted back that he had seen it all before, and then he was not walking, but running towards the crowded downtown streets, pursued not by police, but by other days. It wasn't that he considered Russo an ass for having sent him to visit the Court House—Albie respected teachers too much for that—rather I think he felt Russo had tried to rub his nose in it.

No surprise, then, when the next day after gym Albie announced his assault on the Occupations teacher; it was the first crime he had planned since his decision to go straight back in September. He outlined the action to me and indicated that I should pass the details on to the other members of the class. As liaison between Albie and the well-behaved, healthy nonconvicts like myself who made up the rest of the class, I was stationed at the classroom door and as each member passed in I unfolded the plot into his ear: "As soon after ten-fifteen as Russo turns to the blackboard, you bend over to tie your shoelace." If a classmate looked back at me puzzled, I would motion to Pelagutti hulking over his desk; the puzzled expression would vanish and another accomplice would enter the room. The only one who gave me any trouble was the Duke. He listened to the plan and then scowled back at me with the look of a man who's got his own syndicate, and, in fact, has never even heard of yours.

Finally the bell rang; I closed the door behind me and moved noiselessly to my desk. I waited for the clock to move to a quarter after; it did; and then Russo turned to the board to write upon it the salary range of aluminum workers. I bent to tie my shoe-laces—beneath all the desks I saw other upside-down grinning faces. To my left behind me I heard Albie hissing; his hands fumbled about his black silk socks, and the hiss grew and grew until it was a rush of Sicilian, muttered, spewed, vicious. The exchange was strictly between Russo and himself. I looked to the front of the classroom, my fingers knotting and unknotting my shoelaces, the blood pumping now to my face. I saw Russo's legs turn. What a sight he must have seen—where there had been twenty-five faces, now there was nothing. Just desks. "Okay," I heard Russo say, "okay." And then he gave a little clap with his hands. "That's enough now, fellas. The joke is over. Sit up." And then Albie's hiss traveled to all the blood-pinked ears below the desks; it rushed about us like a subterranean stream—"Stay down!"

While Russo asked us to get up we stayed down. And we did not sit up until Albie told us to; and then under his direction we were singing—

> Don't sit under the apple tree
> With anyone else but me,
> Anyone else but me,
> Anyone else but me,
> Oh, no, no, don't sit under the apple tree . . .

And then in time to the music we clapped. What a noise!

Mr. Russo stood motionless at the front of the class, listening, astonished. He wore a neatly pressed dark blue pin-striped suit, a tan tie with a collie's head in the center, and a tieclasp with the initials R.R. engraved upon it; he had on the black wingtipped shoes; they glittered. Russo, who believed in neatness, honesty, punctuality, planned destinies—who believed in the future, in Occupations! And next to me, behind me, inside me, all over me—Albie! We looked at each other, Albie and I, and my lungs split with joy: *"Don't sit under the apple tree—"* Albie's monotone boomed out, and then a thick liquid crooner's voice behind Albie bathed me in sound: it was the Duke's; he clapped to a tango beat.

Russo leaned for a moment against a visual aids chart—"Skilled Laborers: Salaries and Requirements"—and then scraped back his chair and plunged down into it, so far down it looked to have no bottom. He lowered his big head to the desk and his shoulders curled forward like the ends of wet paper; and that was when Albie pulled his coup. He stopped singing "Don't Sit Under the Apple Tree"; we all stopped. Russo looked up at the silence; his eyes black and baggy, he stared at our leader, Alberto Pelagutti. Slowly Russo began to shake his head from side to side: this was no Capone, this was a Garibaldi! Russo waited, I waited, we all waited. Albie slowly rose, and began to sing *"Oh, say can you see, by the dawn's early light, what so proudly we hailed—"* And we all stood and joined him. Tears sparkling on his long black lashes, Mr. Robert Russo dragged himself wearily up from his desk, beaten, and as the Pelagutti basso boomed disastrously behind me, I saw Russo's lips begin to move, *"the bombs bursting in air, gave proof—"* God, did we sing!

Albie left school in June of that year—he had passed only Occupations—but our comradeship, that strange vessel, was smashed to bits at noon one day a few months earlier. It was a lunch hour in March, the Duke and I were sparring in the hall outside the cafeteria, and Albie, who had been more hospitable to the Duke since the day his warm, liquid voice had joined the others—Albie had decided to act as our referee, jumping between us, separating our clinches, warning us about low blows, grabbing out for the Duke's droopy crotch, in general having a good time. I remember that the Duke and I were in a clinch; as I showered soft little punches to his kidneys he squirmed in my embrace. The sun shone through the window behind him, lighting up his hair like a nest of snakes. I fluttered his sides, he twisted, I breathed hard through my nose, my eyes registered on his snaky hair, and suddenly Albie wedged between and knocked us apart—the Duke plunged sideways, I plunged forward, and my fist crashed through the window that Scarpa had been using as his corner. Feet pounded; in a second a wisecracking, guiltless, chewing crowd was gathered around me, just me. Albie and the Duke were gone. I cursed them both, the honorless bastards! The crowd did not drift back to lunch until the head dietitian, a huge, varicose-veined matron in a laundry-stiff white uniform had written down my name and led me to the nurse's office to have the glass picked out of my knuckles. Later in the afternoon I was called for the first and only time to the office of Mr. Wendell, the Principal.

Fifteen years have passed since then and I do not know what has happened to Albie Pelagutti. If he is a gangster, he was not one with notoriety or money enough for the Kefauver Committee to interest itself in several years ago. When the Crime Committee reached New Jersey I followed their investigations carefully but never did I read in the papers the name Alberto Pelagutti or even Duke Scarpa—though who can tell what name the Duke is known by now. I do know, however, what happened to the Occupations teacher, for when another Senate Committee swooped through the state a while back it was discovered that Robert Russo—among others—had been a Marxist while attending Montclair State Teachers' College circa 1935. Russo refused to answer some of the Committee's questions, and the Newark Board of Education met, chastised, and dismissed him. I read now and then in the Newark *News* that Civil Liberties Union attorneys are still trying to appeal his case, and I have even written a letter to the Board of Education swearing that if anything subversive was ever done to my character, it wasn't done by my ex-high school teacher, Russo; if he was a Communist I never knew it. I could not decide whether or not to include in the letter a report of the "Star-Spangled Banner" incident: who knows what is and is not proof to the crotchety ladies and chainstore owners who sit and die on Boards of Education?

And if (to alter an Ancient's text) a man's history is his fate, who knows whether the Newark Board of Education will ever attend to a letter written to them by me. I mean, have fifteen years buried that afternoon I was called to see the Principal?

. . . He was a tall, distinguished gentleman and as I entered his office he rose and extended his hand. The same sun that an hour earlier had lit up snakes in the Duke's hair now slanted through Mr. Wendell's blinds and warmed his deep green carpet. "How do you do?" he said. "Yes," I answered, non sequiturly, and ducked my bandaged hand under my unbandaged hand. Graciously he said, "Sit down, won't you?" Frightened, unpracticed, I performed an aborted curtsy and sat. I watched Mr. Wendell go to his metal filing cabinet, slide one drawer open, and take from it a large white index card. He set the card on his desk and motioned me over so I might read what was typed on the card. At the top, in caps, was my whole name—last, first, and middle; below the name was a Roman numeral one, and beside it, "Fighting in corridor; broke window (3/19/42)." Already documented. And on a big card with plenty of space.

I returned to my chair and sat back as Mr. Wendell told me that the card would follow me through life. At first I listened, but as he talked on and on, the drama went out of what he said, and my attention wandered to his filing cabinet. I began to imagine the cards inside, Albie's card and the Duke's, and then I understood—just short of forgiveness—why the two of them had zoomed off and left me to pay penance for the window by myself. Albie, you see, had always known about the filing cabinet and these index cards; I hadn't; and Russo, poor Russo, has only recently found out.

A: I'm not sure whether the title of this story applies to Albie, to the Duke, or to Russo.

B: Do you think there's an index card in a filing cabinet somewhere for me?

# To an Athlete Dying Young

*A. E. Housman*

The time you won your town the race
We chaired you through the market-place;
Man and boy stood cheering by,
And home we brought you shoulder-high.

Today, the road all runners come,
Shoulder-high we bring you home,
And set you at your threshold down,
Townsman of a stiller town.

Smart lad, to slip betimes away
From fields where glory does not stay          10
And early though the laurel grows
It withers quicker than the rose.

280

Eyes the shady night has shut
Cannot see the record cut,
And silence sounds no worse than cheers
After earth has stopped the ears:

Now you will not swell the rout
Of lads that wore their honors out,
Runners whom renown outran
And the name died before the man.          20

So set, before its echoes fade,
The fleet foot on the sill of shade,
And hold to the low lintel up
The still-defended challenge-cup.

And round that early-laureled head
Will flock to gaze the strengthless dead,
And find unwithered on its curls
The garland briefer than a girl's.

From "A Shropshire Lad"—Authorized Edition—from THE COLLECTED POEMS
OF A. E. HOUSMAN Copyright 1939, 1940, © 1959 by Holt, Rinehart and
Winston, Inc. Copyright © 1967, 1968 by Robert E. Symons. Reprinted by
permission of Holt, Rinehart and Winston, Inc., The Society of Authors as the
literary representative of the Estate of A. E. Housman, and Jonathan Cape Ltd.

# EX-BASKETBALL PLAYER

John Updike

Pearl Avenue runs past the high-school lot,
Bends with the trolley tracks, and stops, cut off
Before it has a chance to go two blocks,
At Colonel McComsky Plaza. Berth's Garage
Is on the corner facing west, and there,
Most days, you'll find Flick Webb, who helps Berth out.

Flick stands tall among the idiot pumps—
Five on a side, the old bubble-head style,
Their rubber elbows hanging loose and low.
One's nostrils are two S's, and his eyes                    10
An E and O. And one is squat, without
A head at all—more of a football type.

Once Flick played for the high-school team, the Wizards.
He was good: in fact, the best. In '46
He bucketed three hundred ninety points,
A county record still. The ball loved Flick.
I saw him rack up thirty-eight or forty
In one home game. His hands were like wild birds.

He never learned a trade, he just sells gas,
Checks oil, and changes flats. Once in a while,        20
As a gag he dribbles an inner tube,
But most of us remember anyway.
His hands are fine and nervous on the lug wrench.
It makes no difference to the lug wrench, though.

Off work, he hangs around Mae's Luncheonette.
Grease-grey and kind of coiled, he plays pinball,
Sips lemon cokes, and smokes those thin cigars;
Flick seldom speaks to Mae, just sits and nods
Beyond her face towards bright applauding tiers
Of Necco Wafers, Nibs, and Juju Beads.             30

# The Erl Child

*Andrew Glaze*

I've always voted in elections,
I've been a good democrat all my life.
I am coterminous with everybody, and everybody
is a piece of me. But there is something
in me that doesn't vote.
In the morning it tells me when I walk down to the village
where they give me bad eggs, bad bacon,
bad looks, and a bad reputation,
that this is not where I was born.
There was some perfidious star,
there was flaming at the coffee ring
and white-coated waiters walking about in the dark.
A tall white lady was putting Scottish socks on my feet,
arranging around my head
a silk blanket and jade jacket-fastenings.
I remember being carried down by rushes and a stream.
I keep looking in the attic for a basket.
Someday I shall turn over an old sewing machine
or broken hamper and there it will have been all the time.
I'll open it and find the wristlet,
the enamels, the identification ring, the money,
and (I hope with an intact seal)
the morocco box with the tape and the stamp inside
and the book of the code.

A: Have you ever had the feeling that you're really someone else?

B: *Someone else?* Ya crazy or somethin'?

282

# The Erlking

## Johann Wolfgang von Goethe

*Translated by Sir Walter Scott*

O who rides by night thro' the woodland so wild?
It is the fond Father embracing his child;
And close the boy nestles within his loved arm
To hold himself fast, and to keep himself warm.

"O Father, see yonder! see yonder!" he says;
"My boy, upon what dost thou fearfully gaze?"
"O, 'tis the Erlking with his crown and his shroud."
"No, my son, it is but a dark wreath of the cloud."

"O come and go with me, thou loveliest child;          [The Erlking
By many a gay sport shall thy time be beguiled;          speaks.] 10
My mother keeps for thee full many a fair toy,
And many a fine flower shall she pluck for my boy."

"O Father, my father, and did you not hear
The Erlking whisper so low in my ear?"
"Be still, my heart's darling—my child, be at ease;
It was but the wild blast as it sung thro' the trees."

"O wilt thou go with me, thou loveliest boy?          [The Erlking.]
My daughter shall tend thee with care and with joy;
She shall bear thee so lightly thro' wet and thro' wild,
And press thee, and kiss thee, and sing to my child."          20

"O Father, my father, and saw you not plain
The Erlking's pale Daughter glide past thro' the rain?"
"O yes, my loved treasure, I knew it full soon;
It was the gray willow that danced to the moon."

"O come and go with me, no longer delay,          [The Erlking.]
Or else, silly child, I will drag thee away."
"O Father! O Father! now, now, keep your hold,
The Erlking has seized me—his grasp is so cold!"

Sore trembled the Father; he spurr'd thro' the wild,
Clasping close to his bosom his shuddering child;          30
He reaches his dwelling in doubt and in dread,
But, clasp'd to his bosom, the infant was dead.

Almost as long as there have been people, they have sung songs that told stories. For centuries these song-stories—ballads—were passed from generation to generation by word of mouth. It's only within the last two hundred years or so that ballads have been written down.

This ballad has to do with the mythical king of the elves (the Erlking) of German legend, who lived deep in the forest and who lured children to their death.

9

283

# The Golden Vanity

*Version by Tom Glazer*

For hundreds of years, as you know, ballads were passed from father to son by word of mouth. Each time a child listened to a ballad, he most likely heard a slightly different version—no doubt partly because the balladeer wanted to bring the story in tune with the times.

This ballad, sung since the 1680's, has more than 50 versions. Some have a sad ending; some, a happy ending. No one is sure what the original story of the ballad was like, and no one knows for sure whether the story is true or made up. One thing we do know: The more-than-fifty-versions are now written down. Here's one.

*Oh, there was a lofty ship,*
*And she sailed upon the sea;*
*And the name of our ship*
*Was the Golden Vanity.*
*And we feared she would be taken*
*By the Spanish enemy.*
*As she sailed upon the lowlands, lowlands, low,*
*As she sailed upon the lowland sea.*

*Then up spoke our cabin boy*
*And boldly out spoke he:*                                      10
*And he said to our Captain,*
*"What will ye give to me,*
*If I swim along side*
*The Spanish enemy,*
*And I sink her in the lowlands, lowlands, low,*
*If I sink her in the lowland sea?"*

*"Oh, I will give you silver,*
*And I will give you gold,*
*And my own fair young daughter*
*Your bonny bride shall be,* 20
*If you swim alongside*
*The Spanish enemy*
*And you sink her in the lowlands, lowlands, low,*
*You sink her in the lowland sea."*

*Then the boy he made him ready,*
*And overboard sprang he*
*And he swam alongside*
*The Spanish enemy*
*And with his brace and auger*
*In her side he bore holes three* 30
*And he sank her in the lowlands, lowlands, low,*
*He sank her in the lowland sea.*

*Then quickly he swam back*
*To the cheering of the crew*
*But the captain would not help him*
*For his promise he did rue*
*And he scorned his poor entreatings*
*As boldly he did sue,*
*And he left him in the lowlands, lowlands, low,*
*He left him in the lowland sea.* 40

*Then the boy he turned around*
*And he swam to the port side*
*And up unto his messmates*
*Full bitterly he cried*
*"Oh messmates draw me up*
*For I'm drifting with the tide*
*And I'm sinking in the lowlands, lowlands, low,*
*I'm sinking in the lowland sea."*

*Then his messmates drew him up*
*But on the deck he died* 50
*And they stitched him in his hammock*
*Which was so fine and white*
*And they lowered him overboard*
*And he drifted with the tide*
*And he sank into the lowland, lowland, low*
*He sank into the lowland sea.*

# Get Up and Bar the Door

Anonymous

This ancient ballad comes from Scotland.

It fell about the Martinmas time,
  And a gay time it was then,
When our goodwife got puddings to make,
  And she's boild them in the pan.

The wind sae cauld blew south and north,
  And blew into the floor;
Quoth our goodman to our goodwife,
  "Gae out and bar the door."

"My hand is in my hussyfskap,°
  Goodman, as ye may see;                            ·10
And it should nae be barrd this hundred year,
  It's no be barrd for me."

They made a paction tween them twa,
  They made it firm and sure,
That the first word whaeer shoud speak,
  Shoud rise and bar the door.

Then by there came two gentlemen,
  At twelve o clock at night,
And they could neither see house nor hall,
  Nor coal nor candle-light.                          20

°HUSSYFSKAP: household chores

From THE ENGLISH AND SCOTTISH POPULAR BALLADS by F. J. Child. Reprinted by permission of Dover Publications, Inc.

*"Now whether is this a rich man's house,*
  *Or whether is it a poor?"*
*But neer a word wad ane o them speak,*
  *For barring of the door.*

*And first they ate the white puddings,*
  *And then they ate the black;*
*Tho muckle° thought the goodwife to hersel,*
  *Yet neer a word she spake.*

*Then said the one unto the other,*
  *"Here, man, tak ye my knife;*                    30
*Do ye tak aff the auld man's beard,*
  *And I'll kiss the goodwife."*

*"But there's nae water in the house,*
  *And what shall we do than?"*
*"What ails ye at the pudding-broo,°*
  *That boils into the pan?"*

*O up then started our goodman,*
  *An angry man was he:*
*"Will ye kiss my wife before my een,*
  *And scad me wi pudding-bree?"*                   40

*Then up and started our goodwife,*
  *Gied three skips on the floor:*
*"Goodman, you've spoken the foremost word,*
  *Get up and bar the door."*


°MUCKLE: much

°WHAT . . . PUDDING-BROO: What's wrong with (using) the sausage broth?

287

*Ballade of Lost Objects*

*Phyllis McGinley*

A ballade isn't exactly a ballad. It's a poem written according to special rules about rhyme and other repeated sounds. Making up a ballade is like concocting a sixteen-layer French pastry from scratch instead of using an already-prepared cake mix. The person who writes a ballade— like the person who starts from scratch in his baking of French pastry—is entitled to feel pleased with himself, particularly if he can make others think that what he has done was easy.

Where are the ribbons I tie my hair with?
  Where is my lipstick? Where are my hose—
The sheer ones hoarded these weeks to wear with
  Frocks the closets do not disclose?
Perfumes, petticoats, sports chapeaux,
  The blouse Parisian, the earring Spanish—
Everything suddenly ups and goes.
  *And where in the world did the children vanish?*

This is the house I used to share with
  Girls in pinafores, shier than does.          10
I can recall how they climbed my stair with
  Gales of giggles, on their toptoes.
Last seen wearing both braids and bows
  (But looking rather Raggedy-Annish),
When they departed nobody knows—
  Where in the world did the children vanish?

Two tall strangers, now I must bear with,
  Decked in my personal furbelows,
Raiding the larder, rending the air with
  Gossip and terrible radios.                   20

Neither my friends nor quite my foes,
  Alien, beautiful, stern, and clannish,
Here they dwell, while the wonder grows:
  Where in the world did the children vanish?

Prince, I warn you, under the rose,
  Time is the thief you cannot banish.
These are my daughters, I suppose.
  But where in the world did the children vanish?

# The Computer's First Birthday Card

*Edwin Morgan*

```
many  returns  happy
many  turns  happier
happy  turns  remain
happy  remains  turn
turns  remain  happy
turn  happy  remains
remains  turn  happy
mains  return  happy
happy  mains  return
main  happy  returns
main  turns  happier
happier  main  turns
happier  many  turns
many  happier  turns
many  happier  turns
many  happier  turns
er  turns  er  turns?
happy  er  er  happy?
er  error  er  check!
turn  er  pre  turns!
many  happy  turners
```

$$+ \$ - ! = 0\tfrac{1}{2} \dagger^* / \pounds \,(\&?$$

```
many  gay  whistlers
no no no no no no!
many  gainsboroughs
stop  stop  stop  stp
happier  constables
01 01 01 01 01 01 01
raise  police  pay  p
ost  early  for  chri
stmas  watch  forest
fires  get  well  soo
n bon voyage KRGK
many  happy  returns
eh? eh? eh? eh? eh?
```

Edwin Morgan's "The Computer's First Birthday Card" was published in *The Beloit Poetry Journal*, and is reprinted with their permission.

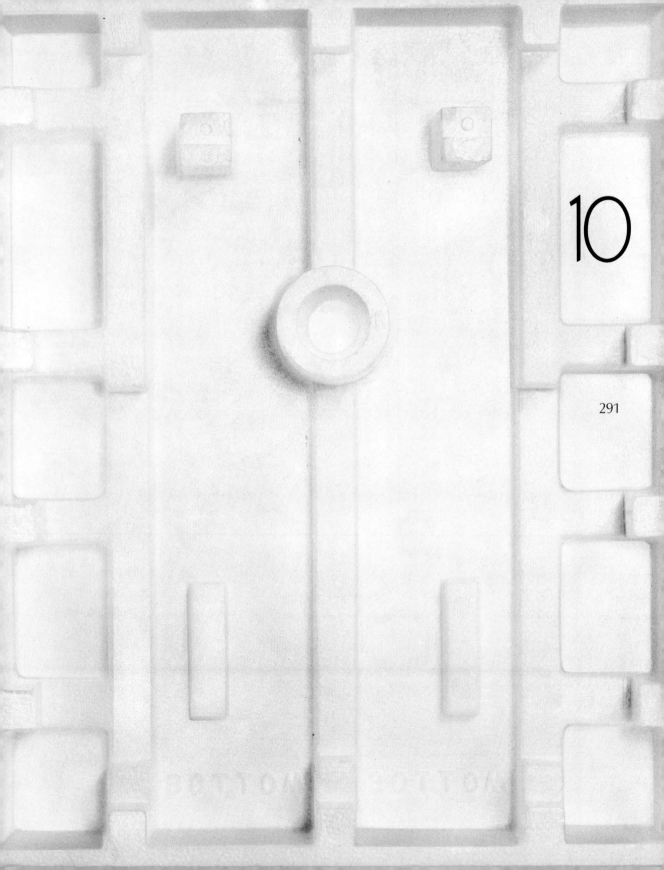

10

291

# The
# Great
# Automatic
# Grammatisator

Roald Dahl

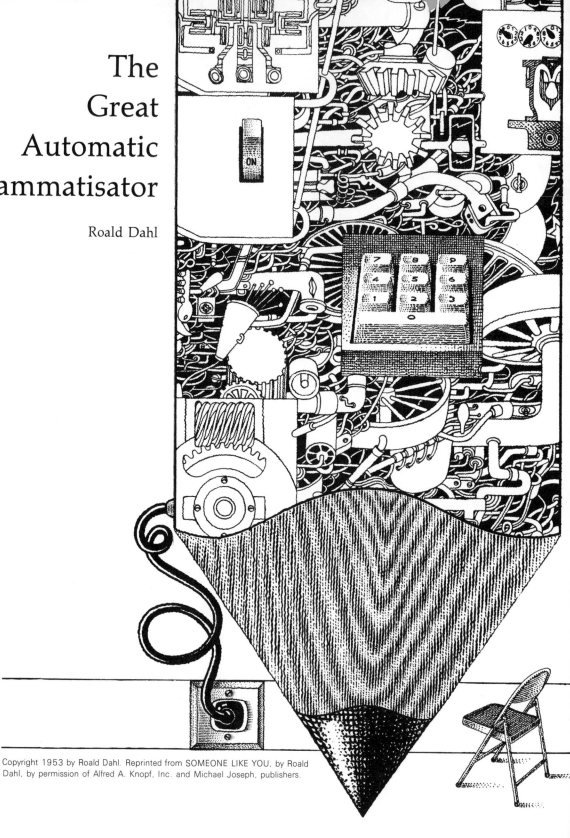

292

"Well, Knipe, my boy. Now that it's all finished, I just called you in to tell you I think you've done a fine job."

Adolph Knipe stood still in front of Mr. Bohlen's desk. There seemed to be no enthusiasm in him at all.

"Aren't you pleased?"

"Oh yes, Mr. Bohlen."

"Did you see what the papers said this morning."

"No sir, I didn't."

The man behind the desk pulled a folded newspaper toward him, and began to read: "The building of the great automatic computing engine, ordered by the government some time ago, is now complete. It is probably the fastest electronic calculating machine in the world today. Its function is to satisfy the ever-increasing need of science, industry, and administration for rapid mathematical calculation which, in the past, by traditional methods, would have been physically impossible, or would have required more time than the problems justified. The speed with which the new engine works, said Mr. John Bohlen, head of the firm of electrical engineers mainly responsible for its construction, may be grasped by the fact that it can provide the correct answer in five seconds to a problem that would occupy a mathematician for a month. In three minutes, it can produce a calculation that by hand (if it were possible) would fill half a million sheets of foolscap paper. The automatic computing engine uses pulses of electricity, generated at the rate of a million a second, to solve all calculations that resolve themselves into addition, subtraction, multiplication, and division. For practical purposes there is no limit to what it can do . . ."

Mr. Bohlen glanced up at the long, melancholy face of the younger man. "Aren't you proud, Knipe? Aren't you pleased?"

"Of course, Mr. Bohlen."

"I don't think I have to remind you that your own contribution, especially to the original plans, was an important one. In fact, I might go so far as to say that without you and some of your ideas, this project might still be on the drawing boards today."

Adolph Knipe moved his feet on the carpet, and he watched the two small white hands of his chief, the nervous fingers playing with a paper clip, unbending it, straightening out the hairpin curves. He didn't like the man's hands. He didn't like his face either, with the tiny mouth and the narrow purple-colored lips. It was unpleasant the way only the lower lip moved when he talked.

"Is anything bothering you, Knipe? Anything on your mind?"

"Oh no, Mr. Bohlen. No."

"How would you like to take a week's holiday? Do you good. You've earned it."

"Oh, I don't know, sir."

The older man waited, watching this tall, thin person who stood so sloppily before him. He was a difficult boy. Why couldn't he stand up straight? Always drooping and untidy, with spots on his jacket, and hair falling all over his face.

"I'd like you to take a holiday, Knipe. You need it."

"All right, sir. If you wish."

"Take a week. Two weeks if you like. Go somewhere warm. Get some sunshine. Swim. Relax. Sleep. Then come back, and we'll have another talk about the future."

Adolph Knipe went home by bus to his two-room apartment. He threw his coat on the sofa, poured himself a drink of whiskey, and sat down in front of the typewriter that was on the table. Mr. Bohlen was right. Of course he was right. Except that he didn't know the half of it. He probably thought it was a woman. Whenever a young man gets depressed, everybody thinks it's a woman.

He leaned forward and began to read through the half-finished sheet of typing still in the machine. It was headed "A Narrow Escape," and it began, *The night was dark and stormy, the wind whistled in the trees, the rain poured down like cats and dogs . . ."*

Adolph Knipe took a sip of whiskey, tasting the malty-bitter flavor, feeling the trickle of cold liquid as it traveled down his throat and settled in the top of his stomach, cool at first, then spreading and becoming warm, making a little area of warmness in the gut. To hell with Mr. John Bohlen anyway. And to hell with the great electrical computing machine. To hell with . . .

At exactly that moment, his eyes and mouth began slowly to open, in a sort of wonder, and slowly he raised his head and became still, absolutely motionless, gazing at the wall opposite with this look that was more perhaps of astonishment than of wonder, but quite fixed now, unmoving, and remaining thus for forty, fifty, sixty seconds. Then gradually (the head still motionless), a subtle change spreading over the face, astonishment becoming pleasure, very slight at first, only around the corners of the mouth, increasing gradually, spreading out until at last the whole face was open wide and shining with extreme delight. It was the first time Adolph Knipe had smiled in many, many months.

"Of course," he said, speaking aloud, "it's completely ridiculous." Again he smiled, raising his upper lip and baring his teeth in a queerly sensual manner.

"It's a delicious idea, but so impracticable it doesn't really bear thinking about at all."

From then on, Adolph Knipe began to think about nothing else. The idea fascinated him enormously, at first because it gave him a promise— however remote—of revenging himself in a most devilish manner upon his greatest enemies. From this angle alone, he toyed idly with it for perhaps ten or fifteen minutes; then all at once he found himself examining it quite seriously as a practical possibility. He took paper and made some preliminary notes. But he didn't get far. He found himself, almost immediately, up against the old truth that a machine, however ingenious, is incapable of original thought. It can handle no problems except those that resolve themselves into mathematical terms—problems

294

that contain one, and only one, correct answer.

This was a stumper. There didn't seem any way around it. A machine cannot have a brain. On the other hand, it *can* have a memory, can it not? Their own electronic calculator had a marvelous memory. Simply by converting electric pulses, through a column of mercury, into supersonic waves, it could store away at least a thousand numbers at a time, extracting any one of them at the precise moment it was needed. Would it not be possible, therefore, on this principle, to build a memory section of almost unlimited size?

Now what about that?

Then suddenly, he was struck by a powerful but simple little truth, and it was this: *That English grammar is governed by rules that are almost mathematical in their strictness!* Given the words, and given the sense of what is to be said, then there is only one correct order in which those words can be arranged.

No, he thought, that isn't quite accurate. In many sentences there are several alternative positions for words and phrases, all of which may be grammatically correct. But what the hell. The theory itself is basically true. Therefore, it stands to reason that an engine built along the lines of the electric computer could be adjusted to arrange words (instead of numbers) in their right order according to the rules of grammar. Give it the verbs, the nouns, the adjectives, the pronouns, store them in the memory section as a vocabulary, and arrange for them to be extracted as required. Then feed it with plots and leave it to write the sentences.

There was no stopping Knipe now. He went to work immediately, and there followed during the next few days a period of intense labor. The living room became littered with sheets of paper: formulae and calculations; lists of words, thousands and thousands of words; the plots of stories, curiously broken up and subdivided; huge extracts from *Roget's Thesaurus;* pages filled with the first names of men and women; hundreds of surnames taken from the telephone directory; intricate drawings of wires and circuits and switches and thermionic valves; drawings of machines that could punch holes of different shapes in little cards, and of a strange electrical typewriter that could type ten thousand words a minute. Also, a kind of control panel with a series of small pushbuttons, each one labeled with the name of a famous American magazine.

He was working in a mood of exultation, prowling around the room amidst this littering of paper, rubbing his hands together, talking out loud to himself; and sometimes, with a sly curl of the nose, he would mutter a series of murderous imprecations in which the word *editor* seemed always to be present. On the fifteenth day of continuous work, he collected the papers into two large folders which he carried—almost at a run—to the offices of John Bohlen Inc., electrical engineers.

Mr. Bohlen was pleased to see him back.

"Well Knipe, good gracious me, you look a hundred per cent better. You have a good holiday? Where'd you go?"

He's just as ugly and untidy as ever, Mr. Bohlen thought. Why doesn't he stand up straight? He looks like a bent stick. "You look a hundred per cent better, my boy." I wonder what he's grinning about. Every time I see him, his ears seem to have got larger.

Adolph Knipe placed the folders on the desk. "Look, Mr. Bohlen!" he cried. "Look at these!"

Then he poured out his story. He opened the folders and pushed the plans in front of the astonished little man. He talked for over an hour, explaining everything, and when he had finished, he stepped back, breathless, flushed, waiting for the verdict.

"You know what I think, Knipe? I think you're nuts." Careful now, Mr. Bohlen told himself. Treat him carefully. He's valuable, this one is. If only he didn't look so awful, with that long horse face and the big teeth. The fellow had ears as big as rhubarb leaves.

"But Mr. Bohlen! It'll work! I've proved to you it'll work! You can't deny that!"

"Take it easy now, Knipe. Take it easy, and listen to me." Mr. Bohlen watched his man, disliking him more every second.

"This idea," Mr. Bohlen's lower lip was saying, "is very ingenious—I might almost say brilliant—and it only goes to confirm my high opinion of your abilities, Knipe. But don't take it too seriously. After all, my boy, what possible use can it be to us? Who on earth wants a machine for writing stories? And where's the money in it, anyway? Just tell me that."

"May I sit down, sir?"

"Sure, take a seat."

Adolph Knipe seated himself on the edge of a chair. The older man watched him with alert brown eyes, wondering what was coming now.

"I would like to explain something, Mr. Bohlen, if I may, about how I came to do all this."

"Go right ahead, Knipe." He would have to be humored a little now, Mr. Bohlen told himself. The boy was

really valuable—a sort of genius, almost—worth his weight in gold to the firm. Just look at these papers here. Darndest thing you ever saw. Astonishing piece of work. Quite useless, of course. No commercial value. But it proved again the boy's ability.

"It's a sort of confession, I suppose, Mr. Bohlen. I think it explains why I've always been so . . . so kind of worried."

"You tell me anything you want, Knipe. I'm here to help you—you know that."

The young man clasped his hands together tight on his lap, hugging himself with his elbows. It seemed as though suddenly he was feeling very cold.

"You see, Mr. Bohlen, to tell the honest truth, I don't really care much for my work here. I know I'm good at it and all that sort of thing, but my heart's not in it. It's not what I want to do most."

Up went Mr. Bohlen's eyebrows, quick like a spring. His whole body became very still.

"You see, sir, all my life I've wanted to be a writer."

"A writer!"

"Yes, Mr. Bohlen. You may not believe it, but every bit of spare time I've had, I've spent writing stories. In the last ten years I've written hundreds, literally hundreds of short stories. Five hundred and sixty-six, to be precise. Approximately one a week."

"Good heavens, man! What on earth did you do that for?"

"All I know, sir, is I have the urge."

"What sort of urge?"

"The creative urge, Mr. Bohlen." Every time he looked up he saw Mr. Bohlen's lips. They were growing thinner and thinner, more and more purple.

"And may I ask you what you do with these stories, Knipe?"

"Well sir, that's the trouble. No one will buy them. Each time I finish one, I send it out on the rounds. It goes to one magazine after another. That's all that happens, Mr. Bohlen, and they simply send them back. It's very depressing."

Mr. Bohlen relaxed. "I can see quite well how you feel, my boy." His voice was dripping with sympathy. "We all go through it one time or another in our lives. But now—now that you've had proof—positive proof—from the experts themselves, from the editors, that your stories are—what shall I say—rather unsuccessful, it's time to leave off. Forget it, my boy. Just forget all about it."

"No, Mr. Bohlen! No! That's not true! I *know* my stories are good. My heavens, when you compare them with the stuff some of those magazines print—oh my word, Mr. Bohlen!—the sloppy, boring stuff that you see in the magazines week after week—why, it drives me mad!"

"Now wait a minute, my boy . . ."

"Do you ever read the magazines, Mr. Bohlen?"

"You'll pardon me, Knipe, but what's all this got to do with your machine?"

"Everything, Mr. Bohlen, absolutely everything! What I want to tell you is, I've made a study of the magazines, and it seems that each one tends to have its own particular type of story. The writers—the successful ones—know this, and they write accordingly."

"Just a minute, my boy. Calm yourself down, will you. I don't think all this is getting us anywhere."

"*Please*, Mr. Bohlen, hear me through. It's all terribly important." He paused to catch his breath. He was properly worked up now, throwing his hands around as he talked. The long, toothy face, with the big ears on either side, simply shone with enthusiasm, and there was an excess of saliva in his mouth which caused him to speak his words wet. "So you see, on my machine, by having an adjustable co-ordinator between the 'plot-memory' section and the 'word-memory' section, I am able to produce any type of story I desire simply by pressing the required button."

"Yes, I know, Knipe, I know. This is all very interesting, but what's the point of it?"

"Just this, Mr. Bohlen. The market is limited. We've got to be able to produce the right stuff, at the right time, whenever we want it. It's a matter of business, that's all. I'm looking at it from *your* point of view now—as a commercial proposition."

"My dear boy, it can't possibly be a commercial proposition—ever. You know as well as I do what it costs to build one of these machines."

"Yes sir, I do. But with due respect, I don't believe you know what the magazines pay writers for stories."

"What do they pay?"

"Anything up to twenty-five hundred dollars. It probably averages around a thousand."

Mr. Bohlen jumped.

"Yes *sir*, it's true."

"Absolutely impossible, Knipe! Ridiculous!"

"No sir, it's true."

"You mean to sit there and tell me that these magazines pay out money like that to a man for . . . just for scribbling off a story! Good heavens, Knipe!

297

Whatever next! Writers must all be millionaires!"

"That's exactly it, Mr. Bohlen! That's where the machine comes in. Listen a minute, sir, while I tell you some more. I've got it all worked out. The big magazines are carrying approximately three fiction stories in each issue. Now, take the fifteen most important magazines—the ones paying the most money. A few of them are monthlies, but most of them come out every week. All right. That makes, let us say, around forty big money stories being bought each week. That's forty thousand dollars. So with our machine—when we get it working properly—we can collar nearly the whole of this market!"

"My dear boy, you're mad!"

"No sir, honestly, it's true what I say. Don't you see that with volume alone we'll completely overwhelm them! This machine can produce a five-thousand word story, all typed and ready for despatch, in thirty seconds. How can the writers compete with that? I ask you, Mr. Bohlen, *how?*"

At that point, Adolph Knipe noticed a slight change in the man's expression, an extra brightness in the eyes, the nostrils distending, the whole face becoming still, almost rigid. Quickly, he continued. "Nowadays, Mr. Bohlen, the handmade article hasn't a hope. It can't possibly compete with mass production, especially in this country—you know that. Carpets . . . chairs . . . shoes . . . bricks . . . crockery . . . anything you like to mention—they're all made by machinery now. The quality may be inferior, but that doesn't matter. It's the cost of production that counts. And stories—well—they're just another product, like carpets or chairs, and no one cares how

you produce them so long as you deliver the goods. We'll sell them wholesale, Mr. Bohlen! We'll undercut every writer in the country! We'll corner the market!"

Mr. Bohlen edged up straighter in his chair. He was leaning forward now, both elbows on the desk, the face alert, the small brown eyes resting on the speaker.

"I still think it's impracticable, Knipe."

"Forty thousand a week!" cried Adolph Knipe. "And if we halve the price, making it twenty thousand a week, that's still a million a year!" And softly he added, "You didn't get any million a year for building the old electronic calculator, did you, Mr. Bohlen?"

"But seriously now, Knipe. D'you really think they'd buy them?"

"Listen, Mr. Bohlen. Who on earth is going to want custom-made stories when they can get the other kind at half the price? It stands to reason, doesn't it?"

"And how will you sell them? Who will you say has written them?"

"We'll set up our own literary agency, and we'll distribute them through that. And we'll invent all the names we want for the writers."

"I don't like it, Knipe. To me, that smacks of trickery, does it not?"

"And another thing, Mr. Bohlen. There's all manner of valuable by-products once you've got started. Take advertising, for example. Beer manufacturers and people like that are willing to pay good money these days if famous writers will lend their names to their products. Why, my heavens, Mr. Bohlen! This isn't any children's plaything we're talking about. It's big business."

"Don't get too ambitious, my boy."

"And another thing. There isn't any reason why we shouldn't put *your* name, Mr. Bohlen, on some of the better stories, if you wished it."

"My goodness, Knipe. What should I want that for?"

"I don't know, sir, except that some writers get to be very much respected—like Mr. Erle Gardner or Kathleen Norris, for example. We've got to have names, and I was certainly thinking of using my own on one or two stories, just to help out."

"A writer, eh?" Mr. Bohlen said, musing. "Well, it would surely surprise them over at the club when they saw my name in the magazines—the good magazines."

"That's right, Mr. Bohlen."

For a moment, a dreamy, faraway look came into Mr. Bohlen's eyes, and he smiled. Then he stirred himself and began leafing through the plans that lay before him.

"One thing I don't quite understand, Knipe. Where do the plots come from? The machine can't possibly invent plots."

"We feed those in, sir. That's no problem at all. Everyone has plots. There's three or four hundred of them written down in that folder there on your left. Feed them straight into the 'plot-memory' section of the machine."

"Go on."

"There are many other little refinements too, Mr. Bohlen. You'll see them all when you study the plans carefully. For example, there's a trick that nearly every writer uses, of inserting at least one long, obscure word into each story. This makes the reader think that the man is very wise and clever. So I have the machine do the same

thing. There'll be a whole stack of long words stored away just for this purpose."

"Where?"

"In the 'word-memory' section," he said, epexegetically.

Through most of that day the two men discussed the possibilities of the new engine. In the end, Mr. Bohlen said he would have to think about it some more. The next morning, he was quietly enthusiastic. Within a week, he was completely sold on the idea.

"What we'll have to do, Knipe, is to say that we're merely building another mathematical calculator, but of a new type. That'll keep the secret."

"Exactly, Mr. Bohlen."

And in six months the machine was completed. It was housed in a separate brick building at the back of the premises, and now that it was ready for action, no one was allowed near it excepting Mr. Bohlen and Adolph Knipe.

It was an exciting moment when the two men—the one, short, plump, breviped—the other tall, thin and toothy—stood in the corridor before the control panel and got ready to run off the first story. All around them were walls dividing up into many small corridors, and the walls were covered with wiring and plugs and switches and huge glass valves. They were both nervous, Mr. Bohlen hopping from one foot to the other, quite unable to keep still.

"Which button?" Adolph Knipe asked, eyeing a row of small white discs that resembled the keys of a typewriter. "You choose, Mr. Bohlen. Lots of magazines to pick from—*Saturday Evening Post, Collier's, Ladies' Home Journal*—any one you like."

"Goodness me, boy! How do I know." He was jumping up and down like a man with hives.

"Mr. Bohlen," Adolph Knipe said gravely, "do you realize that at this moment, with your little finger alone, you have it in your power to become the most versatile writer on this continent?"

"Listen Knipe, just get on with it, will you please—and cut out the preliminaries."

"Okay, Mr. Bohlen. Then we'll make it . . . let me see—this one. How's that?" He extended one finger and pressed down a button with the name *TODAY'S WOMAN* printed across it in diminutive black type. There was a sharp click, and when he took his finger away, the button remained down, below the level of the others.

"So much for the selection," he said. "Now—here we go!" He reached up and pulled a switch on the panel. Immediately, the room was filled with a loud humming noise, and a crackling of electric sparks, and the jingle of many, tiny, quickly-moving levers; and almost in the same instant, sheets of quarto paper began sliding out from a slot to the right of the control panel and dropping into a basket below. They came out quick, one sheet a second, and in less than half a minute it was all over. The sheets stopped coming.

"That's it!" Adolph Knipe cried. "There's your story!"

They grabbed the sheets and began to read. The first one they picked up started as follows: "Aifkjmbsaoeg-wcztpplnvoqudskigt&, fuhpekanvbert-yuiolkjhgfdsazxcvbnm,peruitrehdjkgm-vnb,wmsuy . . ." They looked at the others. The style was roughly similar in all of them. Mr. Bohlen began to shout. The younger man tried to calm him down.

"It's all right, sir. Really it is. It only needs a little adjustment. We've got a connection wrong somewhere, that's all. You must remember, Mr. Bohlen, there's over a million feet of wiring in this room. You can't expect everything to be just right first time."

"It'll never work," Mr. Bohlen said.

"Be patient, sir. Be patient."

Adolph Knipe set out to discover the fault, and in four days time he announced that all was ready for the next try.

"It'll never work," Mr. Bohlen said. "I know it'll never work."

Knipe smiled and pressed the selector button marked *Reader's Digest.* Then he pulled the switch, and again the strange, exciting, humming sound filled the room. One page of typescript flew out of the slot into the basket.

"Where's the rest?" Mr. Bohlen cried. "It's stopped! It's gone wrong!"

"No sir, it hasn't. It's exactly right. It's for the Digest, don't you see?"

This time, it began: "Fewpeople-yetknowthatarevolutionarynewcurehas-beendiscoveredwhichmaywellbringper-manentrelieftosufferersofthemostdread-eddiseaseofourtime . . ." And so on.

"It's gibberish!" Mr. Bohlen shouted.

"No sir, it's fine. Can't you see? It's simply that she's not breaking up the words. That's an easy adjustment. But the story's there. Look, Mr. Bohlen, look! It's all there except that the words are joined together."

And indeed it was.

On the next try a few days later, everything was perfect, even the punctuation. The first story they ran off, for a famous women's magazine, was a solid, plotty story of a boy who wanted to better himself with his rich employer. This boy arranged, so the story went, for a friend to hold up the rich man's daughter on a dark night when she was driving home. Then the boy himself, happening by, knocked the gun out of his friend's hand and rescued the girl. The girl was grateful. But the father was suspicious. He questioned the boy sharply. The boy broke down and confessed. Then the father, instead of kicking him out of the house, said that he admired the boy's resourcefulness. The girl admired his honesty—and his looks. The father promised him to be head of the Accounts Department. The girl married him.

"It's tremendous, Mr. Bohlen! It's exactly right!"

"Seems a bit sloppy to me, my boy."

"No sir, it's a seller, a real seller!"

In his excitement, Adolph Knipe promptly ran off six more stories in as many minutes. All of them—except one, which for some reason came out a trifle lewd—seemed entirely satisfactory.

Mr. Bohlen was now mollified. He agreed to set up a literary agency in an office downtown, and to put Knipe in charge. In a couple of weeks, this was accomplished. Then Knipe mailed out the first dozen stories. He put his own name to four of them, Mr. Bohlen's to one, and for the others he simply invented names.

Five of these stories were promptly accepted. The one with Mr. Bohlen's name on it was turned down with a letter from the fiction editor saying, "This is a skillful job, but in our opinion it doesn't quite come off. We would like to see more of this writer's work . . ." Adolph Knipe took a cab out to the factory and ran off another story for the same magazine. He again put Mr. Bohlen's name to it, and mailed it out immediately. That one they bought.

The money started pouring in. Knipe slowly and carefully stepped up the output, and in six months' time he was delivering thirty stories a week, and selling about half.

He began to make a name for himself in literary circles as a prolific and successful writer. So did Mr. Bohlen; but not quite such a good name, although he didn't know it. At the same time, Knipe was building up a dozen or more fictitious persons as promising young authors. Everything was going fine.

At this point it was decided to adapt the machine for writing novels as well as stories. Mr. Bohlen, thirsting now for greater honors in the literary world, insisted that Knipe go to work at once on this prodigous task.

"I want to do a novel," he kept saying. "I want to do a novel."

"And so you will, sir. And so you will. But please be patient. This is a very complicated adjustment I have to make."

"Everyone tells me I ought to do a novel," Mr. Bohlen cried. "All sorts of publishers are chasing after me day and night begging me to stop fooling around with stories and do something really important instead. A novel's the only thing that counts—that's what they say."

"We're all going to do novels," Knipe told him. "Just as many as we want. But please be patient."

"Now listen to me, Knipe. What I'm going to do is a *serious* novel, something that'll make 'em sit up and take notice. I've been getting rather tired of the sort of stories you've been putting my name to lately. As a matter of fact, I'm none too sure you haven't been trying to make a monkey out of me."

"A monkey, Mr. Bohlen?"

"Keeping all the best ones for yourself, that's what you've been doing."

"Oh no, Mr. Bohlen! No!"

"So this time I'm going to make damn sure I write a high class intelligent book. You understand that."

"Look, Mr. Bohlen. With the sort of switchboard I'm rigging up, you'll be able to write any sort of book you want."

And this was true, for within another couple of months, the genius of Adolph Knipe had not only adapted the machine for novel writing, but had constructed a marvelous new control system which enabled the author to pre-select literally any type of plot and any style of writing he desired. There were so many dials and levers on the thing, it looked like the instrument panel of some enormous airplane.

First, by depressing one of a series of master buttons, the writer made his primary decision: historical, satirical, philosophical, political, romantic, erotic, humorous, or straight. Then, from the second row (the basic buttons), he chose his theme: army life, pioneer days, civil war, world war, racial problem, Wild West, country life, childhood memories, seafaring, the sea bottom, and many, many more. The third row of buttons gave a choice of literary style: classical, whimsical, racy, Hemingway, Faulkner, Joyce, feminine, etc. The fourth row was for characters, the fifth for wordage—and so on and so on—ten long rows of pre-selector buttons.

But that wasn't all. Control had also to be exercised during the actual writing process (which took about fifteen minutes per novel), and to do this the author had to sit, as it were, in the driver's seat, and pull (or push) a battery of labeled stops, as on an organ. By so doing, he was able continually to modulate or merge fifty different and variable qualities such as tension, surprise, humor, pathos, and mystery. Numerous dials and gauges on the dashboard itself told him throughout exactly how far along he was with his work.

Finally, there was the question of "passion." From a careful study of the books at the top of the best-seller lists for the past year, Adolph Knipe had decided that this was the most important ingredient of all—a magical catalyst that somehow or other could transform the dullest novel into a howling success—at any rate financially. But Knipe also knew that passion was powerful, heady stuff, and must be prudently dispensed—the right proportions at the right moments; and to ensure this, he had devised an independent control consisting of two sensitive sliding adjustors operated by footpedals, similar to the throttle and brake in a car. One pedal governed the percentage of passion to be injected, the other regulated its intensity. There was no doubt, of course—and this was the only drawback—that the writing of a novel by the Knipe method was going to be rather like flying a plane and driving a car and playing an organ all at the same time, but this did not trouble the inventor. When all was ready, he proudly escorted Mr. Bohlen into the machine house and began to explain the operating procedure for the new wonder.

"Good God, Knipe! I'll never be able to do all that! Dammit, man, it'd be easier to write the thing by hand!"

"You'll soon get used to it, Mr. Bohlen, I promise you. In a week or two, you'll be doing it without hardly thinking. It's just like learning to drive."

Well, it wasn't quite as easy as that, but after many hours of practice, Mr. Bohlen began to get the hang of it, and finally, late one evening, he told Knipe to make ready for running off the first novel. It was a tense moment, with the fat little man crouching nervously in the driver's seat, and the tall toothy Knipe fussing excitedly around him.

"I intend to write an important novel, Knipe."

"I'm sure you will, sir. I'm sure you will."

With one finger, Mr. Bohlen carefully pressed the necessary pre-selector buttons:

Master button—*satirical*
Subject—*racial problem*
Style—*classical*
Characters—*six men, four women,*
*one infant*
Length—*fifteen chapters.*

At the same time he had his eye particularly upon three organ stops marked *power, mystery, profundity.*

"Are you ready, sir?"

"Yes, yes, I'm ready."

Knipe pulled the switch. The great engine hummed. There was a deep whirring sound from the oiled movement of fifty thousand cogs and rods and levers; then came the drumming of the rapid electrical typewriter, setting up a shrill, almost intolerable clatter. Out into the basket flew the typewritten pages—one every two seconds. But what with the noise and the excitement, and having to play upon the stops, and watch the chapter-counter and the pace-indicator and the passion-gauge, Mr. Bohlen began to panic. He reacted in precisely the way a learner driver does in a car—by pressing both feet hard down on the pedals and keeping them there until the thing stopped.

"Congratulations on your first novel," Knipe said, picking up the great bundle of typed pages from the basket.

Little pearls of sweat were oozing out all over Mr. Bohlen's face. "It sure was hard work, my boy."

"But you got it done, sir. You got it done."

"Let me see it, Knipe. How does it read?"

He started to go through the first chapter, passing each finished page to the younger man.

"Good heavens, Knipe! What's this!" Mr. Bohlen's thin purple fish-lip was moving slightly as it mouthed the words, his cheeks were beginning slowly to inflate.

"But look here, Knipe! This is outrageous!"

"I must say it's a bit fruity, sir."

"*Fruity!* It's perfectly revolting! I can't possibly put my name to this!"

"Quite right, sir. Quite right."

"Knipe! Is this some nasty trick you've been playing on me?"

"Oh no, sir! No!"

"It certainly looks like it."

"You don't think, Mr. Bohlen, that you mightn't have been pressing a little hard on the passion-control pedals, do you?"

"My dear boy, how should *I* know."

"Why don't you try another?"

So Mr. Bohlen ran off a second novel, and this time it went according to plan.

Within a week, the manuscript had been read and accepted by an enthusiastic publisher. Knipe followed with one in his own name, then made a dozen more for good measure. In no time at all, Adolph Knipe's Literary Agency had become famous for its large stable of promising young novelists.

And once again the money started rolling in.

It was at this stage that young Knipe began to display a real talent for big business.

"See here, Mr. Bohlen," he said. "We still got too much competition. Why don't we just absorb all the other writers in the country?"

Mr. Bohlen, who now sported a bottle-green velvet jacket and allowed his hair to cover two-thirds of his ears, was quite content with things the way they were. "Don't know what you mean, my boy. You can't just absorb writers."

"Of course you can, sir. Exactly like Rockefeller did with his oil companies. Simply buy 'em out, and if they won't sell, squeeze 'em out. It's easy!"

"Careful now, Knipe. Be careful."

"I've got a list here, sir, of fifty of the most successful writers in the country, and what I intend to do is offer each one of them a lifetime contract with pay. All *they* have to do is undertake never to write another word; and, of course, to let us use their names on our own stuff. How about that?"

"They'll never agree."

"You don't know writers, Mr. Bohlen. You watch and see."

"What about that creative urge, Knipe?"

"It's bunk! All they're really interested in is the money—just like everybody else."

In the end, Mr. Bohlen reluctantly agreed to give it a try, and Knipe, with his list of writers in his pocket, went off in a large chauffeur-driven Cadillac to make his calls.

He journeyed first to the man at the top of the list, a very great and

wonderful writer, and he had no trouble getting into the house. He told his story and produced a suitcase full of sample novels, and a contract for the man to sign which guaranteed him so much a year for life. The man listened politely, decided he was dealing with a lunatic, gave him a drink, then firmly showed him to the door.

The second writer on the list, when he saw Knipe was serious, actually attacked him with a large metal paperweight, and the inventor had to flee down the garden followed by such a torrent of abuse and obscenity as he had never heard before.

But it took more than this to discourage Adolph Knipe. He was disappointed but not dismayed, and off he went in his big car to seek his next client. This one was a female, famous and popular, whose fat romantic books sold by the million across the country. She received Knipe graciously, gave him tea, and listened attentively to his story.

"It all sounds very fascinating," she said. "But of course I find it a little hard to believe."

"Madam," Knipe answered. "Come with me and see it with your own eyes. My car awaits you."

So off they went, and in due course, the astonished lady was ushered into the machine house where the wonder was kept. Eagerly, Knipe explained its workings, and after a while he even permitted her to sit in the driver's seat and practice with the buttons.

"All right," he said suddenly. "You want to do a book now?"

"Oh yes!" she cried. "Please!"

She was very competent and seemed to know exactly what she

wanted. She made her own pre-selections, then ran off a long, romantic, passion-filled novel. She read through the first chapter and became so enthusiastic that she signed up on the spot.

"That's one of them out of the way," Knipe said to Mr. Bohlen afterwards. "A pretty big one too."

"Nice work, my boy."

And you know *why* she signed?"

"Why?"

"It wasn't the money. She's got plenty of that."

"Then why?"

Knipe grinned, lifting his lip and baring a long pale upper gum. "Simply because she saw the machine-made stuff was better than her own."

Thereafter, Knipe wisely decided to concentrate only upon mediocrity. Anything better than that—and there were so few it didn't matter much—was apparently not quite so easy to seduce.

In the end, after several months of work, he had persuaded something like seventy per cent of the writers on his list to sign the contract. He found that the older ones, those who were running out of ideas and had taken to drink, were the easiest to handle. The younger people were more troublesome. They were apt to become abusive, sometimes violent when he approached them; and more than once Knipe was slightly injured on his rounds.

But on the whole, it was a satisfactory beginning. This last year—the first full year of the machine's operation—it was estimated that at least one half of all the novels and stories published in the English language were produced by Adolph Knipe upon the Great Automatic Grammatisator.

Does this surprise you?

I doubt it.

And worse is yet to come. Today, as the secret spreads, many more are hurrying to tie up with Mr. Knipe. And all the time the screw turns tighter for those who hesitate to sign their names.

This very moment, as I sit here listening to the howling of my nine starving children in the other room, I can feel my own hand creeping closer and closer to that golden contract that lies over on the other side of the desk.

Give us strength, oh Lord, to let our children starve.

A: I wonder if a computer really could write a short story?

B: I read where computers now handle a lot of business correspondence. Do you think they'll ever make people obsolete?

# AUTO WRECK

Karl Shapiro

Its quick soft silver bell beating, beating,
And down the dark one ruby flare
Pulsing out red light like an artery,
The ambulance at top speed floating down
Past beacons and illuminated clocks
Wings in a heavy curve, dips down,
And brakes speed, entering the crowd.
The doors leap open, emptying light;
Stretchers are laid out, the mangled lifted
And stowed into the little hospital.                    10
Then the bell, breaking the hush, tolls once,
And the ambulance with its terrible cargo
Rocking, slightly rocking, moves away,
As the doors, an afterthought, are closed.

We are deranged, walking among the cops
Who sweep glass and are large and composed.
One is still making notes under the light.
One with a bucket douches ponds of blood
Into the street and gutter.
One hangs lanterns on the wrecks that cling,     20
Empty husks of locusts, to iron poles.

Our throats were tight as tourniquets,
Our feet were bound with splints, but now,
Like convalescents intimate and gauche,
We speak through sickly smiles and warn
With the stubborn saw of common sense,
The grim joke and the banal resolution.
The traffic moves around with care,
But we remain, touching a wound
That opens to our richest horror.                       30
Already old, the question Who shall die?
Becomes unspoken Who is innocent?
For death in war is done by hands;
Suicide has cause and stillbirth, logic;
And cancer, simple as a flower, blooms.
But this invites the occult mind,
Cancels our physics with a sneer,
And splatters all we knew of denouement
Across the expedient and wicked stones.

306

# Demolition Derby

Stan Isaacs

In a society where the automobile threatens to become the master of the human being, the special madness known as the Demolition Derby deserves an exalted place. It is man's revenge against the machine.

Reprinted with permission from Newsday, Inc.

The Demolition Derby, as conceived by Islip Speedway's Larry Mendelsohn, is a grand elimination contest of autos bashing each other to shrapnel. It is the Coney Island bumping ride elevated to its creative sense. It has been called "a sport that ranks with the gladiatorial games of Rome as a piece of national symbolism."

The Demolition Derby is the vicarious answer to the inherent desire of every driver to smash into other cars. Gloriously, the Demolition Derby is, at once, as wild and hilarious and relatively harmless as it is violent.

Mendelsohn's contribution is in raising the Demolition Derby horizon. From eight-car crash competitions, Mendelsohn upped the fields to 100-car derbies broken down into four 25-car heats. Mendelsohn now lines up cars and drivers for derbies in 108 cities. There were Demolition Derbies in four cities Saturday night, including one at Islip, the center of Mendelsohn's burgeoning demolition dynasty.

The cars at Islip Saturday generally were early 1950 models that had been beefed up, but not so much that the eye could see. The start was initiated by the public-address announcer leading the crowd in a countdown of "10-9-8-7-6-5-4-3-2-1-Bingo!"

Most of the entries drove backward toward the center of the arena. All at once there was a banging, crunching, juicy collison of metal. Groups of two, three, four, and five cars seemingly all collided at once, and the arena was strewn with smoking and battered wrecks—an instant junkyard.

The survivors of the first crashes then putt-putted out in search of further prey, crashing fore, aft, and amid cars with exhilarating crunches. The drivers rarely seemed the worse for wear, and an aficionado claimed that nobody ever has been seriously hurt in a Demolition Derby: "It's like two boxers swinging in a telephone booth; they can't get up enough steam to hurt each other."

There is a bullfight quality about one car bearing down on another, only to have the target ease out of the way just in time. The sight of one car zigzagging in reverse after a retreating opponent, between wrecks, is like one chipmunk scurrying after another in the underbrush.

The crowd broke up at the sight of two cars, both of them wrecked almost beyond recognition, having at each other, in a corner, like two punch-drunk fighters. Both were ever in mortal danger of being knocked off by any of the cars cruising within fender distance. But they only had fenders for each other.

The crowd assumed an instant identification with cars that aggressively sought out adversaries. A car that was being attacked by two opponents at the same time was sure to gain the sympathy and support of the spectators.

The battle for survival conjured up the aura of the gladiators, and there was a certain sentimental attachment formed for a beaten-up machine that limped off from a crash to lock fenders with another foe. A little white car, No. 707, was a particularly gallant entry in one of the Saturday heats. He met and defeated one heavier car after another, seemingly at the point of extinction after every collision.

Finally after one rugged encounter, 707 did not start up again. He appeared to be finished. But, after a moment, the driver got him going again, and back he went into the fray—as noble and pathetic as Don Quixote—only to be done under finally by a heavier and fresher foe.

Mendelsohn, the demoniacal genius, has devised it so that a gallant loser like 707 can be voted into the finals by the crowd. The survivor of each heat is accompanied into the final along with a fallen warrior that wins the voice vote of the fans answering the public-address announcer.

Saturday's final came down to eight cars, including the Carlson brothers and Ted Wesnofske, Demolition Derby stars. These three then outlasted the other five, and the action then developed into an elementary drama, the Brothers Carlson against Wesnofske.

Time and time again, it seemed that the 2-against-1 odds were too much for Wesnofske. Once, when the two Carlsons hit him at once, it seemed as if he was out for good. The crowd groaned. But as the two brothers moved out to the middle to do battle with each other, Wesnofske's car revived, and he rejoined the fray.

It seemed too much to believe that he could continue to avoid the two-car attack. Yet Wesnofske picked off one brother's radiator, causing the car to go up in flames. The crowd roared. Once Wesnofske was on even terms, he was able to knock out the second brother without too much trouble.

Pocketing the $500 first prize, Wesnofske, a 24-year-old landscape worker from Huntington Station, promised to be back for the 200-car World Demolition Derby championship at Islip September 18. "You know," he said, "I think those brothers were out just to get me at first."

It is the ". . . inherent desire of every driver to smash into other cars."
AGREE?
DISAGREE?

# IS THERE LIFE ON EARTH?

Art Buchwald

There was great excitement on the planet of Venus this week. For the first time Venusian scientists managed to land a satellite on the planet Earth, and it has been sending back signals, as well as photographs, ever since.

The satellite was directed into an area known as Manhattan (named after the great Venusian astronomer Professor Manhattan, who first discovered it with his telescope 200,000 light-years ago).

Because of excellent weather conditions and extremely strong signals, Venusian scientists were able to get valuable information on the feasibility of a manned flying saucer's landing on Earth. A press conference was held at the Venus Institute of Technology.

"We have come to the conclusion, based on last week's satellite landing," Professor Zog said, "that there is no life on Earth."

"How do you know this?" the science reporter of the Venus *Evening Star* asked.

"For one thing, Earth's surface in the area of Manhattan is composed of solid concrete, and nothing can grow there. For another, the atmosphere is filled with carbon monoxide and other deadly gases, and nobody could possibly breathe this air and survive."

"What does this mean as far as our flying saucer program is concerned?"

"We shall have to take our own oxygen with us, which means a much heavier flying saucer than we originally planned."

"Are there any other hazards that you discovered in your studies?"

"Take a look at this photo. You see this dark black cloud hovering over the surface of Earth? We call this the Consolidated Edison Belt. We don't know what it is made of; but it could give us a lot of trouble, and we shall have to make further tests before we send a Venus being there.

"Over here you will notice what seems to be a river, but the satellite findings indicate it is polluted, and the water is unfit to drink. This means we shall have to carry our own water, which will add even greater weight to the saucer."

"Sir, what are all those tiny black spots on the photographs?"

"We're not certain. They seem to be metal particles that move along certain paths. They emit gases, make noise, and keep crashing into each other. There are so many of these paths and so many metal particles that it is impossible to land a flying saucer without being smashed by one."

"What are those stalagmite projections sticking up?"

"They're some type of granite formation that gives off light at night. Professor Glom has named them skyscrapers since they seem to be scraping the skies."

"If all you say is true, won't this set back the flying saucer program several years?"

"Yes, but we shall proceed as soon as the Grubstart gives us the added funds."

"Professor Zog, why are we spending billions and billions of Zilches to land a flying saucer on Earth when there is no life there?"

"Because if we Venusians can learn to breathe in an Earth atmosphere, then we can live anywhere."

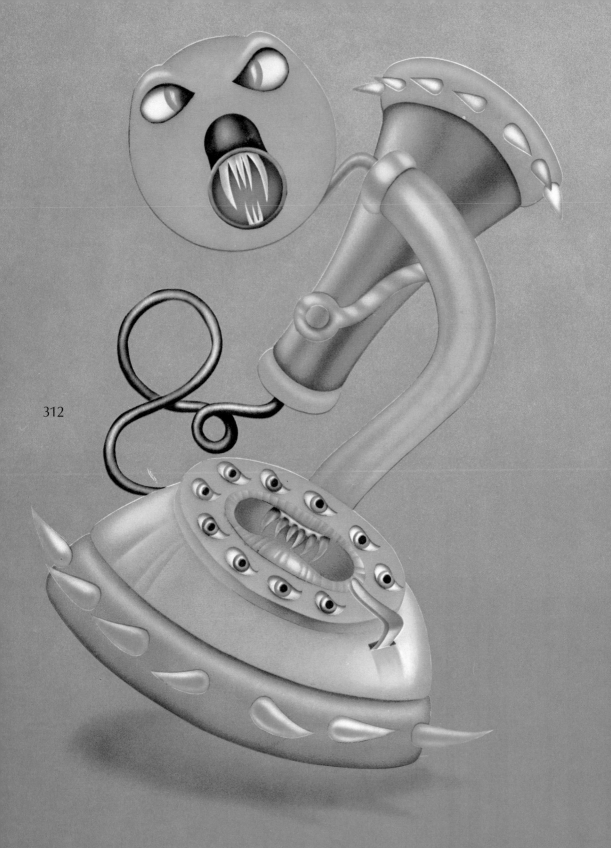

312

# NIGHTMARE NUMBER THREE

*Stephen Vincent Benét*

We had expected everything but revolt
And I kind of wonder myself when they started thinking—
But there's no dice in that now.
                              I've heard fellows say
They must have planned it for years and maybe they did.
Looking back, you can find little incidents here and there,
Like the concrete-mixer in Jersey eating the wop
Or the roto press that printed "Fiddle-dee-dee!"
In a three-color process all over Senator Sloop,
Just as he was making a speech. The thing about that          10
Was, how could it walk upstairs? But it was upstairs,
Clicking and mumbling in the Senate Chamber.
They had to knock out the wall to take it away
And the wrecking-crew said it grinned.
                              It was only the best
Machines, of course, the superhuman machines,
The ones we'd built to be better than flesh and bone,
But the cars were in it, of course . . .
                              and they hunted us
Like rabbits through the cramped streets on that Bloody Monday,    20
The Madison Avenue busses leading the charge.
The busses were pretty bad—but I'll not forget
The smash of glass when the Duesenberg left the show-room
And pinned three brokers to the Racquet Club steps
Or the long howl of the horns when they saw men run,
When they saw them looking for holes in the solid ground . . .

I guess they were tired of being ridden in
And stopped and started by pygmies for silly ends,
Of wrapping cheap cigarettes and bad chocolate bars
Collecting nickels and waving platinum hair                   30
And letting six million people live in a town.
I guess it was that. I guess they got tired of us
And the whole smell of human hands.

313

                                    But it was a shock
To climb sixteen flights of stairs to Art Zuckow's office
(Nobody took the elevators twice)
And find him strangled to death in a nest of telephones,
The octopus-tendrils waving over his head,
And a sort of quiet humming filling the air. . . .
Do they eat? . . . There was red . . . But I did not stop to look.          40
I don't know yet how I got to the roof in time
And it's lonely, here on the roof.
                                    For a while, I thought
That window-cleaner would make it, and keep me company.
But they got him with his own hoist at the sixteenth floor
And dragged him in, with a squeal.
You see, they cooperate. Well, we taught them that
And it's fair enough, I suppose. You see, we built them.
We taught them to think for themselves.
It was bound to come. You can see it was bound to come.          50

And it won't be so bad, in the country. I hate to think
Of the reapers, running wild in the Kansas fields,
And the transport planes like hawks on a chickenyard,
But the horses might help. We might make a deal with the horses.
At least, you've more chance, out there.
                                    And they need us, too.
They're bound to realize that when they once calm down.
They'll need oil and spare parts and adjustments and tuning up.
Slaves? Well, in a way, you know, we were slaves before.
There won't be so much real difference—honest, there won't.          60
(I wish I hadn't looked into that beauty-parlor
And seen what was happening there.
But those are female machines and a bit high-strung.)
Oh, we'll settle down. We'll arrange it. We'll compromise.
It wouldn't make sense to wipe out the whole human race.
Why, I bet if I went to my old Plymouth now
(Of course you'd have to do it the tactful way)
And said, "Look here! Who got you the swell French horn?"
He wouldn't turn me over to those police cars;
At least I don't think he would.          70
                                    Oh, it's going to be jake.
There won't be so much real difference—honest, there won't—
And I'd go down in a minute and take my chance—
I'm a good American and I always liked them—
Except for one small detail that bothers me
And that's the food proposition. Because, you see,
The concrete-mixer may have made a mistake,
And it looks like just high spirits.
But, if it's got so they like the flavor . . . well . . .

314

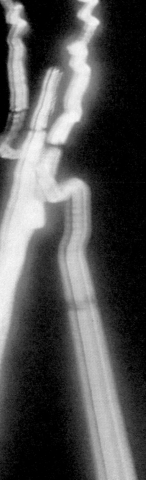

# Southbound on the Freeway

A tourist came in from Orbitville,
parked in the air, and said:

The creatures of this star
are made of metal and glass.

Through the transparent parts
you can see their guts.

Their feet are round and roll
on diagrams—or long

measuring tapes—dark
with white lines.                    10

They have four eyes.
The two in the back are red.

Sometimes you can see a 5-eyed
one, with a red eye turning

on the top of his head.
He must be special—

the others respect him,
and go slow,

when he passes, winding
among them from behind.          20

They all hiss as they glide,
like inches, down the marked

tapes. Those soft shapes,
shadowy inside

the hard bodies—are they
their guts or their brains?

—May Swenson

316

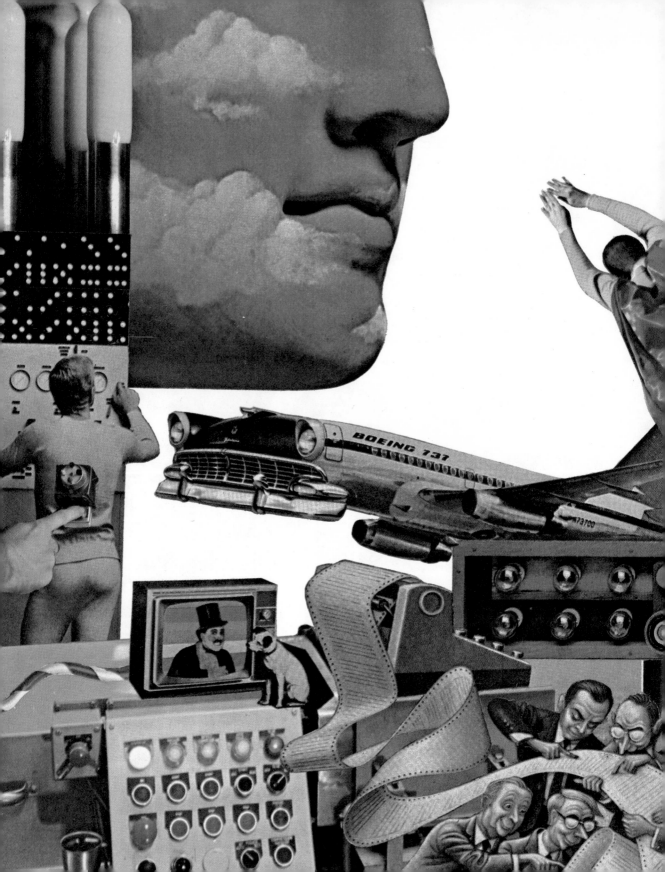

**11**

# The Last Night of the World

Ray Bradbury

"What would you do if you knew that this was the last night of the world?"

"What would I do? You mean seriously?"

"Yes, seriously."

"I don't know. I hadn't thought."

He poured some coffee. In the background the two girls were playing blocks on the parlor rug in the light of the green hurricane lamps. There was an easy, clean aroma of the brewed coffee in the evening air.

"Well, better start thinking about it," he said.

"You don't mean it!"

He nodded.

"A war?"

He shook his head.

"Not the hydrogen or atom bomb?"

"No."

"Or germ warfare?"

"None of those at all," he said, stirring his coffee slowly. "But just, let's say, the closing of a book."

"I don't think I understand."

"No, nor do I, really; it's just a feeling. Sometimes it frightens me, sometimes I'm not frightened at all but at peace." He glanced in at the girls and their yellow hair shining in the lamplight. "I didn't say anything to you. It first happened about four nights ago."

"What?"

"A dream I had. I dreamed that it was all going to be over, and a voice said it was; not any kind of voice I can remember, but a voice anyway, and it said things would stop here on Earth. I didn't think too much about it the next day, but then I went to the office and caught Stan Willis looking out the window in the middle of the afternoon, and I said a penny for your thoughts, Stan, and he said, I had a dream last night, and before he even told me the dream I knew what it was. I could have told him, but he told me and I listened to him."

"It was the same dream?"

"The same. I told Stan I had dreamed it too. He didn't seem surprised. He relaxed, in fact. Then we started walking through the office, for the hell of it. It wasn't planned. We didn't say, 'Let's walk around.' We just walked on our own, and everywhere we saw people looking at their desks or their hands or out windows. I talked to a few. So did Stan."

"And they all had dreamed?"

"All of them. The same dream, with no difference."

"Do you believe in it?"

"Yes. I've never been more certain."

"And when will it stop? The world, I mean."

"Sometime during the night for us, and then as the night goes on around the world, that'll go too. It'll take twenty-four hours for it all to go."

They sat awhile not touching their coffee. Then they lifted it slowly and drank, looking at each other.

"Do we deserve this?" she said.

"It's not a matter of deserving; it's just that things didn't work out. I notice you didn't even argue about this. Why not?"

"I guess I've a reason," she said.

"The same one everyone at the office had?"

She nodded slowly. "I didn't want to say anything. It happened last night. And the women on the block talked about it, among themselves, today. They dreamed. I thought it was only a coincidence." She picked up the evening paper. "There's nothing in the paper about it."

"Everyone knows, so there's no need."

He sat back in his chair, watching her. "Are you afraid?"

"No. I always thought I would be, but I'm not."

"Where's that spirit called self-preservation they talk so much about?"

"I don't know. You don't get too excited when you feel things are logical. This is logical. Nothing else but this could have happened from the way we've lived."

"We haven't been too bad, have we?"

"No, nor enormously good. I suppose that's the trouble—we haven't been very much of anything except us, while a big part of the world was busy being lots of quite awful things."

The girls were laughing in the parlor.

"I always thought people would be screaming in the streets at a time like this."

"I guess not. You don't scream about the real thing."

"Do you know, I won't miss anything but you and the girls. I never liked cities or my work or anything except you three. I won't miss a thing except perhaps the change in the weather, and a glass of ice water when it's hot, and I might miss sleeping. How can we sit here and talk this way?"

"Because there's nothing else to do."

"That's it, of course; for if there were, we'd be doing it. I suppose this is the first time in the history of the world that everyone has known just what they were going to do during the night."

"I wonder what everyone else will do now, this evening, for the next few hours."

"Go to a show, listen to the radio, watch television, play cards, put the children to bed, go to bed themselves, like always."

"In a way that's something to be proud of—like always."

They sat a moment and then he poured himself another coffee. "Why do you suppose it's tonight?"

"Because."

"Why not some other night in the last century, or five centuries ago, or ten?"

"Maybe it's because it was never October 19, 1969, ever before in history, and now it is and that's it; because this date means more than any other date ever meant; because it's the year when things are as they are all over the world and that's why it's the end."

"There are bombers on their schedules both ways across the ocean tonight that'll never see land."

"That's part of the reason why."

"Well," he said, getting up, "what shall it be? Wash the dishes?"

They washed the dishes and stacked them away with special neatness. At eight-thirty the girls were put to bed and kissed good night and the little lights by their beds turned on and the door left open just a trifle.

"I wonder," said the husband, coming from the bedroom and glancing back, standing there with his pipe for a moment.

"What?"

"If the door will be shut all the way, or if it'll be left just a little ajar so some light comes in."

"I wonder if the children know."

"No, of course not."

They sat and read the papers and talked and listened to some radio music and then sat together by the fireplace watching the charcoal embers as the clock struck ten-thirty and eleven and eleven-thirty. They thought of all the other people in the world who had spent their evening, each in his own special way.

"Well," he said at last.

He kissed his wife for a long time.

"We've been good for each other, anyway."

"Do you want to cry?" he asked.

"I don't think so."

They moved through the house and turned out the lights and went into the bedroom and stood in the night cool darkness undressing and pushing back the covers. "The sheets are so clean and nice."

"I'm tired."

"We're *all* tired."

They got into bed and lay back.

"Just a moment," she said.

He heard her get out of bed and go into the kitchen. A moment later, she returned. "I left the water running in the sink," she said.

Something about this was so very funny that he had to laugh.

She laughed with him, knowing what it was that she had done that was funny. They stopped laughing at last and lay in their cool night bed, their hands clasped, their heads together.

"Good night," he said, after a moment.

"Good night," she said.

Lo! 'tis a gala night.
　Within the lonesome latter years!
An angel throng, bewinged, bedight
　In veils, and drowned in tears,
Sit in a theater, to see
　A play of hopes and fears,
While the orchestra breathes fitfully
　The music of the spheres.

Mimes, in the form of God on high,
　Mutter and mumble low,
And hither and thither fly—
　Mere puppets they, who come and go
At bidding of vast formless things
　That shift the scenery to and fro,
Flapping from out their Condor wings
　Invisible Woe!

That motley drama—oh, be sure
　It shall not be forgot!
With its Phantom chased for evermore,
　By a crowd that seize it not,
Through a circle that ever returneth in
　To the self-same spot,
And much of Madness, and more of Sin,
　And Horror the soul of the plot.

But see, amid the mimic rout
　A crawling shape intrude!
A blood-red thing that writhes from out
　The scenic solitude!
It writhes!—it writhes!—with mortal pangs
　The mimes become its food,
And seraphs sob at vermin fangs
　In human gore imbued.

Out—out are the lights—out all!
　And, over each quivering form,
The curtain, a funeral pall,
　Comes down with a rush of a storm,
While the angels, all pallid and wan,
　Uprising, unveiling, affirm
That the play is the tragedy, "Man,"
　And its hero the Conqueror Worm.

# The Conqueror Worm

Edgar Allan Poe

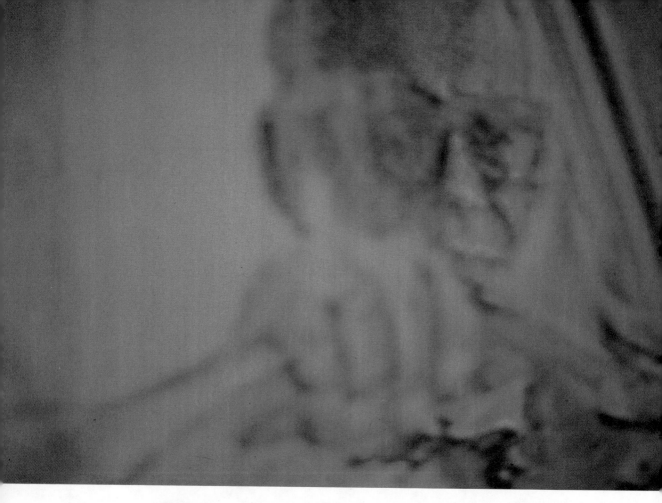

# The Jam

*Henry Slesar*

They left Stukey's pad around eight in the morning; that was the kind of weekend it had been. Early to bed, early to rise. Stukey laughed, squinting through the dirt-stained windshield of the battered Ford, pushing the pedal until the needle swung 20, 30 miles over the speed limit. It was all Mitch's fault, but Mitch, curled up on the seat beside him like an embryo in a black leather womb, didn't seem to care. He was hurting too much, needing the quick jab of the sharp sweet point and the hot flow of the stuff in his veins. Man, what a weekend, Stukey thought, and it wasn't over yet. The fix was out there, someplace in the wilds of New Jersey, and Stukey, who never touched the filthy stuff himself, was playing good Samaritan. He hunched over the wheel like Indianapolis, pounding the horn with the heel of his right hand, shouting at the passing cars to *move over, move over you . . . watch where you're going, stupid, pull over, pull over, you lousy . . .*

"You tell 'em, man," Mitch said softly, "you tell 'em what to do."

Stukey didn't tell them, he showed them. He skinned the paint off a Buick as he snaked in and out of the line, and crowded so close to the tail of an MG that he could have run right over the little red wagon. Mitch began to giggle, urging him on, forgetting for the moment his destination and his need, delighting in the way Stukey used the car like a buzz saw, slicing a path through the squares in their Sunday driving stupor. "Look out, man," Mitch cackled, "here comes old Stukey, here comes nothin'."

The traffic artery was starting to clot at the entrance to the tunnel, and Stukey poured it on, jockeying the car first left and then right, grinning at the competitive game. Nobody had a chance to win with Stukey at the controls; Stukey could just shut his eyes and gun her; nobody else could do that. They made the tunnel entrance after sideswiping a big yellow Caddy, an episode that made Mitch laugh aloud with glee. They both felt better after that, and the tunnel was cool after the hot morning sun. Stukey relaxed a little, and Mitch stopped his low-pitched giggling, content to stare hypnotically at the blur of white tiles.

"I hope we find that fix, man," Mitch said dreamily. "My cousin, he says that's the place to go. How long you think, Stukey? How long?"

*Whish!* A Chevy blasted by him on the other lane, and Stukey swore. *Whish!* went an Oldsmobile, and Stukey bore down on the accelerator, wanting his revenge on the open road outside the tunnel. But the tunnel wound on, endlessly, longer than it ever had before. It was getting hot and hard to breathe; little pimples of sweat covered his face and trickled down into his leather collar; under the brass-studded coat, the sport shirt clung damply to his back and underarms. Mitch started to whine, and got that wide-eyed fishmouth look of his, and he gasped: "Man, I'm suffocating. I'm passing out . . ."

"What do you want me to do?" Stukey yelled. Still the tunnel wound on. *Whish!* went the cars in the parallel lane, and Stukey cursed his bad choice, cursed the heat, cursed Mitch, cursed all the Sundays that ever were. He shot a look at the balcony where the cops patrolled the traffic, and decided to take a chance. He slowed the car down to 35, and yanked the wheel sharply to the right to slip the car into a faster lane, right in front of a big, children-filled station wagon. Even in the tunnel roar they could hear its driver's angry shout, and Stukey told him what he could do with his station wagon and his children. Still the tunnel wound on.

They saw the hot glare of daylight at the exit. Mitch moaned in relief, but nothing could soften Stukey's ire. They came out of the tunnel and turned onto the highway, only to jerk to a halt behind a station wagon with a smelly exhaust. "Come on, come on!" Stukey muttered, and blew his horn. But the horn didn't start the cars moving, and Stukey, swearing, opened the door and had himself a look.

"Oh, man, man, they're stacked up for miles!" he groaned. "You wouldn't believe it, you wouldn't think its possible . . ."

"What is it?" Mitch said, stirring in his seat. "What is it? An accident?"

"I dunno, I can't see a thing. But they just ain't movin', not a foot——"

"I'm sick," Mitch groaned. "I'm sick, Stukey."

"Shut up! Shut up!" Stukey said, hopping out of the car to stare at the sight again, at the ribbon of automobiles vanishing into a horizon 10, 15 miles away. Like one enormous reptile it curled over the highway, a snake with multicolored skin, lying asleep under the hot sun. He climbed back in again, and the station wagon moved an inch, a foot, and greedily, he stomped the gas pedal to gobble up the gap. A trooper on a motorcycle bounced between the lanes, and Stukey leaned out of the window to shout at him, inquiring; he rumbled on implacably. The heat got worse, furnace-like and scorching, making him yelp when his hands touched metal. Savagely, Stukey hit the horn again, and heard a dim chorus ahead. Every few minutes, the station wagon jumped, and every few minutes, Stukey closed the gap. But an hour accumulated, and more, and they could still see the tunnel exit behind them. Mitch was whimpering now, and Stukey climbed in and out of the car like a madman, his clothes sopping with sweat, his eyes wild, cursing whenever he hit the gas pedal and crawled another inch, another foot forward . . .

"A cop! A cop!" he heard Mitch scream as a trooper, on foot, marched past the window. Stukey opened the car door and caught the uniformed arm. "Help us, will ya?" he pleaded. "What the hell's going on here? How do we get outa this?"

"You don't," the trooper said curtly. "You can't get off anyplace. Just stick it out, Mac."

"We'll even leave the . . . car. We'll walk, . . . I don't care about the damn car . . ."

"Sorry, mister. Nobody's allowed off the highway, even on foot. You can't leave this heap here, don't you know that?" He studied Stukey's sweaty face, and grinned suddenly. "Oh, I get it. You're new here, ain't you?"

"What do you mean, new?"

"I thought I never saw you in the Jam before, pal. Well, take it easy, fella."

"How long?" Stukey said hoarsely. "How long you think?"

"That's a stupid question," the trooper sneered. "Forever, of course. Eternity. Where the hell do you think you are?" He jabbed a finger into Stukey's chest. "But don't give *me* a hard time, buster. That was your *own* wreck back there."

"Wreck?" Mitch rasped from inside the car. "What wreck? What's he talkin' about, man?"

"The wreck you had in the tunnel." He waved his gloved hand toward the horizon. "That's where *all* these jokers come from, the tunnel wrecks. If you think this is bad, you ought to see the Jam on the turnpike."

"Wreck? Wreck?" Mitch screamed, as Stukey climbed behind the wheel. "What's he talking about wrecks for, Stukey?"

"Shut up, shut up!" Stukey sobbed, pounding his foot on the gas pedal to gain yet another inch of road. "We gotta get outa here, we gotta get out!" But even when the station wagon jerked forward once more, he knew he was asking for too much, too late.

# The Landlady

Roald Dahl

Billy Weaver had traveled down from London on the slow afternoon train, with a change at Reading on the way, and by the time he got to Bath it was about nine o'clock in the evening and the moon was coming up out of a clear starry sky over the houses opposite the station entrance. But the air was deadly cold and the wind was like a flat blade of ice on his cheeks.

"Excuse me," he said, "but is there a fairly cheap hotel not too far away from here?"

"Try The Bell and Dragon," the porter answered, pointing down the road. "They might take you in. It's about a quarter of a mile along on the other side."

Billy thanked him and picked up his suitcase and set out to walk the quarter-mile to The Bell and Dragon. He had never been to Bath before. He didn't know anyone who lived there. But Mr. Greenslade at the Head Office in London had told him it was a splendid town. "Find your own lodgings," he had said, "and then go along and report to the Branch Manager as soon as you've got yourself settled."

Billy was seventeen years old. He was wearing a new navy blue overcoat, a new brown trilby hat, and a new brown suit, and he was feeling fine. He walked briskly down the street. He was trying to do everything briskly these days. Briskness, he had decided, was *the* one common characteristic of all successful businessmen. The big shots up at Head Office were absolutely fantastically brisk all the time. They were amazing.

There were no shops on this wide street that he was walking along, only a line of tall houses on each side, all of them identical. They had porches and pillars and four or five steps going up to their front doors, and it was obvious that once upon a time they had been very swanky residences. But now, even in the darkness, he could see that the paint was peeling from the woodwork on their doors and windows, and that the handsome white façades were cracked and blotchy from neglect.

Suddenly, in a downstairs window that was brilliantly illuminated by a street lamp not six yards away, Billy caught sight of a printed notice propped up against the glass in one of the upper panes. It said BED AND BREAKFAST. There was a vase of yellow chrysanthemums, tall and beautiful, standing just underneath the notice.

He stopped walking. He moved a bit closer. Green curtains (some sort of velvety material) were hanging down on either side of the window. The chrysanthemums looked wonderful beside them. He went right up and peered through the glass into the room, and the first thing he saw was a bright fire burning in the hearth. On the carpet in front of the fire, a pretty little dachshund was curled up asleep

with its nose tucked into its belly. The room itself, so far as he could see in the half-darkness, was filled with pleasant furniture. There was a baby grand piano and a big sofa and several plump armchairs; and in one corner he spotted a large parrot in a cage. Animals were usually a good sign in a place like this, Billy told himself; and all in all, it looked to him as though it would be a pretty decent house to stay in. Certainly it would be more comfortable than The Bell and Dragon.

On the other hand, a pub would be more congenial than a boarding house. There would be beer and darts in the evenings, and lots of people to talk to, and it would probably be a good bit cheaper, too. He had stayed a couple of nights in a pub once before and he had liked it. He had never stayed in any boarding houses, and, to be perfectly honest, he was a tiny bit frightened of them. The name itself conjured up images of watery cabbage, rapacious landladies, and a powerful smell of kippers in the living room.

After dithering about like this in the cold for two or three minutes, Billy decided that he would walk on and take a look at The Bell and Dragon before making up his mind. He turned to go.

And now a queer thing happened to him. He was in the act of stepping back and turning away from the window when all at once his eye was caught and held in the most peculiar manner by the small notice that was there. BED AND BREAKFAST, it said. BED AND BREAKFAST, BED AND BREAKFAST, BED AND BREAKFAST. Each word was like a large black eye staring at him through the glass, holding him, compelling him, forcing him to stay where he was and not to walk away from that house, and the next thing he knew, he was actually moving across from the window to the front door of the house, climbing the steps that led up to it, and reaching for the bell.

He pressed the bell. Far away in a back room he heard it ringing and then *at once*—it must have been at once because he hadn't even had time to take his finger from the bell button—the door swung open and a woman was standing there.

Normally you ring the bell and you have at least a half-minute's wait before the door opens. But this dame was like a jack-in-the-box. He pressed the bell—and out she popped! It made him jump.

She was about forty-five or fifty years old, and the moment she saw him, she gave him a warm welcoming smile.

"*Please* come in," she said pleasantly. She stepped aside, holding the door wide open, and Billy found himself automatically starting forward. The compulsion or, more accurately, the desire to follow after her into that house was extraordinarily strong.

"I saw the notice in the window," he said, holding himself back.

"Yes, I know."

"I was wondering about a room."

"It's *all* ready for you, my dear," she said. She had a round pink face and very gentle blue eyes.

"I was on my way to The Bell and Dragon," Billy told her. "But the notice in your window just happened to catch my eye."

"My dear boy," she said, "why don't you come in out of the cold?"

"How much do you charge?"

"Five and sixpence a night, including breakfast."

It was fantastically cheap. It was less than half of what he had been willing to pay.

"If that is too much," she added, "then perhaps I can reduce it just a tiny bit. Do you desire an egg for breakfast? Eggs are expensive at the moment. It would be sixpence less without the egg."

"Five and sixpence is fine," he answered. "I should like very much to stay here."

"I knew you would. Do come in."

She seemed terribly nice. She looked exactly like the mother of one's best school friend welcoming one into the house to stay for the Christmas holidays. Billy took off his hat, and stepped over the threshold.

"Just hang it there," she said, "and let me help you with your coat."

There were no other hats or coats in the hall. There were no umbrellas, no walking sticks—nothing.

"We have it *all* to ourselves," she said, smiling at him over her shoulder as she led the way upstairs. "You see, it isn't very often I have the pleasure of taking a visitor into my little nest."

The old girl is slightly dotty, Billy told himself. But at five and sixpence a night, who gives a damn about that? "I should've thought you'd be simply swamped with applicants," he said politely.

"Oh, I am, my dear, I am, of course I am. But the trouble is that I'm inclined to be just a teeny weeny bit choosy and particular—if you see what I mean."

"Ah, yes."

"But I'm always ready. Every-thing is always ready day and night in this house just on the off-chance that an acceptable young gentleman will come along. And it is such a pleasure, my dear, such a very great pleasure when now and again I open the door and I see someone standing there who is just *exactly* right." She was halfway up the stairs, and she paused with one hand on the stair-rail, turning her head and smiling down at him with pale lips. "Like you," she added, and her blue eyes traveled slowly all the way down the length of Billy's body, to his feet, and then up again.

On the second floor landing she said to him, "This floor is mine."

They climbed up another flight. "And this one is *all* yours," she said. "Here's your room. I do hope you'll like it." She took him into a small but charming front bedroom, switching on the light as she went in.

"The morning sun comes right in the window, Mr. Perkins. It *is* Mr. Perkins, isn't it?"

"No," he said. "It's Weaver."

"Mr. Weaver. How nice. I've put a water bottle between the sheets to air them out, Mr. Weaver. It's such a comfort to have a hot water bottle in a strange bed with clean sheets, don't you agree? And you may light the gas fire at any time if you feel chilly."

"Thank you," Billy said. "Thank you ever so much." He noticed that the bedspread had been taken off the bed, and that the bedclothes had been neatly turned back on one side, all ready for someone to get in.

"I'm so glad you appeared," she said, looking earnestly into his face. "I was beginning to get worried."

"That's all right," Billy answered brightly. "You mustn't worry about me." He put his suitcase on the chair and started to open it.

"And what about supper, my dear? Did you manage to get any-thing to eat before you came here?"

"I'm not a bit hungry, thank you," he said. "I think I'll just go to bed as soon as possible because to-morrow I've got to get up rather early and report to the office."

"Very well, then. I'll leave you now so that you can unpack. But before you go to bed, would you be kind enough to pop into the sitting room on the ground floor and sign the book? Everyone has to do that because it's the law of the land, and we don't want to go breaking any laws at *this* stage in the proceedings, do we?" She gave him a little wave of the hand and went quickly out of the room and closed the door.

Now, the fact that his landlady appeared to be slightly off her rocker didn't worry Billy in the least. After all, she not only was harmless—there was no question about that—but she was also quite obviously a kind and generous soul. He guessed that she had probably lost a son in the war, or something like that, and had never gotten over it.

So a few minutes later, after unpacking his suitcase and washing his hands, he trotted downstairs to the ground floor and entered the liv-ing room. His landlady wasn't there, but the fire was glowing in the hearth, and the little dachshund was still sleeping soundly in front of it. The room was wonderfully warm and cozy. I'm a lucky fellow, he thought, rubbing his hands. This is a bit of all right.

He found the guest book lying open on the piano, so he took out his pen and wrote down his name and address. There were only two other entries above his on the page, and, as one always does with guest books, he started to read them. One was a Christopher Mulholland from Cardiff. The other was Gregory W. Temple from Bristol.

That's funny, he thought suddenly. Christopher Mulholland. It rings a bell.

Now where on earth had he heard that rather unusual name before?

Was it a boy at school? No. Was it one of his sister's numerous young men, perhaps, or a friend of his father's? No, no, it wasn't any of those. He glanced down again at the book.

*Christopher Mulholland*
*231 Cathedral Road, Cardiff*

*Gregory W. Temple*
*27 Sycamore Drive, Bristol*

As a matter of fact, now he came to think of it, he wasn't at all sure that the second name didn't have almost as much of a familiar ring about it as the first.

"Gregory Temple?" he said aloud, searching his memory. "Christopher Mulholland? . . ."

"Such charming boys," a voice behind him answered, and he turned and saw his landlady sailing into the room with a large silver tea tray in her hands. She was holding it well out in front of her, and rather high up, as though the tray were a pair of reins on a frisky horse.

"They sound somehow familiar," he said.

"They do? How interesting."

"I'm almost positive I've heard those names before somewhere. Isn't that odd? Maybe it was in the newspapers. They weren't famous in any way, were they? I mean famous cricketers or footballers or something like that?"

"Famous," she said, setting the tea tray down on the low table in front of the sofa. "Oh no, I don't think they were famous. But they were incredibly handsome, both of them, I can promise you that. They were tall and young and handsome, my dear, just exactly like you."

Once more, Billy glanced down at the book. "Look here," he said, noticing the dates. "This last entry is over two years old."

"It is?"

"Yes, indeed. And Christopher Mulholland's is nearly a year before that—more than *three years* ago."

"Dear me," she said, shaking her head and heaving a dainty little sigh. "I would never have thought it. How time does fly away from us all, doesn't it, Mr. Wilkins?"

"It's Weaver," Billy said. "W-e-a-v-e-r."

"Oh, of course it is!" she cried, sitting down on the sofa. "How silly of me. I do apologize. In one ear and out the other, that's me, Mr. Weaver."

"You know something?" Billy said. "Something that's really quite extraordinary about all this?"

"No, dear, I don't."

"Well, you see, both of these names—Mulholland and Temple—I not only seem to remember each one of them separately, so to speak, but somehow or other, in some peculiar way, they both appear to be sort of connected together as well. As though they were both famous for the same sort of thing, if you see what I mean— like . . . well . . . like

Dempsey and Tunney, for example, or Churchill and Roosevelt."

"How amusing," she said. "But come over here now, dear, and sit down beside me on the sofa and I'll give you a nice cup of tea and a ginger biscuit before you go to bed."

"You really shouldn't bother," Billy said. "I didn't mean you to do anything like that." He stood by the piano, watching her as she fussed about with the cups and saucers. He noticed that she had small, white, quickly moving hands, and red finger nails.

"I'm almost positive it was in the newspapers I saw them," Billy said. "I'll think of it in a second. I'm sure I will."

There is nothing more tantalizing than a thing like this that lingers just outside the borders of one's memory. He hated to give up.

"Now wait a minute," he said. "Wait just a minute. Mulholland . . . Christopher Mulholland . . . wasn't *that* the name of the Eton schoolboy who was on a walking tour through the West Country, and then all of a sudden . . ."

"Milk?" she said. "And sugar?"

"Yes, please. And then all of a sudden . . ."

"Eton schoolboy?" she said. "Oh no, my dear, that can't possibly be right because *my* Mr. Mulholland was certainly not an Eton schoolboy when he came to me. He was a Cambridge undergraduate. Come over here now and sit next to me and warm yourself in front of this lovely fire. Come on. Your tea's all ready for you." She patted the empty place beside her on the sofa, and she sat there smiling at Billy and waiting for him to come over.

He crossed the room slowly, and sat down on the edge of the sofa. She placed his teacup on the table in front of him.

"*There* we are," she said. "How nice and cozy this is, isn't it?"

Billy started sipping his tea. She did the same. For half a minute or so, neither of them spoke. But Billy knew that she was looking at him. Her body was half turned toward him, and he could feel her eyes resting on his face, watching him over the rim of her teacup. Now and again, he caught a whiff of a peculiar smell that seemed to emanate directly from her person. It was not in the least unpleasant, and it reminded him—well, he wasn't quite sure what it reminded him of. Pickled walnuts? New leather? Or was it the corridors of a hospital?

At length, she said, "Mr. Mulholland was a great one for his tea. Never in my life have I seen anyone drink as much tea as dear, sweet Mr. Mulholland."

"I suppose he left fairly recently," Billy said. He was still puzzling his head about the two names. He was positive now that he had seen them in the newspapers—in the headlines.

"Left?" she said, arching her brows. "But my dear boy, he never left. He's still here. Mr. Temple is also here. They're on the fourth floor, both of them together."

Billy set his cup down slowly on the table and stared at his landlady. She smiled back at him, and then she put out one of her white hands and patted him comfortingly on the knee. "How old are you, my dear?" she asked.

"Seventeen."

"Seventeen!" she cried. "Oh, it's the perfect age! Mr. Mulholland was also seventeen. But I think he was a trifle shorter than you are; in fact I'm sure he was, and his teeth weren't *quite* so white. You have the most beautiful teeth, Mr. Weaver, did you know that?"

"They're not as good as they look," Billy said. "They've got simply masses of fillings in them at the back."

"Mr. Temple, of course, was a little older," she said, ignoring his remark. "He was actually twenty-eight. And yet I never would have guessed it if he hadn't told me, never in my whole life. There wasn't a *blemish* on his body."

"A what?" Billy said.

"His skin was *just* like a baby's."

There was a pause. Billy picked up his teacup and took another sip of his tea, then he set it down again gently in its saucer. He waited for her to say something else, but she seemed to have lapsed into another of her silences. He sat there staring straight ahead of him into the far corner of the room, biting his lower lip.

"That parrot," he said at last. "You know something? It had me completely fooled when I first saw it through the window. I could have sworn it was alive."

"Alas, no longer."

"It's most terribly clever the way it's been done," he said. "It doesn't look in the least bit dead. Who did it?"

"I did."

"*You* did?"

"Of course," she said. "And have you met my little Basil as well?" She nodded toward the dachshund curled up so comfortably in front of the fire. Billy looked at it. And suddenly, he realized that this animal had all the time been just as silent and motionless as the parrot. He put out a hand and touched it gently on the top of its back. The back was hard and cold, and when he pushed the hair to one side with his fingers, he could see the skin underneath, greyish-black and dry and perfectly preserved.

"Good gracious me," he said. "How absolutely fascinating." He turned away from the dog and stared with deep admiration at the little woman beside him on the sofa. "It must be most awfully difficult to do a thing like that."

"Not in the least," she said. "I stuff *all* my little pets myself when they pass away. Will you have another cup of tea?"

"No, thank you," Billy said. The tea tasted faintly of bitter almonds, and he didn't much care for it.

"You did sign the book, didn't you?"

"Oh, yes."

"That's good. Because later on, if I happen to forget what you were called, then I could always come down here and look it up. I still do that almost every day with Mr. Mulholland and Mr. . . . Mr. . . . ."

"Temple," Billy said. "Gregory Temple. Excuse my asking, but haven't there been *any* other guests here except them in the last two or three years?"

Holding her teacup high in one hand, inclining her head slightly to the left, she looked up at him out of the corners of her eyes and gave him another gentle little smile.

"No, my dear," she said. "Only you."

# A WIRELESS MESSAGE

Ambrose Bierce

In the summer of 1896 Mr. William Holt, a wealthy manufacturer of Chicago, was living temporarily in a little town of central New York, the name of which the writer's memory has not retained. Mr. Holt had had "trouble with his wife," from whom he had parted a year before. Whether the trouble was anything more serious than "incompatibility of temper," he is probably the only living person that knows: he is not addicted to the vice of confidences. Yet he has related the incident herein set down to at least one person without exacting a pledge of secrecy. He is now living in Europe.

One evening he had left the house of a brother whom he was visiting, for a stroll in the country. It may be assumed—whatever the value of the assumption in connection with what is said to have occurred—that his mind was occupied with reflections on his domestic infelicities and the distressing changes that they had wrought in his life. Whatever may have been his thoughts, they so possessed him that he observed neither the lapse of time nor whither his feet were carrying him; he knew only that he had passed far beyond the town limits and was traversing a lonely region by a road that bore no resemblance to the one by which he had left the village. In brief, he was "lost."

Realizing his mischance, he smiled; central New York is not a region of perils, nor does one long remain lost in it. He turned about and went back the way that he had come. Before he had gone far he observed that the landscape was growing more distinct—was brightening. Everything was suffused with a soft, red glow in which he saw his shadow projected in the road before him. "The moon is rising," he said to himself. Then he remembered that it was about the time of the new moon, and if that tricksy orb was in one of its stages of visibility it had set long before. He stopped and faced about, seeking

Reprinted by permission of Citadel Press, Inc. from THE COLLECTED WRITINGS OF AMBROSE BIERCE.

the source of the rapidly broadening light. As he did so, his shadow turned and lay along the road in front of him as before. The light still came from behind him. That was surprising; he could not understand. Again he turned, and again, facing successively to every point of the horizon. Always the shadow was before—always the light behind, "a still and awful red."

Holt was astonished—"dumfounded" is the word that he used in telling it—yet seemed to have retained a certain intelligent curiosity. To test the intensity of the light whose nature and cause he could not determine, he took out his watch to see if he could make out the figures on the dial. They were plainly visible, and the hands indicated the hour of eleven o'clock and twenty-five minutes. At that moment the mysterious illumination suddenly flared to an intense, an almost blinding splendor, flushing the entire sky, extinguishing the stars and throwing the monstrous shadow of himself athwart the landscape. In that unearthly illumination he saw near him, but apparently in the air at a considerable elevation, the figure of his wife, clad in her night-clothing and holding to her breast the figure of his child. Her eyes were fixed upon his with an expression which he afterward professed himself unable to name or describe, further than that it was "not of this life."

The flare was momentary, followed by black darkness, in which, however, the apparition still showed white and motionless; then by insensible degrees it faded and vanished, like a bright image on the retina after the closing of the eyes. A perculiarity of the apparition, hardly noted at the time, but afterward recalled, was that it showed only the upper half of the woman's figure: nothing was seen below the waist.

The sudden darkness was comparative, not absolute, for gradually all objects of his environment became again visible.

In the dawn of the morning Holt found himself entering the village at a point opposite to that at which he had left it. He soon arrived at the house of his brother, who hardly knew him. He was wild-eyed, haggard, and gray as a rat. Almost incoherently, he related his night's experience.

"Go to bed, my poor fellow," said his brother, "and—wait. We shall hear more of this."

An hour later came the predestined telegram. Holt's dwelling in one of the suburbs of Chicago had been destroyed by fire. Her escape cut off by the flames, his wife had appeared at an upper window, her child in her arms. There she had stood, motionless, apparently dazed. Just as the firemen had arrived with a ladder, the floor had given way, and she was seen no more.

The moment of this culminating horror was eleven o'clock and twenty-five minutes, standard time.

# THE MAN AT THE WALL

John Morressy

I used to read back over the inscription whenever I had some spare time like this, but that was long ago, when I was near a part that I understood. If I want to see that part now, I have to go past the pictures. So I stay right here, at the place where the inscription ends.

The wall runs from horizon to horizon as straight and even as a ruled line drawn across the sky. Off to the right, the surface is smooth. There are no words, no letters, not a single mark from where I stopped yesterday to the far end. To the left, as far as the eye can follow and beyond, the inscription is chiseled into the wall, but it stops right here. I can't do any more because they haven't come with my supplies and my instructions.

This is what I don't like, the waiting out here with no work to do. I want to keep busy, and when they're late there's nothing for me to do but sit here idle and wait for them to come.

There's not much to look at. Behind me are the dunes, low dunes tufted with little knots of dry grass, and beyond them, far off in the distance, I can see what look like mountains, although they may be nothing more than higher dunes. Someday I'm going to go out there and look around and see if there's anybody out there or anything worth looking at besides the dunes and the grass and the mountains, or the higher dunes, if that's all they are. But I can't spare the time now. I have a little extra time like this once in a while, when I'm waiting for my food and my instructions, but it's not enough to allow me to wander off out of sight of the wall. It's not good to get too far from the wall.

I don't know what's on the other side. It's not my side and I don't want to know about it. But I don't think they have any inscription over there. I never hear the sound of mallet and chisel, and I would if someone were working on an inscription. Sounds carry in the silence out here, and that's one sound I couldn't miss. The only familiar sound from the other side of the wall comes when they arrive with my food and my instructions—sometimes a new chisel—and I don't always hear that. There are other noises, but I try not to pay attention to them.

They ought to be here soon. I can't tell they're coming until they're actually here, because they never come out on my side of the wall. They always use the other side, whether intentionally or not I don't know, but whatever their reason is, it keeps me from anticipating their arrival. I can't see them and I don't know they've come until my things are lowered in a basket. That may be their reason for coming out on the opposite side of the wall: they may assume that once I know they're coming I'll slow down or perhaps stop working altogether. That's something they don't have to worry about, not with me. I want to get the job done, and done properly.

The other side of the wall must be different in at least one respect. It must have a road, or a track, or a path of some sort, otherwise they'd have a difficult time making the trip out here every day. I wonder why I'm on this side, while the road is on that side, though. I wonder did they station me on this side of the wall because the road is on the other side, or did they build the road on the other side because the inscription is on this side. It might all be pure chance. Perhaps there's a man on the other side right now wondering why he was stationed on that side and not on this. Or maybe he's finished his job and gone now, and that's why I never hear him working. I'd like to talk to him sometime. It would be good to know if there are other stonecutters working on the wall, and what sort of instructions they get, and what they do when they finish. He might know about the sound I heard, too, that sound like a scream, only cut short.

I shouldn't be thinking like this, though. If they wanted me thinking about what's on the other side they'd have put me there, and they didn't, they put me on this side to cut the inscription, and that's what I do.

The inscription is my responsibility. I cut it just at eye level; in regulation letters six inches high and an inch deep. I'm careful, but I can work quickly without sacrificing quality, and there aren't many who can do that. It's probably the main reason why I was chosen for this job. I'm only guessing at that, I really don't know why I was chosen, and it's been so long that it's getting hard to remember what they said to me, but I know I've always had a reputation as a fine stonecutter. From here, I can sight down the row of letters and numbers I've inscribed, and the line of tops and bottoms is as straight as a ruler. It's a perfect piece of work, and I'm proud of it. I'm really glad to be working on this wall, even though it means being out here alone with nobody to talk to. This is a good wall, the kind you don't see being built these days. Today everything is wire fences, or wooden paling, or flimsy things like that. Not this wall, though. This wall is built to last a thousand years.

The surface is absolutely smooth, except for the inscription and the pictures. I have a little box that I stand on in order to be able to work near the top, but even when I stand the box on end and stretch as far as I can, I can't reach the top of the wall. Once I grew so curious I tried to jump from the box and get a grip to pull myself up and look over, but it didn't work. I fell and bruised my leg badly.

They knew about it. I don't know how they found out, but they knew. My rations were cut to two slices of bread and a cup of water a day for the next ten days. I don't try anything like that any more especially now that I know it's useless. With just this box to stand on, a man couldn't hope to reach the top of the wall. And even if he did, he'd never be able to get a grip and climb over, because the top of the wall isn't flat, it slopes upward and rounds off so a man can't get a fingergrip to pull himself up. Nobody's going to get past this wall.

The only bad thing is the pictures. I don't mind working hard and being out here alone under the hot sun and through the cold nights, but having to work on the pictures is hard. Some of them nearly got me sick when I was cutting them. What makes it a little better is that pictures only come up once in a while, so I have a good break between them, a few weeks sometimes,

long enough to forget the details. I don't have any trouble with the inscription, and I'm especially glad of that because the inscription is something I have to work on every day. I don't understand the meaning of some of the words I put down, but that doesn't make any difference, I'm not required to understand them, just cut them into the stone, and the words are no problem to cut even when I don't understand them. They never give me any trouble. It's the pictures that give me the bad dreams. To do the inscription, I just follow the instructions and cut whatever they say. Lately the letters have been changing here and there, and sometimes the spelling looks strange. But then, there may be new official spellings for the words I'm being given. That's possible. And they don't keep to one language in the inscription, either. That's another thing. The part I've just been working on reads *ta hranxlux qlda, ta obrtlo di fuom qldoan.* I don't understand it. I don't even know what language it's in, and I'm not curious to learn. I was given that wording in my instructions, enclosed with my rations, written on a plain yellow card and sealed in an envelope, so I know it's right and it belongs on the wall. I don't have to know the meaning.

Sometimes the inscription calls for numbers, and they're harder because of the curving lines, especially in the threes and the eights; I don't like to do threes and eights, but then, when they give me numbers to cut I don't get as much to do each day, so it all comes out even. The symbols are the hardest part. The ones like the triangle or the dagger are no trouble at all, but there are others that can take a lot of time to get just right. Some of the symbols I can't even describe. There was one that made me dizzy when I looked at it, and I had to stop a few times, four or five times it must have been, and come right down off the box and stretch out on the ground and take a drink of water before I was able to finish it. I don't know how I ever did that one, I never thought I'd be able to, but I have my quota to fill and they don't accept excuses. That was a hard one, though.

However much trouble the symbols may be sometimes, I'd rather do them for the rest of my life than do more pictures like the ones I had to do that time a few months ago. I don't go near that section of the wall any more. I want to be able to sleep. I'm a man who's never in his life had trouble sleeping. I work hard all day in the open air in all kinds of weather, and when I crawl into my sleeping bag I'm sound asleep in a minute and I don't stir until morning. But after I worked on those pictures I didn't sleep right for weeks. One night I woke up screaming. I was drenched in cold sweat and I could hear my heart beating. I think what affected me most was the picture with the children and the spikes. I don't want to think about it any more.

The sun is at the point where I can see it if I step back about five paces, just the upper edge of it bright against the top of the wall. This is late for them to be coming out. It can't be that today's a holiday; they always announce holidays in advance and give me special rations and an extra day's supplies, and sometimes a bottle of whisky. We haven't had a holiday for a long time, though, not since the day when I heard

all that noise off in the distance on the other side of the wall, first the clanking and the loud rumbling, and then the noise that sounded like a lot of people moving. It was then that I thought I heard the scream, but the sound was cut short, so I can't be sure. It could have been an animal, or a machine creaking. It doesn't make any difference, anyway, because it stopped right away. Just after that came the holiday, a two-day holiday, and they sent me a bottle, no, two bottles of whisky and said I could go ahead and get good and drunk, and I did, but I was ready for work on the third morning. They gave me a funny order that morning, I remember, it said "You are to repeat the word TRIUMPHANT until otherwise ordered," and I cut that word in a hundred and thirty-one consecutive times until they sent orders to stop and begin a new inscription immediately, a list of names it was, and I stopped in the middle of a word, right at TRIUM, and went on to the list of names that they kept sending me for months. Then the pictures came and the bad part started. I don't want to think about the pictures.

It's not very pleasant being out here alone with nothing to do. I could go back into my tent and sleep while I'm waiting, but I don't like to sleep during working hours, it's not natural. A man ought to work by day and sleep by night.

There's not a sound from the other side. It's not like them to be so late. They're usually punctual. Something must be wrong.

They'll come, sooner or later. They always do. That time I was writing TRIUMPHANT over and over I didn't hear from them for weeks, but they kept right on sending my rations. Even if there's a problem over the inscription, they have to come out with the rations. I can hold out for a few days. I've learned to set aside a little food in case they cut me back to bread and water for some reason. I have scraps of food and a few unopened tins and some water, enough to last for two days, maybe four if I go easy on my meals. So there's really nothing for me to worry about. I can hold out if they don't make it for a few days. But that's all speculation. They'll come out today, a little later than usual, maybe, but they'll be here. There's no reason for them not to come. The inscription has to keep on, and I'm the only one to do it, and I can't do it if they don't tell me what I'm to do and give me food and drink to keep up my strength. I can't do it. It's not a matter of whether I want to do the job or not. They know that.

Maybe if I rest for a while I'll feel better. I'd hate to be asleep when they come, after waiting all this time, though. They'll probably expect me to get right to work, and if they don't hear my tools immediately they might cut down on my food again. I don't want that. Still, I'm hungry and I'm feeling tired now, thinking about sleep so much. I don't want to go into my supplies yet. I'll just squat at the base of the wall, that's a good idea, instead of going all the way back to my tent where I wouldn't have a chance of hearing them when they come. This way I'll wake up as soon as I hear the basket land, and I can get right to work. I'll just settle myself right here at the base of the wall.

The sun is just barely showing over those distant mountains or high dunes or whatever they are, I never found out, it will be going down in a few minutes, and no one has come.

They'll be here tomorrow morning, though, right on time, I'm sure of that. I'm not going to lose confidence in them over something like this. They'll come.

They have to come, there's no two ways about it. They have to. I haven't got enough supplies to last for a trip all the way back to the gate. I'm weeks away from the gate, maybe months, maybe even years, I can't tell any more because I lose track of time out here where every day is just like every other. There may be another gate nearer in the opposite direction, but then again there may not and I don't see any reason to take a chance.

I could try cutting steps in the wall and climbing over, so I could wait by the road or the path or the highway they must have on the other side. I couldn't do any worse over there. There's no one else on this side and no road, so I really couldn't lose and I might be picked up by someone and be back at the gate by tomorrow night.

But I don't have any orders to cut steps into the wall. I could get into serious trouble for something like that.

They might be testing me, to see if I can act without orders. They could be waiting back at the gate right now, timing me to see how long it takes me to get there on my own.

But maybe they're testing my loyalty, and if I leave my post, I lose everything. I'm a stonecutter, and if they take me away from the inscription there won't be anything for me to do and if there's no work for me they won't have any reason to feed me.

I think it was a scream I heard that time. It could have been something else, but I think it was a scream.

Would I be loyal to stay here, though, when there's no work for me to do, and there may be serious trouble back at the gate? They might need me there more than they need me here, that's possible. I'm a stonecutter, but I can fight as well as the next man when the time comes, and one good man, if he's on the spot at the right time, can make all the difference.

If I walk back I'll have to pass by the pictures.

They have to come. I'm the only one who can do the inscription the way it has to be done, and the symbols, and even the pictures, it doesn't matter that they frighten me, I still do them perfectly.

They can't get along without me. They'll never get anyone else to do those pictures, never, nobody else would be willing to stay at the job and keep working the way I did even though I felt that I was going to faint or vomit or just throw away my tools and run off beyond the dunes to where I'd never have to see the wall again. But I stayed at the job and finished it, and it was perfect. Every line was absolutely perfect. I did my job.

I'll wait right here, where the inscription ends. They'll come. They have to. They need me.

\*    \*    \*

# 12

*It's a large stairway . . .*

Erik Satie

*Translated by John Cage*

It's a large stairway, very large.
It has more than a thousand steps, all made of ivory.
It is very handsome.
Nobody dares use it
For fear of spoiling it.

The King himself never does.
Leaving his room
He jumps out the window.

So, he often says:
I love this stairway so much
I'm going to have it stuffed.

Isn't the King right?

Sam Martin

## wind wind wind wind wind

*Pedro Xisto*

```
wind   wind   wind   wind   wind
wind   leaf   wind   leaf   wind
leaf   wind   leaf   wind   leaf
wind   leaf   wind   leaf   wind
leaf   wind   leaf   wind   leaf
wind   leaf   wind   leaf   wind
leaf   wind   leaf   wind   leaf
leaf   leaf   leaf   leaf   leaf
```

# O where are you going?

*W. H. Auden*

"O where are you going?" said reader to rider,
"That valley is fatal when furnaces burn,
Yonder's the midden whose odors will madden,
That gap is the grave where the tall return."

"O do you imagine," said fearer to farer,
"That dusk will delay on your path to the pass,
Your diligent looking discover the lacking
Your footsteps feel from granite to grass?"

"O what was that bird," said horror to hearer,
"Did you see that shape in the twisted trees?
Behind you swiftly the figure comes softly,
The spot on your skin is a shocking disease?"

"Out of this house"—said rider to reader,
"Yours never will"—said farer to fearer,
"They're looking for you"—said hearer to horror,
As he left them there, as he left them there.

Pedro Xisto's "wind wind wind wind wind" was published in *The Beloit Poetry Journal,* and is reprinted with their permission.

# SANCTUARY

*My land is bare of chattering folk;*
*The clouds are low along the ridges,*
*And sweet's the air with curly smoke*
*From all my burning bridges.*

—Dorothy Parker

## *Reason*

Said, Pull her up a bit will you, Mac, I want to unload there.
Said, Pull her up my rear end, first come first serve.
Said, Give her the gun, Bud, he needs a taste of his own bumper.
Then the usher came out and got into the act:

Said, Pull her up, pull her up a bit, we need this space, sir.
Said, For God's sake, is this still a free country or what?
You go back and take care of Gary Cooper's horse
And leave me handle my own car.

Saw them unloading the lame old lady,
Ducked out under the wheel and gave her an elbow,
Said, All you needed to do was just explain;
*Reason, Reason* is my middle name.

—*Josephine Miles*

# AFTER THE DENTIST

May Swenson

*My left upper*
*lip and half*

*my nose is gone.*
*I drink my coffee*

*on the right from*
*a warped cup*

*whose left lip dips.*
*My cigarette's*

*thick as a finger.*
*Somebody else's.*

*I put lip-*
*stick on a cloth-*

*stuffed doll's*
*face that's*

*surprised when one*
*side smiles.*

## Besides That

*If I could get to heaven*
*By eating all I could,*
*I'd become a pig,*
*And I'd gobble up my food!*

*Or, if I could get to heaven*
*By climbing up a tree,*
*I'd become a monkey,*
*And I'd climb up rapidly!*

*Or, if I could get to heaven*
*By any other way*
*Than the way that's told of,*
*I'd 'a been there yesterday!*

*But the way that we are told of*
*Bars the monkey and the pig!*
*And is very, very difficult,*
*Besides that!*

*—James Stephens*

348

# Museum Piece

The good grey guardians of art
Patrol the halls on spongy shoes,
Impartially protective, though
Perhaps suspicious of Toulouse.

Here dozes one against the wall,
Disposed upon a funeral chair.
A Degas dancer pirouettes
Upon the parting of his hair.

See how she spins! The grace is there,
But strain as well is plain to see.
Degas loved the two together:
Beauty joined to energy.

Edgar Degas purchased once
A fine El Greco, which he kept
Against the wall beside his bed
To hang his pants on while he slept.

—Richard Wilbur

349

# SONNET 29

William Shakespeare

When in disgrace with fortune and men's eyes,
I all alone beweep my outcast state,
And trouble deaf heaven with my bootless cries,
And look upon myself, and curse my fate,
Wishing me like to one more rich in hope,
Featur'd like him, like him with friends possess'd,
Desiring this man's art and that man's scope,
With what I most enjoy contented least;
Yet in these thoughts myself almost despising,
Haply I think on thee, and then my state,
Like to the lark at the break of day arising
From sullen earth, sings hymns at heaven's gate;
   For thy sweet love remember'd such wealth brings
   That then I scorn to change my state with kings.

# TO A BROWN GIRL

*Ossie Davis*

Since I care naught for what is pale and cold,
My heart must hunger when the snows are down
For dearer climates, where the sun, of old,
Taught us that love is something warm and brown.

Here, like a stranger, stranded in the north,
I dream the scarlet dream of purple skies,
And strain for glimpses, as I hurry forth,
Of shy reports: rich-black, and passion-wise.

And laugh to plumb the deep-remembered flood
of tropic heats, where winter cannot come.
And feel within the pulses of my blood
The white-eyed throbbings of some ancient drum.

And I can treasure this: to catch a trace,
Still burning hot and bright beneath the chill—
Beneath the bosom of your brown embrace
Hot suns of Africa are burning still!

From SOON, ONE MORNING, edited by Herbert Hill, 1963. Reprinted by
permission of the author.

Sam Martin

# DÉJEUNER SUR L'HERBE°

## Tu Fu

*Translated by Carolyn Kizer*

### I

It's pleasant to board the ferry in the sunscape
As the late light slants into afternoon;
The faint wind ruffles the river, rimmed with foam.
We move through the aisles of bamboo
Towards the cool water-lilies.

The young dandies drop ice into the drinks,
While the girls slice the succulent lotus root.
Above us, a patch of cloud spreads, darkening
Like a water-stain on silk.

*Write this down quickly, before the rain!*

### II

Don't sit there! The cushions were soaked by the shower.
Already the girls have drenched their crimson skirts.
Beauties, their powder streaked with mascara, lament their ruined faces.

The wind batters our boat, the mooring-line
Has rubbed a wound in the willow bark.
The edges of the curtains are embroidered by river foam.
Like a knife in a melon, Autumn slices Summer.

*It will be cold, going back.*

° "Breakfast on the Grass"

From KNOCK UPON SILENCE by Carolyn Kizer. Copyright © 1963 by Carolyn Kizer. Reprinted by permission of Doubleday & Company, Inc. and Brandt & Brandt.

# FIREWORKS

Not guns, not thunder, but a flutter of clouded drums
That announce a fiesta: abruptly, fiery needles
Circumscribe on the night boundless chrysanthemums.
Softly, they break apart, they flake away, where
Darkness, on a svelte hiss, swallows them.
Delicate brilliance: a bellflower opens, fades,
In a sprinkle of falling stars.
Night absorbs them
With the sponge of her silence.

—*Babette Deutsch*

# TRIPLE FEATURE

*Denise Levertov*

*Innocent decision: to enjoy.*
*And the pathos*
*of hopefulness, of his solicitude:*

*—he in mended serape,*
*she having plaited carefully*
*magenta ribbons into her hair,*
*the baby a round half-hidden shape*
*slung in her rebozo, and the young son steadfastly*
*gripping a fold of her skirt,*
*pale and severe under a*
*handed-down sombrero—*

                *all regarding*
*the stills with full attention, preparing*
*to pay and go in—*
*to worlds of shadow-violence, half-*
*familiar, warm with popcorn, icy*
*with strange motives, barbarous splendors!*

354

# The Eagle

*Alfred, Lord Tennyson*

He clasps the crag with crooked hands;
Close to the sun in lonely lands,
Ring'd with the azure world, he stands.

The wrinkled sea beneath him crawls;
He watches from his mountain walls.
And like a thunderbolt he falls.

# A narrow fellow...

Emily Dickinson

A narrow fellow in the grass
Occasionally rides;
You may have met him,—did you not?
His notice sudden is.

The grass divides as with a comb,
A spotted shaft is seen;
And then it closes at your feet
And opens further on.

He likes a boggy acre,
A floor too cool for corn.                    10
Yet when a child, and barefoot,
I more than once, at morn,

Have passed, I thought, a whip-lash
Unbraiding in the sun,—
When, stooping to secure it,
It wrinkled, and was gone.

Several of nature's people
I know, and they know me;
I feel for them a transport
Of cordiality;                                20

But never met this fellow,
Attended or alone,
Without a tighter breathing,
And zero at the bone.

# SNAKE

D. H. Lawrence

A snake came to my water-trough
On a hot, hot day, and I in pajamas for the heat,
To drink there.

In the deep, strange-scented shade of the great dark
    carob tree
I came down the steps with my pitcher
And must wait, must stand and wait, for there he was
    at the trough before me.

He reached down from a fissure in the earth-wall in
    the gloom
And trailed his yellow-brown slackness soft-bellied
    down, over the edge of the stone trough
And rested his throat upon the stone bottom,
And where the water had dripped from the tap, in a
    small clearness,                                          10
He sipped with his straight mouth,
Softly drank through his straight gums, into his slack
    long body,
Silently.

Someone was before me at my water-trough,
And I, like a second-comer, waiting.

He lifted his head from his drinking, as cattle do,
And looked at me vaguely, as drinking cattle do,
And flickered his two-forked tongue from his lips, and
    mused a moment,
And stooped and drank a little more,
Being earth-brown, earth-golden from the burning
    bowels of the earth                                       20
On the day of Sicilian July, with Etna smoking.

357

From THE COMPLETE POEMS OF D. H. LAWRENCE, Vol. I, edited by Vivian
de Sola Pinto and F. Warren Roberts. Copyright 1923, renewed 1951 by Frieda
Lawrence. Reprinted by permission of The Viking Press, Inc., William Heinemann
Ltd., the estate of the late Mrs. Frieda Lawrence and Laurence Pollinger Limited.

The voice of my education said to me
He must be killed,
For in Sicily the black black snakes are innocent, the
    gold are venomous.

And voices in me said, If you were a man
You would take a stick and break him now, and finish
    him off.

But must I confess how I liked him,
How glad I was he had come like a guest in quiet, to
    drink at my water-trough
And depart peaceful, pacified, and thankless
Into the burning bowels of this earth?             30

Was it cowardice, that I dared not kill him?
Was it perversity, that I longed to talk to him?
Was it humility, to feel so honored?
I felt so honored.

And yet those voices:
*If you were not afraid, you would kill him!*

And truly I was afraid, I was most afraid,
But even so, honored still more
That he should seek my hospitality
From out the dark door of the secret earth.       40

He drank enough
And lifted his head, dreamily, as one who has drunken,
And flickered his tongue like a forked night on the air,
    so black,
Seeming to lick his lips,
And looked around like a god, unseeing, into the air,
And slowly turned his head,
And slowly, very slowly, as if thrice adream
Proceeded to draw his slow length curving round
And climb again the broken bank of my wall-face.

And as he put his head into that dreadful hole,     50
And as he slowly drew up, snake-easing his shoulders,
    and entered further,
A sort of horror, a sort of protest against his with-
    drawing into that horrid black hole,
Deliberately going into the blackness, and slowly
    drawing himself after,
Overcame me now his back was turned.

I looked round, I put down my pitcher,
I picked up a clumsy log
And threw it at the water-trough with a clatter.

I think it did not hit him;
But suddenly that part of him that was left behind
    convulsed in undignified haste,
Writhed like lightning, and was gone                                    60
Into the black hole, the earth-lipped fissure in the wall-
    front
At which, in the intense still noon, I stared with
    fascination.

And immediately I regretted it.
I thought how paltry, how vulgar, what a mean act!
I despised myself and the voices of my accursed
    human education.

And I thought of the albatross,
And I wished he would come back, my snake.

For he seemed to me again like a king,
Like a king in exile, uncrowned in the underworld,
Now due to be crowned again.                                           70

And so, I missed my chance with one of the lords
Of life.
And I have something to expiate:
A pettiness.

# 13

# Laughing at Animals

Konrad Lorenz

How much difference is there between animal and human behavior?
What do we mean when we say that someone is "acting like an animal"?
Konrad Lorenz, working at a scientific institute in Austria, has devoted
a lifetime seeking answers to these questions. This selection is an excerpt
from his book, *King Solomon's Ring*.

It is seldom that I laugh at an animal, and when I do, I usually find out afterwards that it was at myself, at the human being whom the animal has portrayed in a more or less pitiless caricature, that I have laughed. We stand before the monkey house and laugh, but we do not laugh at the sight of a caterpillar or a snail, and when the courtship antics of a lusty greylag gander are so incredibly funny, it is only our human youth that behaves in a very similar fashion.

The initiated observer seldom laughs at the bizarre in animals. It often annoys me when visitors at a Zoo or Aquarium laugh at an animal that, in the course of its evolutionary adaptation, has developed a body form which now deviates from the usual. The public is then deriding things which, to me, are holy: the riddles of the Genesis, the Creation and the Creator. The grotesque forms of a chameleon, a puffer or an anteater awake in me feelings of awed wonder, but not of amusement.

Of course I have laughed at unexpected drollness, although such amusement is in itself not less stupid than that of the public that annoys me. When the queer, land-climbing fish Periophthalmus was first sent to me and I saw how one of these creatures leaped, not out of the water basin, but on to its edge and, raising its head with its pug-like face towards me, sat there perched, staring at me with its goggling, piercing eyes, then I laughed heartily. Can you imagine what it is like when a fish, a real and unmistakable vertebrate fish, first of all sits on a perch, like a canary, then turns its head towards you like a higher terrestrial animal, like anything but a fish, and then, to crown all, fixes you with a binocular stare? This same stare gives the owl its characteristic and proverbially wise expression, because, even in a bird, the two-eyed gaze is unexpected. But here, too, the humor lies more in the caricature of the human, than in the actual drollness of the animal.

In the study of the behavior of the higher animals, very funny situations are apt to arise, but it is inevitably the observer, and not the animal, that plays the comical part. The comparative ethologist's method in dealing with the most intelligent birds and mammals often necessitates a complete neglect of the dignity usually to be expected in a scientist. Indeed, the uninitiated, watching the student of behavior in operation, often cannot be blamed for thinking that there is madness in his method. It is only my reputation for harmlessness, shared with the other village idiot, which has saved me from the mental home. But in defense of the villagers of Altenberg I must recount a few little stories.

I was experimenting at one time with young mallards to find out why artificially incubated and freshly hatched ducklings of this species, in contrast to similarly treated greylag goslings, are unapproachable and shy. Greylag goslings unquestioning accept the first living being whom they meet as their mother, and run confidently after him. Mallards, on the contrary, always refused to do this. If I took from the incubator freshly hatched mallards, they invariably ran away from me and pressed themselves in the nearest dark corner. Why? I remembered that I had once let a muscovy duck hatch a clutch of mallard eggs and that the tiny mallards had also failed to accept this foster mother. As soon as they were dry, they had simply run away from her and I had trouble enough to catch these crying, erring children. On the other hand, I once let a fat white farmyard duck hatch out mallards and the little wild things ran just as happily after her as if she had been their real mother. The secret must have lain in her call note, for, in external appearance, the domestic duck was quite as different from a mallard as was the muscovy; but what she had in common with the mallard (which, of course, is the wild progenitor of our farmyard duck) were her vocal expressions. Though, in the process of domestication, the duck has altered considerably in color pattern and body form, its voice has remained practically the same. The inference was clear: I must quack like a mother mallard in order to make the little ducks run after me. No sooner said than done. When, one Whit-Saturday, a brood of purebred young mallards was due to hatch, I put the eggs in the incubator, took the babies, as soon as they were dry, under my personal care, and quacked for them the mother's call-note in my best Mallardese. For hours on end I kept it up, for half the day. The quacking was successful. The little ducks lifted their gaze confidently towards me, obviously had no fear of me this time, and as, still quacking, I drew slowly away from them, they also set themselves obediently in motion and scuttled after me in a tightly huddled group, just as ducklings follow their mother. My theory was indisputably proved. The freshly hatched ducklings have an inborn reaction to the call-note, but not to the

363

optical picture of the mother. Anything that emits the right quack note will be considered as mother, whether it is a fat white Pekin duck or a still fatter man. However, the substituted object must not exceed a certain height. At the beginning of these experiments, I had sat myself down in the grass amongst the ducklings and, in order to make them follow me, had dragged myself, sitting, away from them. As soon, however, as I stood up and tried, in a standing posture, to lead them on, they gave up, peered searchingly on all sides, but not upwards towards me and it was not long before they began that penetrating piping of abandoned ducklings that we are accustomed simply to call "crying." They were unable to adapt themselves to the fact that their foster mother had become so tall. So I was forced to move along, squatting low, if I wished them to follow me. This was not very comfortable; still less comfortable was the fact that the mallard mother quacks unintermittently. If I ceased for even the space of half a minute from my melodious "Quahg, gegegegeg, Quahg, gegegegeg," the necks of the ducklings became longer and longer corresponding exactly to "long faces" in human children—and did I then not immediately recommence quacking, the shrill weeping began anew. As soon as I was silent, they seemed to think that I had died, or perhaps that I loved them no more: cause enough for crying! The ducklings, in contrast to the greylag goslings, were most demanding and tiring charges, for, imagine a two-hour walk with such children, all the time squatting low and quacking without interruption! In the interests of science I submitted myself literally for hours on end to this ordeal. So it came about, on a certain Whit-Sunday, that, in company with my ducklings, I was wandering about, squatting and quacking, in a May-green meadow at the upper part of our garden. I was congratulating myself on the obedience and exactitude with which my ducklings came waddling after me, when I suddenly looked up and saw the garden fence framed by a row of dead-white faces: a group of tourists was standing at the fence and staring horrified in my direction. Forgivable! For all they could see was a big man with a beard, dragging himself, crouching, round the meadow, in figures of eight, glancing constantly over his shoulder and quacking—but the ducklings, the all-revealing and all-explaining ducklings, were hidden in the tall spring grass from the view of the astonished crowd.

. . . Jackdaws long remember someone who has laid hands on them and thereby elicited a "rattling" reaction. Therein lay a considerable impediment to the ringing of the young jackdaws reared in my colony. When I took them out of the nest to mark them with aluminum rings, I could not help the older jackdaws seeing me and at once raising their voices to a wild rattling concert. How was I to stop the birds developing a permanent shyness for me as a result of the ringing procedure, a state of affairs which would have been immeasurably detrimental to my work? The solution was obvious: disguise. But what? Again quite easy. It lay ready to hand in a box in the loft and was very well suited for my purpose, although, normally, it was only brought out every sixth of December to celebrate the old Austrian festival of St. Nicholas and the Devil. It was a gorgeous, black, furry devil's costume with a mask covering the whole head, complete with horns and tongue, and a long devil's tail which stuck well out from the body. I wonder what you would think if, on a beautiful June day, you suddenly heard from the gabled roof of a high house a wild rattling noise and, looking up, you saw Satan himself, equipped with horns, tail and claws, his tongue hanging out with the heat, climbing from chimney to chimney, surrounded by a swarm of black birds making ear-splitting rattling cries. I think this whole alarming impression disguised the fact that the devil was fixing, by means of a forceps, aluminum rings to the legs of young jackdaws, and then replacing the birds carefully in their nests. When I had finished the ringing, I saw for the first time that a large crowd of people had collected in the village street, and were looking up with expressions just as aghast as those of the tourists at the garden fence. As I would have defeated my own object by now disclosing my identity, I just gave a friendly wag of my devil's tail and disappeared through the trapdoor of the loft.

The third time that I was in danger of being delivered up to the psychiatric clinic was the fault of my big yellow-crested cockatoo Koka. I had bought this beautiful and very tame bird shortly before Easter, for a considerable sum of money. It was many weeks before the poor fellow had overcome the mental disturbances caused by his long imprisonment. At first he could not realize that he was no longer fettered and could now move about freely. It was a pitiable sight to see this proud creature sitting on a branch, ever and anon preparing himself for flight, but not daring to take off, because he could not believe that he was no longer on the chain. When at last he had overcome this inward resistance, he became a lively and exuberant being and developed a strong attachment for my person. As soon as he was let out of the room in which we still shut him up at nighttime, he flew straight off to find me, displaying thereby an astonishing intelligence. In quite a short time he realized where I was probably to be found. At first he flew to my bedroom window, and, if I was not there, down to the duck pond; in short he visited all the sites of my morning inspection at the various animal pens in our research station. This determined quest was not without danger to the cockatoo because, if he failed to find me, he extended his search farther and farther and had several times lost his way on such occasions. Accordingly, my fellow workers had strict instructions not to let the bird out during my absence.

One Saturday in June, I got off the train from Vienna at Altenberg station, in the midst of a gathering of bathers, such as often flock to our village at fine weekends. I had gone only a few steps along the street and the crowd had not yet dispersed when, high above me in the air, I saw a bird whose species I could not at first determine. It flew with slow, measured wing-beats, varied at set intervals by longer periods of gliding. It seemed too heavy to be a buzzard; for a stork, it was not big enough and, even at that height, neck and feet should have been visible. Then the bird gave a sudden swerve so that the setting sun shone for a second full on the underside of the great wings which lit up like stars in the blue of the skies. The bird was white. By Heaven, it was my cockatoo! The steady movements of his wings clearly indicated that he was setting out on a long-distance flight. What should I do? Should I call to the bird? Well, have you ever heard the flight-call of the greater yellow-crested cockatoo? No? But you have probably heard pig-killing after the old method. Imagine pig squealing at its most voluminous, taken up by a microphone and magnified many times by a good loudspeaker. A man can imitate it quite successfully, though somewhat feebly, by bellowing at the top of his voice "O-ah." I had already proved that the cockatoo understood this imitation and promptly "came to heel." But would it work at such a height? A bird always has great difficulty in making the decision to fly downwards at a steep angle. To yell, or not to yell, that was the question. If I yelled and the bird came down, all would be well, but what if it sailed calmly on through the clouds? How would I then explain my song to the crowd of people? Finally, I did yell. The people around me stood still, rooted to the spot. The bird hesitated for a moment on outstretched wings, then, folding them, it descended in one dive and landed upon my outstretched arm. Once again I was master of the situation.

On another occasion, the frolics of this bird gave me quite a serious fright. My father, by that time an old man, used to take his siesta at the foot of a terrace on the south-west side of our house. For medical reasons, I was never quite happy to think of him exposed to the glaring midday sun, but he would let nobody break him of his old habit. One day, at his siesta time, I heard him, from his accustomed place, swearing like a trooper, and as I raced round the corner of the house, I saw the old gentleman swaying up the drive in a cramped position, bending forwards, his arms tightly folded about his waist. "In heaven's name, are you ill?" "No," came the embittered response, "I am not ill, but that confounded creature has bitten all the buttons off my trousers while I was fast asleep!" And that is what had happened. Eyewitnesses at the scene of the crime discovered, laid out in buttons, the whole outline of the old professor: here the arms, there the waistcoat, and here, unmistakably, the buttons off his trousers.

One of the nicest cockatoo-tricks which, in fanciful inventiveness, equaled the experiments of monkey or human children, arose from the ardent love of the bird for my mother who, so long as she stayed in the garden in summertime, knitted without stopping. The cockatoo seemed to understand exactly how the soft skeins worked and what the wool was for. He always seized the free end of the wool with his beak and then flew lustily into the air, unraveling the ball behind him. Like a paper kite with a long tail, he climbed high and then flew in regular circles round the great lime tree which stood in front of our house. Once, when nobody was there to stop him he encircled the tree, right up to its summit, with brightly colored woolen strands which it was impossible to disentangle from the wide-spreading foliage. Our visitors used to stand in mute astonishment before this tree, and were unable to understand how and why it had been thus decorated.

The cockatoo paid court to my mother in a very charming way, dancing round her in the most grotesque fashion, folding and unfolding his beautiful crest and following her wherever she went. If she were not there, he sought her just as assiduously as he had been used, in his early days, to search for me. Now my mother had no less than four sisters. One day these aunts, in company with some equally aged ladies of their acquaintance, were partaking of tea in the veranda of our house. They sat at a huge round table, a plate of luscious home-grown strawberries in front of each, and in the middle of the table, a large, very shallow bowl of finest icing sugar. The cockatoo, who was flying accidentally or wittingly past, espied, from without, my mother who was presiding at this festive board. The next moment, with a perilous dive, he steered himself through the doorway, which, though wide, was nevertheless narrower than the span of his wings. He intended to land before my mother on the table where he was accustomed to sit and keep her company while she knitted; but this time he found the runway encumbered with numerous obstacles to flying technique and, into the bargain, he was in the midst of unknown faces. He considered the situation, pulled himself up abruptly in midair, hovering over the table like a helicopter, then turning on his own axis, he opened the throttle again and the next second had disappeared. So also had the icing sugar from the shallow bowl, out of which the propeller wind had wafted every grain. And around the table sat seven powdered ladies, seven rococo ladies whose faces, like lepers', were white as snow and who held their eyes tight shut. Beautiful!

# The Presbyterian Choir Singers

William Saroyan

One of the many curious and delightful things about our country is the ease with which our good people move from one religion to another, or from no particular religion at all to any religion that happens to come along, without experiencing any particular loss or gain, and go right on being innocent anyhow.

Myself, I was born, for instance, a kind of Catholic, although I was not baptized until I was thirteen, a circumstance which, I remember clearly, irritated the priest very much and impelled him to ask my people if they were crazy, to which my people replied, We have been away.

Thirteen years old and not baptized! the priest shouted. What kind of people are you?

For the most part, my uncle Melik replied, we are an agricultural people, although we have had our brilliant men, too.

It was a Saturday afternoon. The whole thing took no more than seven minutes, but even after I was baptized it was impossible for me to feel any change.

Well, my grandmother said, you are now baptized. Do you feel any better?

For some months, I believe I ought to explain, I had been feeling intelligent, which led my grandmother to suspect that I was ill with some mysterious illness or that I was losing my mind.

I think I feel the same, I said.

Do you believe now? she shouted. Or do you still have doubts?

I can easily *say* I believe, I said, but to tell you the truth I don't know for sure. I want to be a Christian of course.

Well, just believe then, my grandmother said, and go about your business.

My business was in some ways quaint and in other ways incredible.

I sang in the Boys Choir at the Presbyterian Church on Tulare Street. For doing so I received one dollar a week from an elderly Christian lady named Balaifal who lived in sorrow and solitude in the small ivy-covered house next to the house in which my friend Pandro Kolkhozian lived.

This boy, like myself, was loud in speech. That is to say, we swore a good deal—in all innocence of course—and by doing so grieved Miss or Mrs. Balaifal so much that she sought to save us while there was still time. To be saved was a thing I for one had no occasion to resent.

Miss Balaifal (I shall call her that from now on, since while I knew her she was certainly single, and since I do not know for sure if she ever married, or for that matter if she ever thought of marrying, or if she ever so much as fell in love—earlier in life of course, and no doubt with a scoundrel who took the whole matter with a grain of salt)—Miss Balaifal, as I began to say, was a cultured woman, a reader of the poems of Robert Browning and other poets and a woman of great sensitivity, so that coming out on the porch of her house to hear us talk she could stand so much and no more, and when the limit had been reached, cried out, Boys, boys. You must not use profane language.

Pandro Kolkhozian, on the one hand, seemed to be the most uncouth boy in the world and on the other—and this was the quality in him which endeared him to me—the most courteous and thoughtful.

Yes, Miss Balaifum, he said.

Balaifal, the lady corrected him. Please come here. Both of you.

We went to Miss Balaifal and asked what she wanted.

What do you want, Miss Balaifum? Pandro said.

Miss Balaifal went into her coat pocket and brought out a sheaf of pamphlets, and without looking at them handed one to each of us. My pamphlet was entitled *Redemption, The Story of a Drunkard.* Pandro's was entitled *Peace at Last, The Story of a Drunkard.*

What's this for? Pandro said.

I want you boys to read those pamphlets and try to be good, Miss Balaifal said. I want you to stop using profane language.

It doesn't say anything here about profane language, Pandro said.

There's a good lesson for each of you in those pamphlets, the lady said. Read them and don't use profane language any more.

Yes, ma'am, I said. Is that all?

One thing more, Miss Balaifal said. I wonder if you boys would help me move the organ from the dining room to the parlor?

Sure, Miss Balaifum, Pandro said. Any time.

So we went into the lady's house and, while she instructed us in just how to do it without damaging the instrument or ourselves, we moved it, by slow degrees, from the dining room to the parlor.

Now read those pamphlets, Miss Balaifal said.

Yes, ma'am, Pandro said. Is that all?

Well, now, the lady said. I want you to sing while I play the organ.

I can't sing, Miss Balaifum, Pandro said.

Nonsense, the lady said. Of course you can sing, Pedro.

Pandro, not Pedro, Pandro said. Pedro is my cousin's name.

As a matter of fact Pandro's name was Pantalo, which in Armenian means pants. When he had started to school his teacher hadn't cared for, or hadn't liked the sound of, the name, so she had written down on his card Pandro. As for his cousin's name, it was Bedros, with the *b* soft, which in turn had been changed at school to Pedro. It was all quite all right of course, and no harm to anybody.

Without answering him, the elderly lady sat on the stool, adjusted her feet on the pedals of the organ, and without any instructions to us, began to play a song which, from its dullness, was obviously religious. After a moment she herself began to sing. Pandro, in a soft voice, uttered a very profane, if not vulgar, word, which fortunately Miss Balaifal did not hear. Miss Balaifal's voice was, if anything, not impressive. The pedals squeaked a good deal louder than she sang, the tones of the organ were not any too clear, but even so, it was possible to know that Miss Balaifal's voice was not delightful.

Galilee, bright Galilee, she sang.

She turned to us, nodded, and said, Now sing. Sing, boys.

We knew neither the words nor the music, but it seemed that common courtesy demanded at least an honest effort, which we made, trying as far as possible to follow the music coming out of the organ and the dramatic words coming out of Miss Balaifal.

Ruler of the storm was He, on the raging Galilee, she sang.

In all, we tried to sing three songs. After each song, Pandro would say, Thank you very much, Miss Balaifum. Can we go now?

At last she got up from the organ and said, I'm sure you're the better for it. If evil friends invite you to drink, turn away.

We'll turn away, Miss Balaifum, Pandro said. Won't we, Aram?

*I* will, I said.

I will too, Pandro said. Can we go now, Miss Balaifum?

Read the pamphlets, she said. It's not too late.

We'll read them, Pandro said. Just as soon as we get time.

We left the lady's house and went back to the front yard of Pandro's house and began to read the pamphlets. Before we were

370

half through reading, the lady came out on the porch and in a very high and excited voice said, Which of you was it?

Which of us was *what?* Pandro said.

He was very bewildered.

Which of you was it that *sang?* Miss Balaifal said.

We both sang, I said.

No, Miss Balaifal said. Only one of you sang. One of you has a beautiful Christian voice.

Not me, Pandro said.

*You,* Miss Balaifal said to me. Eugene. Was it you?

Aram, I said. Not Eugene. No, I don't think it was me either.

Boys, come here, Miss Balaifal said.

Who? Pandro said.

Both of you, the lady said.

When we were in the house and Miss Balaifal was seated at the organ again Pandro said, I don't want to sing. I don't like to sing.

*You* sing, the lady said to me.

I sang.

Miss Balaifal leaped to her feet.

You are the one, she said. You must sing at church.

I won't, I said.

You mustn't use profane language, she said.

I'm not using profane language, I said, and I promise not to use profane language again as long as I live, but I won't sing in church.

Your voice is the most Christian voice I have ever heard, Miss Balaifal said.

It isn't, I said.

Yes, it is, she said.

Well, I won't sing anyway, I said.

You must, you must, Miss Balaifal said.

Thanks very much, Miss Balaifum, Pandro said. Can we go now? He doesn't want to sing in church.

He must, he must, the lady insisted.

Why? Pandro said.

For the good of his soul, the lady said.

Pandro whispered the profane word again.

Now tell me, the lady said. What is your name?

I told her.

You are a Christian of course? she said.

I guess so, I said.

A Presbyterian of course, she said.

I don't know about that, I said.

You are, the lady said. Of course you are. I want you to sing in the Tulare Street Presbyterian Church—in the Boys' Choir—next Sunday.

Why? Pandro said again.

371

We need voices, the lady explained. We must have young voices. We must have singers. He must sing next Sunday.

I don't like to sing, I said. I don't like to go to church either.

Boys, Miss Balaifal said. Sit down. I want to talk to you.

We sat down. Miss Balaifal talked to us for at least thirty minutes.

We didn't believe a word of it, although out of courtesy we kept answering her questions the way we knew she wanted us to answer them, but when she asked us to get down on our knees with her while she prayed, we wouldn't do it. Miss Balaifal argued this point for some time and then decided to let us have our way—for a moment. Then she tried again, but we wouldn't do it. Pandro said we'd move the organ any time, or anything else like that, but we wouldn't get down on our knees.

Well, Miss Balaifal said, will you close your eyes?

What for? Pandro said.

It's customary for everybody to close his eyes while someone is praying, Miss Balaifal said.

Who's praying? Pandro said.

No one, *yet*, Miss Balaifal said. But if you'll promise to close your eyes, *I'll* pray, but you've got to promise to close your eyes.

What do you want to pray for? Pandro said.

I want to pray for you boys, she said.

What for? Pandro said.

A little prayer for you won't do any harm, Miss Balaifal said. Will you close your eyes?

Oh! all right, Pandro said.

We closed our eyes and Miss Balaifal prayed.

It wasn't a little prayer by a long shot.

Amen, she said. Now, boys, don't you feel better?

In all truth, we didn't.

Yes, we do, Pandro said. Can we go now, Miss Balaifum? Any time you want the organ moved, we'll move it for you.

Sing for all you're worth, Miss Balaifal said to me, and turn away from any evil companion who invites you to drink.

Yes, ma'am, I said.

You know where the church is, she said.

What church? I said.

The Tulare Street Presbyterian Church, she said.

I know where it is, I said.

Mr. Sherwin will be expecting you Sunday morning at nine-thirty, she said.

Well, it just seemed like I was cornered.

Pandro went with me to the church on Sunday, but refused to stand with the choir boys and sing. He sat in the last row of the church and watched and listened. As for myself, I was never more unhappy in my life, although I sang.

Never again, I told Pandro after it was all over.

The following Sunday I didn't show up of course, but that didn't do any good, because Miss Balaifal got us into her house again, played the organ, sang, made us try to sing, prayed, and was unmistakably determined to keep me in the Boys' Choir. I refused flatly, and Miss Balaifal decided to put the whole thing on a more worldly basis.

You have a rare Christian voice, she explained. A voice needed by religion. You yourself are deeply religious, although you do not know it yet. Since this is so, let me ask you to sing for *me* every Sunday. I will *pay* you.

How much? Pandro said.

Fifty cents, Miss Balaifal said.

We usually sang four or five songs. It took about half an hour altogether, although we had to sit another hour while the preacher delivered his sermon. In short, it wasn't worth it.

For this reason I could make no reply.

Seventy-five cents, Miss Balaifal suggested.

The air was stuffy, the preacher was a bore, it was all very depressing.

One dollar, Miss Balaifal said. Not a cent more.

Make it a dollar and a quarter, Pandro said.

Not a cent more than a dollar, Miss Balaifal said.

He's got the best voice in the whole choir, Pandro said. *One* dollar? A voice like that is worth *two* dollars to any religion.

I've made my offer, Miss Balaifal said.

There are other religions, Pandro said.

This, I must say, upset Miss Balaifal.

His voice, she said bitterly, is a Christian voice, and what's more it's Presbyterian.

The Baptists would be glad to get a voice like that for two dollars, Pandro said.

The Baptists! Miss Balaifal said with some—I hesitate to say it—contempt.

They're no different than the Presbyterams, Pandro said.

One dollar, Miss Balaifal said. One dollar, and your name on the program.

I don't like to sing, Miss Balaifal, I said.

Yes, you do, she said. You just think you don't. If you could see your face when you sing—why—

He's got a voice like an angel, Pandro said.

I'll fix you, I told Pandro in Armenian.

That's no one-dollar voice, Pandro said.

All right, boys, Miss Balaifal said. A dollar and fifteen cents, but no more.

A dollar and a quarter, Pandro said, or we go to the Baptists.

All right, Miss Balaifal said, but I must say you drive a hard bargain.

Wait a minute, I said. I don't like to sing. I won't sing for a dollar and a quarter or anything else.

A bargain is a bargain, Miss Balaifal said.

I didn't make any bargain, I said. Pandro did. Let *him* sing.

He *can't* sing, Miss Balaifal said.

I've got the worst voice in the world, Pandro said with great pride.

His poor voice wouldn't be worth ten cents to anybody, Miss Balaifal said.

Not even a nickel, Pandro said.

Well, I said, I'm not going to sing—for a dollar and a quarter or anything else. I don't need any money.

You made a bargain, Miss Balaifal said.

Yes, you did, Pandro said.

I jumped on Pandro right in Miss Balaifal's parlor and we began to wrestle. The elderly Christian lady tried to break it up, but since it was impossible to determine which of us was the boy with the angelic voice, she began to pray. The wrestling continued until most of the furniture in the room had been knocked over, except the organ. The match was eventually a draw, the wrestlers exhausted and flat on their backs.

Miss Balaifal stopped praying and said, Sunday then, at a dollar and a quarter.

It took me some time to get my breath.

Miss Balaifal, I said, I'll sing in that choir only if Pandro sings too.

But his voice, Miss Balaifal objected. It's horrible.

I don't care what it is, I said. If I sing, he's got to sing too.

I'm afraid he'd ruin the choir, Miss Balaifal said.

He's got to go up there with me every Sunday, I said, or nothing doing.

Well, now, let me see, Miss Balaifal said.

She gave the matter considerable thought.

Suppose he goes up and stands in the choir, Miss Balaifal said, but *doesn't* sing? Suppose he just *pretends* to sing?

That's all right with me, I said, but he's got to be there all the time.

What do *I* get? Pandro said.

Well, now, Miss Balaifal said, I surely can't be expected to pay you, too.

If I go up there, Pandro said, I've got to be paid.

All right, Miss Balaifal said. One dollar for the boy who sings; twenty-five cents for the boy who doesn't.

I've got the worst voice in the world, Pandro said.

You must be fair, Miss Balaifal said. After all, you won't be singing. You'll just be standing there with the other boys.

Twenty-five cents isn't enough, Pandro said.

We got off the floor and began rearranging the furniture.

All right, Miss Balaifal said. One dollar for the boy who sings. Thirty-five cents for the boy who doesn't.

Make it fifty, Pandro said.

Very well, then, Miss Balaifal said. A dollar for *you*. Fifty cents for *you*.

We start working next Sunday? Pandro said.

That's right, Miss Balaifal said. I'll pay you here after the services. Not a word of this to any of the other boys in the choir.

We won't mention it to anybody, Pandro said.

In this manner, in the eleventh year of my life, I became, more or less, a Presbyterian—at least every Sunday morning. It wasn't the money. It was simply that a bargain had been made, and that Miss Balaifal had her heart set on having me sing for religion.

As I began to say six or seven minutes ago, however, a curious thing about our country is the ease with which all of us—or at least everybody I know—are able to change our religions, without any noticeable damage to anything or anybody. When I was thirteen I was baptized into the Armenian Catholic Church, even though I was still singing for the Presbyterians, and even though I myself was growing a little skeptical, as it were, of the whole conventional religious pattern, and was eager, by hook or crook, to reach an understanding of my own, and to come to terms with Omnipotence in my own way. Even after I was baptized, I carried in my heart a deep discontent.

Two months after I was baptized my voice changed, and my contract with Miss Balaifal was canceled—which was a great relief to me and a terrible blow to her.

As for the Armenian Catholic Church on Ventura Avenue, I went there only on Easter and Christmas. All the rest of the time I moved from one religion to another, and in the end was none the worse for it, so that now, like most Americans, my faith consists in believing in every religion, including my own, but without any ill-will toward anybody, no matter what he believes or disbelieves, just so his personality is good.

# The Yellow Bus

## Lillian Ross

A few Sundays ago, in the late, still afternoon, a bright-yellow school bus, bearing the white-on-blue license plate of the State of Indiana and with the words "BEAN BLOSSOM TWP MONROE COUNTY" painted in black letters under the windows on each side, emerged into New York City from the Holland Tunnel. Inside the bus were eighteen members of the senior class of the Bean Blossom Township High School, who were coming to the city for their first visit. The windows of the bus, as it rolled out into Canal Street, were open, and a few of the passengers leaned out, dead-pan and silent, for a look at Manhattan. The rest sat, dead-pan and silent, looking at each other. In all, there were twenty-two people in the bus: eleven girls and seven boys of the senior class; their English teacher and her husband; and the driver (one of the regular bus drivers employed by the township for the school) and his wife. When they arrived, hundreds of thousands of the city's eight million inhabitants were out of town. Those who were here were apparently minding their own business; certainly they were not handing out any big hellos to the visitors. The little Bean Blossom group, soon to be lost in the shuffle of New York's resident and transient summer population, had no idea of how to elicit any hellos—or, for that matter, any goodbyes or how-are-yous. Their plan for visiting New York City was divided into three parts: one, arriving; two, staying two days and three nights; three, departing.

Well, they had arrived. To get here, they had driven eight hundred and forty miles in thirty-nine and a half hours, bringing with them, in addition to spending money of about fifty dollars apiece, a fund of $957.41, which the class had saved up collectively over the past six years. The money represented the profits from such enterprises as candy and ice-cream concessions at school basketball games, amusement booths at the class (junior) carnival, and ticket sales for the class (senior) play, "Mumbo-Jumbo." For six years, the members of the class had talked about how they would spend the money to celebrate their graduation. Early this year, they voted on it. Some of the boys voted for a trip to New Orleans, but they were outvoted by the girls, all of whom wanted the class to visit New York. The class figured that the cost of motels and hotels—three rooms for the boys, three rooms for the girls, one room for each of the couples—would come to

about four hundred dollars. The bus driver was to be paid three hundred and fifty dollars for driving and given thirty for road, bridge, and tunnel tolls. Six members of the class, who were unable to participate in the trip, stayed home. If there should be any money left over, it would be divided up among all the class members when the travelers returned to Bean Blossom Township. The names of the eighteen touring class members were: R. Jay Bowman, Shelda Bowman (cousin of R. Jay), Robert Britton, Mary Jane Carter, Lynn Dillon, Ina Hough, Thelma Keller, Wilma Keller (sister of Thelma), Becky Kiser, Jeanne Molnar, Nancy Prather, Mike Richardson, Dennis Smith, Donna Thacker, Albert Warthan, Connie Williams, Larry Williams (not related to Connie), and Lela Young.

It was also a first visit to New York for the English teacher, a lively young lady of twenty-eight named Polly Watts, and for her husband, Thomas, thirty-two, a graduate student in political science at Indiana University, in Bloomington, which is about twelve miles from the Bean Blossom Township school. The only people on the bus who had been to New York before were the driver, a husky, uncommunicative man of forty-nine named Ralph Walls, and his wife, Margaret, thirty-nine and the mother of his seven children, aged twenty-one to two, all of whom were left at home.

Walls was the only adviser the others had on what to do in New York. His advice consisted of where to stay (the Hotel Woodstock, on West Forty-third Street, near Times Square) and where to eat (Hector's Cafeteria, around the corner from the hotel).

The Bean Blossom Township school is in the village of Stinesville, which has three hundred and fifty-five inhabitants and a town pump. A couple of the seniors who made the trip live in Stinesville; the others live within a radius of fifteen miles or so, on farms or in isolated houses with vegetable gardens and perhaps a cow or two. At the start of the trip, the travelers gathered in front of their school shortly after midnight, and by one in the morning, with every passenger occupying a double seat in the bus (fifty-four-passenger, 1959 model), and with luggage under the seats, and suits and dresses hung on a homemade clothes rack in the back of the bus, they were on their way.

The senior-class president, R. (for Reginald) Jay Bowman, was in charge of all the voting on the trip. A wiry, energetic eighteen-year-old with a crew haircut, he had been president of the class for the past five years, and is one of two members of the class who intend to go to college. He wants to work, eventually, for the United States Civil Service, because a job with the government is a steady job. Or, in a very vague way, he thinks he may go into politics. With the help of a hundred-and-two dollar-a-year scholarship, he plans to pay all his own expenses at Indiana University. The other student who is going to college has also chosen Indiana University. She is Nancy Prather, an outdoorsy, freckle-faced girl whose father raises dairy and beef cattle on a two-hundred-and-fifty-acre farm and who is the class salutatorian. As for the valedictorian, a heavyset, firm-mouthed girl named Connie Williams, she was planning to get married a week after returning home from New York. The other class members expected, for the most part, to get to work at secretarial or clerical jobs, or in automobile or electronic-parts factories in Bloomington. The New York trip was in the nature of a first and last fling.

Ralph Walls dropped the passengers and their luggage at the Woodstock and then took the bus to a parking lot on Tenth Avenue, where he was going to leave it for the duration of the visit. His job, he had told his passengers, was to drive *to* New York, not *in* it. He had also told them that when he got back to the Woodstock he was going to sleep, but had explained how to get around the corner to Hector's Cafeteria. The boys and girls signed the register and went to their rooms to get cleaned up. They all felt let down. They had asked Walls whether the tall buildings they saw as they came uptown from the Holland Tunnel made up the skyline, and Walls had said he didn't know. Then they had asked him which was the Empire State Building, and he had said they would have to take a tour to find out. Thus put off, they more or less resigned themselves to saving any further questions for a tour. Jay Bowman said that he would see about tours before the following morning.

Mrs. Watts and her husband washed up quickly and then, notwithstanding the bus driver's advice, walked around the Times Square area to see if they could find a reasonably priced and attractive place to have supper. They checked Toffenetti's, almost across the street from the hotel, but decided it was too expensive (hamburger dinners at two dollars and ten cents, watermelon at forty cents) and too formidable. When they reconvened with the senior class in the lobby of the Woodstock, they recommended that everybody have this first meal at Hector's. The party set out—for some reason, in Indian file—for Hector's, and the first one inside was Mike Richardson, a husky, red-haired boy with large, swollen-looking hands and sunburned forearms. A stern-voiced manager near the door, shouting "Take your check! Take your check!" at all incomers, gave the Indiana group the same sightless once-over he gave everybody else. The Bean Blossom faces, which had been puzzled, fearful, and disheartened since Canal Street, now took on a look of resentment. Mike Richardson led the line to the counter. Under a sign reading "BAKED WHITEFISH," a white-aproned counterman looked at Mike and said, "Come on, fella!" Mike glumly took a plate of fish and then filled the rest of his tray with baked beans, a roll, iced tea, and strawberry shortcake (check— $1.58). The others quickly and shakily filled their trays with fish, baked beans, a roll, iced tea, and strawberry short-cake. Sweating, bumping their trays and their elbows against other trays and other elbows, they found seats in twos and threes with strangers, at tables that still had other people's dirty dishes on them. Then, in a nervous clatter of desperate and noisy eating, they stuffed their food down.

"My ma cooks better than this," said Albert Warthan, who was sitting with Mike Richardson and Larry Williams. Albert, the eldest of seven children of a limestone-quarry worker, plans to join the Army and become a radar technician.

"I took this filet de sole? When I wanted somethin' else, I don't know what?" Mike said.

"I like the kind of place you just set there and decide what you want," said Larry, who is going to work on his grandfather's farm.

"My ma and pa told me to come home when it was time to come home, and not to mess around," Albert said. "I'm ready to chuck it and go home right now."

"The whole idea of it is just to see it and get it over with," Mike said.

"You got your money divided up in two places?" Albert asked. "So's you'll have some in one place if it gets stolen in t'other?"

The others nodded.

"Man, you can keep this New York," said Larry. "This place is too hustly, with everybody pushin' and no privacy. Man, I'll take the Big Boy any old day."

Frisch's Big Boy is the name of an Indiana drive-in chain, where a hamburger costs thirty cents. The general effect of Hector's Cafeteria was to give the Bean Blossom Class of 1960 a feeling of unhappiness about eating in New York and to strengthen its faith in the superiority of the Big Boys back home.

Jay Bowman went from table to table, polling his classmates on what they wanted to do that evening. At first, nobody wanted to do anything special.

Then they decided that the only special thing they wanted to do was to go to Coney Island, but they wanted to save Coney Island for the wind-up night, their last night in New York. However, nobody could think of anything to do that first night, so Jay took a revote, and it turned out that almost all of them wanted to go to Coney Island right away. Everybody but three girls voted to go to Coney Island straight from Hector's. Mrs. Watts was mildly apprehensive about this project, but Mike Richardson assured her it was easy; somebody at the hotel had told him that all they had to do was go to the subway and ask the cashier in the booth which train to take, and that would be that. Mrs. Watts said she was going to walk around a bit with her husband. The three girls who didn't want to go to Coney Island explained that they firmly believed the class should "have fun" on its last night in the city, and not before. The three were Ina Hough, whose father works in an R.C.A.-television manufacturing plant in Indianapolis (about fifty miles from Stinesville); Lela Young, whose foster father works in a Chevrolet-parts warehouse in Indianapolis; and Jeanne Molnar, whose father is a draftsman at the Indiana Limestone Company, in Bloomington. All three already knew that they disliked New York. People in New York, they said, were all for themselves.

At nine o'clock, while most of their classmates were on the Brighton B.M.T. express bound for Coney Island, the three girls walked to Sixth Avenue and Fiftieth Street with Mr. and Mrs. Watts, who left them at that point to take a walk along Fifth Avenue. The girls stood in a long line of people waiting to get into the Radio City Music Hall. After twenty minutes, they got out of the line and walked over to Rockefeller Plaza, where they admired the fountain, and to St. Patrick's Cathedral, which looked bigger to them than any church they had ever seen. The main church attended by the Bean Blossom group is the Nazarene Church. No one in the senior class had ever talked to a Jew or to more than one Catholic, or—with the exception of Mary Jane Carter, daughter of the Nazarene minister in Stinesville—had ever heard of an Episcopalian. At ten o'clock, the three girls returned to the Music Hall line, which had dwindled, but when they got to the box office they were told that they had missed the stage show, so they decided to skip the Music Hall and take a subway ride. They took an Independent subway train to the West Fourth Street station, which a subway guard had told them was where to go for Greenwich Village. They decided against getting out and looking, and in favor of going uptown on the same fare and returning to their hotel. Back at the Woodstock, where they shared a room, they locked themselves in and started putting up their hair, telling each other that everybody in New York was rude and all for himself.

At Coney Island, the Indiana travelers talked about how they could not get over the experience of riding for forty-five minutes, in a shaking, noisy train, to get there.

"The long ride was a shock to what I expected," said Albert Warthan.

Nancy Prather said she didn't like the looks of the subway or the people on it. "You see so many different people," she said. "Dark-complected ones one minute, light-complected ones the next."

"I hate New York, actually," Connie Williams said. "I'm satisfied with what we got back home."

"Back home, you can do anything you please in your own back yard any time you feel like it, like hootin' and hollerin' or anything," said Larry Williams. "You don't ever get to feel all cooped up."

"I sort of like it here in Coney Island," said Dennis Smith. "I don't feel cooped up."

Dennis's buddies looked at him without saying anything. His "sort of liking" Coney Island was the first sign of defection from Indiana, and the others did not seem to know what to make of it. Dennis is a broad-shouldered boy with large, beautiful, wistful blue eyes and a gold front tooth.

"I hate it," Connie said.

Jay Bowman organized as many of the group as he could to take a couple of rides on the Cyclone. Most of the boys followed these up with a ride on the parachute jump, and then complained that it wasn't what they had expected at all. Some of the boys and girls went into the Spookorama. They all rode the bobsled, and to top the evening off they rode the bumper cars. "The Spookorama was too imitation to be frightening," Albert said. Before leaving Coney Island, Jay got to work among his classmates, polling them on how much money they were prepared to spend on a tour of the city the next day. They stayed in Coney Island about an hour. Nobody went up to the boardwalk to take a look at the ocean, which none of the class had ever seen. They didn't feel they had to look at the ocean. "We knew the ocean was there, and anyway we aim to see the ocean on the tour tomorrow," Jay said later.

When Ina, Lela, and Jeanne got in line for the Music Hall, the Wattses took their stroll along Fifth Avenue and then joined a couple of friends, Mike and Ardis Cavin. Mike Cavin plays clarinet with the United States Navy Band, in Washington, D.C., and is studying clarinet—as a commuter—at the Juilliard School of Music. At Madison Avenue and Forty-second Street, the two couples boarded a bus heading downtown, and while talking about where to get off they were taken in hand by an elderly gentleman sitting near them, who got off the bus when they did and walked two blocks with them, escorting them to their destination—the Jazz Gallery, on St. Mark's Place. Mike Cavin wanted to hear the tenor-saxophone player John Coltrane. The Wattses stayed at the Jazz Gallery with the Cavins for three hours, listening, with patient interest, to modern jazz. They decided that they liked modern jazz, and especially Coltrane. Leaving the Jazz Gallery after one o'clock, the two couples took buses to Times Square, walked around for twenty minutes looking for a place where they could get a snack, and finally, because every other place seemed to be closed, went to Toffenetti's. Back at the hotel, the Wattses ran into one of the Coney Island adventurers, who told them that Ina, Lela, and Jeanne were missing, or at least were not answering their telephone or knocks on their door. Mr. Watts got the room clerk, unlocked the girls' door, and found them sitting on their beds, still putting up their hair. Everybody was, more or less unaccountably, angry—the three girls who hadn't gone to Coney Island, the girls who had, the boys who had, the Wattses, and the room clerk. The Wattses got to bed at 3:30 A.M.

At 6:30 A.M., Mrs. Watts was called on the telephone. Message: One of the anti-Coney Island trio was lying on the floor of the room, weeping and hysterical. Mrs. Watts called the room clerk, who called a doctor practicing in the Times Square area, who rushed over to the hotel, talked with the weeping girl for twenty minutes, and left her with a tranquilizing pill, which she refused to take.

By the time everybody had settled down enough to eat breakfast in drugstores and get ready to start out, it was after nine in the morning, half an hour behind time for the scheduled (by unanimous vote) all-day tour of the city by chartered sightseeing bus, at six dollars per person. The tour was held up further while Mrs. Watts persuaded the weeper to take a shower, in an effort to encourage her to join the tour. After the shower, the unhappy girl stopped crying and declared that she would go along. By the time the group reached the Bowery, she felt fine, and in Chinatown, like the other boys and girls, she bought a pair of chopsticks, for thirty-five cents. The Cathedral of St. John the Divine was the highlight of the tour for many of the students, who were delighted to hear that some of the limestone used in the cathedral interior had very likely come from quarries near Stinesville. Mrs. Watts, on the other

hand, who had studied art, had taught art for five years at Huntington College, in Huntington, Indiana, and had taken an accredited art tour of Europe before her marriage, indignantly considered the cathedral "an imitation of European marvels."

Mrs. Watts took the Bean Blossom teaching job, at thirty-six hundred dollars a year, last fall, when her husband decided to abandon a concrete-building-block business in Huntington in order to study for a Ph.D. in political science, a subject he wants to teach. Since he had decided that Indiana University was the place to do this, they moved from Huntington—where Mr. Watts had won the distinction of being the youngest man ever to hold the job of chairman of the Republican Party of Huntington County—to Bloomington. Mrs. Watts drives the twelve miles from Bloomington to Stinesville every day. She teaches English to the tenth, eleventh, and twelfth grades, and, because the school had no Spanish teacher when she signed up for the job, she teaches Spanish, too. She considers the Bean Blossom Township school the most democratic school she has ever seen. "They vote on everything," she says. "We have an average of two votes on something or other every day." Having thus been conditioned to voting as a way of life, Mrs. Watts left the voting on day-to-day plans for the group visit in the capable hands of Jay Bowman. He solved the problem of the tour's late start that morning by taking a vote on whether or not to leave out the Empire State Building. It was promptly voted out of the tour, and voted in for some later time as a separate undertaking.

The tour included a boat trip to the Statue of Liberty, where the group fell in with crushing mobs of people walking to the top of the torch. Mrs. Watts found the experience nightmarish, and quit at the base of the torch. Most of the boys and girls made it to the top. "There are a hundred and sixty-eight steps up the torch, and there were forty thousand people ahead of me, but I was determined to climb up it," Jay Bowman reported to Mrs. Watts. "It took me twenty minutes, and it was worthwhile. The thing of it was I had to do it."

For the tour, Jay, like the other boys, had put on dress-up clothes bought specially, at a cost of about twenty-five dollars an outfit, for the trip to New York—white beachcomber pants reaching to below the knee, white cotton-knit shirt with red and blue stripes and a pocket in one sleeve, white socks with red and blue stripes, and white sneakers. The girls wore cotton skirts, various kinds of blouses, white cardigan sweaters, and low heeled shoes. Mrs. Watts wore high-heeled pumps, even for sightseeing. Everyone else on the tour was astonished at the way New York City people dressed. "They look peculiar," Nancy Prather said. "Girls wearing high heels in the daytime, and the boys here always got a regular suit on, even to go to work in."

"I wouldn't trade the girls back home for any of the girls here," Jay Bowman says. "New York girls wear too much makeup. Not that my interests are centered on any of the girls in the senior class. My interests are centered on Nancy Glidden. She's in the *junior* class. I take her to shows in Blooming-

ton. We eat pizzas, listen to Elvis Presley—things of that nature—and I always get her home by twelve. Even though my interests are centered on the junior class, I'm proud to say my classmates are the finest bunch of people in the world."

Jay lives with his parents and two brothers in an old nine-room house on thirty acres of land owned by Jay's father, who works in the maintenance department of the Bridgeport Brass Company, in Indianapolis. His mother works in Bloomington, on the R.C.A. color-television-set assembly line. Jay's grandfather, who has worked in limestone quarries all his life, lives across the road, on five acres of his own land, where he has a couple of cows and raises beans and corn for the use of the family. The Bowman family had no plumbing in their house while Jay was a child, and took baths in a tub in the kitchen with water from a well, but a few years ago, with their own hands, they installed a bathroom and a plumbing system, and did other work on the house, including putting in a furnace. Jay's parents get up at four in the morning to go to work. Jay, who hasn't been sick one day since he had the mumps at the age of twelve, never sleeps later than seven. He is not in the least distressed at having to work his way through college. He plans to get to school in his own car. This is a 1950 Chevrolet four-door sedan, which he hopes to trade in, by paying an additional four hundred dollars, for a slightly younger model before the end of the year.

"The thing of it is I feel proud of myself," Jay says. "Not to be braggin' or anything. But I saved up better than a thousand dollars to send myself to college. That's the way it is. I scrubbed floors, put up hay, carried groceries, and this last winter I worked Saturdays and Sundays in a country store on the state highway and got paid a dollar an hour for runnin' it."

The Bowman family has, in addition to a kind of basic economic ambition, two main interests—basketball and politics. Jay, like most of the other boys on the trip, played basketball on the school basketball team, which won the first round in its section of the Wabash Valley tournament last season. Jay talks about basketball to his classmates but never about politics. Talk about the latter he saves for his family. His grandfather is a Democrat. "If it was up to my grandpa, he'd never want a single Republican in the whole country," he says. "And my Dad agrees with him. I agree with my Dad. My Dad thinks if Franklin D. Roosevelt was still President, this country wouldn't be in the trouble it finds itself in."

At 5 P.M. of this second day in the City of New York, the members of the Bean Blossom senior class returned to their hotel and stood in the lobby for a while, looking from some distance at a souvenir-and-gift stand across from the registration desk. The stand was stocked with thermometers in the form of the Statue of Liberty, in two sizes, priced at seventy-nine cents and ninety-eight cents; with silver-plated charm bracelets; with pins and compacts carrying representations of the Empire State Building; with scarves showing the R.C.A. Building and the U.N. Building; and with ashtrays showing the New York City skyline. Mike Richardson edged over to the stand and

picked up a wooden plaque, costing ninety-eight cents, with the Statue of Liberty shown at the top, American flags at the sides, and, in the middle, a poem, inscribed "Mother," which read:

To one who bears the sweetest name
And adds a luster to the same
Who shares my joys
Who cheers when sad
The greatest friend I ever had
Long life to her, for there's no other
Can take the place of my dear mother.

After reading the poem, Mike smiled.

"Where ya from?" the man behind the stand asked him.

"Indiana," Mike said, looking as though he were warming up. "We've been on this tour. The whole day."

"Ya see everything?" the man asked.

"Everything except the Empire State Building," said Mike.

"Yeah," said the man, and looked away.

Mike was still holding the plaque. Carefully, he replaced it on the stand. "I'll come back for this later," he said.

Without looking at Mike, the man nodded.

Mike joined Dennis Smith and Larry Williams, who were standing with a tall, big-boned, handsome girl named Becky Kiser. Becky used to be a cheerleader for the Bean Blossom Township basketball team.

"We was talkin' about the way this place has people layin' in the streets on that Bowery sleepin'," Larry said.

"You don't see people layin' in the streets back home."

"I seen that in Chicago," Dennis said. "I seen *women* layin' in the streets in Chicago. That's worse."

The others nodded. No argument.

Mike took a cigarette from his sleeve pocket and lit it with a match from the same pocket. He blew out a stream of smoke with strength and confidence. "I'll be glad when we light out of here," he said. "Nothin' here feels like the farm."

Becky Kiser, with an expression of terrible guilt on her attractive, wide-mouthed face, said, "I bet you'd never get bored here in New York. Back home, it's the same thing all the time. You go to the skating rink. You go to the Big Boy. In the winter, there's basketball. And that's all."

"When I was in Chicago, I seen a man who shot a man in a bar," Dennis said. "I stood right across the street while the man who was shot the people drug him out." He looked at Becky Kiser. The other boys were also looking at her, but with condemnation and contempt. Dennis gave Becky support. "In Stinesville, they see you on the streets after eleven, they run you home," he said. "Seems like here the city never closes."

"Man, you're just not lookin' ahead," Mike said to Dennis, ignoring Becky.

"You like it here?" Larry asked, in amazement. "Taxes on candy and on everything?"

The Nazarene minister's daughter, Mary Jane Carter, came over with Ina Hough.

"Dennis, here, likes New York," Mike announced.

"*I* don't," said Ina. "I like the sights, but I think they're almost ruined by the people."

"The food here is expensive, but I guess that's life," said Mary Jane, in a mood of forbearance.

"Oh, man!" said Mike.

"Oh, man!" said Larry. "Cooped up in New York."

Ina said stiffly, "Like the guide said today, you could always tell a New Yorker from a tourist because a New Yorker never smiles, and I agree with him."

"After a while, you'd kinda fit in," Dennis said mildly.

Before dinner that night, Mr. Watts walked through the Times Square area checking prices and menus at likely restaurants. He made tentative arrangements at The Californian for a five-course steak or chicken dinner, to cost $1.95 per person, and asked Jay Bowman to go around taking a vote on the proposition. Half an hour later, Jay reported to Mr. Watts that some of the boys didn't want to go to The Californian, because they thought they'd have to do their own ordering. So Mr. Watts talked to the boys in their rooms and explained that the ordering was taken care of; all they had to say was whether they wanted steak or chicken. On the next ballot, everybody was in favor of The Californian. The class walked over. When the fifth course was finished, it was agreed that the dinner was all right, but several of the boys said they thought the restaurant was too high-class.

After dinner, it started to rain, and it rained hard. The Wattses and seven of the girls decided that they wanted

385

to see "The Music Man." The four other girls wanted to see "My Fair Lady." None of the boys wanted to see a musical show. In the driving rain, the Wattses and the girls ran to the theatres of their choice, all arriving soaked to the skin. By good luck, each group was able to buy seats. At "The Music Man," the Wattses and the seven girls with them sat in the balcony, in the direct path of an air-conditioning unit that blew icy blasts on their backs. At "My Fair Lady," the four girls sat in the balcony, where an air-conditioning unit blew icy blasts at their legs. The girls liked their shows. The "My Fair Lady" group was transported by the costumes. Ina Hough, who went to "The Music Man," thought that it was just like a movie, except for the way the scenes changed.

The boys split up, some of them taking the subway down to Greenwich Village, the others heading for the Empire State Building, where they paid a dollar-thirty for tickets to the observatory and, once up there, found that the fog and rain blotted out the view completely. "We stood there about an hour and a half messin' around, me and my buddies," Jay later told Mrs. Watts. "Wasn't no sense in leavin' at that price." In Greenwich Village, Mike Richardson, Dennis Smith, and Larry Williams walked along the narrow streets in a drizzling rain. All were still wearing their beachcomber outfits. Nobody talked to them. They didn't see anybody they wanted to talk to. They almost went into a small coffeehouse; they changed their minds because the prices looked too high. They went into one shop, a bookstore, and looked at some abstract paintings, which ap-

pealed to them. "Sort of interestin', the way they don't look like nothin'," Mike said. Then they took the subway back to Times Square, where they walked around for a while in the rain. Toward midnight, Mike and Dennis told each other they were lonesome for the smell of grass and trees, and, the rain having stopped, they walked up to Central Park, where they stayed for about an hour and got lost.

The next morning, a meeting of the class was held in the hotel lobby to take a vote on when to leave New York. Jay Bowman reported that they had enough money to cover an extra day in the city, plus a side trip to Niagara Falls on the way home. Or, he said, they could leave New York when they had originally planned to and go to Washington, D.C., for a day before heading home. The bus driver had told Jay that it was all one to him which they chose. The class voted for the extra day in New York and Niagara Falls.

"I'm glad," Becky Kiser said, with a large, friendly smile, to Dennis Smith. Several of her classmates overheard her and regarded her with a uniformly deadpan look. "I like it here," she went on. "I'd like to live here. There's so much to see. There's so much to do."

Her classmates continued to study her impassively until Dennis took their eyes away from her by saying, "You get a feelin' here of goin' wherever you want to. Seems the city never closes. I'd like to live here, I believe. People from everyplace are here."

"Limousines all over the joint," Albert Warthan said.

"Seems like you can walk and walk and walk," Dennis went on dreamily. "I like the way the big build-in's crowd you in. You want to walk and walk and never go to sleep."

"I hate it," Connie Williams said, with passion.

"Oh, man, you're just not lookin' ahead," Mike Richardson said to Dennis. "You got a romantic notion. You're not realistic about it."

"This place couldn't hold me," Larry Williams said. "I like the privacy of the farm."

"I want to go to new places," said Becky, who had started it. "I want to go to Europe."

"Only place I want to go is Texas," Larry said. "I got folks in Texas."

"There's no place like home," Mike said. "Home's good enough for me."

"I believe the reason of this is we've lived all of our lives around Stinesville," Dennis said. "If you took Stinesville out of the country, you wouldn't be hurt. But if you took New York out of the country, you'd be hurt. The way the guide said, all our clothes and everything comes from New York."

Becky said, "In Coney Island, I saw the most handsome man I ever saw in my whole life. I think he was a Puerto Rican or something, too."

Albert said, "When we get back, my pa will say, 'Well, how was it?' I'll say, 'It was fine.'"

"I'd like to come back, maybe stay a month," Jay Bowman said diplomatically. "One thing I'd like to do is come here when I can see a major-league baseball game."

"I'd like to see a major-league baseball game, but I wouldn't come back just to see *it*," Mike said.

"I hate New York," Connie said.

"Back home, everybody says 'Excuse me,'" Nancy Prather said.

"I like it here," Dennis said stubbornly.

This day was an open one, leaving the boys and girls free to do anything they liked, without prearranged plan or vote. Mike passed close by the souvenir-and-gift stand in the hotel lobby, and the proprietor urged him to take home the Statue of Liberty.

"I'd like to, but it won't fit in my suitcase," Mike said, with a loud laugh.

A group formed to visit the zoo in Central Park, got on the subway, had a loud discussion about where to get off, and were taken in hand by a stranger, who told them the zoo was in the Bronx. Only the boy named Lynn Dillon listened to the stranger. The others went to the zoo in Central Park. Lynn stayed on the subway till it reached the Bronx, and spent the entire day in the Bronx Zoo by himself. The rest of the zoo visitors, walking north after lunch in the cafeteria, ran into the Metropolitan Museum of Art and went in. "It was there, and it was free, so we did it," Nancy Prather said. "There were these suits of armor and stuff. Nothin' I go for myself."

That morning, the Wattses had tried to get some of the boys and girls to accompany them to the Guggenheim Museum or the Museum of Modern Art, but nobody had wanted to pay the price of admission. "Why pay fifty cents to see a museum when they got them free?" the class president asked. Mrs. Watts reported afterward that the Guggenheim was the most exciting museum she had ever seen, including all the museums she had seen in Europe on her accredited art tour. "There aren't big crowds in there, for one thing," she said. "And I don't think the building overpowers the paintings at all, as I'd heard." From the Guggenheim, the Wattses went to Georg Jensen's to look at silver, but didn't buy anything. Then they went to the Museum of Modern Art and had lunch in the garden. "Lovely lunch, fabulous garden, fabulous sculpture, but I'm disappointed in the museum itself," Mrs. Watts said. "Everything jammed into that small space! Impossible to get a good view of Picasso's *Girl Before a Mirror*."

By dinnertime, more than half of the Bean Blossomers had, to their relief, discovered the Automat. Jay Bowman had a dinner consisting of a ham sandwich (forty cents), a glass of milk (ten cents), and a dish of fresh strawberries (twenty cents). Then, with a couple of buddies, he bought some peanuts in their shells and some Cokes, and took them up to his room for the three of them to consume while talking about what to do that night. They decided, because they had not yet had a good view of the city from the Empire State observatory, that they would go back there. They were accompanied by most of the girls and the other boys, and this time the group got a cut rate of sixty-five cents apiece. Dennis went off wandering by himself. He walked up Fifth Avenue to Eighty-fifth Street, over to Park Avenue, down Park to Seventy-second Street, across to the West Side, down Central Park West to Sixty-sixth Street, over behind the Tavern-on-the-Green (where he watched people eating outdoors), and down Seventh Avenue to Times Square, where he stood around on corners looking at the

people who bought papers at newsstands.

The Wattses had arranged to meet anybody who was interested under the Washington Arch at around nine-thirty for an evening in Greenwich Village. The boys had decided to take a walk up Broadway after leaving the Empire State Building, but the girls all showed up in Washington Square, along with two soldiers and three sailors they had met in the U.S.O. across the street from the Woodstock. The Wattses led the way to a coffeehouse, where everybody had coffee or lemonade. Then the girls and the servicemen left the Wattses, saying they were going to take a ride on the ferry to Staten Island. The Wattses went to the Five Spot, which their jazz friend had told them had good music.

After breakfast the following morning, the bus driver, Ralph Walls, showed up in the hotel lobby for the first time since the group's arrival in New York and told Jay Bowman to have everyone assembled at five-forty-five the following morning for departure at six o'clock on the dot. The driver said that he was spending most of his time sleeping, and that before they left he was going to do some more sleeping. He had taken his wife on a boat trip around Manhattan, though, he said, and he had taken a few walks on the streets. After reminding Jay again about the exact time planned for the departure, he went back upstairs to his room.

Mrs. Watts took nine of the girls (two stayed in the hotel to sleep) for a walk through Saks Fifth Avenue, just looking. Mr. Watts took three of the boys to Abercrombie & Fitch, just looking. Everybody walked every aisle on every floor in each store, looking at everything on the counters and in the showcases. Nobody bought anything. The two groups met at noon under the clock in Grand Central; lunched at an Automat; walked over to the United Nations Buildings, where they decided not to take the regular tour; and took a crosstown bus to the Hudson River and went aboard the liner S.S. Independence, where they visited every deck and every lounge on the boat, and a good many of the staterooms. Then they took the bus back to Times Square and scattered to do some shopping.

Mike Richardson bought all his gifts—eleven dollars' worth—at the hotel stand, taking not only the plaque for his mother but a set of salt and pepper shakers, with the Statue of Liberty on the salt and the Empire State Building on the pepper, also for his mother; a Statue of Liberty ashtray for his father; a George Washington Bridge teapot for his sister-in-law; a mechanical dog for his niece; a City Hall teapot-cup-and-saucer set for his grandparents; and a cigarette lighter stamped with the Great White Way for himself. At Macy's, Becky Kiser bought a dress, a blouse, and an ankle chain for herself, and a necklace with matching bracelet and earrings for her mother, a cuff-link-and-tie-clasp set for her father, and a bracelet for her younger sister. Albert Warthan bought a miniature camera for himself and a telephone-pad-and-pencil set stamped with the George Washington Bridge and a Statue of Liberty thermometer, large-size, as general family gifts, at the hotel stand. Jay Bowman bought an unset cultured pearl at Macy's for his girl friend in the junior class, as well as silver-looking earrings for his married sister and for his mother, and at a store called King of Slims, around the corner from the hotel, he bought four ties—a red toreador tie (very narrow) for his older brother, a black toreador tie for his younger brother, a conservative silk foulard for his father, and a white toreador tie for himself. Dennis Smith bought a Statue of Liberty ashtray for his mother and a Statue of Liberty cigarette lighter for his father. Connie Williams bought two bracelets and a Statue of Liberty pen for herself. The bus driver and his wife spent sixty dollars on clothes for their children, six of whom are girls. Nancy Prather didn't buy anything. The Wattses spent about a hundred dollars in the course of the visit, most of it on meals and entertainment.

On their last evening in New York, all the boys and girls, accompanied by the Wattses, went to the Radio City Music Hall, making it in time to see the stage show. Then they packed and went to bed. The bus driver, after an early dinner with his wife at Hector's Cafeteria, brought the yellow school bus over from Tenth Avenue and parked it right in front of the hotel, so that it would be there for the early start.

Next morning at five-forty-five, the Bean Blossomers assembled in the lobby; for the first time since the trip had started, nobody was late. The bus pulled out at exactly 6 A.M., and twenty minutes after that, heading west over the George Washington Bridge, it disappeared from the city.

Does this selection strike you as a true account, or as one that's made up? Why?

# The Boy Who Painted Christ Black

*John Henrik Clarke*

He was the smartest boy in the Muskogee County School—for colored children. Everybody even remotely connected with the school knew this. The teacher always pronounced his name with profound gusto as she pointed him out as the ideal student. Once I heard her say: "If he were white he might, some day, become President." Only Aaron Crawford wasn't white; quite the contrary. His skin was so solid black that it glowed, reflecting an inner virtue that was strange, and beyond my comprehension.

In many ways he looked like something that was awkwardly put together. Both his nose and his lips seemed a trifle too large for his face. To say he was ugly would be unjust and to say he was handsome would be gross exaggeration. Truthfully, I could never make up my mind about him. Sometimes he looked like something out of a book of ancient history . . . looked as if he was left over from that magnificent era before the machine age came and marred the earth's natural beauty.

His great variety of talent often startled the teachers. This caused his classmates to look upon him with a mixed feeling of awe and envy.

Before Thanksgiving, he always drew turkeys and pumpkins on the blackboard. On George Washington's birthday, he drew large American flags surrounded by little hatchets. It was these small masterpieces that made him the most talked-about colored boy in Columbus, Georgia. The Negro principal of the Muskogee County School said he would some day be a great painter, like Henry O. Tanner.

For the teacher's birthday, which fell on a day about a week before commencement, Aaron Crawford painted the picture that caused an uproar, and a turning point, at the Muskogee County School. The moment he entered the room that morning, all eyes fell on him. Besides his torn book holder, he was carrying a large-framed concern wrapped in old newspapers. As he went to

390

his seat, the teacher's eyes followed his every motion, a curious wonderment mirrored in them conflicting with the half-smile that wreathed her face.

Aaron put his books down, then smiling broadly, advanced toward the teacher's desk. His alert eyes were so bright with joy that they were almost frightening. The children were leaning forward in their seats, staring greedily at him; a restless anticipation was rampant within every breast.

Already the teacher sensed that Aaron had a present for her. Still smiling, he placed it on her desk and began to help her unwrap it. As the last piece of paper fell from the large frame, the teacher jerked her hand away from it suddenly, her eyes flickering unbelievingly. Amidst the rigid tension, her heavy breathing was distinct and frightening. Temporarily, there was no other sound in the room.

Aaron stared questioningly at her and she moved her hand back to the present cautiously, as if it were a living thing with vicious characteristics. I am sure it was the one thing she least expected.

With a quick, involuntary movement I rose up from my desk. A series of submerged murmurs spread through the room, rising to a distinct monotone. The teacher turned toward the children, staring reproachfully. They did not move their eyes from the present that Aaron had brought her. . . . It was a large picture of Christ—painted black!

Aaron Crawford went back to his seat, a feeling of triumph reflecting in his every movement.

The teacher faced us. Her curious half-smile had blurred into a mild bewilderment. She searched the bright faces before her and started to smile again, occasionally stealing quick glances at the large picture propped on her desk, as though doing so were forbidden amusement.

"Aaron," she spoke at last, a slight tinge of uncertainty in her tone, "this is a most welcome present. Thanks. I will treasure it." She paused, then went on speaking, a trifle more coherent than before. "Looks like you are going to be quite an artist. . . . Suppose you come forward and tell the class how you came to paint this remarkable picture."

When he rose to speak, to explain about the picture, a hush fell tightly over the room, and the children gave him all of their attention . . . something they rarely did for the teacher. He did not speak at first; he just stood there in front of the room, toying absently with his hands, observing his audience carefully, like a great concert artist.

"It was like this," he said, placing full emphasis on every word. "You see, my uncle who lives in New York teaches classes in Negro History at the Y.M.C.A. When he visited us last year, he was telling me about the many great black folks who have made history. He said black folks were once the most powerful people on earth. When I asked him about Christ, he said no one ever proved whether he was black or white. Somehow a feeling came over me that he was a black man, 'cause he was so kind and forgiving, kinder than I have ever seen white people be. So, when I painted his picture I couldn't help but paint it as I thought it was."

After this, the little artist sat down, smiling broadly, as if he had gained entrance to a great storehouse of knowledge that ordinary people could neither acquire nor comprehend.

The teacher, knowing nothing else to do under prevailing circumstances, invited the children to rise from their seats and come forward so they could get a complete view of Aaron's unique piece of art.

When I came close to the picture, I noticed it was painted with the kind of paint you get in the five and ten cent stores. Its shape was blurred slightly, as if someone had jarred the frame before the paint had time to dry. The eyes of Christ were deep-set and sad, very much like those of Aaron's father, who was a deacon in the local Baptist Church. This picture of Christ looked much different from the one I saw hanging on the wall when I was in Sunday School. It looked more like a helpless Negro, pleading silently for mercy.

For the next few days, there was much talk about Aaron's picture.

The school term ended the following week and Aaron's picture, along with the best handwork done by the students that year, was on display in the assembly room. Naturally, Aaron's picture graced the place of honor.

There was no book work to be done on commencement day and joy was rampant among the children. The girls in their brightly colored dresses gave the school the delightful air of spring awakening.

In the middle of the day all the children were gathered in the small assembly. On this day we were always favored with a visit from a man whom all the teachers spoke of with mixed esteem and fear. Professor Danual, they called him, and they always pronounced his name with reverence. He was supervisor of all the city schools, including those small and poorly equipped ones set aside for colored children.

393

The great man arrived almost at the end of our commencement exercises. On seeing him enter the hall, the children rose, bowed courteously, and sat down again, their eyes examining him as if he were a circus freak.

He was a tall white man with solid gray hair that made his lean face seem paler than it actually was. His eyes were the clearest blue I have ever seen. They were the only lifelike things about him.

As he made his way to the front of the room the Negro principal, George Du Vaul, was walking ahead of him, cautiously preventing anything from getting in his way. As he passed me, I heard the teachers, frightened, sucking in their breath, felt the tension tightening.

A large chair was in the center of the rostrum. It had been daintily polished and the janitor had laboriously recushioned its bottom. The supervisor went straight to it without being guided, knowing that this pretty splendor was reserved for him.

Presently the Negro principal introduced the distinguished guest and he favored us with a short speech. It wasn't a very important speech. Almost at the end of it, I remember him saying something about he wouldn't be surprised if one of us boys grew up to be a great colored man, like Booker T. Washington.

After he sat down, the school chorus sang two spirituals and the girls in the fourth grade did an Indian folk dance. This brought the commencement program to an end.

After this the supervisor came down from the rostrum, his eyes tinged with curiosity, and began to view the array of handwork on display in front of the chapel.

Suddenly his face underwent a strange rejuvenation. His clear blue eyes flickered in astonishment. He was looking at Aaron Crawford's picture of Christ. Mechanically he moved his stooped form closer to the picture and stood gazing fixedly at it, curious and undecided, as though it were a dangerous animal that would rise any moment and spread destruction.

We waited tensely for his next movement. The silence was almost suffocating. At last he twisted himself around and began to search the grim faces before him. The fiery glitter of his eyes abated slightly as they rested on the Negro principal, protestingly.

"Who painted this sacrilegious nonsense?" he demanded sharply.

"I painted it, sir." These were Aaron's words, spoken hesitantly. He wetted his lips timidly and looked up at the supervisor, his eyes voicing a sad plea for understanding.

He spoke again, this time more coherently. "Th' principal said a colored person have jes as much right paintin' Jesus black as a white person have paintin' him white. And he says. . . ." At this point he halted abruptly, as if to search for his next words. A strong tinge of bewilderment dimmed the glow of his solid black face. He stammered out a few more words, then stopped again.

The supervisor strode a few steps toward him. At last color had swelled some of the lifelessness out of his lean face.

"Well, go on!" he said, enragedly, ". . . I'm still listening."

Aaron moved his lips pathetically but no words passed them. His eyes wandered around the room, resting finally, with an air of hope, on the face of the Negro principal. After a moment, he jerked his face in another direction, regretfully, as if something he had said had betrayed an understanding between him and the principal.

Presently the principal stepped forward to defend the school's prize student.

"I encouraged the boy in painting that picture," he said firmly. "And it was with my permission that he brought the picture into this school. I don't think the boy is so far wrong in painting Christ black. The artists of all other races have painted whatsoever God they worship to resemble themselves. I see no reason why we should be immune from that privilege. After all, Christ was born in that part of the world that had always been predominantly populated by colored people. There is a strong possibility that he could have been a Negro."

But for the monotonous lull of heavy breathing, I would have sworn that his words had frozen everyone in the hall. I had never heard the little principal speak so boldly to anyone, black or white.

The supervisor swallowed dumfoundedly. His face was aglow in silent rage.

"Have you been teaching these children things like that?" he asked the Negro principal, sternly.

"I have been teaching them that their race has produced great kings and queens as well as slaves and serfs," the principal said. "The time is long overdue when we should let the world know that we erected and enjoyed the benefits of a splendid civilization long before the people of Europe had a written language."

The supervisor coughed. His eyes bulged menacingly as he spoke. "You are not being paid to teach such things in this school, and I am demanding your resignation for overstepping your limit as principal."

George Du Vaul did not speak. A strong quiver swept over his sullen face. He revolved himself slowly and walked out of the room towards his office.

The supervisor's eyes followed him until he was out of focus. Then he murmured under his breath: "There'll be a lot of fuss in this world if you start people thinking that Christ was a nigger."

Some of the teachers followed the principal out of the chapel, leaving the crestfallen children restless and in a quandary about what to do next. Finally we started back to our rooms. The supervisor was behind me. I heard him murmur to himself: "Damn, if niggers ain't getting smarter."

A few days later I heard that the principal had accepted a summer job as art instructor of a small high school somewhere in south Georgia and had gotten permission from Aaron's parents to take him along so he could continue to encourage him in his painting.

I was on my way home when I saw him leaving his office. He was carrying a large briefcase and some books tucked under his arm. He had already said good-by to all the teachers. And strangely, he did not look brokenhearted. As he headed for the large front door, he readjusted his horn-rimmed glasses, but did not look back. An air of triumph gave more dignity to his soldierly stride. He had the appearance of a man who had done a great thing, something greater than any ordinary man would do.

Aaron Crawford was waiting outside for him. They walked down the street together. He put his arms around Aaron's shoulder affectionately. He was talking sincerely to Aaron about something, and Aaron was listening, deeply earnest.

I watched them until they were so far down the street that their forms had begun to blur. Even from this distance I could see they were still walking in brisk, dignified strides, like two people who had won some sort of victory.

396

# Read to the Last Line

## William Stafford

Suppose a heroic deed—
at a big picnic, say, you save a child;
later the child is killed while being a hero;
then you meet the beautiful sister,
and all . . . ; you have a son who wakes
in the middle of the night and cries;
you hear him—strange—there in the dark, and—

Suppose all the supposes.
You find your self-story patch-quilted
all over the place; and after that          10
you are reading an author who tells
your whole story, around all the spirals,
till you come face to face and recognize you.

397

Grateful, you find yourself
identified, so clearly named that you decide
to bring other patches together by
rounding on that author, too, with some
greatest, ultimate deed: he deserves something.

So you in turn begin a story,
but then you stop—what goes on?          20
"I'll not tell nor be told what I think," you cry,
"None of it's true, anyway."

And all the time it's your own story,
even when you think: "It's all just made up, a trick.
What is the author trying to do?"

Reader, we are in such a story:
all of this is trying to arrange a kind of a prayer for you.

Pray for me.

# INDEX

## TITLES
## AUTHORS
## TRANSLATORS

398

399

400

# INDEX

## TYPES OF LITERATURE

## NONFICTION: ARTICLES, ESSAYS, AUTOBIOGRAPHY

## DRAMA

402

## POEMS

## CONCRETE POEMS

404

## GRAPHICS

# CREDITS

406

ABCDEFGH 0765432
Printed in the United States of America